Optimize Now
(or else!)

Optimize Now
(or else!)

How to Leverage
Processes and Information to
Achieve Enterprise Optimization
(and Avoid Enterprise Extinction)

David M. Fisher

iUniverse, Inc.
New York Lincoln Shanghai

Optimize Now
(or else!)
How to Leverage Processes and Information to Achieve Enterprise Optimization
(and Avoid Enterprise Extinction)

iUniverse, Inc.

For information address:
iUniverse, Inc.
2021 Pine Lake Road, Suite 100
Lincoln, NE 68512
www.iuniverse.com

ISBN: 0-595-29837-0 (Pbk)
ISBN: 0-595-66062-2 (Cloth)

Printed in the United States of America

For Helene, Robin, and Brian
You are my everything!

Contents

Acknowledgements

I would like to extend my sincere thanks to the people who contributed to the creation of this book. First is my primary motivator, Paul Brinkley, who helped inspire many of the core concepts contained throughout the text. Paul is the closest thing I know to a CPIO, and his example of leading an organization with a focus on processes and information has guided many of the ideas expressed in the book. I would also like to thank my colleagues and clients who helped contribute insights, case studies, and feedback as the book has grown and evolved over the last year. This includes the following group of extremely talented folks: Mandeep Sirohi, Paul Hooper, Steve Fisher, Jack Ahuja, Mark Lee, Lee Jones, Rob Schoenthaler, Tomi Miller, Tariq Choudry, and Russ Thomas.

The list of people from whom I have learned my craft and who have inspired me throughout my career would be too long to mention here, but I am proud to extend my gratitude to the following people who have been mentors in more ways than one throughout the years: Karin Maday, Paul Ciandrini, Stan Blaustein, Tony Muller, Joe Riera, and Ged Fox, along with John Abel—the best "right-hand man" with whom I have ever worked. Much of my success is due to the personal and professional guidance and assistance I have received from this amazing group. In addition, my thanks to the countless consultants from BearingPoint who have joined me in serving clients in the true spirit of partnership, and those special clients who allowed us to collaborate with them in this very same spirit. Finally, I would like to extend my thanks to the members of my family, who are my true inspiration and provide meaning to my life (Helene, Robin, Brian, Paul, Dena, and Steve).

Foreword

In October 2002, I was involved in an off-site executive session focusing on the strategic trends for information technology (IT) organizations and issues facing chief information officers (CIOs) and their companies. Joining me in the session were a couple of colleagues from BearingPoint (formerly KPMG Consulting), a vice-president from one of the leading analyst organizations, and a CIO from a prominent high-tech company. We covered a variety of interesting topics and discussed a number of examples in the marketplace in terms of how companies were organized in the context of processes, information, and systems.

We kept coming back to one question: Who does all of this well? We kept coming back to it because we could never come up with an answer. And we're talking about nearly 100 years of collective experience in business and IT management in this small group, so there was a broad range of research and experience from which to draw. For every example of a company that excelled in one particular area, there also seemed to be known drawbacks to that overall environment. Try as we did, we were unable to identify one company that had the complete package and was operating in a truly optimal environment. Let's call this non-existent organization the *Optimal Enterprise*. For all practical purposes, no company will ever attain a true optimal state. But from this conversation patterns of optimization were starting to emerge. It became my objective to begin to document some of these trends, and to see if I could highlight those elements that were most likely to provide a path along what I called *Enterprise Optimization*. I also sought a means by which to highlight those pitfalls that typically inhibit companies in their search for the optimal state, and the all-too-common devastating results of these unfortunate scenarios.

Enterprise Optimization is a collection of components, all of which are interrelated in how an organization can effectively and continually improve its overall capabilities. While the original off-site session focused initially on topics related to traditional Information Technology Departments, it quickly became obvious to me that the path to optimization went far beyond the walls of IT. In fact, as I will discuss, traditional IT is one of the problems itself, and something that needs to undergo significant changes if companies as a whole will ever be able to achieve the desired levels of optimization.

My experiences and my research have also continued to bring me back to a common theme whereby the KISS ("Keep It Simple, Stupid") approach is highly correlated with optimal environments. Complexity is often the result of the conflicting wants and desires of various constituents within organizations, but the overall cost of these complex environments will usually outweigh the benefits. While the KISS method will typically lead to optimal results, the corresponding takeaway is that "complexity kills." Along these lines, here are some sayings to keep in mind throughout the reading of this book:

- Any intelligent fool can make things bigger and more complex. It takes a touch of genius—and a lot of courage—to move in the opposite direction.—*Albert Einstein*

- Truth is ever to be found in the simplicity, and not the multiplicity and confusion of things.—*Sir Isaac Newton*

- Simplicity is the ultimate sophistication.—*Leonardo da Vinci* [1]

The core components of the discussion of Enterprise Optimization will be broken down into the following sections:

- The Organization
- The Framework:
  o Process Optimization
  o Information Optimization
  o Total Cost Optimization
- Outsourcing
- Information Technology

The first two sections of the book (The Organization and The Framework) are timeless. These concepts are appropriate today, and I believe they will continue to be appropriate for many years to come. The third and fourth sections (Outsourcing and Information Technology) are particularly timely, and are meant as specific ways in which companies can move to be able to take advantage of the guidelines presented in the first two sections of the book. The sections are summarized as follows:

- Section I: The Organization
  o This section builds the case on the importance of processes and information in terms of the degree to which companies can be optimized.

Specifically, the organizational gaps prevalent in our companies today with respect to these two fundamental business imperatives are exposed. Part of the current condition is linked to the totally ineffective nature of the role of the CIO. This position does not warrant a C-level title. The role needs to be eliminated.

- o What we are missing in the C-level executive suite is a business-focused leader who has the vision and mandate to provide an enterprise-wide view of the organization around processes and information. Companies break down at all points of intersection with respect to these two areas. We need to have executive business leadership to fill these gaps and achieve enterprise-wide alignment across each of the following organization essentials: Strategy, Controls, People, Process, and Technology. That role belongs to the Chief Process and Information Officer (CPIO) and the Process and Information Department (PI Department). While some CIOs may make good CPIOs, many may not. This is fundamentally a *different* role with different responsibilities and a different charter. The book explores these differences in detail.
- o The PI Department, an organization focused on *business* (not technology), has four major components, each of which is explored in detail in this section:
  - Process Department
  - Information Department
  - Information Technology Department
  - Office of Program/Project Management
- o Case studies and concrete examples bring each of these concepts to life.

- Section II: The Framework
  - o Most companies lack a rigorous framework in which to guide the decision-making process. This section makes the case that all decisions fundamentally come down to whether or not the *net* effect of an initiative will improve the bottom line of the company as a whole by means of the following three areas:
    - Process Optimization
    - Information Optimization
    - Total Cost Optimization
  - o This is what I call the *Enterprise Optimization Framework*, as depicted below:

o The framework is meant to provide a high-level, philosophical approach to decision-making guidelines that can be referenced by anyone in a company, as well as a very detailed guideline for members of the PI Department who will use it for project opportunity analysis.

   ▪ Case studies are explored in significant detail to bring to life the analytical components of the framework, and to demonstrate how the business-focused PI Department can appropriately use the framework in reviewing and tracking the progress of opportunities.

   ▪ The case is made that the impact of a project must be measurable in order to be meaningful. The concept of quantifying "hard to measure" metrics is discussed with specific suggestions on how to utilize these measurements with multiple scenarios providing the basis for an ultimate decision.

   ▪ The concepts of the framework are then extended to each of the following areas, with specific guidance on how each of

these components should be utilized, including multiple discussions on the common inappropriate usage of today:
- Budgeting
- Staffing
- Steering committees
- Competitive advantage

- Section III: Outsourcing
  - o There is a lot of buzz in the marketplace today about the opportunities presented by outsourcing, including both information technology and business process outsourcing. This section explores what's real and what isn't real in the marketplace today, along with what's failed (and why) and what is going to lead to success in this space. It opens the door to the world of offshore outsourcing in terms of what makes sense and what doesn't for companies today, uncovering common misconceptions at both extremes.
  - o Service and solution provider outsourcing is featured in this section, including application service providers and the concept of software vs. service, as well as end-to-end, multi-platform managed services solutions. We are finally seeing viable business models emerge in these spaces, ones that finally deserve some consideration within the framework.
  - o The section concludes with an emphasis on what it means to establish a true partnership with an outsourcing arrangement—what that means, how it can be achieved, and what can happen if it is ignored. I believe anyone who has ever worked with an external vendor will feel the impact of this powerful section.

- Section IV: Information Technology
  - o The final section explores the world of information technology, and how it impacts our ability to achieve increasingly higher degrees of optimization relative to processes and information. I take a look at the typical IT infrastructure in place with companies today and identify why many of the decisions made in the last few years are no longer optimal and need to be reviewed. I make the case that Enterprise Optimization is strongly aided by an IT architecture that demonstrates a commitment to simple, single instance, common infrastructures.
  - o I also explore some of the latest IT innovations hitting the marketplace. Every PI Department needs to be aware of the latest and

greatest technology, but also needs to be cautious about unsubstan-
tiated hype. Among the areas discussed in this section are:
- On-demand services
- Web services
- Business process management (BPM)

o Once again, timely research and case studies provide insights to companies on how they can attack their current environmental problems
(which are often extensive), and how decisions relative to information
technology can assist in yielding improvements in all three areas of
the Enterprise Optimization Framework.

The four appendices featured at the end of the book provide the reader with additional depth to a particular topic, but may be at a level of detail that is beyond some
of the audience. As such, I included these areas in a more optional format for those
who are particularly interested in the details of that particular section.

My purpose with this book is not to simply regurgitate what the analyst community is saying. While I have leveraged some insights as provided by the analyst community to help substantiate and add depth to the analysis, this is by no means the
focus of the book. I am not an analyst and this is not a research paper. I have
attempted to articulate my thoughts on how companies can move down a path
toward optimization within the framework highlighted above. I have seen success
stories in some of these areas, some of which will be highlighted. I have also seen failure, and I will attempt to demonstrate many of the hard lessons that have been
learned by organizations that have struggled to move forward down this path.

Most discussions around IT involve getting out of a mess, or making sense of
the mess in which organizations find themselves. There are many common elements to "the mess." There are also a number of specific ways in which companies
can move beyond their current struggles. But make no mistake: this will involve
change, even significant change for many organizations. Companies are going to
need to recreate the norm in terms of organizational structure, decision-making
framework, and technology management. The good thing is that all of this is
doable. It may be harder for some organizations than others, and therefore may
take longer for some, but the opportunities are there for everyone. Those who
take advantage of this opportunity will thrive. Those who don't will die. Neither
extreme result will be immediate, but success or failure in this area will be representative of the fundamental lifeline of the business. I firmly believe that a strong
commitment behind this approach can move any company along the path
toward Enterprise Optimization. True believers may even approach the ultimate
state of the "Optimal Enterprise."

Section I: The Organization

The Criticality of Processes and Information

A couple of years ago, I had the opportunity to make a nighttime visit to the Santa Clara County, CA, 911 Emergency Call Center. This is one of the most technologically advanced 911 centers in the country. But what is truly amazing is the absolute commitment to processes and information integrity indicated by each and every action taken by the staff on duty that night. The stakes are the highest possible when calls come in on 911, and failure to stick to procedures or failure to provide the right information to the right people at the right time may quite literally mean the difference between life and death. When those dispatchers take a call, they must remain completely focused on their tried-and-true procedures. They need to quickly ascertain the situation and then follow explicit guidelines on what to say and who to contact based on the information they can obtain. Some of the information is provided by their systems (such as the phone number and location of the caller), but much of the critical information is case specific and must be elicited from the caller regardless of his or her state of panic. Based on the information retrieved, the dispatcher needs to follow the appropriate steps on what additional questions to ask, what advice to give, whom to contact, and to do so in a calm and straightforward manner. Deviation from process or the inability to capture the appropriate information can lead to catastrophic results.

Another element that caught my eye at the 911 center was the relatively simplistic nature of the process itself. By this I mean that the dispatchers have all the tools they need right at their fingertips, and the decision tree they were following had very few decision points before they could respond appropriately to any given call. The process designers have effectively narrowed the choices for these dispatchers so that virtually any call can be routed to the first line of response in a matter of seconds. Adding complexity, including more questions and more decision points, might be able to narrow the specific issue at hand in a more detailed fashion, but the inefficiency created by this added complexity would significantly impede the ability to achieve the ultimate objective, which is to provide immediate aid to the person on the phone.

1

Especially when time is of the essence, robust but simple procedures lead to optimal results. Complex procedures that slow things down can lead to death.

It was further apparent during my visit that this commitment to the highest standards for processes and information extends to the emergency service organizations that respond to the dispatches. Be it the fire department, police, or ambulance service, each of these entities must quickly absorb the information provided and then begin to execute its own reliable set of procedures. The response teams take the hand-off from dispatch and then take action in the next set of steps in this end-to-end process. What would happen if this complex set of processes and information flow broke down somewhere along the way? What would be the result if the fire department did not follow procedures in terms of preparedness and response time? What would be the result if the ambulance driver was taking a break and failed to notify dispatch, so was not ready to go when the call came in? What would be the result if the police were unclear on the information provided, failed to double-check, and ended up unprepared for the criminal activity underway? Simply put, these failures could lead to disaster. Moreover, repeated failures along these lines could lead to a total loss of confidence in the emergency response system. And it probably wouldn't take many failures to lead to this result, which could mean chaos for the community. When it's a matter of life and death, there is no margin for error, and strict adherence to processes and the highest commitment to Information Optimization can make all the difference in the world.

Now consider what it takes to successfully land a commercial airplane. Talk about the criticality of process and information. Have you ever listened on the in-flight audio system to the communication between the pilots and the air traffic control team? Here you'll find a classic example of rigorous attention to detail, all within the strict guidelines of a tightly controlled process. These aren't casual conversations. There is a focus on information flow that is restricted to neither more nor less than what is required. And everyone plays by the same rules, regardless of air carrier, nationality, or culture. In this case, the universal adoption of standards is a fundamental component of the end-to-end process. The traffic controllers call the shots based on rigid procedural guidelines, which allow for timely adjustments based on the latest and greatest available information. No one is allowed to deviate. Imagine one pilot who decides to ignore procedures and simply land his plane whenever he wants, regardless of instructions from the ground. Imagine the outcome.

This disciplined approach extends to all the other activities associated with these landings as well. The officers in the cockpit run through their checklists, with no deviation, for each and every landing. Why the discipline? It's just routine, right? Well, no, because even slight deviation can mean disaster. And what about the landing crews? Imagine if the signals from one crew differed from those of another. A lapse in either process discipline or adherence to standards on the ground could lead to information confusion in the cockpit, which could easily lead to a devastating result. An airplane landing is not an isolated act, limited to the free-wheeling responsibility of the single individual flying the plane. Rather, it is a complex process founded on the integrated needs of multiple participants performing a variety of distinct but highly connected roles. In a case where success is the only option, these functional process participants (pilots, flight attendants, air traffic controllers, ground crew members, etc.) are all relying on flawless execution from each other, supported by the continuous flow of timely and accurate information.

A rigorous commitment to well-defined processes and reliance and confidence in the information available is the difference between life and death in these high-risk areas. When the margin for error is small, so is the allowable deviation from standards. Plus, with everyone relying on everyone else in these multi-step, integrated processes, a single lapse anywhere along the line can prove catastrophic. This conclusion may seem obvious in these specific examples, but companies of all shapes and sizes need to be aware that things can turn just as catastrophic in the world of business when it comes to the suboptimal state of most of our processes and the quality of our information. Suboptimal performance in the 911 call center or in the air traffic control tower can clearly result in death. It is my contention that similar levels of suboptimal performance in our corporate processes and information quality can just as easily result in death—the death of our businesses. Death may not be immediate in the business world. It may be a gradual, slow erosion, but the result can be just as painful and just as final. The cancer may start small and grow by incremental amounts over long periods of time, but without preventative care, that tumor can grow exponentially and the patient (your business, in this case) goes on life support with high-risk emergency surgery as the only option to keep the patient (the business!) alive. And even then, it may be too late.

The strength in our companies and the way in which we achieve competitive advantage stems from two primary sources: (1) our ability to innovate and bring superior products and services to the marketplace, and (2) our ability to optimize processes and information in the realm of lowest total cost. While I acknowledge the importance of the first source, that is not what this book is about. Far too many companies focus exclusively on the first with complete disregard for the second, usually until an operations crisis surfaces and puts the company in serious jeopardy. As such, this book is focused on generating the maximum benefits that can be achieved with the second source, on how we can find the optimal balance between processes, information, and total cost to achieve operational excellence and gain competitive advantage. (By the way, optimization in these three areas related to the *processes* associated with product innovation is certainly in scope for discussion, just not the innovations themselves.) The book will also explore the downside with respect to lapses in these areas, which can lead directly to our downfall. We need to make a choice. We need to optimize our environments, or we need to prepare to meet our demise. It really is that simple. The economy, price pressures, global competition, and the marketplace in general will no longer support mediocrity. We may be able to sustain for a while in this state, but that's just prolonging the inevitable downward spiral to extinction. *Optimize now (or else!)*—that's our choice, and the "or else" could be devastating.

The good news is that there are things we can do to stand out amongst our peers to move down the path toward Enterprise Optimization. There are ways to organize our companies to eliminate much of the inefficiency that infects us today. There are ways to analyze and frame our key decisions to ensure an optimal degree of success. And there are ways for us to utilize existing solutions and technologies to further enhance our environments without engaging in unnecessary and destructive risk. We need to ask ourselves hard questions and be prepared for fundamental change.

Here are some basic questions to ponder based on the earlier examples:

- Why can't all our call centers be as efficient and effective as the 911 call centers?
- Why can't our global businesses settle on industry standards, such as with air traffic control, so that we can all become more efficient and effective?

More specifically:

- How can we be effective as organizations if our information flow is corrupted, such as with disconnects in the order-to-cash process flow from Order Management to Shipping to Customer Service?
  - o How is that any different from the 911 dispatcher providing incorrect information to the fire department regarding an emergency call?
- How can we be effective as organizations if our systems are unreliable and we execute our processes based on faulty information? Examples include denying credit to one of our best customers or consistently providing the wrong shipping date to customers.
  - o How is that any different from the 911 system providing the wrong address for the current emergency?
  - o How is that any different from air traffic control or systems in the cockpit providing faulty weather or distance information to pilots trying to land?

- How can we be effective as organizations if the norm is for everyone to constantly try to expedite what is important to *them*, making the rest of the company (and its customers) suffer?
  - o How is that any different from all the pilots trying to land their planes at the same time, regardless of procedural standards and the specific information provided by air traffic control?

Obviously death is more immediate in the latter case of each scenario, but the business scenarios can just as surely lead companies to the same death march if these occurrences become the norm. What is the real cost of customer dissatisfaction? How many times can you get away with one part of your company telling a customer one thing and another part of the company telling that same customer something completely different? What is the patience level for customers in your business? Companies that had previously competed solely based on superior products, most notably in the high tech industry, are now experiencing a commoditization of their products. As a result, one of the few remaining ways in which to differentiate themselves is through high quality, reliable service. If processes are such that it becomes to difficult to do business with these companies, it will become easy pickings for competitors to take market share by offering similar products but superior service based on more efficient processes and more effective use of information. In these hard economic times, your margin for error is razor thin, and customer loyalty may be the only thing keeping you alive, so it's up to you to never give these loyal customers a reason to look elsewhere.

Throughout this book the impact of processes and information in the business world will be explored, including:

- The attention that companies pay (or don't pay!) to these critical elements of survival.
- The lack of leadership in most companies in each of these key areas, and what should be done to alleviate this leadership gap.
- A framework in which to evaluate opportunities for optimization centered around the impact on processes, information, and total cost.
- Several initiatives to pursue that can help optimize our environments and avoid the slow death that can result from the failure to execute.

Various details of the quantifiable impacts of Process and Information Optimization in our environments will be explored to demonstrate the opportunities that effort and discipline can provide, as well as the damage that can result from lack of attention to these areas. And while discrete quantification is important when opportunities are evaluated at the project level in this framework, one must never forget the big picture. For each and every process or information failure, you're taking yet another step toward the extinction of your enterprise. The hardest part of these scenarios to quantify often represents the most devastating—things such as customer satisfaction and customer loyalty. What is the benefit when we succeed in these areas, and what is the cost when we don't? We need satisfied customers to drive revenue and profitability for our companies. Failure in these areas drives us right out of business. And the more complicated we make things, the harder it will be for us to be successful. So, welcome to a world where the means to avoid these slow, painful deaths will be identified, and where the fruits of your labor can be enjoyed by making some fundamental changes to your choices in organizational alignment and decision-making with regard to processes, information, and total cost. This represents the overall context of what I call Enterprise Optimization.

Current State of Affairs

Business models and the technologies that support them have gone through a number of cycles throughout the twentieth century. For a long time we focused on strong, centralized organizations that ran everything from corporate headquarters. These organizations were well suited for the mainframe technology of the day, which provided powerful capabilities for these highly centralized organizations, but very little for those "out in the field" in terms of capabilities and flexibility. These business models were also straining organizations due to the inefficiencies of always having to contact the home office for timely decisions (which were rarely very timely). By the early 1990s, companies were beginning to focus on the critical importance of geographic-based capabilities, requiring more distributed technical architectures to match the growing independence of these regionalized organizations. Technology morphed into the client-server model, which provided the ability for graphical user interfaces running on top of fully functional applications tailored to each region, with roll-up capabilities at the corporate level. That phase didn't last all that long, however, as we realized that this approach made our regional entities seem like separate companies to our customers, and the leverage we received from being part of a single enterprise was being lost. So, as we moved to the Internet age, our information technology moved to a model that could emphasize both centralized control as well as regional flexibility. These solutions were typically built around functional areas, which allowed us to become global entities again for our Customer Service, Finance, Manufacturing, Human Resources, etc., divisions across the globe. We arrived at a mix of centralized control over certain functions, while others maintained the freedom to respond to the immediate and dynamic needs of the local environment. In each case the business *function* was the entity around which our business models and supporting technology revolved. This is where many organizations around the world are today.

The question we must ask is whether any of these business or technology models is truly optimal for individual companies or even entire industries. Have we reached an optimal state, or are we still in the midst of another inevitable transition to yet another variation on the current model, or even a reversion back to something from the past? One element that has remained relatively constant throughout the organization models is that we have organized our companies around functional areas. It was nearly ten years ago when Michael Hammer and James Champy set out to change the way we organize our businesses, as well as how we use information technology to support the new model. They made the following claim at the outset of their best selling book, *Reengineering the Corporation*:

> The core message of our book, then, is this: It is no longer necessary or desirable for companies to organize their work around Adam Smith's division of labor. Task-oriented jobs in today's world of customers, competition, and change are obsolete. Instead, companies must organize work around *process*....The contemporary performance problems that companies experience are the inevitable consequences of process fragmentation.[1]

I agree with a lot in their revolutionary approach to business, yet by and large we still find ourselves structured around functions. It appears that change does not come easily. While many companies have increased their focus on processes in the past decade, we still have not rearranged our organization models around processes. We still have CFOs in charge of Finance and COOs in charge of Operations, yet no one is specifically in charge of most of our end-to-end processes, such as "order to cash" or "procure to pay." We still have silos that must be integrated by people, processes, and technologies in order to complete the overall activities for the company. As a result, despite some more legitimate concern around processes, we still encounter many of the same organizational inefficiencies that we have seen for decades. It appears that the following Hammer and Champy claim may not be as on target as they had imagined, or companies simply have yet to be able to get to this state of nirvana:

> In companies that have reengineered, however, organization structure isn't such a weighty issue. Work is organized around processes and the teams that perform them. Lines of communication? People communicate

with whomever they need. Control is vested in the people performing the process.[2]

The fact is, organization structure does matter, and that's one of the reasons we haven't been able to evolve into process-focused organizations. What CFOs have been willing to give up accounts receivable (part of "order to cash") or accounts payable (part of "procure to pay")? Not many. The same can be said for most of our org chart leadership positions. Organization structure matters to these people, and these are the folks in charge. My guess is that Hammer and Champy would simply state that this just means these organizations don't understand the benefits of a complete focus around processes, and that their resistance to change is killing their businesses. They may be right. But they also may be naïve to think that dramatically altering the focus of the company without a corresponding change in the organization structure could ever work. Leaders haven't been willing to give up their domains, and process-oriented teams haven't been able to become self-governing with respect to their processes. Just as they claimed that we didn't have a lot of "vice presidents of order fulfillment" in 1993,[3] we still don't have many of them today. Optimal or not, fundamental organization structure changes around processes have not permeated our companies, and we still have many of the same process fragmentation inefficiencies that we have had for years.

Another area where the prophecies of Hammer and Champy have yet to bear fruit relates to the people in whom power and authority is entrusted with respect to process definition. They suggested that the individuals closest to the customer should have this control, providing greater ability to be responsive to the needs of the moment and dramatically cut out the unnecessary cycles of centralized managerial decision-making. In theory, this sounds great. In reality, the decentralization of company authority has often yielded problematic results when measured on an enterprise-wide scale. The problem begins when decisions that are perceived as optimal at a local or functional level are in conflict with the optimization of the enterprise as a whole, especially for global entities that have the market-driven mandate to provide "one face to the customer." Constant process variation at the local level can result in inconsistencies that become problematic for the rest of the organization, and, in turn, for customers and business partners. They can also actually result in slower overall response times when local processes are in conflict with inter-connected local processes from other parts of the business, a not uncommon phenomenon for global enterprises.

Hammer and Champy felt that enterprise-wide data repositories within global information systems would be able to help overcome some of these challenges of decentralization, but once again reality has stepped in with some unwanted surprises. Those organizations that have centralized information management have certainly benefited from such a move; however, the more common response to the decentralization of processes and controls has been to decentralize information systems as well. That has left organizations with multiple instances of the same system, as well as different systems around the company for essentially the same function. These systems have become customized and disconnected, and even if they have been integrated, the integration is typically extremely fragile, unreliable, and inflexible. Decentralized systems of this nature, while appearing to provide for the unique needs of the individual functions and business units, are not only incredibly costly for the organization to deploy and maintain, but are also inhibitors to optimal information management in terms of providing an enterprise-wide view of the company's data. With this approach, you may win the local battles, but you're likely to lose the global war. To be clear, I am not advocating a police state whereby all activity is mandated by Big Brother at corporate headquarters. However, without some degree of centralization and standardization of processes and information management, companies will never be able to yield Enterprise Optimization when measured from an end-to-end, company-wide perspective.

I like to use an analogy of the structure of government with my clients when discussing this topic of centralization vs. decentralization of processes and controls. Every company should have a constitution in which the bedrock strategic principles of the organization are articulated, and the fundamental definitions and controls around processes and information are codified. Elements that make their way into this constitution are mandates that need to be followed throughout the organization. Elements that relate to end-to-end processes and key information components that yield the critical decision-making capabilities of the company should be spelled out for all to see, and adherence to the constitution should be monitored and correlated to performance evaluations. Beyond this centralized governance structure, there will be other structures that are more dispersed throughout the organization. There may be further governing boards at the regional, country, business unit, or functional levels that prescribe standards for activities that are appropriate for these more localized levels. The common theme must be that no rules at the lower levels can be in conflict with any of the mandates stemming from the higher levels of the organization. Moreover, nothing about this type of structure will be static. Processes must exist for the modifications of these guidelines and standards at all levels of the organization. Certain events may stimulate a further push to centralization, while other environmental changes may yield the need for more decentralized control. None of this is locked in stone. But the overall structure provides an excellent guideline for the means to establish the ways in which the company can balance the needs for flexibility at the local level, while also maintaining the necessary standards and controls that are fundamental for the optimal performance of the organization as a whole.

Finally, let's not take this governmental analogy too far. This structural mindset is not an analogy relative to the specific processes themselves or the execution of those processes. Far be it from me to suggest that our organizations begin to operate like traditional government agencies which have often been plagued with bloated bureaucracies. We'd probably all go out of business at that point. Think about the structure—that's the key part of the message. Do you have an enterprise model for your organization that articulates global standards for processes and information? Would your *overall* level of performance improve with a global constitution in place to address these concerns? Of course it's a balance when it comes down to this approach of centralization vs. decentralization. But the balance has swayed too much to the functional entities and the local teams. The move toward decentralization of processes and systems has been taken to the extreme. We need to refocus our organizations around optimal end-to-end processes, and that will require some movement toward standardization and consolidation of definitions, responsibilities, controls, and systems.

I heartily endorse the reengineering focus around processes in terms of achieving Enterprise Optimization. I agree that the optimal end state for companies may be to organize and operate completely as a collection of end-to-end business processes, and not as independent functional silos. This represents a vision worth pursuing, and some companies have done just that. Canada Post, for example, the publicly owned national postal service provider for Canada, went through a massive business transformation project starting in 1999, which included organizational realignment around four enterprise-wide processes: market, sell, serve, and fulfill. Canada Post now identifies itself as a "process enterprise [which] demands that every role from the executive on down can define not just its tasks and its success, but its very existence according to its relationship with one or more of these core processes."[4]

Another example is U.K.-based Electrocomponents plc, an international distributor of a wide range of electrical and electronic components. This organization adopted a process focus in the year 2000 when it introduced the leadership role of the Chief Process Officer (CPO). This multi-national collection of operating companies leverages what it calls "group processes" to drive end-to-end operational success. The operational processes include: product management, supply chain, media publishing, and facilities. These are supported by the following additional enterprise-wide processes: e-commerce, human resources, information systems, finance, and legal and company secretarial. Each process area has a specific set of metrics upon which it is evaluated, with metric categories ranging from efficiency to effectiveness to gross profit contribution to cost targets to benefits achieved. The company states: "By leveraging off our common process infrastructure we have been able to expand globally and accelerate the development of all our businesses. We can enter new markets with unmatched levels of service and confidence and at much lower cost than our competitors, and can disseminate best practice around the Group with speed and confidence." This organization has gone beyond just becoming a *process aware* organization and has ventured into the rare space of a truly *process-centric* company, and has rallied around this structure as the optimal means for expansion and rapid growth.[5]

Other large U.S.-based organizations have also generated significant benefits for their companies based on adopting a process-based path toward optimization. IBM, Dow, Wal-Mart, FedEx, and Dell are among those companies that have created a competitive advantage by instituting optimization initiatives wrapped around the fundamentals of process and information, and I'm sure there are others. But this has not been the norm. If it were, we all might be better off, as the process-focused enterprise could eliminate many of the bottlenecks and headaches that we encounter within businesses focused around functional and geographic silos. But the fact is most companies have not made the leap toward becoming process enterprises, and in the need for practical solutions, where manageable change needs to be reasonable and wholesale revolution is probably unrealistic, I'm not prepared to simply advocate a change that so few have chosen to adopt. There is another way to achieve process-focused optimal results without changing the entire structure of the organization. The approach in this book will explore in detail the opportunities available to organizations based on a focus of optimizing three critical elements of their environments (Process Optimization, Information Optimization, and Total Cost Optimization), and will do so based on changes most organizations can begin to act upon almost immediately. In this first section, I will explore the Organization aspect of this approach. In subsequent sections, I will discuss in detail a framework for decision-making in the context of Enterprise Optimization, as well as the impact outsourcing and information technology can have in optimizing our environments.

The Role of Information Technology Departments: Present and Future

As mentioned, most of our organizations have yet to evolve into completely process-driven structures. We still map processes from one functional unit to the next, with the corresponding hand-offs at each point of intersection. These intersection points represent some of the greatest deficiencies of our overall operations. One of the reasons is that most organizations simply do not have anyone overseeing these end-to-end processes to ensure that these points of failure are reviewed and improved. The only group that typically has any sense of these process gaps is the Information Technology (IT) Department, and this is more by default than anything else. This group typically gets involved when data gets stuck going from one system to the next, or when data integrity is called into question somewhere along the way. So IT has some role in helping us through our process challenges, but this organization has never been defined in a position of authority such that it can truly drive organizational change on a path to optimization. IT's role is generally to fix a problem, often receive blame for causing the problem in the first place, and then be sent on its merry way until the next problem pops up that brings the business to its knees. That's a typical IT cycle, often because IT is rarely empowered to bring interrelated functional groups together and drive fundamental process change.

Now, it's important to give IT organizations their due. IT has done a pretty effective job enabling companies to grow from completely siloed organizations into what I like to call "tactically integrated." Siloed companies are those that operate in a disconnected, non-cohesive fashion, with work being managed largely independently within a functional or geographic silo. The silo itself may operate in an efficient manner, but siloed organizations are very rarely efficient when it comes to end-to-end processes, and rarely effective when trying to provide a single face to its customers and business partners. Also, with information sharing at a minimum in these organizations, decision-making is both slow and based on incomplete data, thereby making those decisions often far less than optimal. As companies mature in their capabilities and cohesiveness, both efficiency and effectiveness tend to improve, often to a much higher level than in a siloed state, and IT has helped many companies make this leap. The implementation of Enterprise Resource Planning (ERP), Supply Chain Management (SCM), and Customer Relationship Management (CRM) systems have all helped organizations by at least providing an integrated data flow, and certain elements of governance as defined and maintained by these enterprise-level systems. So, even if various elements within organizations (such as functions and/or geographic units) still remain relatively autonomous, these "tactically integrated" companies do have the opportunity to reap some benefits with standards and controls in place at least with respect to the system-specific components of their end-to-end activities.

While IT organizations and these enterprise systems have enabled performance improvement both with respect to functional execution and information-based decision-making, there is a limit as to how far IT can lead companies with respect to organizational maturity. The problem is that to grow from "tactically integrated" to "process driven," which is a big part of what this book is about, it isn't sufficient to just thrown in a new IT system. To become a "process driven" organization requires alignment around more than just information technology. Truly "process driven" organizations must broaden the scope of optimization to include each of the following elements, and further ensure that each of these elements is aligned with the other four:

- **Strategy:** The strategic vision for the organization, along with the understanding of the role, positioning, and focus for enterprise-wide decision-making in support of the company's overall objectives
- **Controls:** The governance model for the management, administration, and evaluation of initiatives, with a strong focus on the appropriate metrics applied for measurement
- **People:** The human resource environment, including skills, organizational culture, and organization structure
- **Process:** Operating methods and practices, including policies and procedures, which determine the way activities are performed
- **Technology:** Enabling information systems, applications, tools, and infrastructure

Only when *all five* of these organizational elements are aligned toward the enterprise-wide goal of process and information optimization will the true benefits of a "process driven" organization be realized. Companies can't simply proclaim a strategic intent to become "process driven" and achieve the desired results without accounting for the operational components of the strategy. A governance model without a supporting strategy or organization model won't work either. And a new IT system without these other elements will enable you to automate elements of your environment, but that doesn't mean you'll ever be able to achieve truly breakthrough levels of improvement. This is one of the fundamental reasons why IT organizations are not well-suited to leading an enterprise's transformation from "tactically integrated" to "process driven." In most companies, the only one of the five levers identified above that is truly owned and controlled by IT is Technology. In fact, not only does IT not own the Strategy, Controls, People, or Process elements, it often doesn't even have much influence on any of those four components. IT is often asked to step in at times and provide guidance in some of these areas (usually because no other entity is available to address these elements), but the positioning of IT within most companies today does not provide a real opportunity to *lead* decision-making in most of these areas. Even when IT is staffed by business savvy, process-focused professionals, more often than not, "the business" is not receptive to attempts at organizational leadership from IT based on the perception that those individuals are basically the "technology people," and not much more than that.

Consider that IT represents the only department in most companies that is distinguished as being distinct from "the business." In every IT project in which I have ever participated, you invariably hear the discussion about how "IT" thinks things should be vs. how "the business" thinks it should be. "Are you a member of IT or are you from the business?" is a common question in understanding someone's role and motivations in a project. How is that anything but counterproductive? Aren't all of these employees part of "the business?" Let's face it, this distinction does not come with a positive twist. If you're part of IT, and therefore not part of "the business," then you're always starting one step behind the rest of the team in terms of credibility, presumed bias, buy-in, etc. This dynamic is what I call the "Grand IT/Business Divide," and it exists in one degree or another in most companies today. In IT shops of the future (which need to be renamed, of course), these core process- and information-focused individuals will be just as much a part of "the business" as anyone in Finance, Manufacturing, or Human Resources. What needs to happen is that the nuts and bolts of the technology must truly go into the background, and the business focus of these organizations needs to come front and center, leading with the two principle needs of the company: (1) Process Optimization, and (2) Information Optimization.

Why do companies invest in projects? The objective is generally to improve on capabilities by way of increased efficiency or effectiveness. These capabilities may be internally focused (primarily affecting the performance of employees) or externally focused (primarily touching the needs of customers, suppliers, various partners, etc.). In either case, the projects come down to allocating funds to improve the *performance* or *experience* of one of these constituencies. That boils down to what I call **Process Optimization**. Imbedded in this title is the concept that your company will improve its overall standing if it can improve the capability or efficiency of one or more of these entities, or enhance their experience in a material way. The ability to do that comes down to the processes by which these entities interact with (or within) your company, where a *process* is defined as a set of continuous activities that are interconnected for the purpose of achieving a specific outcome. For example, the "order-to-cash" process encompasses a number of specific tasks that follow a logical progression in order to provide a product or service to a customer and ultimately receive payment for that product or service. Typically, this process will cross multiple functional units within an organization, and include many of the following sub-processes or tasks:

- Create Customer Accounts
- Manage Contracts
- Maintain Customers
- Manage Credit
- Maintain Pricing
- Manage Sales Orders
- Pick Products
- Ship to Customer
- Create Install Base
- Bill Customers
- Collections
- Aging Analysis
- Receive Payments

As suboptimal components throughout this process are identified, concrete and quantifiable opportunities for improvement can be evaluated and pursued in the spirit of Process Optimization. This concept applies to any process within an organization, including those that cross organizational barriers and those that extend to customers and/or partners. If a company can operate more efficiently, then its cost burden should be reduced, and the company's bottom line will be enhanced. If the customer-related processes are enhanced, then the top line should grow, and, again, the company will see the benefits. (A detailed list of a number of additional core processes will be provided later in this section.)

One additional point about process definition is that there is generally a vast difference between a "complex process" and an "optimal process." As mentioned, you're much more likely to achieve an optimal result based on keeping things as simple as possible, rather than adding layers of complexity. It may appear that adding sophistication to a process may be increasing capabilities, but mostly it just makes things confusing and harder to execute. This may be counter to conventional wisdom, which seeks to gain competitive advantage through unique, multi-faceted, highly complex, exhaustive processes. More often than not, this approach yields a false prophecy. You will often find yourself managing the majority of your transactions as exceptions instead of the other way around, and all sense of efficiency is tossed aside. The preferred method is commonly referred to as the KISS methodology ("Keep It Simple, Stupid"). "Keeping it simple" will be a common theme throughout this book as a means to achieve an optimal result.

Just as important as Process Optimization are a company's needs in the areas of information and reporting. All too often today it is the IT analysts who are making the key decisions about the reporting requirements for a company. Partly this is because "the business" is too busy with other things to focus on reporting.

The common expression during project implementations is, "Just give me what I've got today." The problem, of course, is that with new systems come new data structures, new data elements, new transactional flows, etc., so it's never quite as simple as "Just give me what I've got today." Plus, "what you've got today" may not represent the optimal information set that could be available. Information requirements are all too often afterthoughts in the context of current IT projects, and they're among the very first things that "the business" points to after a go-live in terms of what isn't working with a new system.

Information and Reporting need to come out of the dark hole in which they find themselves, usually buried somewhere within the bowels of IT organizations, where people tend to be off on their own trying the best they can to figure out what "the business" wants. It's an impossible task based on the typical organization structure of today. Companies are run by their processes and their information, so just as optimal transaction flow is critical to bottom line success, so is getting the right information to the right people at the right time. In order to accomplish this task effectively, **Information Optimization** needs to become a core competence of companies, with *information* defined in this context as the assimilation of data from all sources within an organization and the presentation of that data in a timely and accurate fashion so that members of the organization can make informed decisions. Business executives need to take a leadership role in defining standards around information, and facilitating the appropriate distribution and consumption of that information. This is not the role of a technical team with data warehouse training. This is a critical role of business leadership, providing the business community with the essential tools that are needed to enable effective decision-making.

In reviewing IT environments of today in terms of the technology itself, we have witnessed tremendous advances in capabilities, but we are also still paying the price for deploying solutions that are currently inhibiting our ability to achieve optimal results for our businesses. For example, decentralized systems development has brought IT shops down the path of supporting variations of systems, instances, customizations, etc., for different regional entities around the world. For each variance, corporate-wide optimization takes a step back, in terms of process and information management as well as total cost of ownership. One reason we have gone down this path is the limitation of the software and infrastructure tools that have been available over the years. One primary limitation has arisen from the inability to provide truly global systems due to inadequate network capabilities. Global instances weren't practical because of network latency, but once you're onto different instances, you're talking different support organizations, different decision-making, and ultimately different systems—even when you're using the same basic software applications. A new technology paradigm now exists with the pervasive nature of high-speed Internet access bringing the world closer together, at least from a systems perspective. Global application instances are now viable and should be strongly encouraged. In addition, the world has gotten smaller with the widespread availability of low-cost, high-quality software development resources located in a variety of pockets around the world, providing further incentive to rethink our current IT structures.

With these new capabilities and the opportunities they present, it is finally time to take a look at the traditional IT organization of today. It is time to throw out old assumptions, and be prepared to pursue a new organizational model. It is time to align around core competencies of the company, such as process and information management, and to do so at the lowest total cost as possible. This is not the way we are structured today. But it is time to change, to focus on what matters most, and to move from an IT focus to a process and information focus that will yield competitive advantage over those organizations that remain stuck in the older, traditional IT model.

The Call for Fundamental Change

One of the most glaring weaknesses in our typical organizational structures of today revolves around the role of the Chief Information Officer (CIO). This comment is both with respect to what the CIO role *is*, and what the CIO role *is not*. Let's take a look at this title and try to provide a link between the title and the actual role.

Any C-level executive in an organization should be a strategic leader who has broad responsibility across the enterprise, and should have direct accountability to the company's Chief Executive Officer (CEO). Why else put the "C" in front of the title? Tactical individuals have no business being a "chief" in any company. People who aren't important enough to report directly to the CEO simply shouldn't be labeled a "chief." These are the people on whom we rely to steer the ship and make the strategic decisions about the direction of the entire organization. This definition usually is appropriate for Chief Operating Officers (COOs), Chief Financial Officers (CFOs), and Chief Technology Officers (CTOs). Most of these individuals have broad levels of responsibilities, often crossing multiple functional organizations, and most report directly to the CEO. For some reason we don't have a C-level title for our top executive in Sales, but maybe we should, as this individual typically fulfills this kind of broad-based strategic role as well.

So what about CIOs? How many CIOs are truly strategic leaders in their organizations? How strategic are the people in these roles when recent surveys indicate that more than half of all CIOs report to someone other than the CEO?[6]

What other C-level executive doesn't report directly to the CEO? Is there one? Moreover, the trend is not positive, as the percentage of CIOs reporting to the CFO *doubled* from 2002 to 2003.[7] What kind of message does it send to CIOs who report to the CFO? Doesn't that just perpetuate the fact that CIOs and their organizations are viewed simply as cost centers that are subservient to Finance, as opposed to strategic leaders within the organization? In fact, that's exactly how most CIOs view themselves. According to *CIO* magazine's 2003 survey, *The State of the CIO, 84%* of the more than 500 CIOs who participated in the survey said that "their IT function is currently being budgeted as a cost center that generates expenses rather than an investment center that generates new business capabilities."[8] Does this describe a role that merits a strategic, C-level position in an organization?

C-level executives are responsible for running the company. CEOs, CFOs, COOs, CTOs—these people run the company. CIOs don't run the company. CIOs run the Help Desk. And let me be clear. This is not an indictment of the *people* in this role. No, this is an indictment of the *role itself* and how the individuals placed in these roles have become perceived and utilized in most organizations today. It's sad to say, but the CIO is much more likely to get a call from his CEO when the latter can't log into his e-mail from home than when he has a strategic business imperative that he would like to bounce off one of his senior advisors. The reason? Because, despite the lofty title, CIOs continue to be viewed inside most organizations as simply the head of IT, and that is a much more tactical role than one would ever expect for a true C-level executive.

What are most CIOs expected to do? Primarily, it is to design, implement, support, and enhance the company's information technology assets. To the degree that this role supports the strategic direction of the company tends to vary from one organization to the next, but the fundamental expectation is basically the same. Some of these folks have a seat at the table when the major decisions are made, but many do not. They are typically handed some requirements, and then tasked with finding the optimal approach to bringing those requirements to life. Most of the time, the value the CIO is expected to add is focused on the technology component of the solution, not the strategy itself. The IT Departments that CIOs manage are usually evaluated based on their *cost structure* (i.e., IT spend as a percent of revenue) and are rarely evaluated in terms of the overall *value* they bring to the organization.

I struggle with the CIO title on another level as well. The title implies that the CIO is the chief of the company's *information*. But, let's face it, it's the *technology* that supports the management of the information for which the CIO is primarily responsible. How many times have you heard IT organizations claim, "We don't own the data, we just manage the systems. If *they* put in lousy data, don't hold *us* accountable." (There's that "they" and "us" divide again.) CIOs and IT don't manage the information assets—they manage the systems that support those assets. Really, if this were a C-level role, then the more appropriate title would be CIT or CITO, for Chief Information Technology Officer. After all, CIOs lead Information *Technology* Departments, not Information Departments. My guess is memories of our childhood days at camp with Counselors in Training (CITs) had something to do with the unwillingness to adopt the moniker, but it would be more appropriate. Semantics aside, however, the distinction is important. It goes to the conflict between the lofty title and the actual role that CIOs are expected to fulfill.

So, how did we get here, and what should we be doing about it? Initially, when CIOs started coming onto the scene, it was at a time when information technology was new, exciting, and appeared to hold the cards for competitive advantage. Leaders in this space who could understand the benefits of these new technologies, and could effectively manage projects throughout the enterprise, were thought of as strategic players for the company, especially those who could find the links between the technologies and the strategic business initiatives and core processes that required optimization. The early adopters who leveraged breakthroughs in information technology in this business-focused manner had the correct notion of promoting these sophisticated individuals to the upper levels of the organization.

Unfortunately, a handful of things transpired as time moved on. Many companies that created spots for CIOs still did not actually allow these individuals to take a leadership role in process-oriented actions. The functional leaders still owned the processes, and relied on the CIOs to support them with the technology. Moreover, over the past decade, many business functions found themselves inundated with huge technology initiatives where the technology often led the design of the solution rather than the specific process or information challenges in place. As a result, CIOs and IT became easy targets for blame when results fell short of expectations, regardless of whether they deserved that blame or not. This blame game has further hurt IT organizations with respect to their credibility in fulfilling a leadership role in subsequent process-focused initiatives. In some cases, this perception has been warranted, while in others it's a case of perception overtaking reality. In either case, IT's credibility as a leader in the drive for enterprise optimization has been diminished. Another dynamic that must be recognized is that we found over the years that if one company in an industry had a CIO, then every other company needed to demonstrate its prowess by promoting or hiring its own CIO. As a result, we found ourselves inundated with a ton of really smart IT directors sitting in C-level positions. This method of promoting talented but tactically focused individuals into what should be a strategic and process-driven role helped perpetuate the reality that CIOs are rarely more than the leader of the IT support organization. This helps to yield the widespread belief that IT is here to *serve* its customers in "the business," rather than function as a strategic organization that is part of "the business" and that should work collaboratively from the very beginning on strategic initiatives.

The fact is, in most cases:

- CIOs are not used as strategic decision-makers.
- CIOs are expected to focus much more on the technology side of IT than the information (or process) imperatives of the business.
- CIOs run an organization that is expected to *serve* the business, rather than *lead* the business.
- Many CIOs would not be able to serve in a strategic capacity even if given the opportunity because their background is often in technology and not in the essential process and information elements of business.

Moreover, as will be discussed in greater detail in Section III (Outsourcing), IT is in many ways no longer a strategic element, especially as far as the actual technology is concerned. Many components of the traditional IT organization have become largely commoditized, and must, therefore, be treated differently. Finally, IT is simply not a core competence of most organizations. As such, I strongly advocate the outsourcing of many of the traditional IT functions as a path toward the overall optimization of the enterprise.

Given all this, the following questions must be asked:

- Why is the leader of IT given a C-level title without C-level responsibilities?
- How we can change the title, role, and structure of this leadership position to help organizations achieve optimal results?

While we should not be satisfied with what the CIO's role has become, there is a desperate need in most organizations for a C-level role that is *not* being fulfilled. That role includes information management as one of its core requirements, coupled with the area of end-to-end process leadership. Processes and information are absolutely strategic elements on which companies can rise and fall. However, very few companies have leaders and internal organizations in place to be both the driver and the watchdog of these fundamental business requirements. We have functional leaders who own limited organizations, and may serve to optimize those environments quite well. However, what good is that optimization if things constantly fall apart when processes span from one functional area to the next (as they often do)? Rarely is anyone in the company looking after these touch points, which is precisely where leadership is needed—to manage through the tough spots where ownership is unclear and responsibility falls to the side. We need alignment around all five levers discussed earlier in this section (Strategy, Controls, People, Process, and Technology) to have a chance at achieving breakthrough levels of efficiency and effectiveness, yet rarely is any individual or group assigned this responsibility, either at the top of the organization or throughout the management structure. Sometimes IT organizations are forced into this role by default, but they are rarely empowered to make key decisions that affect the functional organizations. This is the problem of the "Grand IT/Business Divide." IT is a service organization that is often shot down when it tries to lead. Even when CIOs and their IT personnel have the right focus and the right answers for the organization, they are rarely put in a position where they have enough authority to fill these gaps. I have encountered numerous CIOs who could provide this leadership based on personal experience, skills, and vision, but are thwarted in their attempts by a business community that doesn't respect this kind of leadership from the head of IT. They may be the right people, but the organization structure identifies them as "support," so at best they can influence others but rarely can they drive effective decision-making.

Everything about this structure is suboptimal. It's suboptimal in that no one is looking out for end-to-end processes to begin with, creating process inefficiencies and information management nightmares. It's suboptimal because there may be individuals within the organization who can provide this leadership, but they are stuck under the label of "IT" and therefore not deemed up to the task. And in some cases, since there's no spot on the org chart for process and information leadership, some companies simply lack this skill set altogether. That may be the most suboptimal component of all. All of this conspires against the health of our organizations, leaving us in a situation where the whole adds up to far *less* than the sum of the parts. We need to leverage each of the elements of our entire organizations in a way such that the whole is *greater* than the sum of the parts.

So here's where the call for fundamental change enters the discussion. It is time to call for an organizational change to address this gap in our corporate leadership structures, one that has a corresponding impact on our present-day CIOs and their IT organizations. It is time to call for the introduction of the Process and Information Department (PI Department) as a strategic entity within our organizations, led by a true C-level executive, the Chief Process and Information Officer (CPIO).

The Process and Information Department

One of the key differences between IT organizations of today and PI organizations of tomorrow is that PI Departments are *part of the business,* breaking down the barriers that exist in the world of the IT/Business Divide. These are not separate service organizations. They are groups of business professionals, with business backgrounds and leadership skills, who are out front on many initiatives within the company. These are strategic groups that have a seat at the table at the top of the org chart and are very much involved in the overall direction of the enterprise. Some organizations have clearly begun to take a deeper look into the organizational imperatives around processes with newly defined leadership in this area, but often this is viewed as an operational role, and not a strategic one reporting directly to the CEO. Further, these organizations typically introduce this process leadership alongside the existing CIO structure, which tends to just create further territorial conflict. We need a new structure. Something needs to be added, and something needs to be altered. We need CPIOs. We need PI Departments. We don't need CIOs. We don't need IT Departments as they exist today.

The appropriate organization structure for a company today entails the introduction of the role of the Chief Process and Information Officer as a peer to the other C-level executives in the company (see Figure I-1). The executive leadership team (including the CPIO) is responsible for the establishment of the strategic objectives of the organization, and also has the ultimate responsibility for the implementation of initiatives and tasks that are consistently supportive of those enterprise-wide goals. The CPIO then communicates those objectives to the PI Department, which has multiple responsibilities in terms of evaluating, approving, prioritizing, implementing, and supporting those initiatives across the organization. The organization structure depicted in Figure I-1 provides a view on the relationships of these various entities across the company. These relationships will be explored further throughout this section.

Figure I-1: Company Organization Structure, including the CPIO, the PI Department, and the Inter-relationships with the Rest of the Organization

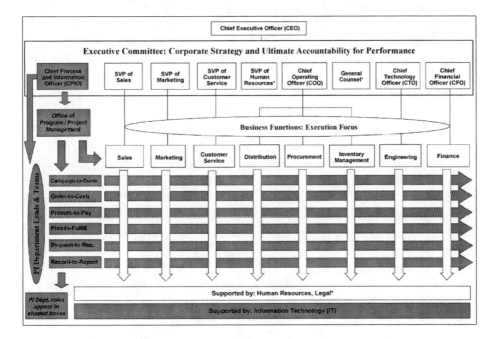

As mentioned, most organizations today do not have a specific entity tasked with overseeing end-to-end business processes. Yet it was established long ago that many of our most profound business stumbling blocks occur when processes cross from one functional silo to another. A customer is concerned with the entire life cycle for "order-to-cash" or "issue-to-resolution," not just with one component of those processes. Unfortunately, we are constantly letting these customers down by allowing gaps in these processes to exist and not be actively addressed. We lose credibility with our customers each and every time we fail at these functional touch points, which can be clearly seen in Figure I-1. A failure to provide "one face to the customer" is a common deficiency of our organizational capabilities today, yet it is one of the most desired capabilities in the marketplace. We can't provide "one face to the customer" with companies founded on functional silos, especially without anyone overlooking the connections and dependencies between those entities. There are similar challenges when processes cross geographic regions (more silos), even when within the same functional unit. In terms of process effectiveness, consider the following:

- Who is responsible for ensuring that what your engineers design can actually be built (manufactured) in a repeatable and profitable manner?
- Who is responsible for ensuring that forecasts from Sales are effectively communicated to the Manufacturing organizations as inputs to their build plans?
- Who is responsible for ensuring that the Customer Service organization obtains accurate information with respect to a customer's install base immediately upon shipment?
- Who is responsible for ensuring that the Sales organization is informed of credit and/or collections issues related to a specific customer?
- Who is responsible for tracking the life cycle of marketing campaigns, as they pass from leads to opportunities to quotes to orders, and acting upon issues along the way?
- Who is responsible for ensuring that changes within Human Resources regarding organization structure are communicated to the Purchasing organizations, which require such information for approval hierarchies?

In terms of master data, consider the following:

- Who owns the customer master (Operations, Order Management, Sales, Customer Service, or Accounts Receivable)?
- Who owns the vendor master (Purchasing or Accounts Payable)?
- Who owns the item master (Operations, Order Management, Document Control, or Marketing)?
- Who owns the price lists (Order Management, Marketing, Sales, or Customer Service)?

In light of these questions, the following must also be asked:

- What happens when no one is able to definitively answer the above questions?
- What happens when multiple groups claim responsibility or ownership? Does that lead to an optimal environment or does that lead to things falling through the cracks?
- What happens when IT is thrust into the middle of these border disputes? Can IT effectively lead these silo organizations to agree to solutions that would be optimal for the company, but may not be optimal for one or both individual parties? Can current IT organizations lead, in the absence of any alternative leadership, without real authority from above?

The fact is, these process gaps occur in most organizations, whenever processes cross functional areas (or geographies), and yet rarely does anyone have direct control over the gaps. Even COOs and CFOs may only have ultimate responsibility for parts of a process. IT is often the only organization that is truly cross-functional in its nature, but rarely does IT have the clout in the organization to drive resolution, even when it does arrive at the optimal solution for the enterprise. While these process gaps are commonplace, they are clearly not compatible with an enterprise trying to optimize its environment. And this is just for processes that are managed primarily inside the walls of the company itself. What about all the processes that extend to external partners and outsource service providers? Who is responsible for ensuring Process Optimization and appropriate decision-making for these complicated tasks? This is why we need the horizontal focus in Figure I-1, to provide the leadership and cohesion to bring our companies together for optimal effectiveness.

What makes matters even more challenging in this context these days is that suboptimal performance around processes and information no longer is limited to inflicting pain on the organization in the marketplace. This new law affectionately known as Sarbanes-Oxley, which was passed in 2002 to address the concerns of integrity in our corporate governance structures and processes, has senior executives worried about serious lapses landing them in prison. This act of Congress has companies now finally focusing on their long-neglected processes and controls. However, just seeking compliance with the act does not represent a truly optimal response. Some organizations have responded to Sarbanes-Oxley with new internal audit functions, but these teams are typically focused on compliance, not optimization. It is a defensive approach based on a premise of staying out of trouble. Compliance is certainly important, but it is actually even more important for companies to implement best practices around processes and information, and then remain compliant in what can be considered an optimal environment. Having an audit function trying to ensure compliance in a suboptimal structure doesn't appear to provide a lot of benefit for these executives, their employees, or their shareholders. The typical result is a set of binders full of process flows and policy statements that end up sitting on a shelf and rarely, if ever, receiving any practical attention from anyone in the company. In other words, other than keeping you out of jail, most Sarbanes-Oxley initiatives that are purely focused on compliance will add very little real value to the organization.

In order to turn these efforts into tangible benefits, companies should focus not just on compliance and controls, but also on extending these themes into *optimal* processes that encompass appropriate compliance and controls. If you're going to go through the effort to become compliant, why not get your Process and Information professionals aligned in an enterprise-wide initiative that actually analyzes these documented processes, and look for opportunities for improvement? Don't just document what you have today and make insignificant adjustments just in the name of compliance—optimize for the future! That's where real benefits can be had, with the focus shifting from compliance to optimization. That's where all this effort and cost will actually yield material benefits for your organization, rather than just be a government-mandated waste of time and money. And that's where the leadership from the Process and Information Department kicks in.

Then there's the issue of information security. At first you may think that this is IT's responsibility, but guess again. Many of a company's information assets are completely outside the realm of IT. Sure, IT supports the core systems, but there is a great deal of critical information within an organization that typically extends far beyond these core systems. Who is responsible for the security of these "off-line" information assets? Some areas that may be particularly exposed include Engineering, Legal, and Human Resources, which often use off-line means to manage critical information for which IT has no insight or responsibility. Is anybody looking after this stuff? The PI Department is the solution to this gap.

Finally, what about technology, specifically traditional information technology? If we need a new organization to look after processes and information, what happens to our current IT organizations, which have responsibility for the selection, implementation, integration, maintenance, and enhancement of our systems infrastructure? This responsibility surely does not go away, but it will be managed differently in companies that adopt the vision of a PI Department. As will be discussed in sections III and IV, information technology becomes one of the responsibilities of the PI Department, but with a different focus and different alignment.

At this point one may have a concern about the type of organizational model depicted in Figure I-1 simply as a shift of control from functional leadership within an organization to this newly created central body, and that the likely result will be continuous conflict. If executed poorly, this could, in fact, be the result. So let me be clear on how to implement a PI Department in your organization, as well as the division of responsibilities between this group and the functional units that will continue to exist and operate in conjunction with this new team. The PI Department is an umbrella organization that must receive its mandate from the top of the company. This means the CEO, President, and maybe even the Board of Directors will need to publicly announce and support this structure in the best interests of the overall company. The CEO, in both words and actions, must send a strong signal to the entire organization regarding the strategic value of the Process and Information Department. This message needs to resonate at the leadership level and on down throughout the entire company. Without this top-level support, companies shouldn't even try—they simply won't succeed. These are not bottom-up changes being proposed. This kind of change will only work from the top down, and not just by changing a few business cards and org charts. A lot of this comes down to leadership. If a new organization unit is created without a mandate from the company's leadership, it is doomed to fail. You'll simply be back to "us" and "them" with no one in charge and no progress being made. The organization's leadership must rally around this structure, and the correct set of individuals must be placed into the leadership roles in this new department. (The profile of the key roles in the PI Department will be discussed in detail later in this section.)

I'd like to believe that this kind of top-down mandate will be sufficient to empower the new organization and gain universal buy-in, but I'm realistic enough to understand that this will only get you so far. No matter how much verbal support is provided in launching this fundamental change, and no matter the depth of business talent that is poured into the make-up of this new organization, there will still be resistance that will only grow as time wears on and the verbal support begins to wane as focus moves into other directions. Companies need to understand that the acceptance of transformational change must be facilitated and managed by experienced professionals. This is the only way to achieve real alignment around Strategy, Controls, People, Process, and Technology, and this requires an organizational commitment and investment that becomes an additional responsibility of the PI Department. CPIOs should ease into their new roles and pick small, high-value opportunities to begin asserting their new responsibilities. Quick wins will yield trust and respect which will serve CPIOs and their teams well for the long haul. A full-bore enterprise-wide transformation initiative right out of the gate may provide positive results, but too much change too fast coming from "corporate" may be resented and, therefore, yield obstructionist responses. Company cultures vary widely in terms of being able to adapt to dramatic changes quickly. My experience has taught me that the temptations to institute dramatic change all at once usually results in strong pockets of resistance. A well-directed, well-managed phased approach is often much more effective, and tends to pave the way for more rapid acceptance to transformational initiatives in the future. By the way, effectively managing the approach and alignment around transformational change may require a concerted effort at the very top of the organization in the first place. As mentioned, without this alignment in the executive suite, most transformational initiatives are doomed before they even begin. You should not assume that this alignment will happen naturally. In fact, alignment at this level is often the most difficult to achieve. Just as the PI

Department needs to guide the rest of the organization through an alignment exercise, it will likely also be needed to first address this thorny issue with the executives themselves. Don't underestimate the need for this alignment! Lack of a concerted effort up front in this area will likely yield numerous roadblocks throughout the life of the initiative, and will significantly inhibit your ability to achieve alignment throughout the rest of the organization.

It must also be recognized that even these efforts directed at alignment and ensuring top down support may not be enough to achieve the required level of institutional buy-in to support these fundamental shifts in the organization. Ultimately, *financial* incentives and budgetary control will also be needed to foster real support. **As such, the PI Department needs to become the central decision-making body for approving and prioritizing all relevant initiatives throughout the company.** The key word in that statement is *relevant*, which may have different definitions based on the size and complexity of the organization. Companies should identify a monetary cap that if exceeded would initiate the PI Department approval process. For some companies that number may be $1,000. For others, it may be $50,000 or $100,000 and so on. My suggested path is to initially institute this cap at a very low number, and then consider increasing the number over time as the policies, procedures, and disciplines become institutionalized throughout the organization. The point is that in order to truly empower the PI Department, it must have fiscal control over the initiatives across the organization. Moreover, the PI Department must control not only the budgetary approval process, but also the allocation of those expenditures to the functional units that will receive the benefits from the initiatives. Someone needs to own this responsibility to avoid endless bickering over these allocations, and the PI Department is the answer. (The process for the appropriate allocation of project budgets will be discussed in detail in Section II.)

As for prioritization, this, too, must fall into the hands of the PI Department for all relevant initiatives (as defined above). Some group must be empowered to align the strategic imperatives of the company with the opportunities for optimization, and not only provide approval at the individual project level, but also identify the optimal staging of these initiatives for deployment. The decision-making framework, which will be introduced in Section II, will be one of the primary tools used by the PI Department in this regard, but the closed-loop approach to prioritization must account for the overall objectives set by senior management. Typically there is too much risk associated with trying to implement all of a company's initiatives at the same time, not to mention constraints around personnel, capital, etc., so a company must make choices. Often this is a matter of balancing the current sense of urgency with respect to three fundamental concerns: time, cost, and performance/quality. The PI Department needs to evaluate the tradeoffs based on the approach and prioritization of the project opportunities that have been approved, and quite often something needs to give based on current constraints. And who yells the loudest should have nothing to do with this decision-making process.

As an example, many companies may want to launch a full business process transformation initiative, including dramatic changes to the supporting IT infrastructure, and to include business process outsourcing (BPO) as part of the total solution. That's a lot to do all at once, based on cost, coordination, personnel, and risk. So what should come first, and how should the phasing of initiatives be prioritized to achieve optimal results? The answer to these questions comes back to the strategic objectives set by the senior leadership of the organization. If immediate cost reduction is the primary goal in addressing market pressures to improve the P&L, and a big portion of the cost structure today is based on high labor costs, then the BPO option would likely be the correct choice for the first phase of the program, because that will generate the greatest immediate savings based on dramatic reduction in overall labor cost. If, however, decreases in customer and partner satisfaction are driving business to competitors, and that's the current source of greatest pain, then the business process/systems transformation projects should be positioned at the top of the list to quickly improve the company's effectiveness in working with its customers and partners. All of these components of the business transformation program have the potential to increase the overall optimization of the enterprise, but the PI Department needs to balance the maximum amount of change that can be introduced into the company at any given time, and then evaluate *what's possible* with *what's most important* from a strategic company perspective. Leaving these decisions in the hands of the functional teams and general managers will result in biased outcomes that tend to optimize components of the organization, but not the organization as a whole. Further, this traditional approach to prioritization rarely takes a step back and looks at the overall strategic objectives of the entire company. This myopic view needs to change, and the CPIO and the PI Department will be the agents of that change.

One final point for companies that establish a minimum threshold for triggering the project approval process is to watch out for abuse of that system. I have seen a common pattern of behavior in some companies where, for example, if the minimum threshold is set at $100,000, there will be an amazing number of projects which come in at $99,900, and then get renewed at that amount over and over. If you want to truly gain control, a process needs to be put into place to monitor recurring activity just below the threshold amount, or else the control will be more fiction than reality.

There will undoubtedly be objections regarding this transition of budgetary and prioritization control from the functional teams and general managers who are used to having much more freedom with respect to spending authority. But that's exactly the point. Far too often that spending has been misguided, based on "gut feel" decision-making instead of rigorous analysis and meaningful business cases, and often not in synch with the strategic imperatives of the company. We need to reign in this kind of behavior, and the way to do it is to empower the PI Department with budgetary authority over all projects (over some minimum dollar amount) across the enterprise. This step is a necessary piece of the puzzle to truly empower this critical new business entity across organizations.

Beyond the verbal support from the corporate executives and authority for budget authorization and prioritization of initiatives, there are other specific steps that should be taken to align the PI Department with the functional organizations across the company. There are real people involved here, and that means incentives need to have an impact at the individual level to encourage appropriate behavior. Specific roles and responsibilities must be clearly articulated (as I will explain later in this section), and must be consistently applied across the organization. While these roles and responsibilities will be different, they must be compatible. One of the ways of ensuring cooperation is to think carefully about the performance management evaluation process that applies to all employees, and to establish goals and bonus plans which reward a partnership approach by the PI Department and the functional units. Both entities need to understand that neither will be successful without the other, and alignment of goals and rewards is a necessary and logical step to make it clear to these individuals that the executives really mean it when they claim support for cooperation in this newly-defined organizational structure. To this end, the relevant metrics are the ones that pertain to end-to-end processes but cross specific functional areas. If you want order management, planning, manufacturing, and shipping to work together as a cohesive unit, then you should measure each of these entities on common metrics such as book-to-ship cycle time and schedule date variance. Each of those functional entities have an execution role which drives performance for those metrics, so it's perfectly appropriate to measure their individual performance based on the outcome of the team. If the team wins, then everyone wins. If one part stumbles, then the rest of the value chain is incented to help get through that stumble, all in the best interest of the customer. You may also have function-specific metrics which account for part of the performance evaluation of the individuals and the teams, but the more emphasis you place on the end-to-end process metrics for performance management, the more likely you're going to achieve enhanced performance throughout the entire process. Remember, the PI Department must be established as *part of the business*, not just another "us" and "them" relationship. Alignment of individual financial incentives is perhaps the best way to get this message across.

Companies must also consider the participation that is required at the individual level in implementing the initiatives that are authorized by the PI Department. The PI Department leadership and deployment teams may be responsible for driving these initiatives, but they will also need the input and commitment from many individuals in the functional units. Design input, testing, validation, and training all will require participation from the functional teams. A clear understanding needs to be established between the leaders of the PI Department and the leaders of the functional teams in terms of how this participation is going to be managed and adjusted as necessary based on the overall demands of the business. This must become a partnership, or else it will simply be another failed attempt of a matrix organization. This will require change. Functional leaders need to understand the importance of these end-to-end initiatives, which cross functional boundaries, and these leaders need to be incented to adopt this mindset, just as the members of their teams. Further, the PI Department needs to understand that just trying to bully the functional teams into submission will defeat the purpose as well. The PI Department must work within the established governance framework, and must factor realistic expectations for the functional teams into their project plans. The PI Department must be empowered with decision-making responsibilities, but it must also collaborate with the functional teams, as depicted in Figure I-1. One group doesn't work for the other. While they operate under distinct roles and responsibilities, they must share common objectives, governance, and evaluations in order to obtain the necessary alignment for organizational success.

As mentioned, one way to achieve buy-in is to give the PI Department control of initiative authorization, prioritization, and budgetary control. This effort remains an important first step in establishing the new focus around end-to-end processes. But other important steps have also have been discussed which can be taken in which to achieve this buy-in, as summarized as follows:

- Top down mandate which is consistently delivered across the leadership of the entire organization;
- Change management approach that educates the business community on the merits and benefits of this new organization;
- Governance model which applies equally to the PI Department and the functional teams, including clearly articulated roles and responsibilities;
- Goals and rewards which are aligned between the PI Department and the functional teams, to constantly remind these individuals that they are working toward a common set of objectives;
- Realistic project plans which take into consideration the time demands on the functional teams.

Companies which implement matrix components as part of their organization structures actually run the risk of creating more conflict than they had previously. But following the guidelines outlined above will establish the framework in which the focus around processes and information can be manifest throughout the company, empowered by a new entity established around the enterprise-wide optimization of these components *and* supported in thought and action by the functional teams throughout the company.

At this point, the core responsibilities for the PI Department can be identified as follows:

- The definition of the end-to-end processes that exist within an organization;
- The ongoing identification, evaluation, and prioritization of opportunities to optimize the organization via enterprise-wide process changes under the guidance of an objective, metric-driven decision-making framework;
- The definition of key performance indicators that will be used to manage and evaluate the organization;
- The ongoing identification, evaluation, and prioritization of opportunities to optimize the organization via the way information is procured in terms of the right information reaching the right people in the right way at the right time;
- The definition and monitoring of the standards that must be followed to ensure data accuracy and integrity;
- The definition and monitoring of standards related to enterprise-wide information security;
- The definition and monitoring of standards for ongoing knowledge transfer related to processes and systems;
- The definition and ongoing administration of the governance structure for initiatives and the management of these projects;
- The facilitation of organization alignment around transformational initiatives, beginning with the executive suite and cascading throughout the entire organization. This alignment needs to incorporate each of the following five areas: Strategy, Controls, People, Process, and Technology;
- The control of the budgetary approval and budget allocation processes for all initiatives across an organization (possibly over a minimum dollar amount, as determined based on the specific circumstances of the company); and
- The management of relationships with external partners that will become increasingly important as organizations move to outsource non-core business processes and a broad array of IT services.

Conversely, the PI Department is *not* responsible for:

- The execution of processes;
- The execution of data entry into systems or knowledge repositories; or
- The functional component of the delivery of initiatives throughout the organization.

These execution roles remain with the functional units that have been identified as responsible for them. These teams will also participate in the definition phases around process and information requirements, as well as the identification, evaluation, and prioritization of initiatives. But these activities will not be their primary responsibility, which is the flawless execution of their specific roles in end-to-end processes. Stated another way, referring back to the government analogy, the PI Department, with input from the entire organization, is responsible for the definition and maintenance of the global constitution and the enforcement of those standards. There will be plenty of localized activities that occur beyond this group's scope of influence, but the essential components that are necessary for optimal performance across the enterprise, specifically related to processes and information, fall into the responsibility of this global, business-focused organization. They own this living constitution, which contains the fundamental guiding principles for the execution teams throughout the enterprise.

Another way to look at the breakdown of responsibilities is that the PI Department should get called when a process breaks down as in the case of shipments not being properly communicated to the accounts receivable organization for customer invoicing. In this same case, the appropriate functional unit should be called when these invoices are appearing but have the wrong customer addresses or contact information. The former is a process deficiency, whereas the latter is a fault of execution (data entry, in this case). The PI Department needs to provide leadership to the functional units on behalf of the organization as a whole to define these standards and procedures, and to continuously look for opportunities for improvement. The functional leaders and their teams need to work collaboratively with the PI Department to ensure that these prescriptions for optimization are practical for execution. The functional teams are further responsible for high-quality process execution based on these agreed-upon definitions. Working collaboratively on behalf of the company in this fashion will provide numerous opportunities to improve the efficiency and effectiveness of the organization. Working as "us" and "them" will keep us in the suboptimal state in which most of our organizations reside today.

One of the specific areas highlighted above provides a clear distinction between the responsibilities of the PI Department and the rest of the organization. One common occurrence that results in poor execution is a lack of formal training for personnel when they first join the organization or find themselves in a new role. Local domain knowledge is typically passed along from colleague to colleague, often getting the subjective twist to processes and systems (and workarounds) from those who have lived in these environments for some time. While this institutional knowledge is helpful in getting through the day, it does not necessarily drive optimal behavior as designed into accepted best practices. Training curriculum needs to be part and parcel with every process found within a company, and this material should operate on both the detailed process view, as well as on the related systems view. The PI Department is responsible for ensuring that this material is created and maintained throughout the life of the process. The PI Department must also ensure that adequate training is provided to new employees. This can be in the form of Web-based tutorials, easily accessible cheat sheets, formal instructor led courses, etc.—whatever is appropriate for the task at hand. Companies can no longer rely on word-of-mouth training and expect optimal results. What good is taking the time to design an optimal process if you don't take the time to instruct the people who are responsible for the actual execution of the process?

Organizations usually do a reasonably good job of training when new processes and systems come on line, but once the go-live day hits, the formal knowledge transfer program simply disappears. This makes no sense with all the process changes and personnel changes that companies undergo on a daily basis. The PI Department is responsible for institutionalizing an enterprise-wide commitment to process training and ensuring compliance. Being too busy for training is not an acceptable excuse. The long-term cost of blowing off process training is too high for the organization relative to the perceived short-term gain. Articulating processes and standards for training and putting them in place is the responsibility of the PI Department. The functional groups within the company are then responsible for the execution of training and the ongoing participation of all team members. The PI Department can only go so far in charting the path. The functional teams must then participate in and execute these programs, which are all components of the overall optimization of the enterprise.

One of the important elements to address in creating an effective organization is the make-up of the individual teams within the PI Department. As mentioned, unless we make at least some structural changes, we will likely end up in the same suboptimal environment in which we find ourselves today, with warring factions between PI and "the business." One strong way to break down the barriers with "the business" is to bring some of the best and brightest from the functional teams into the PI Department as foundational team members. These may even be the same people who have been fighting with IT for years. Well, now it's time to put their money where their mouths are. There have been many examples of the benefits of moving high-caliber, process-focused individuals from "the business" into IT. Moving these people into the PI Department should be even more valuable, as this new organization will have stronger institutional support as a leadership organization in the company. The PI Department should be one employees aspire to join—a step up in responsibility and acclaim in the organization. My expectation is that these individuals, who already understand the fundamental business challenges of their prior individual domains, will be well-suited to working collaboratively in this new role on across-the-board business optimization opportunities. I further expect that given their prior experience in "the business," these people will be more likely to be accepted by "the business" so that we don't have this "us" vs. "them" mentality when it is time to form teams and work together.

Companies may consider these types of moves as permanent transfers, or as rotational assignments. In the rotational context, individuals may move into the PI Department for a period of one to two years, and then return with that cross-functional experience to the functional unit from which they came. The fact that they are scheduled to return to their business units will provide a constant reminder to keep focused on the business impact of their decisions as they will inherit the outcome of those decisions down the road. This approach should help prevent the ivory tower mentality that has permeated so many IT departments that have become out of touch with the ramifications of their decisions on the day-to-day lives of the business community. This approach should also enable these individuals to bring a new, enterprise-wide view of the world back to their individual functions. It would also open up further opportunities for other individuals to move into these cross-functional, strategic roles. The more people who rotate through the PI Department, the more the company will see adoption of the enterprise-wide view of Process and Information Optimization. In fact, the ultimate state may result when the PI Department can become a very lean team of project leads, but the core set of resources remains in the functional units. As long as the enterprise view becomes an imbedded mindset in the functional teams, then moving employees into this corporate structure may no longer be necessary. But you can't simply declare a mindset to be in place. An environment needs to be created that will nurture it, and then it needs to be allowed to grow and permeate the institution. This will take time. There are no simple shortcuts. Maybe we'll eventually get to a model championed by Hammer and Champy when processes govern the essence of our organizations. Maybe we'll all become "Process Enterprises" such as Canada Post. Maybe someday. But, in the meantime, we have the capability to move in this direction by embarking on a journey that includes organization change and a specific focus around a decision-making framework that will yield immediate positive results. Whether this step is long-term or merely transitional in the move toward a complete "process-driven enterprise" is not important. The point is to recognize the problems associated with our suboptimal structures of today, and make the commitment to immediately begin the change process of formally creating empowerment for a group of individuals focused on enhancing (optimizing!) capabilities in the areas of processes and information.

Over the past couple of years I have observed a number of organizations that have recognized this need for a process focus to their companies, but their organizational response has proved ineffective in addressing the challenge. These companies have established executive-level, process-focused councils or committees to take responsibility for closing our gaps around processes and execution. The problem with this approach is that these organizations tend to operate at a visionary level and not an operational one. In other words, they tend to meet once a quarter and discuss process-focused challenges and opportunities for the organization, but rarely empower specific individuals or teams to act on that vision. The disconnect is the lack of a formal PI Department to enact the strategies as defined.

It is unrealistic to believe that these senior executives will work together to design an operational output of their vision (they're often too removed from the day-top-day activities of the company to do that). It is further naïve to believe that these functionally oriented executives will then go drive cross-functional, process-oriented change across the enterprise. Five minutes after they leave their quarterly sessions, these executives typically recall all the problems for which they are responsible today, and all that end-to-end process stuff gets shoved aside. The vision part of this equation is great. The CPIO needs to be part of that visioning and take the input from the senior executives to craft the organizational strategy. The missing link in these efforts is the ability to hand off the vision to a PI Department, which can then organize programs around its immediate end-to-end execution, based on an analytical framework for approval and prioritization at the individual project level. These senior councils can report their vision upward to their CEOs, but without any formal organization to operationalize the vision, nothing ever gets done. And, as has been discussed, IT is certainly not the answer to filling this gap. We need an empowered organization of business professionals to fill this gap. We need a CPIO and a PI Department.

The final concept that provides the clear distinction between traditional IT Departments and these new PI Departments is the means by which these organizations and their members are evaluated. IT is viewed as a cost center in most organizations, with the "percent of revenue" metric representing the classic benchmark for the evaluation of the performance. It doesn't take much analysis to come to the conclusion that this makes very little sense. Departments should spend the appropriate amount of money based on the relative opportunities to improve the bottom line of the organization. If a project costs $1 million, but will provide a $2-million benefit, then, as long as the initiative is consistent with the strategic goals of the organization, the expenditure should be made, regardless of where it puts the department in terms of spend as a percent of revenue. The percent of revenue view puts IT further into the mold of an entity that truly adds no value. It implies IT is a necessary evil that consumes company funds but really doesn't add anything of meaning to the organization.

Conversely, the Process and Information Department is a business entity that serves a leadership role in the organization. It needs to be evaluated based on the overall *value* it brings to the organization, relative to the cost of producing that value. Rather than just looking at the cost side of the equation, PI Departments and their leaders need to be tasked with goals that enhance the optimal state of the enterprise in concrete and measurable ways. In Section II, I will introduce the details of the Enterprise Optimization Framework, which provides the basis for this kind of evaluation. Basically, this refers to setting objectives relative to tangible improvements in processes and/or information that are greater than the total cost of reaching those objectives. PI Departments should be expected to achieve a quantifiable level of improvement within this framework and that should be the basis of their evaluation. This is so much more than just looking at the budget and spend as a percent of revenue. It is placing expectations of optimization on these individuals and their teams that can be tracked on an ongoing basis. This is an organization that serves to significantly enhance the value of the enterprise, not just spend some of its hard-earned money.

Now that the fundamental purpose of the Process and Information Department has been identified, and a basic approach to building its resource base has been articulated, let's take a more detailed look at the leadership positions and the different segments of the PI Department. To provide some specific structure, we start with an organization chart of a representative PI Department (see Figure I-2).

Figure I-2: Representative Organization Structure for the Process and Information Department

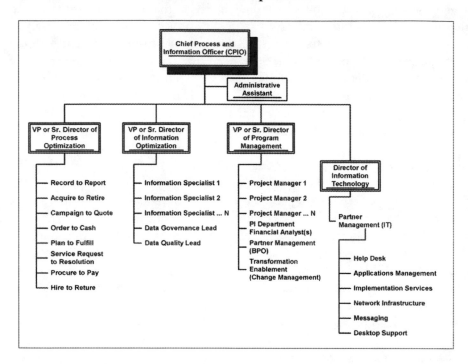

The size and depth of each of these departments will vary based on the size of the company. For small organizations, multi-tasking is always the norm, and the PI Department would be no exception. Project managers may need to overlap in Process or Information roles, as well as in the partner relationship roles in the area of information technology. In some cases, the Process and the Information leads will need to be one and the same. The critical point is the definition of the roles and the assurance that each role will be represented, whether by one or many individuals.

The Chief Process and Information Officer

A company's Chief Process and Information Officer (CPIO) should be among the most senior business executives in the organization, reporting directly to the CEO of the company, and responsible for charting the path to optimize capabilities relative to the company's strategic vision. The CPIO primarily tackles this critical objective by way of two fundamental means:

- The optimal design, implementation, and oversight of all end-to-end processes within the enterprise, and
- The availability and quality of information as required by key decision-makers throughout the organization.

Unlike a CIO, who is primarily concerned with technology, the CPIO is a strategic business leader who understands the core foundation of the company and has the ability to lead his people, as well as those in other parts of the organization, down a path of change based on a never-ending desire to optimize the *overall* enterprise. Maybe this is what CIOs were meant to be, but it is not what they have become. CPIOs are not there to *serve* the business. They are there to *lead* the business. Colin Powell once said, "Leadership is the art of accomplishing more than the science of management says is possible."[9] This is what we need with our CPIOs—leaders who have the personal qualities to take their teams beyond the norm, beyond traditional expectations. This is not just changing the business card of the CIO and making him the process person and expecting everyone to follow. In some cases, the current CIO may be the right person to fill this new role, but just as likely he may not. Many current CIOs are having their talents wasted in these technology-focused roles and would thrive with a new leadership challenge. These individuals are likely aching to get out from under their technology-focused labels and lend their talents to the strategic process and information imperatives of their organizations. However, other CIOs may be well suited as leaders for IT but do not have the skill set or desire (or either) to become a leader for Process and Information Optimization. These individuals would still have a role in the organization, but would need to be repositioned based on the appropriate level of strategic importance to the organization. Regardless of the capabilities of the person currently filling the CIO chair, a clear distinction needs to be made in terms of the responsibility of this new position, vis-à-vis the traditional CIO role. Lack of clarity around this fundamental distinction may ruin any chance for a successful introduction of the new role.

The background of the CPIO should be broad-based business, working in a variety of functional and/or process roles throughout an organization. Just as General Electric is famous for moving its managers around the company before promoting them up the chain, CPIOs should have experience in a number of areas throughout an organization, including regional assignments and functional roles. This experience is the only way to prepare an individual for the end-to-end responsibilities of a CPIO. Further, these need to be business roles, not technology roles. Ideally, CPIOs will have experiences dealing with customer-facing processes, partner-facing processes, employee-facing processes, etc. It's important to understand processes from all sides, including those operating the transactions as well as those on the receiving end. Only a holistic perspective can be expected to yield optimal decision-making with respect to process management.

The focus is not just on processes. The "I" remains in the title because Information Optimization is another core element that is often lacking in many organizations. People are very good about complaining after the fact about the information they cannot get, or how the information is untrustworthy. One reason this happens is that there is no defined leadership in most companies to ensure adherence to standards around data, and no defined leadership to focus on data as it moves from one functional area (or from one information system) to the next. We need leadership for Information Optimization, for which there are hard dollar advantages to be gained if done properly. This should have been a focal point for our CIOs (our Chief *Information* Officers) all along. But their focus has typically been technology, and not information and not processes. And even when CIOs have had the right focus and the right skill sets to lead in these areas, the organization structure and cultural view of IT has typically not been compatible with their ability to lead. The business community was not looking for leadership from the CIO, so it was very difficult to achieve any success in this area. All too often, data quality issues were pushed right back to "the business," where resolution would not be forthcoming. It's time to change this dynamic. It's time for CPIOs and their PI Departments to take the lead in treating information as the highly valued asset it is, and ensure that this asset is receiving the appropriate level of care.

CPIOs don't just need to be selected—they need to be empowered. Quite simply, without a top-down mandate, even the strongest individuals will be unable to provide leadership in the organization. The remaining C-level executives need to buy into the fact that this new dynamic represents a much-needed change on the path to Enterprise Optimization. These other leaders need to accept the mandate that accompanies the leader of the PI Department, which implies that they will need to be open to working with their new peer in areas within their functional groups and for initiatives that cross functional groups. CPIOs and their teams may lead these initiatives, but they will require input and cooperation. The walls of isolation that have formed between these functional groups over the years need to come down. Unless that happens, our organizations will simply remain in their current suboptimal state, which can ultimately lead to a slow and painful death.

This acceptance of the new role has to start at the top of the food chain. CEOs need to call the IT director (or the help desk!) for problems with e-mail, not the CPIO. CEOs need to call the CPIO when they get a call from their biggest customer complaining that their shipment or RMA process is delayed and they can't get a straight answer from Order Management, Finance, or Customer Service. CEOs need to call the CPIO when their on-line dashboards provide conflicting information from the reports they are getting from their staff. CEOs need to call the CPIO when they are considering a strategic business partnership with another organization and fundamental process and information issues need to be discussed and resolved—not just technical integration, but true strategies around end-to-end Process and Information Optimization. CEOs need to stop thinking of one of their C-level executives as the technologist responsible for the plumbing (systems and infrastructure) of the company. There's a need for that role, but it is not a C-level position. This is why CEOs must be very careful about who they put into this new role. If the CIO is going to assume the role, then the CEO must be sure that the CIO has the appropriate business and leadership background to succeed in his fundamentally new duties. Otherwise, it's a waste of time and disappointment will be the only result. Regardless of who fills the role, the CEO needs to position the role with the rest of the organization around the core responsibilities of this leadership function, and then support the CPIO when territorial conflicts arise. Opportunities for optimization will be readily available with the introduction of CPIOs and PI Departments, but only if empowerment and support come with the package, and that needs to start at the top of the organization.

This level of empowerment raises the question of the extent to which CPIOs should be involved in the creation of the overall business strategy of the organization. Typically, this is a major responsibility of C-level executives. The CEO has ultimate responsibility for the vision, but the other C-level executives have valuable roles to play in crafting the overall strategy in support of that vision. The CFO needs to ensure that a strategy is in place that will be profitable for the enterprise as well as in accordance with Generally Accepted Accounting Principles (GAAP). The CTO needs to ensure that the company has the requisite technical knowledge and capabilities to bring the vision to life. The COO needs to ensure that the organization can produce and distribute the product (or service) in a means that will yield a profitable result. Leaders in Marketing and Sales need to ensure that there is a viable market for the offering and that it can be effectively sold, again in the context of eventual profitability. The General Counsel needs to ensure that there are no legal or contractual issues that will prevent any of the functional units from executing the strategy as defined. These leaders need to work together at the executive level to craft a strategy that can be handed down to their teams for ultimate execution, and then they all need to be measured against their ability to execute against the prescribed objectives. Where does the CIO fit into this structure today? Usually as an afterthought. More often than not, the CIO receives the output of the business strategy and is told to ensure that the systems are in place to support it. Rarely does the CIO have a seat at the table offering input into the strategy definition phase.

This approach would change with the introduction of the CPIO. The CPIO must be involved because the processes required to support the strategy will ultimately span most of the functional units identified above. It is unacceptable to merely design a business strategy within the isolated functional silos of the company. How often does it occur that you get to the very last stage of a new product deployment and no one has brought together Marketing, Sales, Order Management, Planning, Operations, Shipping, and Accounts Receivable? Then it's time to place orders and there is no price list, or the product numbers aren't available, or the shipping labels haven't been designed, or the discounting rules haven't been defined, or the customer-specific documentation hasn't been created. How often are the procedures and training related to customer returns, customer support, and customer repairs for a new offering left to the last minute for definition simply because of the disconnect between these groups from those defining the go-to-market portion of the strategy?

New Product Introduction is a classic example of a process related to the deployment of a new strategic imperative that spans multiple functional units and all too often yields a fire drill sequence just as the product is ready to ship for the first time because so many of the critical decisions have been left hanging for lack of a coordinated process. Whether it's a new product launch, a new marketing strategy, a new service offering, or the integration of a newly acquired business—all of these directives require top-down leadership and ultimate execution from the functional units, but that's not all. They also require an entity that can pull it all together. They need an organization that is responsible to ensure that efficient and effective processes are in place to optimize the use of the resources across the functional units, and give the new strategy the greatest opportunity to achieve the profitability goals established by the executive team. They need an organization that can look at these end-to-end processes in a holistic fashion to identify the key performance indicators appropriate for tracking so that the proper feedback can be provided to the various functional units responsible for the success of these initiatives. CIOs and IT Departments certainly don't provide this benefit to organizations. They're likely to participate in the fire drills trying to get things ready at the last minute, but they're rarely invited to the table when these strategies are being formulated and the plans for execution are being developed.

It is for these reasons that CPIOs and PI Departments need to exist, and why CPIOs need to be fully engaged when the business strategy is being developed in the executive suite. CPIOs and their teams need both to provide and receive input from their functional colleagues in a collaborative fashion to ensure that none of these steps are missed when end-to-end solutions are designed. These steps are missed all the time in today's world. Finally, no initiative should be approved unless it is consistent with the business strategy of the organization. As the PI Departments will have a central role in the analysis and recommendation processes relative to initiatives, it is vital that the CPIO be included in the executive strategy sessions for the company. This involvement is not only for his or her valuable business input, but also to ensure that all segments of the organization are on the same page when determining the optimal way to invest the company's money. Companies can dramatically reduce the exposure to potentially poor investments by introducing this key leadership responsibility and providing it a role up front in the definition of the approach to executing on fundamental business strategies.

There is one additional difference between CPIOs and CIOs that merits attention. Many of the CIOs I meet have become frustrated in their jobs. This frustration stems from a number of areas. One cause is that they feel they have reached a C-level position yet are still treated by people throughout the organization mostly as a nuts-and-bolts IT person. Imagine finding out that you've finally been given the promotion you've been waiting years to receive only to discover that you're really doing a director level role with a C-level title. Imagine the frustration of being a C-level executive who must struggle to get functional directors to follow your lead. Frustration also results from the fact that the position of CIO is often a dead-end job. Where do you go from there? You don't see many CIOs getting other C-level titles. It's pretty much the end of the line, and after these folks find out they're not really in the strategic role they longed for, frustration inevitably sets in. CPIOs will certainly encounter frustrations in their jobs as well. Who doesn't? But the frustrations will not be the same (or as depressing) as those of the CIO. If properly positioned, CPIOs will be in a strategic position of leadership and will receive the level of respect appropriate for a C-level executive. Moreover, while the CPIO role is already near the top of the org chart, it is not a dead end. Since this is a business leadership role focused on processes and information, there is no perception in place about the CPIO being unfit outside the realm of IT. Quite the contrary. Being a CPIO is an excellent training ground for positions of general management all the way to the CEO. It would be a great achievement to reach the level of a CPIO, but you won't have to worry about being "stuck" in that position forever. There will be plenty of additional management and leadership opportunities for successful CPIOs. While CIO may stand for "Career is Over," as some have suggested, CPIO may just as well stand for "Career Placed in Orbit," i.e., on its way to the very top.

The Process and Information Department is by no means a one-man show. CPIOs can be successful only with strong teams to initiate and drive engagements with their business colleagues. Among the key decisions for any leader is the appointment of a staff, and the CPIO is no exception. It is now time to explore the four major components of the Process and Information Department, which make up the core team of the CPIO and represent the organizational components of this critical new business environment. These four components include:

- Process Department
- Information Department
- Information Technology Department
- Office of Program/Project Management

Process Department

Commentary was provided earlier in this section on the process focus to business as espoused by Michael Hammer and James Champy in *Reengineering the Corporation*. I firmly agree on the importance of processes in order to achieve Enterprise Optimization. Process inadequacies represent some of our biggest drawbacks as effective organizations, and also, therefore, represent some of the greatest opportunities for optimization. Eliyahu Goldratt told us in *The Goal*, "Any organization should be viewed as a chain. Since the strength of a chain is determined by its weakest link, then the first step to improve an organization must be to identify the weakest link."[10] We often don't identify these specific bottlenecks because no one is looking for them. Functional teams are so busy doing their specific functional roles that they pay little or no direct attention to the up-stream or down-stream components of the processes in which they work. They become aware of issues when things break down, but the firefighting that goes on at those times is often limited to fixing the specific break in the chain, not strengthening the chain for future operations. For organizations to optimize, they need to change this mindset and put someone in charge of identifying these systematic constraints, and then focus intently on ways to alleviate the bottlenecks for the future.

In the structure being proposed, this "someone" is the leader of the Process Department, within the Process and Information Department, and his team of business professionals. These people focus their time on process definition and in identifying areas where overall process efficiency can be improved and, in turn, the enterprise can be optimized. One of the key parts of that statement is the reference to the "overall" process. As will be explored in Section II, there will be plenty of times when the level of efficiency of a *specific* function may need to be *degraded* in order for the enterprise to realize overall improvement. Myopic functional views of processes are not acceptable, but they represent one reason we often don't achieve optimal results today. Functional teams are measured on their own performance, not the overall performance of the end-to-end process in which they participate. This measurement focus needs to change.

Since a process focus is going to be fundamental throughout this book, it is appropriate to take a moment to highlight some of the core processes (and associated sub-processes) typical in many organizations today (see Figure I-3).

Figure I-3: Sample Business Processes

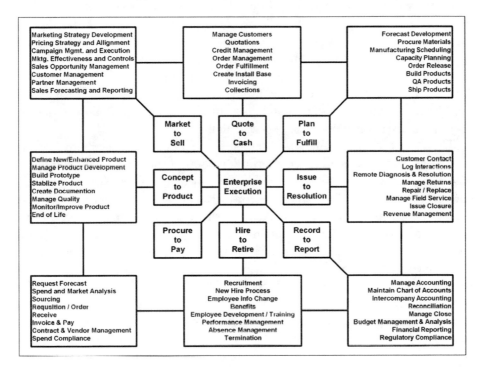

Contributing Source: BearingPoint

Referring to the list in Figure I-3, think through the process gaps discussed earlier in terms of functional disconnects and lack of clearly defined ownership. How can companies be successful in quote-to-cash if the process requires the commitment of multiple functional units that are all operating under different management and different mandates? These gaps in end-to-end process definition and execution are killing our businesses. They need to be closed, and need to be closed permanently. The Process Department must be empowered to lead the way as a means to pursue optimization throughout end-to-end processes.

As mentioned, some members of the Process Department may be on a rotational assignment from one or more of the business functional units. This is perfectly acceptable, and will likely enhance the credibility of this centralized organization and facilitate essential cooperation with the functional teams. There will also be permanent members of the Process Department, including a senior leader who reports directly to the CPIO. These full-time professionals will be *business people*. Just as the CPIO should have an extensive business background, hopefully developed by way of multiple assignments with various functional and regional organizations, the same background is desirable for the full-time members of the Process Department. Remember that the charter for the Process Department is to define the *end-to-end* business processes that exist within an organization, and to identify opportunities to optimize the organization by way of changes in processes on an ongoing basis. They will be held accountable for ensuring the deployment of efficient and effective processes that enhance the overall value of the organization and ensuring that additional opportunities for optimization are continuously being evaluated.

The Process Department is not responsible for the actual execution of the processes. That responsibility remains in the hands of the functional units across the enterprise, which will be evaluated in their own right on their ability to execute. But there must exist a commitment to collaboration between the business professionals in the Process Department and the functional teams if there is to be any chance at overall success. An environment of "us" vs. "them" will never yield optimal results. If there is a fundamental problem with a process, the Process Department has to provide leadership in working with its business colleagues to solve the problem. If there is a problem with the execution of a process, then the issue must be identified and additional emphasis placed on the functional teams to ensure that lapses in execution are quickly corrected. There are distinct responsibilities for these organizations, but unless they work together in the spirit of cooperation, no one will be in a position to achieve optimal results for the enterprise. To encourage this cooperative environment, appropriate metrics need to be identified and evaluated that support the responsibilities and objectives of both the individuals and their teams.

Depending on the size of the company, it may be equally important for these critical roles to be filled by people who can interact effectively with multiple parts of the organization, crossing numerous skill sets. Large companies may be able to afford specialists in specific business processes in their Process Department, but many simply will not be able to afford that luxury. As such, general business experience will be an important trait of these full-time team members. But size and scale are not the determining factors of this organization. The important element is the focus of the individuals—an unrelenting focus on optimization around end-to-end processes, however defined by a specific company. And to be effective in these roles, these individuals will also require exceptional communication and relationship skills. There will be times when the PI Department will be at odds with some element of the rest of the company. Process Department team members need to be able to work effectively with all constituents throughout the enterprise. They will need thick skin and a lot of self-confidence, and must be able to work by way of non-confrontational means. Depth of managerial skills, including many of the so-called "soft skills," will certainly pay dividends for members of the Process Department.

Most importantly, the Process Department cannot be biased. The individuals must be able to look at things from the enterprise-wide view, and to do so as objectively as possible. To guide this effort, the need for quantifiable means in which to base recommendations must once again be stressed. The appropriateness of these decisions should be plain for all to see, or else conflict will surely result. I will provide specific guidelines for the Process Department along these lines when I introduce the Enterprise Optimization Framework in Section II.

One of the key roles for the Process Department is enterprise-wide process definition. So, how do we determine the specifics around an optimal process for an organization? To begin, the ground rules include the fact that processes are end-to-end and cross-functional, and need to be defined and executed with this in mind. Even if the functional boundaries continue to exist in our organization structures, the Process Department needs to be immune to these boundaries when creating these definitions. When you think of the boundaries as a legitimate element in the process definition, you are bound to create inefficient processes. Second, it must be understood that process definition is not just a grab for every little want and desire of one or more parts of the organization. There is a cost to deploying and executing processes, and this absolutely needs to be considered by the Process Department when coming up with these definitions. A process that improves productivity by 10 percent but has a total cost burden of 20 percent should not be pursued. *The process teams must not confuse an optimal solution with simply the fulfillment of a process wish list.* This perspective is often lost on functional teams today, but must be at the forefront of the thought process for the business professionals in the Process Department. Process changes must always be evaluated on the *total* impact to the organization.

While moving along the path of process definition, the Process Department must remember that there is an inevitable link between process definition and information systems. To what degree should systems define the process, or vice versa? My firm belief is that it makes no sense for individual companies to reinvent the wheel over and over again. The leading enterprise software companies and the top consulting organizations have all invested millions into embedding industry-specific best practices into their solutions. Time and money can be saved by leveraging these proven solutions, and that makes perfect sense to me as an ideal way toward optimal process definition. These solutions will never be able to provide everything the way the business community wants things for transactional and reporting purposes, but they can come awfully close. The money saved in adopting these out-of-the-box solutions (to the greatest degree that is practical) will go an awfully long way toward covering the additional value that may be achieved if you went down the path of defining these processes from scratch and force-fitting the technology solutions to those process definitions. The total cost associated with the home grown approach often outweighs the incremental process-related benefits which may be realized.

Process Optimization does not mean creating the "perfect process" with no regard to the cost or information impacts that result. Not at all. The "perfect process" is actually very likely to be suboptimal for the organization as a whole given the cost to define, deploy, train, and maintain it over the life of that process. It's not about the "perfect process" whose cost overwhelms the benefits. It's about being able to deploy simple, efficient processes that satisfy the needs in a cost effective manner, and *flawlessly executing* those processes to achieve optimal results. Enterprise systems and established industry best practices can provide a baseline that satisfies many of these requirements out-of-the-box. The results then become a function of the user community's ability to execute. There will certainly be times when competitive differentiation can be achieved by way of customized elements tied to enterprise systems. This approach may yield some benefits in very specific cases. But be careful. The more you tinker with your processes, the more complex and expensive things become, the more errors result, and the least effective you're likely to be. The Process Department doesn't need to invent everything itself. Quite the contrary. The Process Department needs to understand what's available in the marketplace, ensure that everyone understands those capabilities and how to take advantage of them, and that the functional teams collaborate on execution so things don't fall through the cracks. That's how to achieve Process Optimization (on the path to Enterprise Optimization) in its holistic enterprise-wide state.

What about current IT staff members? Are they appropriate for the Process Department? The answer: It depends. An individual with a strong information technology background, especially one that has focused on the process integration both within and between systems, may be an ideal candidate for the Process Department. The more process- and business-focused the individual has been, the better the fit for the Process Department. Plus, the desire to leverage best practice processes embedded in core systems and knowledge of those systems (including staying up to date on the latest innovations) will be excellent complimentary qualifications, including each of the following areas:

- Enterprise software (integrated suites and/or best of breed solutions)
- Integration tools
- Web services
- Business process management tools
- Business rules engines
- High-speed networks

However, PI leads need to be careful about a blanket approach to transferring people from IT into PI. Individuals in IT who think technology and programming first and processes second, or those who have their roots on the core technology side of IT, may find the transition to the Process Department difficult. This is in many ways the key difference between a business analyst (a good candidate for the Process Department) and a systems analyst (a poor candidate for transfer). Systems analysts typically listen for a set of requirements and then want to start customizing the systems to fit those processes. That's the world they understand best, so it's a comfortable approach to solving a problem and pleasing "the business." After all, it's just software, and with enough programming you can accomplish anything, right? Well yes, but at what cost? While this may appear beneficial from a process standpoint in providing for the needs (wants!) of the functional teams, this approach of "customize first" can be very detrimental to the overall organization. The scalability of this approach is highly suspect, and the cost to deploy and support can quickly get out of control. What the PI Department needs is a set of business analysts who are able to leverage the best practices that are available in their core systems to satisfy the needs of the process execution teams in an efficient and effective way, but without tremendous investment in highly customized solutions. We need people in the Process Department who understand the needs of the functional users and can make suggestions on how to use these systems to their advantage, but not reach for the customization toolkit at each opportunity. That approach is way too costly in the end, and should only be pursued as a last resort.

One of the important decisions of the Process Department will be to select those tools that satisfy the business requirements as much out-of-the-box as possible, and then choose industry and system experts as partners in deploying those solutions for the organization. For optimal results, the Process Department needs to leverage what's embedded in these enterprise solutions and the skills and experience of the implementation practitioners, not try to leverage the programming skills of a team wanting to satisfy each and every whim of the user community. The former approach scales extremely well; the latter just drives up cost and complexity, and will rarely yield an optimal result.

Too many technology-focused leads will also hurt the Process Department in terms of gaining credibility with the organization. A clear distinction must be made between the entire Process and Information Department and IT Departments of today, and that distinction will be undercut if the resources do not live up to the new business-focused image as presented for PI Departments. The leaders of the PI Department may want to consider certain business savvy individuals from legacy IT Departments for membership, but they will want to be careful that the skill set is an appropriate match, and that the decision is not simply based on convenience.

All of these requirements cannot just be words on a page. You can't just throw anyone into a key role in the Process Department. The wrong resource, lacking business knowledge, too bull-headed, or materially biased, will be a disaster for the department and the company as a whole. These individuals need to interact throughout the organization, and they need to be personally equipped to handle the task. Since the Process Department is well-positioned to lead the company in the area of optimization, it is also in a position to do great damage with the wrong individuals or the wrong approach. A poor hire in the Process Department can be particularly detrimental to an organization.

Finally, it should be mentioned again that the optimal end state may be a very small corporate entity known as the Process Department, with the process expertise, coordination, and management residing in an overall business structure built around end-to-end processes. One could envision an organization structure that takes the process roles identified in vertical fashion in the Process Department portion of the org chart in Figure I-1, and moving those to horizontal leadership positions across the company at the very top of the org chart. This may ultimately be the ideal organization structure for optimal results. But we don't have that kind of structure today, despite all the talk about the keys to process focus over the years, and we're not even very close to it. The Process Department provides an environment in which this focus can take shape and actually be applied to our business environments right now. Only when this process focus truly permeates our people and institutions can these roles be embedded in more traditional organization structures and distributed throughout the enterprise. For now, we need centralized leadership to move us forward, and that's a major task for the members of the Process Department.

Information Department

Information assets are true differentiators for organizations. Intellectual property, institutional knowledge, knowledge capital—call it what you will, *information* can make all the difference in the success or failure of an enterprise. All companies have raw data. These days, with databases permeating our organizations, we typically have more data than we know what to do with. And that's part of the problem.

- How do we effectively convert our reams of data into meaningful and useful information?
- How do we ensure data integrity, leading to high-quality information on which all constituents can rely?
- How do we ensure timely and controlled access to the appropriate information for the right people at the right time?

Just as with our end-to-end processes, in our current environments we do not have anyone overlooking all of our information assets who is able to provide answers to these questions. The business functions are focused on their own data, but can't be persuaded to focus on how their data management affects the information downstream in an end-to-end process. Data standards are rarely defined at either a functional or enterprise level, and even when they are defined, rarely does anyone take the time to ensure compliance with these standards. IT tends to focus on ensuring that data successfully passes from one interface point to the next, but does next to nothing to ensure that the appropriate data elements were entered into the systems in the first place. "Data—that's the responsibility of the 'the business!'" is all we hear.

This lack of commitment to data quality needs to stop, or our businesses will continue down that deadly path to extinction. As we will see in some of the case studies that will be introduced later in the book, the biggest advantage that can be generated by many initiatives will be related to the Information Optimization component of the analysis, often much greater than the impact available based on Process Optimization. Let's take a moment to examine the negative impact that poor information management can have on the prospects of an organization. What is the cost to an organization that makes poor decisions based on out-of-date or simply inaccurate information? What is the cost to an organization that finds itself in analysis paralysis because the executives can't reconcile inconsistencies in multiple sets of data? What is the cost to an organization that finds its staff arguing with customers over the status of a shipment or a contract, and it turns out that the customer was right all along while the data available to the employees was actually in error? On the other hand, what advantage can be gained in each of these areas by any individual organization given that most of the competition is mired in a mediocre state with respect to information quality? The opportunity for enhancing the degree of Information Optimization is staggering in most organizations, and given that scenario, it also represents a tremendous opportunity to achieve competitive advantage.

One of the primary roles of the Information Department is to leverage a mandate from the executive leadership of the organization to foster an enterprise-wide commitment to data quality. The Information Department is specifically chartered with establishing the data standards that will be adopted by all segments of the organization. In addition, the Information Department is responsible for providing common definitions for all data elements throughout the organization. What good is a "bookings" report if a universal definition of a "booking" does not exist? What good is reporting on on-time deliveries if Order Management and Planning have different definitions of "promise date" and "schedule date?" There are subtle differences in many of our key data elements throughout an organization's process activities, and these differences create havoc when someone tries to analyze the business at its most basic level.

The Information Department needs to uncover these anomalies and proactively work with the functional teams to ensure widespread understanding of the common definition of each of these data elements. Moreover, the Information Department is tasked with working with the Process Department and with the functional teams to ensure the timely and accurate measurement of the key metrics that have been identified as critical for successful management of tasks and processes throughout the organization. If "on-time delivery" is a key performance indicator for an organization, then the Information Department is ultimately responsible for universal acceptance of the definition of that metric and providing the means for which that information can be accessed by the appropriate personnel. Some metrics are self-contained within an individual functional unit, such as "day sales outstanding" in the Accounts Receivable/Collections team. Some span multiple functional teams, such as "order-to-ship cycle time." The business professionals in the Information Department need both to lead and collaborate with the relevant functional teams to ensure that these definitions are in place and the metrics are accessible, regardless of the number of process leaders or functional units involved. Exposure in this area can easily extend beyond the walls of the enterprise itself. Many processes touch entities such as partners, customers, etc. These constituents must also have the same fundamental understanding of the definitions of these key elements. The Information Department needs to work with the functional teams that touch these external constituents to ensure that gaps not only do not materialize within the organization, but that they also do not exist with these interconnected entities, either.

The Information Department is also responsible for ensuring that all data is captured throughout the organization in such a way that it is accessible for future use. In its basic form, this applies to data management within core applications, which may seem to be reasonably straightforward, but can certainly present a number of challenges. The problem grows considerably, however, for data that is not captured within core systems. All those "off-line" data repositories that are so convenient for the individual turn out to be of little to no value for the rest of the organization. A common example is found with people in the Sales Department who refuse to use corporate information systems for lead management, contact management, opportunity management, etc., because the systems and processes are too cumbersome. Instead they keep this information on their laptops in whatever desktop tool they find convenient, which provides no leverage whatsoever for the rest of the company. Similarly, quality data seems to be tracked in all kinds of desktop applications, often not connected to any systems that provide the ability to aggregate and truly analyze the current state, thereby enabling opportunities for improvement. This includes product quality, supplier quality, etc. These repositories may be Excel, Lotus Notes, or paper and pencil in some cases, none of which provide for the systematic ability to leverage the information beyond that particular individual. Here's another case where the process may be convenient for the individual, but the negative impact on Information Optimization clearly makes these scenarios suboptimal for the company as a whole. Taken to the extreme, consider the loss that is suffered when those individuals decide to leave the company—all of that information simply walks out the door with them.

Let's look at a couple of additional examples. How about legal contracts or human resources information, including things like performance appraisals? How many companies still keep these important documents stored in file cabinets, and then can never find the one they're looking for when they need it? When was the last time your organization reviewed its governance around the storage and cataloging of this kind of information assets? Finally, what about information for the IT organization? Who sets the standards for this group in terms of what documents need to be stored and where? How much trouble do you have finding a critical design document or functional specification that was created a year or two year ago, but requires immediate attention today? We need an Information Department providing governance of these critical topics so that we do know what information is stored where, and how to access it in a timely fashion, regardless of whether or not that data is stored in one of the core business applications.

Information security was briefly mentioned earlier, along with initiatives such as those that have cropped up around Sarbanes-Oxley. In many organizations, there is no individual or team clearly responsible for these imperatives. The Information Department is the right response. Information security must go beyond the core systems managed by IT. Policies need to be defined and institutionalized throughout the enterprise. Compliance must be monitored, and performance evaluations need to be appropriately updated (positively or negatively).

We currently don't do this, largely because no one is in charge. There is an ISO/IEC standard (17799) specifically for information security. The standard contains 10 security domains and more than 100 individual controls for companies to consider. The security domains include the following:

- Business continuity and planning
- System access control
- System development and maintenance
- Physical and environmental safety
- Compliance
- Personnel security
- Security organization
- Computer and network management
- Asset classification and control
- Security policy [11]

Now I'm not saying that attaining 17799 compliance is mandatory for organizations in the framework of Enterprise Optimization, but companies do need to take a detailed look at their information assets and ensure that they do have optimal policies and procedures in place to address the concerns related to information security. A cost/benefit analysis is certainly appropriate before pursuing specific compliance/optimization targets. At the very least, however, the ISO/IEC standard provides an excellent guideline for the critical areas that should be addressed.

It is insufficient for information security to be solely the responsibility of IT, which typically focuses on passwords and firewalls. That's important, but it doesn't address the big picture, which the standard actually addresses quite well. As mentioned, information is everywhere within an organization, both within systems and "off-line." Companies need to formalize how to manage that raw data so that it is accessible to the right people at the right time, with that access restricted based on the appropriate security policies. When IT is put in charge of information security, the approach is usually entirely focused on access to systems, which is too narrow for this requirement. That's why this responsibility needs to go to the Information Department, which will extend its reach across the enterprise, into every corner of the business, to ensure that everyone understands the value of a company's information and how to secure and protect it in accordance with its importance. More than anything, information security needs focus, it needs policies and procedures, and it needs incentives for broad-based compliance. This need will most appropriately be addressed by the members of the Information Department.

As with the Process Department, the information component of the PI Department is not an IT-like role where technologists make determinations about report structures and build cubes for the latest incarnation of the data warehouse. The Information *Technology* component of the PI Department (a *service* organization) is responsible for that stuff. The *Information* Department is a business-focused, *leadership* organization that works collaboratively with its fellow business teams to define, monitor, and enforce standards and rules for the company's information assets. It's time that companies dedicate business-experienced individuals to the task of overseeing these areas and look for opportunities to improve the bottom-line performance of the organization by optimizing the information components of the company. At the same time, it must be recognized that the Information Department can only go so far in managing the accuracy and integrity of an organization's data. The functional units must ultimately take responsibility for the actual data entry into the systems of record. The problem is that no one currently holds those units accountable for the accuracy of their efforts. This issue is of such magnitude in organizations that something drastic has to be done, as described in this section, to turn this dismal record into an opportunity for competitive advantage.

Recent corporate scandals and the Sarbanes-Oxley legislation help to highlight the leadership gap we experience today in terms of appropriate levels of information standards and governance. Instituting an audit function for processes and information is the most common response to these challenges, but it is only part of the answer. Someone needs to take Information Optimization as a strategic imperative for the company, not only from a government compliance standpoint, but also from an opportunity to yield the greatest possible results for the company. That includes defining procedures and disseminating standards throughout the organization that leverage best practices for information management. Information Optimization will never occur as an afterthought. It can only occur based on dedicated leadership from an organization that is focused on the task. That organization is the Information Department as part of the PI Department.

Data Quality—A Corporate Killer

There is one commonality that can be found across virtually all organizations, and that is the terrible disregard for quality with respect to data. Everywhere you go it's a mess. And everywhere you go everyone knows it's a mess. And every time a company tries to clean it up, it becomes a mess again in a matter of days (or even hours). Why is this so difficult? I have been in so many meetings over the years discussing this topic, but everyone is always coming at it from the back end—after things have been fouled up. Once you've got a mess, good luck trying to get yourself out of it. And if you do, it will likely cost you exponentially more in total cost than if you had just enforced standards with some rigor in the first place.

Companies build entire programs around quality of manufacturing. It's easy for them to see the benefits of rigor to standards in this area of quality management. Why isn't the same energy put into place for the quality of data? Is it because they only see the downside after the fact? That seems to be a very thin excuse, given how pervasive the problem is and the degree to which the damage has been done.

That being said, how does this apply to the Process and Information Department? In the past, IT has always maintained that it is not responsible for data—"the business" is. But now that dynamic will begin to change as the PI Department is *part of the business*. It is an organization that is imbedded in the daily function of the business itself. One of the reasons that data becomes such a mess is that no one (no department) has ever taken responsibility for setting standards and enforcing them. Now, it's time for that to change. If the functional areas cannot adequately police themselves in terms of maintaining quality of data, then it's time for that to become a centralized function, and one of the primary responsibilities of the Information Department. While this may appear Draconian to some, and may create conflict between the Information Department and the functional units, companies are in such poor shape in this area that someone has to step in and right the ship. This centralized approach of setting standards, and monitoring and enforcing compliance, is the only way to get everyone to comply with respect to this business imperative. The transaction-focused teams may not like it, but we just don't have any choice until we get our arms around this enterprise-wide disease that is eating away at the capabilities and productivity of our businesses.

Most companies will be starting from a negative position in terms of data quality, with the data already in a substandard state (to put it mildly). For many companies, standards have never even been defined in terms of the key master data elements resident within most organizations. The Information Department needs to take the first step to evaluate the present state, and then work collaboratively with colleagues to once and for all define standards for each of these key data elements. The standards must be defined, published, and taught to all appropriate business users. Adherence to standards needs to be monitored and maintained, and these measurements need to be factored into performance evaluations. What company today has a metric for data standard compliance? Probably very, very few. But the complaining about data quality comes from every corner of every organization. If you don't define standards and hold people accountable for adherence to them, you will never solve this problem. You'll simply find yourself right back to making poor decisions based on lousy data, and then spending a bucket load of additional money with consultants to clean the whole thing up again.

Is it that hard to put such a program in place? Does it sound too much like Big Brother, monitoring the way people type in a customer's name or a street address? Nonsense. Quality of data is fundamental to the success of any company and its ability to make good decisions. So let's do something about solving this widespread nightmare of a problem. Let's build some rigor around it, with rewards and punishments attached. And let's have the Process and Information Department take the lead. Again, not as Big Brother, but as *part of the business*, looking out for the overall best interest of the company. Ultimately, this responsibility may be returned to the functional units, once dramatic improvements have been achieved and a commitment to data quality becomes institutionalized throughout the organization. Until then, it is up to the Information Department to set the standards, provide the definitions, and monitor adherence to those standards and definitions. This may be a cultural change as much as anything else, but with proper leadership and appropriate motivation, the change is very achievable. And in the financial context, the cost of doing this right vs. not doing it right is like night and day to the bottom line of the company.

Here are seven straightforward steps to put a data quality program in place:

- Gain Executive Support
  - o Before you do anything, you must realize that this kind of change will only be successful based on a mandate from the top.
  - o Get senior executives to agree to the importance of the initiative, and provide well-publicized support for the project (preferably with awards attached to success).

- Define Standards for All Master Data Elements
  - o Start with master data areas such as customers, employees, items, and suppliers.
  - o Create definitions that can be applied across the board for each area, as well as some contextual exceptions, which may be needed for known anomalies.

- Define Standards for Process Data Elements
  - o Walk through the major business processes and create standards in terms of what data should default or be entered into what fields in all systems (including both "core" and "off-line" data repositories).
    - What is the definition of a contact (billing contact vs. shipping contact vs. sales contact vs. support contact, etc.)?
    - What is a scheduled date vs. a promised date?

o The process leads need to focus not only on the process flows, but also the definitions of each and every data element applicable to those flows.

o Most importantly, the process leads and the information leads need to be cognizant of all integration points in which data is transferred (and sometimes translated) from one system to the next.

▪ Rigorous testing needs to take place to ensure that data integrity is not lost as a result of the process and system integration components of these flows.

- Create an Education Plan
  o Leverage your mandate from senior management and schedule mandatory training sessions relative to standards for master data and process data.
  o Provide updated definitions via an open and accessible Web site (or comparable communication vehicle).
  o Provide cheat sheets to be used as part of desk-top procedures for those individuals who enter data into systems.

- Initiate a Clean-Up Exercise
  o Create a phased plan for cleaning up your existing data environments.
  o Investigate opportunities to leverage technical tools and outside parties to assist in this process, but be aware that manual activities by your personnel (the people who really know the data) will likely be required.
  o Allocate funds for these activities.
  o Provide time for your teams to commit to a thorough data cleansing exercise.

- Monitor Success
  o Define metrics for data quality and make them widely known throughout the organization.
  o Set benchmarks for data quality for *every individual* who enters data into your systems.
  o Regularly monitor data quality metrics, providing timely feedback to your teams on a continuous basis (weekly at first, then reduced to monthly, as appropriate).

- Correlate Compensation to Performance
  - o Provide individual and/or team awards for measurable success in terms of data quality.
  - o Provide negative financial ramifications for poor performers.
  - o Have a consistent, long-term view of the correlation between data quality and performance rewards.

Just remember, you can put all the other steps into place, but if you don't measure on-going data quality and tie those measurements to performance evaluations and compensation, then you'll likely to be wasting your time. Without a long-standing commitment and support by senior management that is felt throughout every pore of the organization's evaluation process, you will not be successful. It's too easy to fall into old habits, and data integrity can degrade in a matter of minutes, with a result that will be both destructive and painful and likely infect the entire organization. However, adopting this kind of approach and following through from beginning to end can provide incredible advantages in your effort to optimize your enterprise.

Information Technology Department

The first point to make about this group is that it is distinct in purpose and function from the Information Department previously described. This is the traditional IT organization, which focuses on how to optimize the technology components of solutions. The primary roles for this group include the following:

- Systems analysts
- Software developers
- Database administrators
- System administrators
- Network administrators
- Help desk
- Application management analysts
- Desktop maintenance and support

This group remains primarily a service organization that is called upon to work on the design, implementation, support, maintenance, and enhancement of IT projects. This group is expected to engage in opportunities as identified by the other segments of the Process and Information Department. While this is a fairly tactical organization, as most support and service organizations are, it is still a critical component of any PI Department and any overall company.

The role of this organization will be explored later in the book, specifically in the discussion around outsourcing in Section III. Fundamentally, most, if not all, of these functions are not part of the core competence of most organizations. Further, the time has now come where most, if not all, of these functions can be performed optimally by third-party organizations that offer a high quality of service at a significantly reduced cost. In this model, the IT Department role within the PI Department will be primarily one of managing relationships with these third-party vendors. This responsibility will require new training and a new focus as managing third-party partners who fulfill IT functions requires a new set of skills that must be instilled across the remaining team of IT professionals. The abilities to appropriately evaluate, select, negotiate with, and engage third party providers as long-term partners represent important roles in the new outsource model for IT, and ones that should not be trivialized. Selecting outsourcing partners in the IT world is different from procuring hardware and software. The criteria for selecting partners and the entire procurement process represent new elements for this organization. The same is true for managing these long-term partner relationships. These are new skills, and they will have to be developed and formally introduced into the management structure of the PI Department. Many of the components of this outsource model and the critical role of true business partnerships will be discussed in further detail in Section III.

Regardless of whether you use an insource or outsource approach to components of the Information Technology Department, it should be noted that this organization is one that is in constant need of improvements in terms of its own approach to IT-related Process and Information Optimization. Traditional IT organizations spend most of their time implementing and supporting systems for "the business," but typically do very little getting their own house into optimal operational status. Process standards for project deployments rarely exist, as each project manager tends to operate under his or her own policies and procedures. As will be highlighted in just a moment, there is very little in the way of cross-project coordination, usually until it's just about too late (or sometimes after it's too late). Further, traditional IT organizations have few standards in terms of how and where they store the critical information related to their projects. IT shops will grill "the business" over and over again about documentation, but when the microscope is put on them, standards are often very much lacking. The common excuse is that these overworked and understaffed teams simply never have time for documentation. That's often true, but it's not good enough. Information Optimization must apply to the information technology specialists (whether they're insourced or outsourced) as much as anyone else. Standards and procedures must be identified, adopted, and rigorously followed in order to have a chance at arriving at an optimal state. Fortunately, the organization structure being proposed here has a group ready to focus on just that element (and much more!). That's the Office of Program/Project Management.

Office of Program/Project Management

The Office of Program/Project Management provides the glue that unifies the PI Department while providing leadership and consistency across the organization for its initiatives. The **program managers** are those key individuals who are responsible for ensuring that there is coordination throughout the PI Department at all levels of activity. Just as chaos will result if individual functional units or geographies are off implementing individual projects without respect for their impact on the rest of the company, the same chaotic outcome will occur if the individuals in the PI Department are similarly focused only on their own specific initiatives. Coordination is one of the key responsibilities of the Office of Program Management. Someone needs to be responsible for ensuring that all initiatives that are either underway or being evaluated are considered in a holistic fashion, and that the success of one does not negate the success of another. In addition, prioritization becomes a responsibility of the Office of Program Management. As initiatives are evaluated, they must be considered as part of a complete set of opportunities. As funds are often limited, these individuals need to be prepared to make recommendations on the greatest opportunity for an optimal impact based on the options at hand. Individual members of the PI Department may lobby for one initiative over another, just as functional units do in most organizations today. Program managers need to stay above the fray and operate strictly under the decision-making framework adopted by the organization. To do this, the Office of Program Management must be the central body that reviews all project opportunities, as even unintended conflicts may be missed if they are not reviewed in the context of the company as a whole. Unless everything funnels through one organization, then all the diligence around process and framework will likely fall apart.

The Office of Program Management has the further responsibility to define the processes and standards by which initiatives will be driven throughout the organization. Just as the functional units need to adhere to processes and standards, so does the PI Department when leading its initiatives. Specifically, the program managers need to lead the effort, in conjunction with the rest of the PI Department, in defining standards and tools for each of the following areas:

- Communication plans
- Meeting structures
- Training procedures
- Issue management
- Documentation (standards for documents themselves and their storage repositories)
- Risk mitigation
- Change management
- Critical success factors

From a procedural standpoint, each of the following must be addressed as part of an overall governance structure that can be applied throughout an organization:

- How to propose an initiative
- How to evaluate an opportunity
- How to evaluate an initiative throughout its life cycle (before, during, and after go-live)
- How to select the appropriate technology solutions (including software, hardware, etc.)
- How to engage external organizations (such as third-party consultants)
- How to escalate issues (both within the framework of a project and beyond that framework, when necessary)
- How to coordinate multiple projects that are underway at the same time
- How to utilize steering committees effectively
- How to allocate resources for initiatives
- How to allocate the budgetary impact of an initiative appropriately across an organization
- How to work with other project teams to ensure coordination across inter-related initiatives
- How to extend the performance management process to project team members

All of these have a material impact on the success of an initiative, and all too often, in project after project, these areas are addressed differently by different teams as they reinvent the wheel in their own fashion over and over again. Companies need to identify best practices for these components that are critical for all projects, and they need to institutionalize them throughout the organization. The Office of Program Management is responsible for this role, and responsible for ensuring that these standards are appropriately updated as needed, and effectively followed by the rest of the organization.

Another critical area of responsibility for the Office of Program Management is in serving as the communication point in the coordination of concurrent projects (as well as the coordination of new projects as they get underway). Experience has taught me that the natural tendency for project managers is to focus exclusively on their own projects, and pay very little attention to those activities going on around them. I have seen this inside client organizations and I have seen it inside consulting organizations. The rationale is fairly obvious. Projects are not planned or staffed based on excess time or resource capacity. Project managers don't think in terms of having the luxury of time to be able to worry about related projects. They have too much to worry about in terms of what is clearly their responsibility, and they can't be bothered with anything else. Plus, project managers are typically evaluated based solely on the success of their projects, not the success of their colleagues. The flaw in this myopic view is obvious: projects are bound to collide if no one is proactively watching out for the inevitable points of integration and dependencies. Individual projects may succeed, but integrated programs will fail as a result of this mindset. This is just like our functional end-to-end processes, which are constantly on the same collision course, when those in the upstream portion of the process pay no attention to the impact of their actions on those who are downstream in the process. When no one is looking out for the conflicts, they inevitably occur—usually at the worst point in the project, just when you're getting ready to go-live.

Take a look at a typical organization chart that reflects the leadership and deployment teams involved in a number of concurrent projects (see Figure I-4):

Figure I-4: Organization Chart for *Disconnected* Project Environments

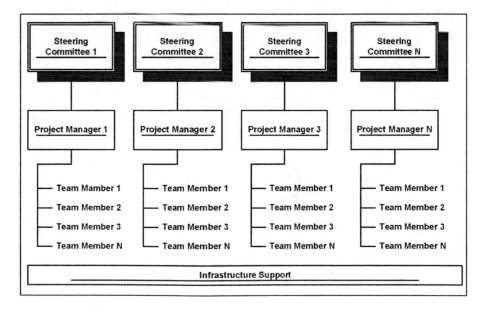

The problem with this "disconnected" structure is that all the lines that serve as connection points are vertical; nothing is formalized horizontally to integrate the individual initiatives in any way. The necessary level of coordination will not occur unless a specific enterprise-wide governance structure and an associated set of policies are put in place by the Program Office. Yet even adding Program Management and a unified steering committee to the structure (as seen in Figure I-5) won't in and of itself solve the problem.

Figure I-5: Organization Chart for Multi-Project Environments with *Unified* Steering Committee and Program Management

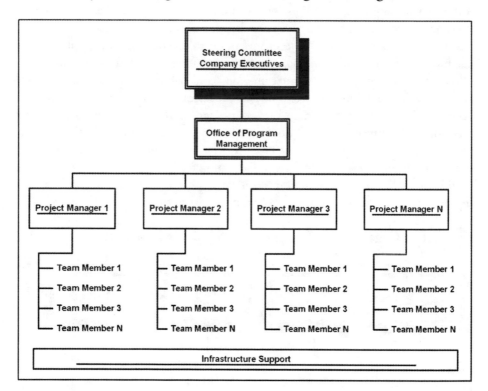

This structure still has mostly vertical communication in place, leaving any sense of coordination simply to the Program Management Office, which is unrealistic for achieving optimal results. Long-term success will only be achieved when the Program Office actively manages this coordination until it becomes truly institutionalized across the enterprise. You may have flawless execution within the confines of individual projects, but unless there are procedures in place to coordinate concurrent projects (which inevitably have some degree of overlap), and at least the individual project managers rigorously adhere to those guidelines, ultimate success will prove elusive for the company as a whole.

This cross-project coordination is depicted in Figure I-6, which highlights the individual coordination between the project managers, and then further highlights the additional component of the Office of Program Management to the coordination equation. Coordination needs to occur on both levels and in a continuous fashion in order to have an opportunity to truly deliver optimal results for the enterprise. Ideally, the coordination extends to the project team members themselves where any overlaps or dependencies occur, but this can be driven by the project managers on a case-by-case basis. What should be mandatory and built into the governance model is the coordination highlighted in Figure I-6.

Figure I-6: Organization Chart for *Integrated* Multi-Project Environments

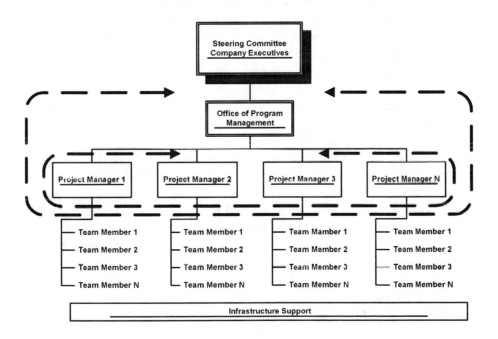

All segments of the PI Department will be involved in identifying opportunities for initiatives, and will have a role in the detailed, metric-driven project justification analysis. But it is the program managers who are ultimately responsible for driving this analysis and standing behind the results and recommendations. Beyond the team of traditional Program Managers in the Office of Program/Project Management, there are three additional distinct responsibilities for this part of the PI Department that span most, if not all, projects undertaken by the organization. These three responsibilities include:

- Financial Analysis and Management
- Transformation Enablement (Change Management)
- Partner Management

PI Departments have the ability to have a tremendous impact on the bottom line of any organization. That statement alone implies a strong desire for these groups to have some focused talent with respect to financial analysis and management. It is important to understand the implications of short-term and long-term budgeting, capital vs. expense, the impact of write-downs and write-offs, and the ability to provide sophisticated analysis when proposals are being generated by the PI Department. Do you know what percentage of a systems implementation should be capitalized and what percentage should be expensed? Many IT shops don't. (In fact, I've encountered a number of accounting departments that don't know this either!) These decisions not only impact compliance with Generally Accepted Accounting Principles in these days of hyper-audit activity, but they can also have dramatic impacts on budgets over the long-term, as encountered these days by IT Departments, which are struggling with huge depreciation schedules balanced against declining company revenues. IT organizations may have this skill set today, but it is usually by chance rather than by design. Others "borrow" these kinds of resources from the Finance organization. The optimal solution is for the skill to be resident within the PI Department itself. This is a strategic organization within the company that is empowered to decide on the approval or rejection of significant corporate investments. The complex financial implications of these decisions need to be well understood, and someone needs to ask the right (tough) questions during these evaluation processes. I strongly encourage the addition of core financial know-how as part of the Program Management team within the PI Department.

The term Change Management has come to mean lots of things to lots of different people. Mostly the term has come to represent something that many companies feel is not needed as a specific discipline. The common misconception is that companies have become so flexible and adept at changing that they don't need to have someone hold their hands through the process—they just do it. If only that was the reality. Organizational transformation, at almost any level, is bound to meet resistance, and those companies that tell me that they've already overcome that inherent problem are the ones that actually cause me the most concern.

They're the ones fooling themselves into believing it, and are usually the hardest ones to help. As stated earlier, resistance to change is natural and will appear whenever the transformation hits close to home. It's easy to define change for others, but it's a whole different story when the change is focused on you. That's when the excuses start to fly. Organizations need transformation experts who can help get stakeholders on board with dramatic change. This is a role for the PI Department, and is often a new skill that needs to be developed and nurtured.

It is critical that these change management professionals understand the strategic intent of the organization's leaders (both in broad terms, as well as in the context of a particular initiative), and assist in the alignment of that strategy with proposed initiatives. Communication plans need to be developed relative to all constituents who will be affected, including those within the project team, outside the project team, across business functions, and with external stakeholders as well. These experts should be consulted in terms of the organization's readiness for change, and at least have input into decisions such as Big Bang vs. a phased approach. Projects fail for many reasons. Resistance to change or lack of preparedness for change are both near the top of the list, often because they aren't addressed head-on with an understanding that these basics can destroy the rest of the great work that is put into an initiative. Don't ignore this component of Program Management (like most companies do)! To become "process driven" organizations and achieve the desired benefits, we need to reach *alignment* across all five areas of Strategy, Controls, People, Process, and Technology. Reaching this goal takes professional focus and dedication to the task. As such, this focus must be an integral part of the management approach of the organization, and it belongs most appropriately in the Process and Information Department (*especially* for those companies that think they don't need it!).

It was mentioned in the previous section that Partner Management will be a new role which will be instrumental in finding the right service provider partners and effectively managing those relationships in the world of IT outsourcing. The same guidance holds for any business functions that are also being reviewed for outsourced solutions. Business Process Outsourcing (BPO), which will be discussed in detail in Section III, also requires a new set of skills for most companies in terms of selecting the optimal partner and then effectively managing that long-term relationship. Just as the procurement and management functions for IT outsourcing services are different from simply procuring hardware and software, the skills and experience needed to select a BPO partner are also different from simply procuring the supplies used by existing business process organizations today. I have seen far too many companies simply insert their existing procurement teams into a BPO vendor selection process, and they run the selection just like they do when they're buying pencils and paper. It's often all about price to them, with little or no understanding of the complexity of the offering or the true capabilities of the service providers. While BPO may be ripe for commoditized process work, BPO as an industry is hardly a commodity. BPO, especially offshore BPO, is an immature industry with lots of suppliers with a wide-ranging degree of capabilities. BPO services represent the procurement of a *relationship* as much as a service, and either the existing procurement teams need to be educated along these lines, or new people should be brought into the PI Department (the preferred route) to run these selections and manage the on-going relationships. I will discuss the "Essence of Partnership" in the context of outsourcing services in Section III. For now, it should be noted that companies need to identify individuals who understand the complexity of these outsource relationships, and how to evaluate competing bids for services. The right place to embed those skills is as part of the team of business professionals in the Process and Information Department.

The Office of Program/Project Management clearly has two tiers. The first, Program Management, as just described, has the responsibility to establish the operational guidelines for projects throughout the organization, and then serves to coordinate those activities on an ongoing basis. The other tier, **Project Management,** then provides the execution leadership for these specific initiatives, and frequently does so in collaboration with other project managers working on related initiatives at the same time. While many roles that traditionally have been performed by IT organizations should be outsourced to providers of high-quality, low-cost services (as will be discussed in detail in Section III), I am reluctant to let Project Management be consumed by that model. Project Management is as much art as it is science. It is every bit as much a political role as it is anything else. While it is reasonable to outsource some of the task management associated with the project manager role, it is unlikely that you will achieve optimal results by outsourcing all elements of Project Management to a third party.

Just as program managers serve as the focal point to unify a number of projects, project managers represent the force that holds individual initiatives together. Most projects will find themselves subject to destabilizing actions that can occur at virtually any time, day or night, from project beginning to project end (and even further after that). In order to succeed in these roles, project managers need to be well-schooled in some fundamental techniques, as well as have the experience and sophistication to understand how to navigate through unique challenges that may pop up at a moment's notice. To this end, it is highly desirable that project managers within an organization have a well-established network of contacts up and down the company org chart in order to be able to openly discuss and evaluate situations directly at the source as they arise.

These individuals need to be as comfortable discussing issues or making presentations with C-level executives, VPs, directors, managers, and so on throughout the organization. They need to be able to understand the motivations for each of these individuals, and to do so not only within the confines of their professional objectives, but also with respect to their personal goals. They need to be able to communicate effectively via a variety of mediums, again with an understanding of the individuals involved and their levels within the organization. They need to be able to understand business processes across the enterprise, and be able to evaluate proposals relative to those processes that touch all facets of the organization. They need to able to rally the troops, but also remain calm during the mightiest of storms. This is a politically charged set of management responsibilities that requires fundamental insight into the organization and an ability to react appropriately to the needs of the moment and in the context of a wide variety of audiences. For these reasons (and more), Project Management should be a skill resident within organizations. Despite the fact that Project Management may not represent a core competence of the company, given the nature of this critical role it should become a core competence of the PI Department and a mainstay of this part of the organization.

Project managers also maintain the responsibility for the change management components of initiatives. Now, I have found that when a consultant utters the words "change management" to a client, there is almost a visceral reaction immediately followed by pronouncements along the lines of "We don't need change management, we're very flexible here and adapt very quickly, so just keep that change management stuff to yourself." As soon as I hear that I start to worry. Contrary to popular belief, change management is not about hand-holding team members and coddling them through an elongated buy-in process. On the contrary, change management is all about ongoing communication associated with any initiative. Team members need to understand the objectives of the initiative in order to make good decisions throughout the life of the project. Team members need to understand the expectations around roles and responsibilities so that the proper work gets done by the proper people, and that gaps are not left to be addressed at the last minute. Team members (and extended team members) need to understand how to perform their new roles based on the outcome of the project, or else the solution will simply come to a crashing halt the day after go-live. Ineffective transition is a common failure of many projects, largely because team members (and extended team members) have not had enough knowledge transfer in which to be able to perform their new duties. When this happens, no matter how well the solution is constructed, the perception is failure because the user community is unprepared for the change in their daily lives. Project managers need to get in front of these issues on each and every project and ensure that adequate communication and education programs are included in the project plans. Flawless execution is a critical element that drives Enterprise Optimization, and that goal can't be achieved unless effective change management techniques are utilized throughout the life of the project.

Many of the important characteristics of the individuals of the Process Department and the Information Department who will lead the organization in designing and evaluating solutions have previously been discussed. These same individuals will certainly be involved in the deployment of those initiatives that pass muster within the decision-making framework. However, while these business-savvy professionals will be critical to project success with their focus on end-to-end business value, that does not necessarily mean they are the right individuals to be the leaders of those deployments. Leading a project is a complex challenge, and subject matter expertise is not always the appropriate prerequisite for the role of Project Management. This is one of the reasons why the scope of the Office of Program/Project Management should extend across the entire organization, and not be limited to initiatives that are focused specifically on Process and Information Optimization. These are specialized skills, and there will be plenty of initiatives focused more on the product development and innovation side of the house that will require these skills. A good engineer does not necessarily make a good project manager. As Project Management becomes a core competency of organizations, this centralized unit needs to be leveraged across the entire enterprise, yielding standards, uniform governance, and management processes that can bring value to all initiatives across the board. A surefire way to have projects fail is to have an unqualified individual leading the effort. We can't afford that risk. Project Management skills need to be fostered in organizations, and then leveraged across the entire enterprise.

In many ways, project managers are the ultimate generalists. Similar to general managers, they have broad responsibilities, including those related to business processes, financial management, human resource management, issue management, and ultimate responsibility for final deliverables. Dr. Harold Kerzner provides the following definition:

> Project management is the planning, organizing, directing, and controlling of company resources for a relatively short-term objective that has been established to complete specific goals and objectives. Furthermore, project management utilizes the systems approach to management by having functional personnel (the vertical hierarchy) assigned to a specific project (the horizontal hierarchy).[12]

Managing a multitude of individuals for whom the project manager does not have direct line responsibility is one of these politically challenging components of the role. Many project team members will not be resident in the PI Department, but the project manager remains ultimately responsible for making sure the correct resources are acquired for the initiative, and that the horizontal and vertical mix of individuals is appropriate and working cohesively. The project manager needs to build relationships throughout the organization to facilitate the appropriate allocation of resources for particular projects, and to foster those relationships in the spirit of long-term trust and cooperation. This concept can be further complicated when one or more third-party service providers enter the mix, which is highly likely given the strong motivation to outsource non-core business and technical functions.

The Office of Program/Project Management is at the center of the universe for many of the most important initiatives in any organization. The criticality of the individuals assigned to this team and the roles that they perform cannot be overemphasized. From the standpoint of guiding principles in this realm, here is my list of the Top Ten Elements of Successful Project Management:

Top Ten Elements of Successful Project Management

- **Leadership**
  - o All initiatives need a leader—not many leaders, one leader. But title alone does not a leader make. Project managers need to earn the respect of their teams in order to lead effectively, and they can't do that by passively watching their projects from the sidelines. These individuals need to be willing to engage in the heat of the most intense issues and provide leadership on how to maneuver through these tough times to get back on track. This component takes decision-making to the next step. It's one thing to make a decision. It's another skill to then lead the team successfully down the path based on that decision. Real leaders provide the way through the toughest times, and do so with everyone running full speed ahead right alongside. Lack of leadership, or confusion over leadership, is a sure way to derail a project.

- **Strong Decision-Maker**
  - o Project managers must be capable of quickly assessing a situation, and then making an informed decision. It is important to be open to input and consider various options, but once the alternatives have been evaluated, a firm decision is critical. Once the decision is made, the project manager must be able to convince all associated constituents on the appropriateness of the decision, and then effectively manage the ramifications of the decision. Analysis paralysis is not an option.

- **Communication**
  - Project managers are the ultimate communicators for a project. They represent the team and the initiative to senior management, the functional leadership, other project managers, and all other participating parties (both inside and outside the organization). They need to determine what to communicate, when, and how, as well as to understand the nature and consequences of those communications. They need to balance the need to escalate issues vs. the implication of crying wolf. They need to understand when to communicate face-to-face, in person, via e-mail, over the phone, etc., and understand that there are subtle differences with each of those mediums. Moreover, project managers need to ensure that the parties themselves are provided the appropriate opportunities for communication. They need to balance the need for meetings vs. the need for time to get work done. Ultimately, they need to ensure that everyone knows what he or she needs to know to effectively complete the project's tasks. If it were only as simple as it sounds. So many projects end up going sideways due to ineffective or inappropriate communication. "No surprises!" That should be one of the mantras of Project Management, and that ties directly to the ability of the project manager to effectively communicate to all appropriate parties.

- **Keep Your Eye On the Prize**
  - Projects are full of distractions. It is easy for everyone to lose focus throughout the life of a project. That can't happen for project managers. It's one of the reasons to advocate the Management by Objective approach, in which specific goals (and related metrics) are identified at the outset of any initiative, and that all aspects of the project should ultimately be related to those objectives. This is the easiest way for project managers to maintain their own focus, and the easiest way to get the team back on track. Project managers can't afford to assume that everyone knows, understands, and focuses on these objectives. They need to proactively communicate these goals on a continuous basis, and be on the lookout for cases where team members may be off struggling with unimportant, tangential details (in other words, wasting precious time). The project manager has to maintain focus, and has to proactively help the team do the same. There's not enough time in the day to allow for distractions to take hold and possibly sidetrack an entire initiative.

- **Versatility**
  - o Projects never follow the prescribed path lock, stock, and barrel. Project managers must be able to effectively navigate the path from beginning to end, despite all the unexpected roadblocks. Oftentimes, the right decision is to change the original plan (anywhere from minor modifications to outright rewrites), and project managers need to be able to distance themselves from the details and provide the appropriate level of flexibility as situations arise. The important thing to remember is that alterations to plans should always be made in the context of the overall strategic objectives of the initiative.

- **Business Management Competence**
  - o Project managers do not need to be functional experts in any one particular area. That's what the functional team members (and/or consulting partners) are for. But effective project managers do need to have a strong sense of business fundamentals in order to be able to understand business issues and proposed solutions. They don't need to be the experts, but they need to be savvy enough to understand when things are on the right path vs. when they're going awry. Oftentimes, people with technical backgrounds who have managed engineering projects stumble when thrust into business project management roles. My observation is that lacking at least some degree of business management competence puts the project manager (and the project!) at a distinct disadvantage.

- **Match the Right People with the Right Jobs**
  - o Project managers are challenged in that they often don't own the resources assigned to their projects. They will often be assigned by the functional leadership or the third-party consulting organizations. While they don't own the resources, they absolutely need to be involved in the resource selection process and should have enough clout in the organization to be able to push back when appropriate. They also need to be savvy enough to understand the pros and cons of swapping out resources in the midst of a project. Sometimes, it's the exact right thing to do to get a project back on track, but sometimes a replacement decision can be devastating to a team environment. My advice in these situations is not to make rash decisions. Think long and hard before making switches midway through a project. Then, once you make the decision, execute quickly and don't look back.

- **Conflict Resolution**
  - I have yet to see a project that didn't require some degree of conflict resolution. Conflicts can range from dueling parties with different objectives pushing a project off course, to an honest disagreement on strategy between parties, both of whom provide compelling cases. Project managers can't just pick a side, declare a winner, and then expect everyone to go about their business happy as a lark. They need to take the time to understand the nature of the conflict, listen attentively to all sides, ask questions, make suggestions, and ideally help the combatants resolve the issue on their own. In some cases, project managers need to take the extra step in deciding the conflict resolution, but need to do so in a manner that yields acceptance from the conflicting parties. One of the most effective means in which to resolve a conflict is to identify it and diffuse it long before it becomes a major issue. Project managers can't hide in their offices waiting for issues to find them. They need to be close enough to their initiatives to see these things coming, and try to help resolve them as early as possible.

- **Time Management (Team)**
  - Time is money, and projects are always constrained by both. Project managers need to ensure that enough time is allocated to get the job done with the people assigned, but also need to be sensitive to being able to provide a rapid return on investment. This doesn't mean working everyone 16 hours a day, seven days a week. Projects will certainly go down this path every once in awhile, and usually that will be okay with the team as long as everyone pitches in together for the common good. But that approach doesn't scale. The project manager is ultimately responsible for making sure that people are pushed to ensure rapid progress, but must also be aware of the breaking point, or those loyal team members will desert him before he knows it.

- **Time Management (Self)**
  - Dr. Kerzner writes, "For most people, time is a resource that, when lost or misplaced, is gone forever. For a project manager, however, time is more of a constraint, and effective time management principles must be employed to make it a resource."[13] Project managers are in a continuous race against the clock. Their time is constantly in demand, and if they try to accommodate all requests, they'll never get anything done. They must empower team members and be willing to delegate responsibility to these key project participants. This is

important for team morale, as well as for project effectiveness. Project managers need to know when to lead, but also know when to back away and allow the team members to perform their roles. Further, project managers need to weigh decisions about how much time to spend amongst the team and how much time to spend behind a closed door getting work done. As I've stated, project managers can't operate in isolation, but they also can't be so deep into everyone's business that they don't get their own work done either. An extreme approach will never be optimal, but finding the right mix can be a challenge. Travel when you must, but be aware that when you're traveling to see one group, all the other groups lose access to you and you lose access to them. This is a constant balancing act, but you can help yourself by some of the following means:

- Keep casual visitors at a minimum.
- Delegate when appropriate.
- Limit travel (Ask: Is this trip necessary?).
- Attend appropriate meetings, but realize you don't need to go to them all.
- Refuse to do the unimportant.
- Proactively plan solid blocks of time for your own important work.
- Train your boss, peers, and subordinates how to work with you.

One of the key responsibilities of the Office of Program/Project Management is to lead the efforts in identifying which projects should be pursued by the company. All too often, these are subjective decisions, rather than ones based on extensive, quantitative analysis. One reason these choices are not very scientific is that companies lack a decision-making framework that serves to guide them through this process. In the next section, I will introduce the Enterprise Optimization Framework, which provides specific guidelines on how initiatives should be properly evaluated in order to achieve a high level of confidence on whether or not an initiative should be pursued.

Summary and Highlights

- Processes and Information are the lifeblood of our businesses. In their optimal state we achieve competitive advantage. In their suboptimal state we move down the painful path toward enterprise extinction. The suboptimal state is the norm, as organizations lack cohesion in their end-to-end processes and are unable to provide timely and accurate information for their employees, customers, and partners.

- Organizations are suffering from a key leadership void, with the Chief Information Officer (CIO) role at the center of the problem. The CIO role has evolved into a tactical, service-focused position, rather than a strategic, leadership function. It is an inappropriate role for a C-level executive and should be eliminated.

- Missing in the executive suite is a role deserving of a C-level title—the Chief Process and Information Officer (CPIO)—who is responsible for the ongoing optimization of these two critical components of successful organizations, and for achieving enterprise-wide alignment when resistance is encountered. Such alignment must incorporate each of the following five organizational elements:
  - Strategy
  - Controls
  - People
  - Process
  - Technology

- CPIOs lead the Process and Information (PI) Department, which consists of the following four components:
  - o Process Department
  - o Information Department
  - o Information Technology Department
  - o Office of Program/Project Management

- The successful introduction of a PI Department will be contingent upon several factors, including an unwavering mandate from top management, which includes buy-in across the senior leadership of the organization. On top of this, financial incentives and budgetary control will be needed to foster real support. As such, the PI Department needs to become the central decision-making body for approving and prioritizing all relevant initiatives throughout the company (as defined in this section). Finally, individual goals and rewards need to be aligned between the PI Department and the functional teams in order to foster the appropriate spirit of partnership that will be necessary for this new organization structure to ultimately be successful.

- The PI Department must focus on end-to-end processes, seeking optimal results for the *entire* organization and not just individual functions or geographic units. The Process Department should look to leverage industry-specific best practices that are embedded in enterprise systems and in the implementation methodologies of the system integration firms as among the most efficient means of establishing Process Optimization, supported by flawless execution by the relevant functional teams. Starting from scratch with a handful of programmers may appear to provide the opportunity for the "perfect process," but the impact on total cost is a major consideration, and it is highly unlikely that this approach will ever yield optimal results for the company as a whole.

- It is not possible to achieve Enterprise Optimization without a rigorous company-wide commitment to data governance and data quality. Information requirements need to be understood at the outset of any initiative, and not addressed as an afterthought, as is the common practice today. Sound decision-making is not possible without the right information being readily accessible by the right people at the right time.

- One of the common downfalls of a set of initiatives is the lack of coordination, in which case an individual project may appear to be successful, but the overall program ends up in failure. The Office of Program Management represents a critical component in the ability to establish the governance structure for company initiatives and then serves to oversee the interrelated execution of those projects. This group also owns responsibilities for financial analysis and management, transformation enablement (change management), and partner management for outsourcing services across the initiatives that involve the PI Department.

- Project Management is both an art and a science. Individuals who take on this responsibility must be well-trained and experienced business professionals in order to be able to handle the myriad of challenges that can crop up at any time throughout the life of a project.

- "Keeping things simple" represents a tried and true recipe for optimization.

Section II: The Framework

Companies have wasted millions on the "gut feel" approach to IT investments. The research is full of examples where IT projects have either had a negative overall impact on an organization, or at least failed to meet the original goals of the project.

- In a Conference Board survey of ERP project managers released in 2001, 40 percent of respondents said they failed to achieve their original business case even after being live for a year or more.[14]
- *Ecommerce Times* reported that, "In 2003, half of all information technology projects involving third-party consulting will be considered unsuccessful by executives who oversee them, according to a new report from Gartner, because they fail to deliver expected return on investment or operational value."[15]
- A survey by Fujitsu Consulting found that two-thirds of the companies that had installed CRM software failed to become any more "customer-centric."[16]
- Even the consulting organizations are coming to grips with the fact that many of these large IT projects are not providing the benefits people thought would be achieved. John Parkinson is the chief technologist for the Americas for Paris-based Cap Gemini Ernst & Young. He said, "Western companies spent north of $300 billion on ERP since the mid-90s, and if you put your hand to your heart, you can't say they got that back."[17]
- Finally, Forrester Research calculates the technology overspend in the years 1998 to 2000 at $65 billion in the U.S. alone.[18]

There are numerous reasons for this noted lack of success, both from a planning perspective as well as in the ultimate management and execution of these initiatives. Sometimes the problem stems from lack of executive support. Sometimes it's lack of user participation. Sometimes it's scope creep. Sometimes it's lack of training and knowledge transfer. Sometimes it's low user adoption where a solution fails to achieve the expected benefits simply because people refuse to use it. Sometimes it's lack of coordination between functional groups, geographies, or other dependent projects. All of these can play a role in achieving less than anticipated results for a particular initiative. But sometimes failure in this regard is the outcome simply because it wasn't a good idea to pursue the project in the first place. That may be because the original plans underestimated the amount of work and resources needed to be successful, so the justification analysis was thrown off, or it may be because no one ever bothered to perform any justification analysis in the first place, instead relying on our good friend "gut feel" for permission to move forward. If that's the case, then shame on those executives. The fact is, "gut feel" decision-making is another surefire way to reach self-inflicted annihilation. It's time to put a stop to that source of corporate suicide right now.

Introducing the Enterprise Optimization Framework

Many of the negative outcomes listed above are caused by flaws in relation to organization structure and governance framework. The organization structure has already been discussed in depth, and how the Process and Information Department is the proposed answer to organizational alignment around end-to-end business processes and providing enterprise-wide leadership in analyzing the expected outcome of initiatives. But that represents only part of the battle. The PI Department needs to further assert itself in providing a framework and governance model in which initiatives can be proposed, evaluated, and approved or rejected based on quantifiable means, and this must be done in the context of the overall strategic business drivers of the company. No projects should be undertaken, even if they satisfy the main criteria in an agreed-upon approval process, unless they are positioned as compatible with the overall strategic direction of the company. That's the first litmus test for any project, and cannot be overemphasized. As mentioned in the previous section, this is one of the reasons why the CPIO needs to be included in the process whereby the overall objectives of the company are translated into an actionable strategy. Just as the other C-level executives need to provide their stamp of approval in these strategic areas, the CPIO must be included to ensure the likelihood that the strategy can be brought to life in a profitable manner. The PI Department must remain constantly in the loop with senior management, as organizational objectives can change rapidly, which can certainly impact the justification and prioritization decisions made by the PI teams.

Once the organization is convinced that an initiative is truly aligned with the company's strategic objectives, then the analysis ultimately comes down to three very specific areas:

- Process Optimization
- Information Optimization
- Total Cost Optimization

This is what I call the Enterprise Optimization Framework, also referred to as "the framework" throughout the book (see Figure II-1).

Figure II-1: Enterprise Optimization Framework

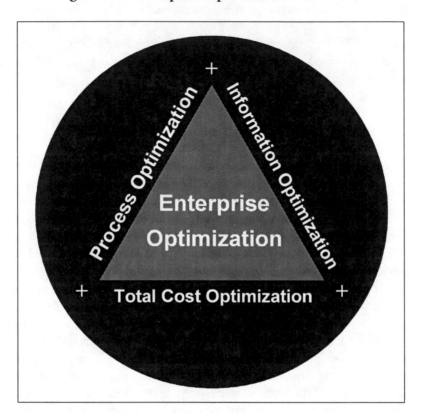

Ideally, an initiative will present benefits in each of these three areas. However, it may be sufficient to approve a project as long as the *overall* benefits are positive (as represented by the combination of these three areas). From a graphical point of view, this refers to maximizing the area of the triangle in Figure II-1, and the true optimal state would be in the case of a fully expanded equilateral triangle. I do not view any one component as more important than the others. They each have an equal impact on Enterprise Optimization. That being said, not all three sides of the triangle need to expand in order to increase the area of the triangle. In order for an initiative to be justified, the increase in one or more of the sides simply needs to outdistance the combined drop from the others. All three components need to be considered, and as long as the total area of the triangle increases, even slightly, then you can be confident that you're adding value to the overall enterprise and the initiative should be pursued.

In this section, I will explore the framework from a number of perspectives, including walking through a detailed case study, as it would be performed by the PI Department. Before venturing into that detail, however, I would like to add a little context to the model. At times there will be additional considerations when making final decisions with respect to the output from the framework. For one thing, each company must determine the appropriate internal rate of return for its opportunities. For some companies, just having a positive net change may be sufficient, but for others that have less confidence in their ability to accurately predict the outcome of such initiatives, a higher bar may be set before a project is approved. Moreover, the company needs to understand the timing of the return on the investment. Some companies may require a one-year payback before approval is granted, while others may have a longer-term view of the decision-making process. Part of this may depend on the economic environment in which the company finds itself. If the company is struggling, is deep in debt, or finds itself worried about making payroll, then the survival of the organization may impact the decision-making process. A company in this situation may reject an opportunity the framework indicates will generate a positive return because the timeframe to realize that return would put the company in peril relative to the initial outlay of funds.

These kinds of considerations all represent an additional reason the PI Department needs to have financial analysis expertise within its organization. It also emphasizes the need for standards in the decision-making process so that all constituents adhere to the same policies regarding the appropriate requirements before a project is approved. Opportunities need to be understood in the context of the environment in which the company resides, and the output of the results needs to be interpreted accordingly. However, none of these subtleties alter the framework itself. The results of the analysis need to be generated by the unbiased professionals in the PI Department. The analysis from the framework remains the core input to the ultimate decision, even though other considerations will be factored in based on the individual circumstances of the organization. But the analysis must come first before any of these other components come into play. The concern about spending a lot of money while you're in a difficult financial situation doesn't excuse not going through the analysis. This is the only way you will truly understand the expected outcome of your proposals, along with the timeframe in which the return will be generated. Companies in these difficult situations may set the bar higher in terms of the expected return and the timing of that return, but if the analysis passes that test, then you should move forward with confidence that your efforts toward optimization are on the right path. Remember, for companies that are struggling, it is virtually impossible to get out of your current hardship without targeted investment in opportunities to improve. This is exactly why we need this framework, to help us objectively identify what the optimal opportunities truly are. Basing decisions purely on "gut feel" surely isn't the answer, especially when available funds are such a precious commodity.

Finally, the framework can, and should, be viewed on *multiple levels*. In this section, specific examples will be explored at length to demonstrate how the framework can be used at its most detailed level for project analysis. But it is important to note that the three-sided structure was chosen for a higher purpose as well. These three components provide an easy-to-remember guide for a simple, generalized thought process regarding initiative opportunities. Part of its beauty is its simplicity, which remains one of my overall objectives. Anyone can remember a three-sided triangle, which makes it easy to socialize the concept of the framework throughout an organization. Long before initiatives are put forth for detailed analysis, individuals should begin thinking through how the project will impact the organization along these lines. This is the first test, and should be common for everyone. Specific members of the PI Department will use the framework in its detailed form for extensive analysis. But the framework itself can be used by anyone when thinking about ways to further optimize your organization.

This broader use of the framework is necessary to understand in that its purpose is not simply to be used in evaluating discrete project opportunities. Yes, that is one major use, but it is not the only use. Companies which adopt this framework as a philosophical guiding principle for business decision-making will find opportunities to create demonstrable competitive advantage, often with little regard to innovation in the area of products or services—just based on the advances in the areas of processes, information, and relative total cost. Let's take a look at Dell Computer, which in less than two decades, has grown to be the biggest, fastest growing, and most profitable computer company in the world.[19]

There are a number of remarkable components of the Dell success story, but one of the most interesting to me is that the company barely spends anything on R&D (just 1.3% of revenue). Dell doesn't gain competitive advantage by innovating on products. Rather, Dell gains competitive advantage by innovating on *process*. "For Michael Dell, inventing the Next Big Thing is not the goal. His mission is to build the Current Big Thing better than anyone else…. 'They're inventing business processes. It's an asset that Dell has that its competitors don't,' says Erik Brynjolfsson, director of the Center for eBusiness at the Massachusetts Institute of Technology's Sloan School of Management."[20] Examples: The company has won 550 business-process patents,[21] and generated more than $800 million in savings in FY03 alone by way of employee-initiated process improvement teams.[22]

Dell follows the five tenets of its *Direct Model* to achieve this tremendous success:

- Most Efficient Path to the Customers
- Single Point of Accountability
- Build-to-Order
- Low-Cost Leader
- Standards-Based Technology

So while other computer makers are investing in product innovation, Dell is focusing on optimizing each of these core components of its process-focused strategy. And it's important to understand that Dell's business model provides not only optimal end-to-end processes, but also provides an optimal utilization of information. The engine behind this smooth running machine is the instantaneous availability of timely information for all constituents who are involved in the supply chain and order fulfillment process, including the many external partners which are critical to their overall success. In doing so it has become the most efficient, effective, and profitable company in the business. It has also become top ranked in terms of overall customer satisfaction, and has held that distinction for every quarter for more than two years.[23]

To get a sense of how Dell differentiates itself from its competition, review Figures II-2, II-3, and II-4.

Figure II-2: Dell vs. Competitors—R&D as a Percent of Revenue

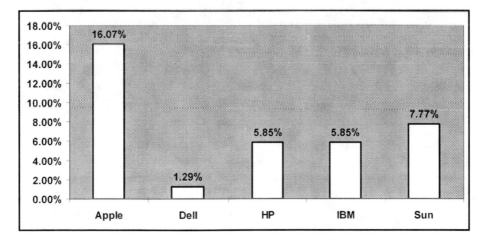

Source: Yahoo! Finance, Most recent annual metrics posted as of October 14, 2003

Figure II-3: Dell vs. Competitors—SG&A as a Percent of Revenue

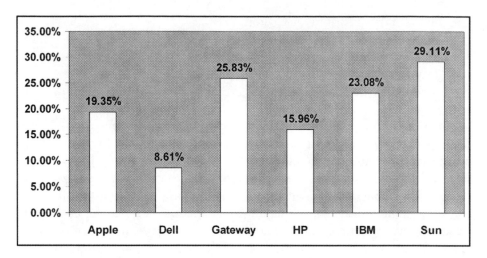

Source: Yahoo! Finance, Most recent annual metrics posted as of October 14, 2003

Figure II-4: Dell vs. Competitors—Revenue per Employee

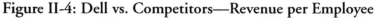

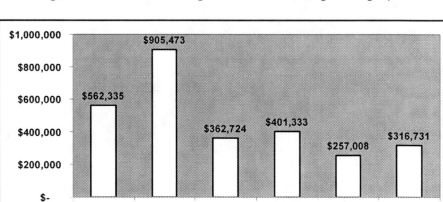

Source: Yahoo! Finance, Most recent annual metrics posted as of October 14, 2003

Little to no R&D or overhead, yet tremendous productivity are evident based on these metrics, which are a testament to the company's commitment to optimizing the way it runs its company. Consistent year-over-year growth and profitability are the results, thanks in large part to the efficiency and effectiveness of this organization which maintains virtually no overhead, invests very little in new product development, but spends incredibly wisely in terms of optimizing the direct relationships with its customers and partners. The competition clearly hasn't cracked this code. Companies like Dell, FedEx, and Amazon.com represent extreme cases where process, information, and execution excellence yield profound differentiation in the marketplace, with very little regard to product innovation. In looking at product-focused companies (by far the majority in the marketplace), optimization in these critical areas tends to take a distant back seat in priorities. To these companies I pose the following questions: What kind of additional differentiation could you achieve by optimizing around both products *and* processes, information, and execution? What kind of impact could this balanced approach have on your bottom line?

With this macro view of the framework in mind, let's now explore each component at a greater level of detail. The first topic is that of **Process Optimization**. The process-focused business professionals in the PI Department are tasked with understanding and supporting the end-to-end business processes throughout the company. As for project opportunity evaluations, this team is responsible for quantifying the benefits associated with a particular initiative. For example, what will it mean to the bottom line for the company to be able to:

- Automatically push a valid sales forecast over to the operations team, and to automatically drive the build plan with no manual intervention?
- Have a customer's entire sales history available at the touch of a button when a customer calls in for support?
- Provide electronic collaboration for a company and its suppliers for forecast and commit information?
- Provide employees self-service capabilities to update human resources data, including benefits, program enrollment, and personnel information?

The list goes on and on. What is the impact that projects in each of these areas can have on the company's bottom line? In other words, what's the overall benefit relative to its cost?

Ultimately, these benefits need to be quantified in order to add value to the analysis. There is a financial amount to all benefits. In the area of Process Optimization, that economic impact relates to the ability to improve the cycle time of whatever process is being reviewed (i.e., *efficiency*), and translating that improvement into the relevant financial metrics (i.e., *effectiveness*). **The objective in Process Optimization, therefore, is to enable a measurable degree of**

improvement in the area of process efficiency, and to effectively translate that impact into a quantifiable financial benefit.

It is also critical to state that this analysis should not be limited to individual functional areas. These processes, and others like them, span multiple functional groups within the enterprise. The total benefit throughout the value chain is what's needed in terms of this analysis. The answer to the typical self-centered, silo approach to project justification analysis is the Process and Information Department. A company needs a group of professionals specifically tasked with looking out for the interests of the entire organization. These folks need to be sensitive to the needs and urgency felt by the individual business units, as well as by the corporate leaders who are ultimately responsible to senior management. All sides need to be considered, and the PI Department is specifically chartered with that focused responsibility.

Along these lines, the Process Department within the PI Department must also be cognizant of the other components of the framework, as nothing takes place in a vacuum. Process Optimization without regard to impacts on information and total cost may, in fact, be *detrimental* to the company. For example, it may appear to narrow-focused individuals that extensive customization to an existing system-supported process may yield a measurable degree of Process Optimization in terms of increased efficiency. That analysis alone, however, cannot be used to justify moving forward with the initiative. The total cost over the life of that solution may be so exorbitant that the negative impact on this part of the framework overwhelms the potential positive result on the process side. Along these same lines, if that custom solution makes it significantly more challenging to preserve data integrity or impedes access to information in a timely fashion, then, again, the solution may not pass the overall test of the framework.

For example, there are many functional units that typically deplore maintaining required levels of information in systems. Salespeople in the field would much rather be selling than entering data into systems. ("Why do I have to enter all this data? It just keeps me from selling more stuff!") The problem, of course, is that without that information, sales management has no means in which to forecast demand to the rest of the organization, which has a trickle-down effect on the effectiveness of the Planning, Inventory, Shipping, and Customer Service organizations. The objective is found in balancing the ability to streamline the process flow, while also capturing the data needed for the company as a whole to operate effectively, and to do so at the point where total cost is not compromised. The Process Department, while primarily focused on Process Optimization, must always act within the guidelines of the framework as a whole, and needs to work collaboratively with the functional teams to ensure they do the same.

The next area that plays into this decision-making process is **Information Optimization**. Your costs may increase and your processes may stay the same (or even get worse), but you may still be able to justify a project if the quality and time-liness of the information you receive is sufficiently improved that it provides an over-all positive impact to the bottom line. As has been discussed, information access and quality are often the last criteria taken into consideration when reviewing a new ini-tiative. People seem to assume that as long as the information is somewhere in the system, they can always get to it. Theoretically that may be true. Practically it may be virtually hopeless to achieve. CIOs have the word *information* right in the middle of their job titles for a reason (and it is retained in the CPIO title for a similar reason). Timely and accurate information is essential for the overall success of the enterprise. In some industries, Information Optimization may represent the determining factor in the overall market success (or failure!) of the company.

What's the company benefit for:

- A CFO to have an updated balance sheet and P&L for any department at the push of a button—and to have complete confidence in the information?
- A COO to have insights into inventory levels not only in-house, but also at the company's major suppliers?
- An HR vice-president to have real-time headcount information on a global basis (especially during dynamic times of rapid growth or contraction)?
- A Sales vice-president to know pipeline and probabilities based on an updated dashboard, rather than a collection of out-dated, disconnected spreadsheets?

As with Process Optimization, these benefits need to be quantifiable in order to be truly helpful in any analysis. **In the case of Information Optimization, there-fore, you're talking about a measurable improvement in the quality and trust-worthiness of the data, as well as the timeliness and accessibility of the data. The result should be better and timelier decision-making that can be measured and quantified.**

There may be a hard dollar cost to providing these benefits, and even some process degradation, but the *overall* benefits may prevail and justify an initiative if the Information Optimization component is significantly compelling. From a process perspective, for example, to obtain the appropriate information on the back-end of a process, the organization may need to add complexity to the data-gathering portion at the front end or middle portion of that process. The front-end team may object, but the *overall* benefit to the company in terms of timely and well-informed deci-sion-making may make such an accommodation worthwhile. This is another reason why projects viewed only in isolation by functional teams may not yield the optimal recommendation on whether or not a project should be approved. It's also why Information Optimization must be included in this analysis right at the front of the process, and not after the fact, as is often the case today.

This area also provides the opportunity to once again stress the importance of data quality throughout an enterprise. Information Optimization cannot exist without a rigorous commitment to data quality standards and controls. Extensive reporting solutions will not yield any value without complete reliability in the underlying data.

Along these same lines of the overall framework, just as the Process Department cannot focus solely on Process Optimization with little or no regard for the impact on information and total cost, the same is true for the focus of the members of the Information Department. In a perfect world we would be able to provide personalized, real-time dashboards for every member of our companies in terms of optimizing the information component of the framework, but clearly that would be cost prohibitive. From a process perspective, it would be inappropriate to mandate that the people processing various transactions be required to capture every single step of those processes in some system in order to be able to report on the ultimate granular level of the process. The negative impact on process efficiency would far outweigh the positive result of enhanced information. This goes back to the need for the Information Department to provide the leadership in identifying the key metrics that will be used to manage and monitor the performance of the company, ensure that standard definitions are in place for these metrics, focus on providing the means to report on these metrics on a consistent and timely basis, and not worry about other irrelevant data capture and reporting requests that are not worth the effort it takes to execute. The Information Department can provide that focal point for gathering agreement on what is important from this perspective, and therefore what is not important, and then make sound judgments based on this analysis. All of this represents a constant balancing act for the members of the PI Department to focus not only on their own areas of expertise, but also to proceed with analysis and recommendations based on all sides of the Enterprise Optimization Framework.

The final area to consider in the framework is **Total Cost Optimization**, which relates to all costs that are required to initiate, deploy, and support a particular initiative throughout its life. It is the specific investment that is made to achieve Process and/or Information Optimization. In today's world, IT projects are typically benchmarked against the software, hardware, and services costs of deploying a project. But clearly this does not represent *all* of the costs associated with an initiative. "Customers can spend up to four times the cost of their software license per year to own and manage their applications," said Brian Zrimsek, research director at Gartner Group. "Over five years, that totals to as much as 20 times their license cost to operate and manage their applications. Ownership costs are often underestimated, in some cases by as much as 70 percent, in many IT budgets."[24]

Typically, each of the following areas must be included in any discussion of a project's total cost:

- Software
- Hardware
- Implementation services (external consulting)
- Implementation services (internal personnel)
- Integration costs (covering each of the above four areas)
- Cost and frequency of future upgrades
- On-going support costs (including software, hardware, and support services)
- Infrastructure costs (including back-ups and disaster recovery)
- Training
- Decommissioned systems (lowers total cost)

The common problem IT shops face today when looking at costs in an ROI model is to limit the analysis to the costs leading up to the go-live point, and stop there. As mentioned, this is a big mistake. Many systems will require additional headcount for support, depending on the complexity of the system as well as the degree to which integration with other systems is required. An Enterprise Resource Planning (ERP) implementation, for example, has a reasonably known and quantifiable investment for initial deployment. But what about the ongoing support and maintenance of the new application vs. the legacy environment? Your in-house IT team, or your outsourced IT services supplier, may need to acquire additional skills to support this new application. The size of the team may need to be increased, at least in the short term, to provide adequate support levels. If the system is unstable, then clearly additional costs will be incurred for support. While it is impossible to predict 100 percent of your current and future costs of an initiative at the time of project proposal, it is incumbent upon the team performing the analysis to factor in as many costs and cost projections as possible. You should leverage experience in the marketplace, as well as insights from your technology and services partners, to understand as much about cost impact as you can. Any ROI calculation will be useless unless the *total* cost is accurately depicted and all foreseeable cost components are accounted for.

Alternatives need to be evaluated in terms of the total cost of the solutions being considered, including the option to leave things as is. It is also important to understand the budgetary impact of each of these costs; i.e., which costs are to be expensed in the current year, and which are to be capitalized and require depreciation over several subsequent budgetary cycles. For example, it would be irresponsible to mortgage the future with a capital-intensive project that results in limited, short-term gains. All of these cost parameters need to be considered when analyzing a potential project for possible pursuit. **The ultimate objective of the PI Department is to determine the optimal amount to invest in an initiative, and then determine if the investment will yield a profitable result for the**

organization based on the combined impact of all three components of the Enterprise Optimization Framework. Only when this analysis is applied on an enterprise-wide basis will you have a reliable perspective on whether or not the initiative will pay dividends to the company, and hence have a positive impact on Enterprise Optimization (the ultimate goal!).

One last point in terms of guiding principles follows the advice of Einstein, da Vinci, and Newton, as mentioned in the book's foreword: Keep it simple! As various scenarios are explored throughout this book, I will continue to stress the theme that simplicity is a tried and true path to optimization, whereas complexity just makes things harder and more costly. In terms of your organization structure, your decision-making framework, your process definitions, and your technology choices—all of these areas can be dramatically aided by a philosophical bias toward simplicity. For some reason people tend to think they can create differentiation and competitive advantage through complexity. My experience has shown over and over again that real advantage is created by keeping things as simple as possible, and then executing better than anyone else.

Metrics

A discussion in this area cannot be complete without some additional focus placed on the foundation of the analysis itself; that is, the metrics that a company uses to evaluate and measure the success of its initiatives.

How does one measure success? First, it must be recognized that many IT organizations today don't really measure anything at all. Metrics are talked about a lot, but just as often IT organizations rarely end up actually digging into the numbers. Based on experience, here's what's typical: A project is proposed by some element of "the business." Requirements are then gathered and maybe a formal proposal is put into place. The proposal would typically include:

- Objectives
- Scope
- Deliverables
- Approach
- Expected benefits
- Areas of risk/critical success factors
- Timeline
- Cost

Some may go through the trouble of creating a Return on Investment (ROI) analysis, but that is often back-of-the-napkin stuff based on broad assumptions and intangible generalizations. On top of that, who actually goes through the rigor of quantifying these potential benefits? Is it done accurately? And, most importantly, how is it actually measured and over what time horizon? Projects may take a year or more to provide a positive return. Is the infrastructure in place to identify and report these metrics over long periods of time? If this is not in place, how can you know if you ever achieved your goals, or even made the project worthwhile? The simple answer is that you don't know, and that's pretty common. You present your back-of-the-napkin approach to some steering committee, which gets a "gut feel" that it's the right thing to do, and then you go forward. There: project justified. A year or two later, do you ever really know if the project added any value to the company? Isn't that what really matters?

The most common excuse for not measuring results is the complaint that obtaining the measurements is anywhere from hard to impossible. How do you measure improved customer satisfaction? How do measure impact on headcount when you don't actually reduce heads as a result of a project, but rather have them focus now on more value-added responsibilities? How do you measure the dollar value of that impact? Many people can't get past these questions, so they never get to any measurements. But if you don't identify measurable benefits, and then proceed to actually measure the impact on those metrics before, during, and after implementation, how do you ever know if what you're doing is adding any value to the bottom line of the company? You know you're hitting the bottom line with expenses associated with the projects. Everyone can see that. But how can you justify your existence to shareholders if you can't identify metric-related improvements that are at least one penny greater than your expenditures? If you can't, then you should probably cease and desist. It's also not good enough to invest in some initiative just because your competitor is doing it. Maybe your competitor is making a mistake. How do you really know you're not just repeating that mistake without being able to measure the impact of your work?

Let's take a look at some of these hard-to-quantify metrics. What about customer satisfaction? Surely there are measurable components that would yield some conclusions about the trending level of customer satisfaction. How about on-time deliveries? How about defect percentages? How about frequency of Return Material Authorizations (RMAs) per customer? How about positive comments via phone, e-mail, or surveys? These should be worth a lot in a total metric calculation! These are just a few of the measurable items that could go into an on overall trended measurement of customer satisfaction. This is not an exact scientific measurement, but *reasonable conclusions* can be drawn, and you could certainly track these kinds of measurements over time and relate them to the impact of some new process or a new piece of technology. Don't ignore things that are hard to measure. Determine a meaningful way to capture these measurements as they may represent the most significant benefits (or costs) of the entire project.

One of the biggest challenges in the area of metrics is the ability to reach a common understanding of the metric in the first place. As asked in Section I, what is the definition of a *booking*? What is the definition of *on-time delivery*? For that matter, what is the definition of *customer satisfaction*? The list goes on and on. Not only do you find different definitions across companies for these and many other common metrics, but you also find similar patterns of variation *within* individual companies themselves. You obviously can't measure anything until you have a definition for what you are trying to measure. So, first things first, you need to undertake a cross-functional, possibly enterprise-wide approach not only to identifying the critical metrics that need to be tracked, but also to articulate the exact definitions that will be applied across the board for each of those metrics. This will not be a trivial task, but one that will require considerable leadership from the Process and Information Department. The value generated by this exercise will be critical to the ability to measure the ongoing success and failure of your initiatives.

Simply put, no project should be initiated without the anticipated benefits being articulated up front, along with the specific metrics that will justify the investment. And those metrics should in one way or another directly impact the P&L or the balance sheet of the company. You're talking about investing shareholders' money. Shareholders should see the fruits of your labor. The best way to show them results is to be able to tie projects to one of these publicly available documents. This is a critical step for the PI Department in terms of being able to positively influence behavior, because simply stating that more efficient processes will result in a positive impact to the bottom line will be insufficient to gain the support necessary to drive action and results. The PI Department needs to break down these metrics into the meaningful inputs that can then be translated into enterprise-wide objectives that can ultimately be measured at not only the process level, but also at the sub-process level. Take the goal of improving gross margin. There are many inputs that ultimately drive the final calculation of gross margin. When that's the overall goal, it is incumbent upon the PI Department to translate that overall objective into its relevant piece parts so that the individuals involved can focus specifically on the components that they can influence and that will ultimately result in improvements to this specific measurement. They can see their personal impact at the sub-process level, and map that impact all the way to the P&L. Further, this kind of breakdown activity (what I call *metric personalization*) can be used for individual performance management, specifically tying bottom-line impacts to the evaluation of the individuals responsible for that very impact. This is how to effectively drive the desired behaviors and get everyone personally involved in meeting the overall objective.

So, what types of metrics are appropriate for this discussion? The most relevant metrics are those that are tied to the efficiency, the effectiveness, and/or the ultimate profitability of the organization. **Efficiency** metrics are concerned with how well the company is executing a particular task or set of tasks. Typically, efficiency metrics will in one way or another link to cycle time of a process or subprocess, or will be concerned with the headcount needed for a particular task. The key point about efficiency metrics is that to be helpful, they need to be as granular as possible, and then be trended over an extended period of time. Goldratt pointed out in *The Goal* that we can optimize our environments by identifying our bottlenecks, and then eliminating those constraints one after another after another.[25] Process efficiency metrics help identify these bottlenecks, and the trends allow us to identify whether we are making any progress. The same thought process follows for headcount analysis. If we're supporting a highly manual process with a disproportionate number of resources relative to other processes, then our metrics can identify and trend our progress in trying to optimize the environment. Furthermore, it is important to remember that we need to broaden our view of efficiency beyond functional silos to extend across end-to-end business processes. Optimizing the efficiency one function at the expense of another within a single business process may yield negative overall results for the company. This is exactly why we need to have measurements for the efficiency of entire processes and not just discrete functions, and we need to apply those measurements to individuals who participate in the execution of any portion of the process. This alignment will ensure the process focus at the individual level, and drive the proper behavior in the overall best interest of the company, not just in the best interest of a discrete business function. Again, granularity will be a key component on how effective these metrics will be for our decision-making processes, and the PI Department will need to work diligently to ensure not only that the correct metrics are being gathered, but that they are also being gathered at the appropriate level of detail.

Efficiency metrics help us determine if we're "doing things right," while **effectiveness** metrics help us determine if we're "doing the right thing." In other words, effectiveness metrics pertain to how well our actions are actually serving to meet our business objectives. We may have fantastically efficient processes (i.e., "doing things right"), but if they are not relevant to our marketplace, or are not resulting in *end-to-end* productivity gains, then we are not being very effective for our customers or shareholders (i.e., not "doing the right thing"). For example, we may have a very efficient manufacturing process in terms of cycle count and headcount ratios, but if our quality is sufficiently poor such that most of our product is returned, then efficiency alone clearly cannot indicate optimal performance. All elements in the end-to-end process value chain must be contributing positively to the ultimate execution of these processes in order for companies to achieve a high level of overall effectiveness. In addition to the product quality example just mentioned, you could consider some of the earlier examples of Information Optimization in this context. For instance, you could have positive trends in the availability of information for management via the implementation of a new data warehouse, but if the data quality is highly suspect then the effectiveness of that solution would be next to nothing. Similarly, you could invest significantly in an on-line store environment that cuts the time for order placement by 70 percent for customers. However, if the adoption rate is minimal, then you probably have not been successful in creating an effective solution. One reason might be that while you've optimized the efficiency of the order placement process for customers, the back-end order fulfillment process may still be terribly inefficient (or, again, product quality could be very poor). The overall end-to-end process, therefore, would be very ineffective for that customer, yielding very little repeat business. This is yet another example whereby the individual alignment of performance management metrics across the entire process value chain is critical in achieving optimal results. Companies are effective when they put the whole process together and it drives results for their customers and partners. That happens when everyone is aligned around the same goals and then execute in a collaborative fashion for effective results. Measuring process effectiveness will provide opportunities for evaluation and improvement. It also provides motivation for the proper alignment for individual execution.

Efficiency is relatively easy to track as those metrics tend to be isolated around a particular action. Effectiveness, however, takes the analysis a step further in quantifying the ultimate impact of a process or set of processes on some additional, higher level objectives of the organization. It's important to do things well (efficiency) in an optimal environment, but things must be done such that a positive overall outcome is also achieved (effectiveness). By the way, effectiveness metrics are also valuable when having to make hard decisions about bringing projects to a halt. If it is determined that the ultimate solution is no longer expected to have an effective result, then it's time to cut your losses and move on. Metric-driven objectivity is the best way to cut to the heart of these otherwise emotional decisions.

The ultimate level of effectiveness is **profitability**. The real goal for companies, as articulated so well in *The Goal*, is to *make money*.

> I make a list of all the items people think of as being goals: cost-effective purchasing, employing good people, high technology, producing

products, capturing market share. I even add some others like communications and customer satisfaction. All of those are essential to running the business successfully. What do they all do? They enable the company to make money. But they are not the goals themselves; they're just the means of achieving the goal....There isn't one item on that list that's worth a damn if the company isn't making money....Money must be the goal. Nothing else works in its place.[26]

We're all in business for a lot of reasons, but the ultimate reason for commercial organizations is to make money. Metrics that are indicative of our ability to be a profitable enterprise must be at the core of the business metrics used by the PI Department. Ultimately, the Enterprise Optimization Framework is all about profitability. Can we find a tradeoff between Process Optimization, Information Optimization, and Total Cost Optimization such that the end result is positive economically for the organization? Why would we invest in something that may improve our process capabilities (likely tied to efficiency) yet will not make us more profitable (for example, if the total cost outweighs the benefit)? These are the kind of metrics that oversee our total analysis and should always have the final say when evaluating opportunities or ongoing activities.

Now that you have the overall components and key metrics associated with Enterprise Optimization, let's put it all together in the form of a definition: **Enterprise Optimization** represents the never-ending pursuit of the ideal state whereby an organization achieves the optimal balance across its capabilities to (1) define and execute processes that maximize both efficiency and ultimate effectiveness, (2) provide the optimal amount of information required for timely and effective decision-making, and (3) do so in the context of the lowest possible total cost, thereby yielding the maximum level of long-term profitability for the company.

Before moving to a couple of specific case studies that demonstrate the framework in action, there are a couple of more points to raise with respect to metrics. One would think that defining appropriate metrics related to the performance of an organization would be relatively straightforward. As mentioned, we're talking about measures that are indicative of the efficiency, effectiveness, and/or ultimate profitability of the organization. Unfortunately, the common practice is not so straightforward, and the breakdown occurs all too often when metrics encourage individuals (people, teams, functional units, etc.) to act in a manner that advocates behavior that supports those individual entities but are actually counter to the objectives or performance of the company as a whole.

As an example, in my own consulting career I used to be confronted with making resource and budgetary decisions based on conflicting objectives; i.e., optimizing my personal metrics vs. optimizing the overall performance of the company. Specifically, I had to make staffing decisions regarding the use of internal resources vs. the use of subcontractor resources. Service quality is always an overriding factor in these types of decisions, but there were cases in the past where I could find comparable quality of resources from outside our company for certain roles, and based on my personal metrics, I would actually achieve more favorable personal results than if I used an available internal resource—even though this was more costly to the company as a whole. Hard to believe? Well, I faced that scenario multiple times before we finally changed the focus of many of our internal accounting controls and performance metrics, which now provide much more alignment between individual and corporate objectives. How would you expect someone to react when his or her personal evaluation is based on specific individual metrics and it turns out that in order to optimize those personal results the metrics for the company as a whole get impacted negatively? While applying metrics to performance management with respect to processes, information, total cost, or any other component of an organization can be extremely compelling and powerful, it can also be destructive if those metrics are not aligned at all levels of the organization.

Incompatible metrics also often materialize in the area of transfer pricing and inter-company accounting, which consumes far too much of our collective energies in a fashion that adds absolutely zero value to our customers or shareholders. The typical scenario is when individual business units or functions are encouraged to treat other elements of their own company as if they were just another supplier. The result is that one division may improve its own standing at the detriment of another division, as well as the detriment of the company as a whole. This makes no sense. There may be times when it is appropriate to source supplies (or people, in the case of service provider organizations) from external organizations in lieu of internal resources, but these decisions should be based on objective measurements in areas such as quality, lead time, and capacity, and not on intensely negotiated pricing between divisions. If other divisions can provide the goods with comparable lead times and quality but at a slightly higher price than an external supplier, then the company as a whole will likely be better served using any available capacity from the other division than with going with the external supplier. The alternative is idle time for the supplier division, which still has to support fixed costs that simply go to waste. But all too often, individual business units are not motivated to look at these big-picture components. They have their own P&Ls that make price the ultimate decision criteria. As mentioned, this translates exactly to the service provider business. If I can call upon an unutilized resource from another business unit to fulfill a requirement vs. going to an external supplier for that resource, I should take the internal route 100 percent of the time (assuming the quality of the resource is comparable and the resource is available). But there was a time when my "internal cost" for that resource from outside my business unit actually was counted as a higher negative impact to my personal metrics than if I used the outside source. This completely ignored the cost to the organization for having that resource remain idle in the other business unit. Whether we're talking about people or materials, this makes no sense. Our personal metrics always need to be consistent with what's good for the company as a whole, and one of the values the Process and Information Department can bring to the table is the ability to analyze these kinds of conflicts and change the internal accounting such that the conflicts are eliminated. Most organizations have no central body that typically looks at these issues. This is how the PI Department is different. It is chartered to do exactly that—to ensure that the company has implemented an organization and procedural environment that supports optimal decision-making for the company as a whole. This is another area where the business understanding and global orientation of the organization is a critical gap to be filled by the introduction of the Process and Information Department.

The scenario described above is fairly obvious in terms of the suboptimal nature of these conflicting metrics, but there is a second, more subtle component (and cost) to this structure that may be less obvious within organizations. There can often be tremendous overhead (again, read "cost") associated with organizations fighting amongst themselves within a company for their personal piece of the pie. Ask yourself how many hours members of your organization, executives on down, spend negotiating deals between divisions. What's the cost of those negotiations in terms of worker productivity? How does the time spent negotiating with yourself add value to your customers or shareholders? The opportunity cost can become huge. Moreover, the infrastructure cost can become huge as well. I have seen companies build extensive system modifications to manage all the permutations to these internal transfer pricing schemes, all of which entail the cost to build, test, deploy, and maintain over time. Out-of-the-box systems tend not to support these processes, as they often evolve over time and tend to be unique to particular companies. Of all things in which to try to reinvent the wheel—something that adds no value to customers, suppliers, or the bottom line of the company!

I spent a brief time at one company that had installed an entire department to oversee the process and home-grown system that had been deployed in support of the transfer pricing and accounting within the company. An entire department! We were brought in to evaluate a possible enterprise-wide system upgrade to the company's existing platform. One of the things we were asked to evaluate was how we would be able to migrate this existing transfer pricing infrastructure so that it would work in the upgraded software environment. My feedback to our team was to recommend getting rid of the process altogether. What a waste of time and money. Why would you upgrade this thing? I suggested implementing a new, simple procedure (Keep It Simple, Stupid!) that focused on the overall success of the organization and rid itself of this costly, wasteful procedure. Needless to say, my recommendation was thoroughly dismissed. After all, that's how they'd always done things, and they weren't about to change, regardless of logical and objective analysis.

Another salient point with respect to metrics is that some metrics are always relevant, some are sometimes relevant, but some common metrics are actually rarely relevant, and you need to be very careful of those. The most common metric mentioned in the same breath as traditional IT projects is the old favorite, "on time, on budget." Let me say right now that this metric, *in and of itself*, is meaningless and should never be used as the sole indicator of the success or failure of a project. First of all, the fact is there is not a project in the world that any of us couldn't complete within the guideline of "on time, on budget." Not one. One technique often used is simply to set the budget too high and estimate too much time. Boom, success. Even better, you just go-live whether you're ready or not. That way you'll make the on time part for sure, and most likely the on budget part as well. Or if you're running over budget, just stop developing the solution a little bit early, and then you can complete the "on budget" component. If your bonus is tied to "on time, on budget" wouldn't you manage the project with this as your primary guiding principle? And everyone will be happy with the result, right? Not exactly. Tell that to all those project managers out there who lost their jobs over failed IT implementations, often because they went live on-time when the *right* decision was to delay.

Take a look at this example straight out of the 10-Q for Agilent Technologies.[27]

> During the current quarter, we implemented a new ERP system which covers over fifty percent of our volume and virtually all of our financial processes. Disruptions from implementing our new ERP system had a negative impact on our orders, revenue and operating profit for the third quarter. Our orders were impacted as customers delayed or did not place purchases due to such issues as our inability to quickly provide accurate shipment dates following the implementation. Our revenues were impacted as a result of orders delayed or lost during the period and due to shipment interruptions and system downtime. In addition to these specific issues, many of our employees were engaged

in learning the system and implementation activities during the quarter, rather than ongoing business activities. We believe that these major system interruptions and conflicts now have been largely resolved.

The table below shows the estimated negative impact on orders, product revenue and operating profits. These estimates were determined using information gathered from many different sources and are provided only as an approximation because the actual impact cannot be determined precisely. In some cases we have generated these estimates from trend data, such as expected orders or shipments per day; in other cases, we have estimated the reductions in orders and revenues based on specific criteria such as information from individual customer actions. In most cases it is difficult to precisely differentiate between the impact of the new system and the impact of the economic environment, but the figures we are presenting below are our best estimate of the impact of the disruptions caused by implementation of our new ERP system.

	Negative Impact during Three Months Ended July 31, 2002 (in millions)		
	Orders	Net Revenue	Operating Profit
Test and Measurement	$40	$75 $100	$45-$70
Semiconductor Products	$50	$10	$5
Total	$90	$85-$110	$50-$75

Do you think Agilent made the right decision to go-live on time? With a stated $50 to $75 million direct hit to Operating Profit, who knows how long it will take to recover from that decision. Sometimes, the *right* thing to do is *not* to finish on time or on budget. Maybe the project wasn't scoped correctly in the first place. The proper thing to do in that case is not to compound that original mistake by sticking with the original project plan, but rather to own up to that forecasting error and adapt to a new schedule that will enable completion under the *right* budget and the *right* timeframe.

Moreover, the focus on "on time, on budget" misses the most important component for the analysis of project success; that is, did you meet your specific *business* objectives? You might complete the project within the original cost and timeframe, but have you positively impacted some business process or reporting capability? Have you lowered total cost of ownership? Is the system usable? Are users appropriately trained? What's the big deal about finishing "on time, on budget" if you haven't demonstrated material success in one or more of these important areas? Meaningful metrics in the Enterprise Optimization Framework must tie back to one or more of the three focus areas: Process Optimization, Information Optimization, and Total Cost Optimization, and no conclusions should be drawn about the success of a project unless *all three components* of the framework are included in the analysis. One segment of the framework cannot be viewed in isolation as an indicator of overall success or failure. "On time, on budget" is merely one of many indicators of performance that factor into just one of the framework's components (Total Cost Optimization). It needs to be viewed in light of this fractional impact on the whole and not as the be-all and end-all arbiter of success. In some cases, investing in another week or an additional month of effort to achieve the desired business results may be exactly what's needed to actually achieve success. "On time, on budget" is not the hallmark of success—it is just *one indicator* of success. Missing the date or being slightly over budget does not automatically imply project failure. It will likely have some impact on the net results vs. what was anticipated, but this impact needs to be evaluated in the context of the entire project and across all sides of the framework. Going over budget with an initiative that was likely to only marginally yield a measurable degree of Enterprise Optimization may have far more impact than a project that is anticipated to yield dramatic improvements. In the former case, the budget overrun may, in fact, represent the difference between success and failure, but in the latter case, it may merely represent a footnote to the total outcome. That is why this often over-quoted and misused statistic should be referenced only in the appropriate context of the whole and not as a sole gauge of success.

Here's an example of just how bad things can get when your ultimate measure of success is simply "on time, on budget." In the wake of a highly publicized debacle where the State of California had entered into a contract with Oracle Corporation without the appropriate internal controls included in the procurement process, state government has been looking into other large high-technology procurement deals. In this case, the California State University (CSU) system had decided in 1999 to launch the Common Management System (CMS) project. The intent of the initiative was to replace the legacy business systems used at its 23 campuses, and serving 407,000 students and 45,000 employees. According to the CSU, "The systems differed by campus, were antiquated, and often were not integrated. Moreover, many were obsolete and no longer serviced by vendors." The CMS scope included replacing systems used for financials and system administration and the installation of a human resources system for the first time.

PeopleSoft was the company picked for the deployment, which was scheduled to be rolled out in phases over a number of years.[28]

In terms of the Enterprise Optimization Framework, this actually sounds like it might be a pretty good idea. The existing environment was clearly suboptimal with outdated, non-integrated technology, and the project as proposed could very well have merited approval based on the combined improvements relative to Process and Information Optimization vs. the Total Cost of the new solution. I say *could* have merited approval because no one really knows. It turns out that no one ever bothered to figure out the expected return on this investment. This is where things get interesting.

Given the climate around these large software contracts in California, the Joint Legislative Audit Committee requested an audit of this project. According to a statement from the CSU after the audit was released, "The audit found that the CSU did not do a cost-benefit analysis or feasibility study before proceeding…but had collected extensive information from the campuses about their technology requirements."[29] There's a novel idea. Now project justification is based simply on a list of user requirements! Sounds like these folks need a framework for this kind of analysis. The auditor, Elaine Howle, concluded, "Without compelling evidence of its need for new administrative software, or a cost-benefit analysis for the project, the university cannot ensure that the CMS project is a worthwhile expenditure of its resources."[30] Despite that perfectly logical conclusion, there's actually no reason to worry according to Richard West, executive vice-chancellor and chief financial officer, who proclaimed in a press release, "We have some disagreement regarding the auditors' determination of the cost, but more important, we remain on budget and on schedule with this project."[31] There it is! "More important, we remain on budget and on schedule with this project." Does that statement validate anything about whether the project will ultimately be beneficial for the CSU? Does that mean you're on schedule to waste a ton of money on the project, or are you on schedule to save the CSU hundreds of millions of dollars over the life of the program? What are you on schedule for? No one has any idea. Mr. West probably said "on budget and on schedule" because he had nothing else to say, or maybe he simply didn't realize that the statement has no meaning relative to whether or not the project is going to generate business success for his organization. Imagine, however, if Mr. West had data from a detailed project justification analysis that demonstrated a significant expected return on the investment. His response to the media could then have been along the lines of, "Despite the seemingly large price tag on this program, we remain on target to achieve $x-million in savings based on the following areas where we anticipate the following metric-driven improvements…." That would have been it. Case closed. No story.

Now, I'll admit that, unlike the business community, a statewide collective of educational institutions is not focused on making money as its core objective. One could argue that there may be some initiatives within education that may warrant pursuit even if they do not project profitability if there is an alternative ultimate objective with the educational benefits outweighing a potential economic loss. The same could be said for opportunities being entertained by various government agencies, with the public welfare serving as a higher goal than profitability. As stated early on, the strategic objectives of the organization must be a key component of this decision-making analysis. But I see none of this at play in this case. This is a financial investment to streamline costs and efficiencies in terms of the financial transaction processing and information management across these institutions. There is no higher value proposition here. This was a business decision based on "gut feel" that is now being called into question because no one has any idea if the investment will prove economically worthwhile.

This group made two fundamental errors. Number one, it based the approval for the project on "gut feel" with no quantifiable targets for improvement on which to justify the significant investment. This failure left the group totally exposed to potential critics. As I stated earlier, my gut tells me that this very likely could represent a wise investment based on the initial premise. But no one's gut is sufficient justification for spending one dollar, let alone several hundred million dollars, of taxpayers' money. Number two, Mr. West makes "on budget and on schedule" the hallmark of success, when we have no idea whether an "on budget, on schedule" completion will yield positive economic results at all. This is a classic example of how projects have been justified in the past, and it cannot continue in the future. It is further an example of how inappropriately people use the phrase "on time, on budget" as if it actually means anything relative to the overall business success of a project. "On time, on budget" is only relevant as one of the many components of the Total Cost Optimization segment of the framework analysis. In and of itself, as it was used in this case and in so many others, "on time, on budget" it is not indicative of anything. Let's stop using it and move on to metrics that are actually meaningful.

There is one other quote from a media account of this story that also caught my eye in terms of the use of meaningful metrics when making comments about an initiative:

> English Professor Susan Meisenhelder, president of the faculty association, said she was saddened by the findings. "Spending close to $700 million would be troubling even in good budget times," she said, "but

it's certainly distressing as we hear about canceling classes and laying off faculty."[32]

Does everyone see how this comment is just as off-base as the "on budget, on schedule" remark from Mr. West? The fact that the state is facing difficult economic times has nothing directly to do with whether or not this is a good investment, and the fact that it costs $700 million doesn't tell us anything, either. What matters is whether or not the organization will increase its degree of Enterprise Optimization as a result of the initiative. Will it improve the status quo in terms of the net impact on Process Optimization, Information Optimization, and Total Cost Optimization? If the likely net result is negative, then it's a bad idea. If the likely net result is positive, then it's a good idea. The economic climate *may* have a role in the decision if the analysis is close, such as when the forecasted outcome is close to a break-even scenario. When it's a close call, then other factors can enter into play to move the decision in one direction or another, since we all must recognize that none of these forecasts will ever be exact. It might also play a role if the institution is cash poor and the projected rate of return is so far in the future that it would cripple the institution in the short run. In that case the short-term risk might outweigh the long-term benefits and, therefore, influence the decision. But those factors aren't pertinent in this case, at least not at this point, since we don't have *any* likely results, including the length of time before the return kicks in. Despite Ms. Meisenhelder's protestations, the price tag isn't the issue here. The issue is whether or not the process and information benefits will outweigh the total cost, and do so in a timeframe that won't cripple the organization in the short-run. If she had evidence that it would, she should have stated so. That might have been a compelling argument for discussion. But all she pointed to was the cost, which, in and of itself, tells us nothing, and I see no evidence that this investment if going to shut down the entire California State University system. What price would be reasonable for Ms. Meisenhelder in these current conditions? Any price, relative to any return? If based on a sound business case, this $700 million investment might generate sufficient returns to *save* jobs and *expand* class offerings. Many organizations seek to invest during difficult economic times, in order to properly prepare for the future. And sometimes that means significant investments even in times of layoffs, as long as the business case warrants such an investment and the cash outlay won't result in overwhelming short-term economic strife. In this case, lacking that business case, we simply don't know the likely short-term and long-term impact, leaving all concerned in a poor position to speak authoritatively either in favor of, or opposed to, the initiative.

Conclusions in cases such as this must be made solely based on a firm understanding of the anticipated costs and benefits of the initiative. Nothing else really matters. Yet it is often these tangential, more emotional issues (like the economic climate and the associated layoffs) that influence our decision-making. We need to weed this stuff out of our thought processes, and focus only on what is pertinent, and PI Departments are chartered to do exactly that. The bottom line on this story is that no one knows if this project is a good idea because no one ever quantified the benefits, so we are unable to make valid recommendations in the context of any objective decision-making framework.

There are a number of other benefits to a metric-driven approach to project evaluations. First, there is no reason that your company needs to assume the entire risk for the success of any particular project. In most cases, there are other partners that play a role in the success of any individual initiative, and those partners should participate in the rewards of success and/or suffer the consequences of failure. The only way to effectively do this is with a metric-driven approach. For example, after you have identified the key metrics for success for a particular project, and then agreed upon the definition of each of those metrics, you can hold all partners (including your employees) responsible for some portion of the risk in reaching those measurable objectives. This approach could affect the compensation or reward system for your employees who are actively engaged in the project. This approach could equally apply to any implementation partners or software vendors to whom you have agreed to pay significant dollars for the project. And the good thing in the metric-driven approach is that you can monitor your success throughout the life cycle of the project, and correct the course along the way if necessary. Since all parties will have some skin in the game, the odds increase that they will give it that extra effort to achieve the forecasted results. To make it really attractive, you could build in an upside for your partners (including your employees) if targeted metrics are exceeded by some percentage. If they're on the hook for reduced compensation for underachieving, they should all be motivated to overachieve, as well.

You'll be amazed what a different environment you will create if you adopt this approach, and you won't have to wait weeks or months to see the impact. Even relatively small risk/reward formulas can yield tangible impacts from the project teams who are subject to the potential consequences (be they positive or negative). Just make sure that everyone is in agreement in what the metrics are and how they are defined up front, so there's no arguing down the road. And remember not to base these rewards on completing the project "on time, on budget." Make sure you base these incentives on metrics that are truly indicative of measurable *business* success.

It's time to take a detailed look at how we can apply the metric-driven approach to project evaluation in the context of the overall Enterprise Optimization Framework. This will be done by way of two real-life case studies (one included here and one included in **Appendix A**). It should be noted that these examples contain detailed, metric-driven analysis, which is essential to achieving meaningful results in the due diligence portion of project evaluations. The intent is to provide a sense of the rigor that is necessary, along with examples of the overriding themes of the framework. These case studies should be reviewed on two levels— for the detail associated with the numerical analysis and for the concepts included in the analysis at a higher level with respect to each of the components of the framework. It is important to always remember the big picture consequences of success or failure in each of these cases. Each and every component of these scenarios will be quantified to the best of my ability, just as would be done by any member of your PI Department. Some may be skeptical when figures are discussed with respect to the impacts on concepts like customer satisfaction. It is good to be skeptical. It is with this in mind that at the end of each case I will also offer some thoughts about the accuracy of this kind of analysis, and some cautionary notes about the sensitivity analysis that should be included as part of a thorough review of any opportunity. It is not acceptable simply to ignore the things that are difficult to quantify. If the analysis is too tactical and just focused on increasing or decreasing headcount by one or two bodies or generating a 15 percent improvement in the cycle time of a process, then you may miss the big picture. Both views are important. One is a good indicator on the tactical impact of the project and is easy to evaluate in terms of project justification. But the larger view may present the true opportunities for optimization, as well as the ever-present danger of a slow, but sure, enterprise collapse. Sophistication is needed in the analysis, and all impacts, both short-term and long-term, need to be considered as part of the process.

Case Study: Solving the Service Returns Calamity— Framework Analysis in Action[33]

A global manufacturing company has its corporate headquarters in California, but operates with multiple factories throughout the world. The largest of these is in New York, which previously had a powerful say in the organization based on its might as the fastest growing, most profitable business unit in the company. That status has been slowly degrading over the past 12 months due to the economic downturn that has hit this unit particularly hard. Partly responsible for this loss of power has been the tremendous inefficiency and poor quality found in the New York operations.

One particular pain point was the clumsy and poorly executed set of processes related to product returns and repairs. Not only was New York suffering from a glut of returns (a quality issue), but it was also struggling with inadequate systems and processes to manage this area of the business. Process cycle times were incredibly poor as material was constantly being lost amongst the multiple warehouses, and the tracking systems were totally inadequate to support the end-to-end processes. The fact is, inventory was lost all the time, with the company having to eat the cost of that inventory and then supply new product to the customer without any ability to provide failure analysis reports. The impact had been dramatic with a staggering increase in customer complaints and a multi-million dollar exposure in inventory-related costs.

The New York unit assigned a team to analyze the situation. The team began its efforts working closely with a consulting team from BearingPoint, which had knowledge of the New York unit by way of assisting in the recent implementation of its new Enterprise Resource Planning (ERP) system (Oracle Applications). The team quickly discovered that the software contained add-on functionality, which was out of scope for the original implementation, but which offered a detailed solution for this particular challenge. While the solution was not deemed a "perfect" fit, the consultants were able to offer a solution that addressed the majority of New York's return/repair process challenges and could be deployed very quickly. Since time was of the essence, this out-of-the-box solution seemed ideal. The project team proposed the implementation to its New York-based leadership team.

Based on "gut feel," the New York leadership team approved the project. However, when the Corporate Quality team heard of this "fast-track" approach, it was unconvinced that this would be the right solution for either the New York unit or for the rest of the units in the company, many of which were facing the very same problem. With budgets being tight and time of the essence, no one could afford to make a mistake on this one, so Corporate Quality pushed back for a more detailed analysis on why this project should be approved. The New York team brought the consultants back in for a short assessment period, which was used to quantify the expected impact of the project. This effort followed the guidelines of the Enterprise Optimization Framework.

Total Cost Optimization

The analysis begins with a detailed breakdown of the cost component of this opportunity, based on the framework provided at the outset of this chapter.

Cost Component	Analysis	Net Impact
Software	It turns out that the company had already acquired the license rights to use the Oracle Service module, but had simply not elected to implement it during the initial deployment. As such there would be no additional expense for software or ongoing software maintenance as a result of this project.	$0
Hardware	No additional hardware required.	$0
Implementation Services (External)	Consulting fees were estimated for process design, system design, system configuration, three testing rounds, core team training, solution validation, and initial post-go-live support. This also included the initial deployment of custom reporting for the new solution.	$800,000
Implementation Services (Internal)	The consulting organization would provide approximately 70 percent of the implementation services, leaving 30 percent for company personnel. The cost for internal personnel for testing, validation, and training is included here. This is in the form of an opportunity cost.	$340,000
Cost and Frequency of Future Upgrades	Negligible impact in light of the scope of this piece in terms of the overall Oracle suite of applications that had been deployed.	$0
Ongoing Support Costs	This company had already outsourced its Application Management responsibilities to a third party. The support contract with this organization included all Oracle modules that were included in the initial software licensing agreement. As such, ongoing support for this newly deployed module had already been accounted for (i.e., no additional charges will be incurred).	$0
Training	Estimated cost for employee-supported end-user training.	$10,000
Decommissioned Systems	The current tracking systems will be decommissioned one month after the go-live of the new system. Currently, approximately 0.5 FTE supports and maintains these off-line systems. This resource will be freed-up to work on other duties.	($50,000)
TOTAL		**$1,100,000**

Based on this analysis, the net impact on the total cost of this solution is an increased cost of $1.1 million, most of which will be incurred during implementation.

Fortunately, this company had already negotiated for expanded services from its software and support vendors, so there would be no increases for either of those cost areas, either now or in the future. A portion of the consulting fees will be capitalized as part of the deployment, so the first year impact of this project will be approximately $500,000, with $600,000 depreciated over the following three years ($200,000 per year). The company was looking for one-year returns on its project investments, so it would be looking for a full $1.1 million return within the first 12 months after go-live in order to authorize the initiative.

Process Optimization

While the New York team felt confident this deployment would achieve a positive impact for the company, it had yet to get into the details and was therefore unable to articulate the specific anticipated impacts (in either business process terms, or in quantifiable measures). Ultimately, during the due diligence phase with Corporate Quality, as well as during the initial stages of the implementation, the New York team and its consultants from BearingPoint generated some of the components of what could be used in this kind of analysis.

From a high level, the teams created process maps that included the current state (see Figure II-5) and the future plan (see Figure II-6). As you can see, the flows are similar in the two scenarios, but the data management has moved from a myriad of off-line systems into one fully integrated environment (in this case, Oracle Applications).

Figure II-5: Current Customer Care Processes

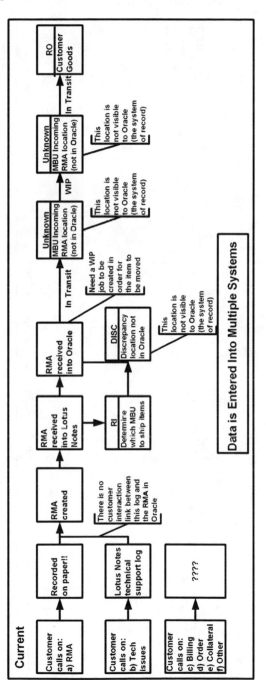

Figure II-6: Future Customer Care Processes

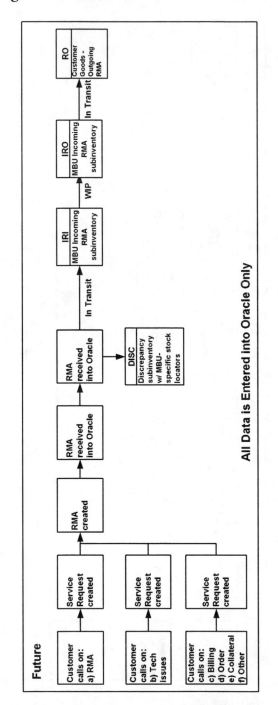

These high-level views provided only the beginning for the analysis. From here, the New York team and its consulting counterparts then stepped through the details of the current and future states, and marveled at the opportunities for process improvement. The improvements came in the form of consolidation of systems and data, process automation, worker efficiency, workflow notifications, and the positive impacts that could be generated by improved quality of data. For those who would like to step through their detailed findings, they are provided in **Appendix B**, which identifies the Current State and Future Expected Benefits for each of the functional units that will be impacted at the New York business unit.

Let's take a few moments to walk through some of the fundamental process-related benefits that are anticipated. Most of these will be generated as a result of consolidating operations within a single system, and where all functions are integrated, moving seamlessly from one operation to the next. First, from a process perspective:

- Data entry and maintenance is consolidated from eight systems to one.
  - o This relates to the following functions, which will all benefit from increased efficiency via system consolidation solely within the Oracle environment:
    - Service requests (currently captured via pencil and paper)
    - Return Material Authorization (RMA) entry
    - Repair charges
    - Interaction history
    - Serial number tracking
    - Material movement
    - Discrepancy receipts
    - Quality results
    - Financial reconciliation
- Transaction processing will be enhanced via the automation of the following processes, which currently require one or more manual steps:
  - o Work order creation (and associated material movement)
    - Note that it currently takes approximately 15 days to move material from the main warehouse to one of the many Manufacturing Business Unit locations. Thanks to the automation that will be built into the new solution, the team anticipates that it will take only one day to process these move transactions.
  - o RMA order creation
  - o Install base updates

- All customer queries will now be available from one system in real time, vs. lengthy off-line reviews as performed in the current state. This is expected to significantly reduce the amount of time spent tracking down information for customers and sales representatives.

In addition to the functionality provided by the integrated solution within Oracle Applications, the team will now have the ability to use the Oracle Workflow tool with which to drive the detailed transaction flow and the all-important in-process notifications and escalations. When the process was spread across multiple systems, this kind of workflow management was extraordinarily difficult to implement (and therefore was nowhere to be found). With the single system approach and the built-in workflow capabilities, these components will become relatively easy to deploy. Use of proactive notifications and escalations is expected to significantly reduce transaction processing delays, which occur in large part in the current state due to the fact that there is no system-enabled tool monitoring these transactions and providing proactive reminders when some action is overdue and still in a state of "pending."

Quantifying the impact the new solution is expected to yield first requires a benchmark relative to the current state of the process. This is the one metric about which the team had become painfully aware. Everyone agreed that the current cycle time for returns processing for the New York business unit was approximately 63 days, although only a fraction of that amount was actually spent hands-on repairing or returning the customer's product. The New York team and its consulting colleagues were convinced that in just three months with the new solution this number could easily be cut in half.

This forecast provides two important values in the justification analysis for this project in the area of Process Optimization, one that impacts the balance sheet and one that impacts the P&L. From a balance sheet perspective, a 50 percent reduction in inventory cycle time should translate to approximately a 50 percent reduction in the RMA inventory that is carried on the company's books at any one time. Prior to the implementation, this figure stood at $4.8 million and had been held at that level in a relatively stable fashion for the past several months. A 50 percent improvement in this area would yield a balance sheet benefit of approximately $2.4 million, freeing up cash for other benefits more productive than the shelf life of repairs-related inventory.

From a P&L perspective, a 50 percent reduction in cycle time should free up 50 percent of the employee time associated with this end-to-end process, allowing for either headcount reduction or enhanced duties. Personnel cost was difficult to estimate for this process, as a number of heads were shared between this process and multiple other processes. That being said, the team took the time to break this down, and determined that 18 full-time equivalents (FTEs), spanning 58 individuals, were tied to the returns process. Based on current salary figures, a 50 percent reduction in the headcount of these 18 individuals would save the company approximately $675,000 per year. Since the team was not convinced that it would receive all of these benefits until four to six months after go-live, it decided to trim this benefit by another 50 percent for the first-year analysis ($337,500), although it was confident that this was a very conservative approach.

Table II-A indicates the analysis at the current stage, which includes the total cost and process components of the Enterprise Optimization Framework.

Table II-A

Total Cost Optimization		($1,100,000)
Process Optimization		
Balance Sheet (Inventory)	$2,400,000	
Head Count Utilization	$337,500	
Net Impact		$2,737,500
Total Impact		$1,637,500

Based on the analysis thus far, focusing just on the total cost and process components, the project would easily pay for itself in less than one year. However, the story gets even better when you factor in the opportunities for Information Optimization.

Information Optimization

As mentioned in the previous section, having all of the data related to these transactions resident in a single system will dramatically improve the company's ability to generate timely information related to these processes, as well as the quality and reliability of that information. Specifically, all parties will now have the same access (security controlled by role) to the same data at the same time. In addition, the team will be able to depend on the fact that all of the information will actually exist, as the processes will require data integrity as enforced by the Oracle system. The various users will no longer have to worry about hunting down off-line databases and spreadsheets, which may have been discarded somewhere along the way. The quality, accessibility, and reliability of the data should improve considerably as a result of this process consolidation in the new environment.

Because the team took the time to work collaboratively on the definition of the new process, it was also able to articulate the specific points in the cycle in which reporting metrics were required for capture. Out of 51 steps that were mapped into the complete end-to-end process, the team identified 16 specific points in which time-based metric capture would be required. Performing this analysis up front enabled easy transition to deployment, as the team now saw that all 16 of these process points occurred within the Oracle solution and would be time-stamped by the system as they occur. This kind of metric gathering was virtually impossible in the multiple system approach that had existed previously. With this new data, the management team will be able to monitor these customer-impacting processes to identify bottlenecks and areas for improvement. In the past, this had been entirely anecdotal, with lots of finger-pointing but very little in the way of common understanding and agreement. Interestingly enough, while the management team was particularly excited about this benefit from the deployment, it was not comfortable adding any quantitative value to it for the benefits calculation. The team felt that these enhancements would yield improvements over time, but were not comfortable with the quantification of such benefits or with the timing of when the benefits would begin to be received. As a result, this optimization component, while important to the appropriate parties, was excluded from the justification analysis. This was in line with the conservative approach in the use of the framework.

The final point identified in **Appendix B** is with respect to financial consolidation. Once again, this had been a Herculean task with marginal accuracy in the past given all the systems and data translations that occurred as the data was passed and massaged from one system to the next. The reconciliation time (as well as the quality of the reconciliation) would be dramatically improved with this new solution.

Information Optimization analysis continues in the context of the all-important balance sheet, specifically with respect to the amount the company had been carrying on its books related to RMA inventory. As mentioned in the Process Optimization section, the team felt that the new solution could cut the cycle time for RMA processing in half, thereby reducing RMA inventory by 50 percent. That being said, the Information Optimization component also provided a benefit relative to the amount of RMA inventory being carried on the books. The team had a strong suspicion that a significant portion of the $4.8 million currently on the books was really outdated material that would be nowhere to be found and for which final disposal had simply never been accounted. The team was convinced that as a result of the due diligence associated with this deployment (including required data conversion) it would be able to provide a one-time decrease to this out-of-control number. Primarily, this would be accomplished through the final disposition of product that had been sitting somewhere on a shelf for who knows how long. The team felt that it could immediately cut this on-hand RMA inventory by a minimum of 20 percent, and as much as 30 percent. This determination actually impacts the overall calculations in the justification analysis in two places. Since a one-time, up-front 20 percent reduction in RMA inventory is assumed as a result of this deployment (taking the more conservative estimate), the company is expected to receive a one-time benefit of $960,000 relative to Information Optimization. This would then lower the current RMA inventory balance to $3.84 million. As such, the inventory balance benefit generated by Process Optimization is slightly reduced to $1.92 million, as seen in Table II-B.

Table II-B

Total Cost Optimization		($1,100,000)
Process Optimization		
Balance Sheet (Inventory)	$1,920,000	
Headcount Utilization	$337,500	
Net Impact		$2,257,500
Information Optimization		
Balance Sheet (one-time)		$960,000
Total Impact		$2,117,500

The final point to discuss, which relates to both Process Optimization and Information Optimization, is customer satisfaction. The motivations for this initiative spanned the areas of cost, efficiency, data access and quality, as well as some of the other areas just mentioned. However, the principle driver that brought the project to the table in the first place was the level of dissatisfaction amongst the company's customers about a variety of topics related to the returns process. As highlighted previously, the frequency of defects was near the top of the list of most customers, and there will need to be other initiatives to address that specific quality control issue. In addition to that concern, though, customers were incredibly frustrated by the inability of the company to provide timely and accurate information relative to the processing of these returns. They had virtually no confidence in what the company was telling them in terms of the status of their returns or expectations for completion of the process. David Meister once compiled what he termed the *Seven Principles of Waiting Time*. Among those principles are:

- "Uncertain waits are longer than known, finite waits."
- "Unexplained waits are longer than explained waits."[34]

It is often the lack of clarity and precision around the timeframe for completing processes that serves to infuriate customers. The longer you go past the expected wait time appears to significantly increase the level of frustration at a rate much greater than a linear impact. That's the position in which this company was finding itself in terms of the reliability of information relative to the returns process. The frustration was reaching a point where calls to site General Management were becoming daily events, and customers were threatening to take their business elsewhere.

So what's the economic impact of this issue of customer satisfaction? How could the team quantify this measure and factor it into the justification analysis? This is clearly the least scientific component of the analysis, although you can't continue to ignore relevant components simply because they are hard to quantify (after all, customer satisfaction had been identified as the original driver for this initiative). Here's what the team came up with:

- The New York business unit was currently operating under a $135 million annual revenue run rate.
- It was estimated that approximately 30 percent of the shipped products were returned at least once for either repair or replacement (i.e., affecting approximately $40 million of annual sales).
- The frequency of unique customer complaints relative to the returns process was linked to approximately 35 percent of the customers who returned product to the company.
  - o This now represented $14 million of the company's annual sales (35 percent of $40 million).
- The Customer Service and Sales organizations, which were putting pressure on Operations to fix this problem, provided an estimate that approximately 20 percent of these customers were threatening to take their business elsewhere unless this problem was fixed immediately.
- As a result, the team concluded that approximately **$2.8 million** in annual sales were at risk due to customer dissatisfaction associated with this problem (20 percent of $14 million).

This figure represents the final component in the analysis as depicted in Table II-C, which clearly indicates a powerful return on investment associated with this initiative.

Table II-C

Total Cost Optimization		($1,100,000)
Process Optimization		
Balance Sheet (Inventory)	$1,920,000	
Head Count Utilization	$337,500	
Net Impact		$2,257,500
Information Optimization		
Balance Sheet (one-time)	$960,000	
Customer Satisfaction	$2,800,000	
Net Impact		$3,760,000
Total Impact		$4,917,500

Before leaving this case study, I want to explore the accuracy of the analysis above, and the context in which it should be used. As stated previously, *this is not pure science*. Assumptions are clearly made throughout this kind of analysis, and those assumptions can have a far-ranging impact on the final results. A quick example can be seen in the percentage estimates just provided for the final portion of the Information Optimization analysis, in terms of the impact based on customer satisfaction. Even small changes to these percentage estimates can yield profound changes to the results of the analysis. But to ignore these critical components because they are hard to estimate can easily sway the outcome of the analysis as well, presenting a false conclusion. This is not acceptable.

To account for the subjectivity and apprehension around specificity in this area, I suggest that best-case, assumed-case, and worst-case scenarios be prepared for each project opportunity. I further recommend adding probabilities to the equations to weight the likelihood of each outcome. Basic spreadsheet scenarios can be performed in very little time to provide meaningful sensitivity analysis and to add some context to the overall result. Finally, I recommend a break-even scenario be developed, so that you can answer the question, "Even if our benefit is only 'X' will the project still pay for itself?" In terms of this case study, taking an extremely conservative approach to the overall benefits, you could create the following scenario, which would *still* generate a break-even result after one year:

- Total Cost Optimization
  - o No change (total cost impact remains negative $1.1 million)
- Process Optimization
  - o Assume just a 10 percent improvement in RMA process cycle time, yielding the following benefits: $432,000 benefit in inventory reduction

(after one-time information benefit is applied) and $135,000 in improved headcount utilization/efficiency

- Information Optimization
  - o Assume a one-time gain of only a 10 percent reduction of RMA inventory balance, and assume *no* further benefit in terms of customer satisfaction. This would still yield a benefit of $480,000.

Even these incredibly modest forecasts yield a near break-even point after just one year. Any benefits beyond that represent pure profit. Compared to the probabilities and expected results identified by the team, this opportunity seems assured to generate an exceptional return, but you also want to be cognizant of the break-even scenario, to understand the minimum benefit required for approval. Assuming that the final project authorization team can be convinced of your break-even and expected results, there should be no challenge in getting a proposal such as this approved within the confines of the Enterprise Optimization Framework.

You should not believe that you're ever going to be able to exactly predict the long-term benefit of any project. There are simply too many moving parts when you deploy things in the real world. What you're trying to do is provide a repeatable context in which the analysis can take place to approximate the long-term results, based on informed assumptions and whatever facts can be determined. Performing this exercise will add rigor to the analysis and help yield decisions in which you can be reasonably confident. While not perfect, it's light years better than the pure "gut feel" approach.

In this particular case, the "gut feel" turned out to be correct. The end result was a phenomenal success, which eventually became the prototype for a company-wide rollout. Table II-D provides a representation of the relevant metrics just six months after the initial go-live:

Table II-D

- Total Cost impact (P&L)   ($1,021,000)

- Process impact
  - Cycle time was reduced from 63 days to 19 days. This provided a *70 percent* reduction benefit in terms of inventory balances and head-count utilization.
  - Ongoing Inventory benefit (after one-time information benefit is applied)

                                                               $1,330,000
  - Headcount utilization benefit (P&L) $945,000

- Information impact
  - During the implementation, the team was able to determine that $2.9 million in the current RMA inventory balance was invalid and was eligible for an immediate write-off (representing 60.4 percent of the current balance) $2,900,000
- Total impact to date $4,154,000

Those figures represent "real dollars" that will be recognized within the balance sheet and P&L of this organization in the first year of this new solution, and do not even account for other areas that were considered, such as improvement in customer satisfaction. The Process Optimization relative to headcount efficiency alone virtually pays for the initiative in the first year, with the other balance sheet and customer-centric benefits being purely additive to the company's overall standing.

In the harder-to-quantify categories, the team was also able to achieve a predictable information flow for its customers, to the point where calls still persisted relative to product quality, but they were reduced to a negligible trickle relative to queries related to in-process returns. Without putting a hard number against this result, the team felt confident that it had covered *at least* a $1-million exposure that easily could have resulted from customer defections if the new solution had not been implemented. Further, the new reporting capabilities based on the single-system solution enabled the local and corporate leadership teams to begin further optimization initiatives, to squeeze even more savings out of the process. The lessons learned were incorporated into the strategy surrounding the subsequent rollout to the rest of the company.

This case has introduced the practical realities of the Enterprise Optimization Framework. In this case the "gut feel" was right, but the project team was even more confident after going through a detailed analysis at the outset of the initiative. I have included an additional detailed case in the book, in which we will see where a different company was not able to realize a significant benefit due to the lack of a decision-making framework and, therefore, no firm support in the organization for a deployment based on nothing but "gut feel." Lacking this framework, this company did *not* pursue its initiative, and all the potential benefits were lost. This case is covered in its entirety in **Appendix A**.

In the case above, as well as in the case covered in **Appendix A**, the projects should have been approved under the guidance of the three-pronged Enterprise Optimization Framework. In both of these cases the framework indicated a positive scenario worth pursuing. Clearly this will not always be the case. The results are the results, and you need to be careful about allowing emotion to step in to overrule the guidance of the framework. Sound business judgment is a critical component of the successful execution of the framework, and various scenarios need to be modeled in order to achieve a good-faith confidence in the results of the analysis. But in the end, if the models are indicating a poor outcome in terms of the overall framework, you have to be prepared to say no and move on to some other alternative.

Along these lines, one must also be very aware of the ability for skilled professionals to use metrics to their advantage. It is easy to highlight the benefits and downplay the costs. Slightly different assumptions may yield dramatically different results. This danger must be acknowledged, and while you can put in procedures to minimize this potential to deceive, you will never be able to completely eliminate it. As a reviewer of such analysis, you must always retain a skeptical eye and be prepared to question assumptions at every turn. This is not being critical of your colleagues. Rather, it is a vital part of the due diligence process in project justification. No one should be offended when assumptions are questioned. Rather, they should be offended if things are simply taken at face value. That usually means that someone isn't working hard enough to poke holes in theories, which is all part of the give and take in arriving at the optimal answer for the company and its shareholders.

Adherence to standards that are in the best interests of the *overall company* must be a guiding principle of the PI Department, and the CPIO is ultimately responsible for driving adherence to this principle. One way to accomplish this is to use metrics as a driver for performance evaluation and compensation. The importance of tracking metrics associated with an initiative long after the project itself goes live has already been discussed. In addition to the benefits described above, these metrics can also be used to track the accuracy of the PI Department in its ability to forecast the economic impact of an initiative (both positive and negative). Just as projects have scorecards, so should the people and teams who analyze projects. While this should not be the sole criterion for evaluating these people, having them held accountable for their analysis may assist in yielding adherence to performing all analysis as objectively as possible. It will also act as a valuable learning tool for these professionals, providing them the ability to benchmark and evaluate their assumptions and forecasts in the context of being able to refine them in the future. Just as metrics should play a role in the performance evaluation and compensation of the deployment teams, they should also play a role for the people who recommend the projects in the first place. If personal compensation is on the line based on measurable impacts, the analysis might turn out to be that much more accurate.

Budgeting for Initiatives

In Section I, I explained that one of the responsibilities of the PI Department is to make decisions on which initiatives within a company will be approved or rejected, and establish the appropriate budgetary amount if the project is approved. The PI Department is also responsible for how those funds get allocated to the appropriate departments within the organization. There are numerous models in existence today that address this often touchy area in the context of IT vs. "the business." Sometimes individual business functions maintain their own budgets for projects, be they process-related or technology-focused. Oftentimes, IT will pick up the tab, but that is usually just the starting point for an ultimate budget allocation of IT expenditures. There is no free lunch. Even when IT or Corporate says it's going to pay for a project, those funds are eventually going to hit someone's P&L. Usually this is in the form of some allocation, often straight across the board based on some metric such as headcount. That approach doesn't always sit well with the various business entities that find themselves starting out deep in the hole in future budgetary cycles based on large IT-related expenses or multi-year depreciation schedules. The PI Department needs to put this issue to rest by becoming the authoritative source on budget allocations for projects, leveraging the detailed output from the project justification analysis, which is based on the Enterprise Optimization Framework.

During that evaluation process, the analysis team is tasked with identifying the total cost of the proposed initiative, as well as the forecasted benefits, which are categorized along the lines of Process and Information Optimization. Those quantifiable measures represent the most accurate budgeting tool in assigning costs to various entities within the organization. Whether the company is organized based on processes or on functions, the findings generated by the framework analysis provide the ability to forecast benefits and therefore appropriately allocate costs. Everyone is aware that the framework-based analysis is not an exact science, but it does provide an informed judgment on the expected outcome of events, and those results can then be prescribed to the appropriate process or functional units. And for the same reason that the projections are not exact, it is appropriate for the PI Department to re-evaluate its allocation findings at least twice a year, and continue to do so well after the go-live of a given initiative.

The PI Department needs to take the leadership in this process, given the likelihood that it will turn into a political dogfight. Everyone wants the benefits, but no one wants to actually foot the bill. Unfortunately, it just can't work that way. Some organization needs to make these budgetary calls, and the PI Department, as has been defined, with its enterprise-wide view of the company, is the appropriate organization for the task. And leveraging the output of the up-front framework analysis as the activity-based component of the cost allocation seems most appropriate as well.

Let's go ahead and apply this technique to the case just reviewed, *Solving the Service Returns Calamity*. The company in this case was organized around functions, so the proposed allocations will also be organized around functions. As you recall from Table II-C, the overall anticipated benefit for this implementation was forecasted to be $6,017,500 (total benefits, with no reflection of cost). Those benefits are broken down across the appropriate organizational functions in Table II-E, both in terms of dollars and percentages:

Table II-E

Business Function	Business Benefit	Benefit ($)	Benefit (%)
Order Management	Head Count Utilization	$ 84,375	1.40%
Shipping	Head Count Utilization	$ 33,750	0.56%
Quality	Head Count Utilization	$ 33,750	0.56%
Operations	Head Count Utilization	$ 185,625	3.08%
Operations	Inventory Reduction	$2,880,000	47.86%
Sales	Customer Satisfaction	$2,800,000	46.53%
		$6,017,500	100.00%

Based on this analysis, the Sales and Operations organizations would be expected to foot the majority of the bill, with the Information Optimization component providing much more in the way of benefits than Process Optimization. Assuming that the scenario above is accepted as the likely outcome, the resulting cost allocation would be as shown in Table II-F:

Table II-F

Business Function	Benefit %	Cost Allocation
Order Management	1.40% $	15,400
Shipping	0.56% $	6,170
Quality	0.56% $	6,170
Operations	50.94% $	560,340
Sales	46.53% $	511,830
	100.00% $	1,100,000

This cost would be allocated over an appropriate schedule based on the capitalized and expensed portions of the engagement.

While it is important to put a stake in the ground with a cost breakdown up front, this does not necessarily have to represent the final outcome for the ultimate cost allocation. Since each of these projects is being approached in a manner that requires benefit measurements before, during, and long after the deployment, you will have actual data from which to make adjustments to your original estimates. In this case, data has been provided that represents a snapshot taken six months after go-live (recall Table II-D). These results yield the benefit and cost allocation breakdowns as shown in Table II-G (benefit) and Table II-H (cost allocation):

Table II-G

Business Function	Business Benefit		Benefit ($)	Benefit (%)
Order Management	Head Count Utilization	$	236,250	3.83%
Shipping	Head Count Utilization	$	94,500	1.53%
Quality	Head Count Utilization	$	94,500	1.53%
Operations	Head Count Utilization	$	519,750	8.42%
Operations	Inventory Reduction	$	4,230,000	68.50%
Sales	Customer Satisfaction	$	1,000,000	16.19%
		$	6,175,000	100.00%

Table II-H

Business Function	Benefit %	Cost Allocation
Order Management	3.83%	$ 39,104
Shipping	1.53%	$ 15,621
Quality	1.53%	$ 15,621
Operations	76.92%	$ 785,353
Sales	16.19%	$ 165,300
	100.00%	$ 1,021,000

As you can see, the allocation changes significantly with respect to Operations (increase) and Sales (decrease). Having this actual data enables the PI Department to make adjustments to the allocation that will be applied to each of these functional units. In the end, the specific business benefits of this initiative have been quantified and then mapped to the appropriate organizations within the company, followed by the corresponding cost allocation to each of those areas as percentages of the total cost of the project. I see this as the optimal approach to budgeting and ultimate cost allocation, and it is a direct byproduct of the metric-driven Enterprise Optimization Framework.

Staffing for Initiatives

The make-up of the Process and Information Department was discussed in Section I, and it was mentioned that a number of the team members of this organization may come from various functional units in the company. That being said, the PI Department should continue to be a relatively lean organization that serves to provide project analysis, recommendations, and leadership throughout the life cycle of company initiatives. More often than not, the PI Department will need to obtain additional resources to effectively complete its implementation projects. Some of these resources may come from external partners (which will be discussed in detail in Section III: Outsourcing), but many of these resources will come from the various functional organizations that are impacted by the projects.

You may recall the definition of project management mentioned in Section I, which included the following statement: "Project management utilizes the systems approach to management by having functional personnel (the vertical hierarchy) assigned to a specific project (the horizontal hierarchy)." Dr. Kerzner continues this thought with respect to incorporating functional resources into projects being driven by cross-functional team leads (from the PI Department, in this case).

> When we say that project managers control project resources, we really mean that they control those resources (which are temporarily loaned to them) *through line managers....* Successful project management is strongly dependent on:
> - A good daily working relationship between the project manager and those line managers who directly assign resources to projects.
> - The ability of functional employees to report vertically to their line managers at the same time that they report horizontally to one or more project managers.[35]

This is no slam dunk, especially for inexperienced project managers. That's another reason why it is important for members of the PI Department's Program Office to have well-established relationships throughout the organization.

The one thing members of the PI Department will rarely control is the ultimate performance evaluation and salary adjustment for line employees assigned to projects. This puts the PI Department in a definite disadvantage compared to the line managers when push comes to shove over the duties of an employee. Project managers need to be aware of this conflict, and need to proactively manage in this environment. Project managers must keep the lines of communication open with the line managers who "own" these resources, and must take the initiative in making sure that everyone continues to operate in the best interests of the overall enterprise. This will not simply happen on its own. It takes energy and commitment, but is essential to making this kind of organizational arrangement work.

Further, it is strongly recommended that PI Departments adopt a performance management culture that affects not only the members of the department, but is also engaged for the resources on loan for project implementations. These individuals need to have clear goals and expectations (preferably driven by hard metrics) and the opportunity to influence their overall evaluation based on their performance during the project. As mentioned in Section I, this approach would need to be driven in a top-down fashion by the leadership team, serving to align the PI Department and the individual contributors from the functional teams around common goals and reward systems. This approach would go a long way in terms of gaining the optimal output (and cooperation) from all of these resources.

The PI Department also needs to understand that it may not get the "best and brightest" resources from the functional teams assigned to each and every project. If these folks are always tabbed, they probably should be moved over to some branch of the PI Department on a full-time basis. Otherwise, if these talented individuals remain assigned to their core functional units, then it must be expected that they will need to spend some portion of their time in their traditional line responsibility. PI

Department leads need to work closely with the line managers to create a balance in terms of which resources are assigned to their projects, and understand that certain projects will get one level of resource while other projects will get different levels of resources. Understanding the skill set being offered is important in the up-front planning and analysis of the initiative, as it may impact the timing (and cost) of the deployment. If PI project managers can afford a second-tier resource on one project or another, they should fess up to that and work with the line managers on the assignments. This will make it that much easier for the project manager to get the top players for the most critical projects.

Finally, the PI Department needs to understand that often these "on loan" resources will only be on loan for part of the time, and that they will still be expected to perform some (or all!) of their regular jobs. The answer is not to work these people 16 hours a day, although that is often what happens. You can do that once in awhile, but beyond that, the workers will revolt. The PI Department needs to be able to plan aggressive schedules, but also ones that are reasonable given the required resource mix. If the PI Department can fulfill most of the requirements with its own members and a set of consultants, with only marginal participation from the functional resources, then one kind of schedule should be established. But if the business users need to be intimately involved, then either those resources need to be moved full-time onto the project (and when I say full-time, I mean *full-time*), or the schedule will need to be adjusted to accommodate an aggressive but *reasonable* schedule. This kind of project planning is one of the fundamental chores of the PI Department, and should be done upfront during the project analysis phase. The cost of resources (internal and/or external) and the overall expected timing of the project all play into the cost justification of the initiative, and therefore must take into consideration the needs and total responsibilities of the functional resources who will participate in the project.

Steering Committees

At this point, it's time we take a look at what specific roles the executive leaders of the organization need to play with respect to these enterprise-wide initiatives. For that we turn to the concept of the steering committee. In principle, the steering committee is the decision-making body of senior executives from across the company who provide direction to the CPIO and the PI Department. This is the group that resolves issues that cannot be resolved at lower levels in the organization and provides the all-important strategic business initiatives around which projects are identified and prioritized. This is also the group that evaluates proposals and is accountable to the CEO and the company's shareholders for ensuring a measurable return on investment related to PI Department projects. That's basically the role of a PI steering committee. But is that the norm in the real world of today's IT steering committees? More often than not, the answer is a resounding "No!"

Typical IT steering committees are composed of a group of executives who occasionally attend meetings scheduled by the CIO, provide very little input other than some casual discussion on topics, take no action items, and often provide little in the way of strategic direction. Meetings with these typical steering committees usually consist of a status report of projects by someone in IT (usually in terms of accomplishments to date against a set of milestones; you know, the typical on-time, on-budget stuff), and then a review of upcoming projects in the pipeline. The members may be asked to approve those projects, typically deciding based on "gut feel." In other words, most of these committees and their meetings are a complete waste of time.

It might be worth exploring why this is the current state of IT steering committees. Partly this is the responsibility of the modern-day CIO. I have found that CIOs often nix any attempt to put issues of substance on the table for review or discussion by the steering committee. Why? Because the CIO typically reports to someone in the room and doesn't want any appearance that there are any issues in his/her domain. Heaven forbid an issue is actually identified and discussed with senior management. The belief, or fear, is that perception will overtake reality, and if one problem is identified, there may be hundreds more just beneath the surface. As a result, these CIOs *manage* the release of information so that nothing of substance is ever discussed. The result is that the IT Department ends up making decisions that should be made by functional (or process) leaders from across the company.

The IT steering committee meetings of today represent one of the few occasions these cross-functional leaders ever gather in a single room, yet the opportunity for meaningful discussion on issues is often wasted. Why not have an open debate with corporate executives and regional general management about tough issues, like global processes and systems vs. the regionalized approach? Shouldn't the steering committee provide the strategic company direction on such difficult topics? All too often the most difficult topics get overlooked in these environments, because the political overtones are too great, and the fear of appearing weak and indecisive is too overwhelming. And this may occur even at levels higher than the CIO. The CIO's peers and bosses may not want to face these challenges in such a forum either. But the question must be asked: If strategic direction is not provided by the leaders of the company, then how will PI Departments ever be able to align initiatives against the appropriate guidelines? Lacking this alignment, self-destruction becomes much more likely than anything to do with optimization.

The concept of an executive steering committee is all the more important these days as I have observed a number of organizations using this vehicle as a key component to becoming a process-driven organization. The concept is a good one, providing a process-focused direction to these global committees (also known as process councils). The problem with this structure, and another reason why we need CPIOs and PI Departments, is that these councils often lack fundamental elements that are necessary for success. First, as with IT steering committees, the executive members of these councils are handed these duties on top of their existing responsibilities. Typically when this happens, the execs engage in their new duties for the 2-3 hours in which they meet each month, but often lose that enterprise-wide focus as soon as they leave those meetings. The incentives to dedicate more time to the council are rarely compelling given the expectations that come with their "day jobs." Second, these executive process councils often lack appropriate leadership and clearly defined roles and responsibilities. It's fine for the execs to get together for process-focused discussions, but if one or two leaders try to dominate the decision-making and there is no one clearly empowered in a leadership role looking out for the broad interests of the organization as a whole, then the effort often deteriorates into a political struggle without any clear direction. Some companies make this situation even worse by designating the CIO as the leader of the global process council, placing someone who lacks the proper enterprise-wide authority in the no-win situation of trying to guide this group of often self-motivated leaders. Process councils with CIOs in charge just perpetuate the challenges that persist in the IT steering committees just described, with even less chance of success due to the new positioning of this leadership group. Finally, perhaps the biggest inhibitor to the success of these process councils is that there is no operational entity sitting under this group to either implement the strategies and tactical initiatives that are approved by the leadership committee, or to provide research, analysis, and due diligence before and after the formal meetings so that the council can be sure that it is making optimal decisions for the organization. Once again, IT is not the answer to this gap. We need empowered teams of business professionals to handle these responsibilities, yet most of the executive process council attempts I have seen have little or nothing in the way of "staff" other than the same old group from IT. It is clear what is keeping these new process councils from really getting anything off the ground; that is, the lack of leadership in the form of a CPIO and the lack of operational support in the form of a PI Department. These councils may appear to be a step in the right direction, but they're not a big enough step that will really make a difference. We need steering committees such as these to guide enterprise-wide business decisions, but we also need CPIOs and their teams to help validate these initiatives, as well as to bring them to life.

So, what should be the make-up of effective steering committees, and how should they engage with the CPIO and the PI Department? First, the onus is on the CPIO to make this an effective organization. It won't happen without leadership, and the CPIO is the person positioned to lead in this area. The mix of committee members is most likely not the issue. The CPIO is looking to staff this committee with C-level and senior VP-level executives from across the company. It is also important to include regional general management for global organizations, under the assumption that these regional general managers have some level of autonomy over their respective regions. One of the most common challenges for the CPIO and his teams is how to resolve conflicts between corporate and regional entities across the enterprise. If both sides are not represented in this forum, then the forum can never be used to resolve such disputes. The result? The CPIO gets stuck in the middle without any legitimate direction from management—in other words, a no-win situation.

What should be expected of this committee? The first responsibility is to provide the PI Department with a set of strategic business initiatives, which will then translate to actions items for the Process and Information Department to evaluate and pursue. No initiative makes sense unless it is aligned with the strategic direction of the enterprise. It should be an ongoing expectation that the PI steering committee provides this direction. And if this direction is not forthcoming, then it is up to the CPIO to raise specific topics around strategic business issues to initiate conversation (and debate, if necessary) that concludes with a summarized approach that can then be acted upon. Remember, the CPIO is a full-fledged member of this steering committee and has a leadership role in ensuring that the group steps up to its strategic responsibilities.

Furthermore, just as all PI projects should operate within the Enterprise Optimization Framework, so should steering committee meetings and discussions. Everything on the table should be able to tie back to one or more components of the framework. That mindset should be well communicated to the executives up front, and be at the forefront of every meeting until it becomes ingrained across the board. Operating within this framework also enables the CPIO to bring discussions back on track from the inevitable rat hole discussions that tend to sidetrack meetings. This also sets the expectation with the executives of how to think about various initiatives. They will be challenged to get away from the generic "gut feel" and "right thing to do" approaches to project justifications, and really see the anticipated tangible benefits related to individual projects. Of course this is where the metrics come in. Steering committee meetings shouldn't focus on milestone checks, as they typically do today. What should be of interest to senior executives is how projects are doing relative to their respective *business objectives*, and progress should be presented in terms of the metrics being measured during the life cycle of an implementation. The meaningful questions should relate to the degree to which the company is going to lower its overall total cost, to improve its processes, and/or to improve its ability to get the right information to the right people at the right time. Status on projects relative to these concepts is what should be shared with senior executives. And, by the way, this reporting should continue well past the go-live date. It may be many months before you see material improvement in your target areas. Most likely, you won't be able to measure success or failure for weeks or months to come. So keep updating the steering committee throughout the appropriate lifetime of the initiative.

It is the responsibility of the PI Department to keep the steering committee informed on the important points of ongoing initiatives, as well as to distinctly identify the opportunities available from projects that are being proposed. Part of this responsibility is to be able to highlight the key elements of the discussion in an organized but concise presentation. In fact, I am partial to the philosophy that steering committee topics should be summarized on a single page. Dwight Eisenhower was famous for the single-page management technique—a method he had seen pioneered by General George Marshall.[36] This "simple" approach forces brief statements pertaining to the most important elements of any project or set of issues. This format may present challenges to those who must concisely prepare the material, but the result provides the reader with a simple summary that focuses on only the most important elements. Plenty of additional detail and further explanation is always available upon request. An example of the type of single-page update that I advocate for project opportunity proposals can be found in Figure II-7. This example ties to the scenario covered in the case study in **Appendix A** (*Integration vs. Integrated, That is the Service Question*). The following have all been concisely articulated on this single page:

- Objectives
- Scope and approach
- Impact on the three legs of the framework
- Resources
- Cost
- Timeline
- Quick bottom line summary

Any project should be able to be presented in this fashion, focusing on the important criteria on which the steering committee can engage in discussion and render a decision. Again, these are the highlights, with the representatives from the PI Department present to add depth and further analysis to the discussion.

Figure II-7: Sample Steering Committee Project Evaluation Page

Insert logo

Oracle Service for Data Entry and Validation

■ Objectives

– Significantly reduce errors in data flow from Oracle to Siebel related to Service entitlements

– Improving accuracy of data will reduce cycle time of entitlement verification

– Enable the company to stop providing free service to those who ask because of lack of confidence in system data without fear of decrease in customer satisfaction

■ Scope and Approach

– Enable Oracle Service functionality within Order Management to capture the following data elements which are currently entered into non-validated fields:

  • Contact Name, Address, Phone Number, and e-Mail Address

  • Product Item and Serial Number of Product for which Service is being ordered or renewed

– Modify data capture processes to validate all of the above elements prior to entry into Order Management using standard Oracle functionality and off-line verifications (as needed)

■ Impact on:

– **TCO:** ($340,000) based on software, implementation, and integration costs

– **PO:** $60,000 based on impacts on Order Management (productivity decrease) and Customer Service (productivity increase)

– **IO:** Up to $3,300,000 based on increased revenue, regained opportunity cost, and positive impact on customer satisfaction

TCO=Total Cost of Ownership; PO=Process Optimization; IO=Information Optimization

■ Resources, Cost, and Timeline

– External: $285,000 for software and consulting, including implementation and integration

– Internal: $60,000 for implementation and training

– Timeline: Eight weeks to test and deploy

■ Bottom Line

– *For this initiative to pay for itself, we need to convert only 0.3% of customers who are currently receiving free service to paying for that service*

Figure II-8: Sample Steering Committee Project Update Page

Oracle Service for Data Entry and Validation *Insert logo*

■Current Status (4/1/03)

– Project went Live on 2/3/03

– Technology is currently stable and operating as expected – process learning curve continues

■Metric Scorecard

	Original	Goal	Current	
– Time to enter Sales Orders (minutes per order)	16 min.	18.5 min.	23 min.	● Red
– Transactions (%) which get stuck between Oracle and Siebel	30%	5%	18%	○ Yellow
– Orders (%) which require manual intervention by Customer Service	60%	20%	24%	● Green
– Contract cycle time from Oracle to Siebel to valid for TAC	3 days	20 min.	6 hours	◐ Yellow
– Customers (%) who receive free Service due to lack of data integrity	10%	0%	2.5%	● Green
– Customers (%) who buy Service after being told that valid contract does not exist	0%	5%	1.5%	○ Yellow

■Impact on:

– **TCO:** ($282,000) based on costs to date – no material incremental costs anticipated

– **PO:** ($12,000) annualized impact (approx.) projected based on *current results* for OM and CS productivity as a result of implementation

– **IO:** $195,000 due to converting free service to paid service

– **Total:** Project on track to pay for itself next quarter

TCO=Total Cost of Ownership; PO=Process Optimization; IO=Information Optimization

■Resources, Cost, and Timeline

– External:$227,000 ($18,000 positive variance)

– Internal: approximately $60,000 (as expected)

– Timeline: Completed on-time (eight weeks)

■Bottom Line

– *Team is still getting used to new process, but significant impact already felt in decrease in manual intervention by CS and in no longer providing free service due to improved data integrity*

Figure II-8 takes this same initiative into the ongoing analysis phase, allowing the PI Department to concisely depict the status of the project relative to the investment. In this case, the PI Department is highlighting the status approximately two months after the go-live. The status update is very metric oriented, including original benchmarks, the project's key target metrics, and the current status of those metrics. Oftentimes, it further helps clarify the current status with graphics, such as the red, yellow, and green lights that are identified in Figure II-8. Additionally, it's important to update the steering committee on the progress relative to the forecasted impacts on Total Cost, Process, and Information Optimization. I also use the "Bottom Line" box for a final summary of the current status. Again, this should be a very straightforward, information-filled one-page summary that focuses on the critical elements of whether or not the project is on track for ultimate success.

When the steering committee convenes, it should be for a purpose, and not just to review status updates. A detailed agenda should be provided at least 48 hours in advance, along with relevant background material for any issues that are going to be discussed. The CPIO should drive the meeting in terms of starting on time, keeping within the guidelines of the agenda, and completing on (or before) the scheduled end time. Beyond that, the committee members should engage actively in the discussion. This should not be a passive event. Passive members don't add to the benefit of such a get-together, and should be weeded out over time. Finally, the PI Department should be responsible for preparing and distributing minutes from the meeting within 48 hours of its conclusion. Just as there should be rigor and discipline in how we run our companies, the same should apply to how we run our meetings. These should be productive events; if these top-level meetings turn into ad hoc, random discussions, then that sets the example for all meetings throughout the organization.

Having the opportunity for open discussion within the context of steering committee meetings in no way limits the need for communication with these senior executives in between the meeting sessions. The point is not to show up for a meeting and thrust a bunch of complex, challenging issues on the table that have not previously been discussed and socialized outside the confines of the meeting environment. Those steps of ongoing communication are still essential to enable productive sessions when you do all meet together. The point is that there is also merit to opening up for some of that discussion with the entire group in attendance, rather than shun that approach entirely for fear of any conflict developing. Lots of companies espouse open and honest communication as a core value. All too often we see those very same companies inhibit this kind of discourse through follow-up punitive words and actions. As a result, this openness is completely stifled, along with the positive results that could flow. This is an opportunity for the CPIO to take the lead to institutionalize the concept of open and honest communication, doing so at the departmental level, as well as with the senior executives of the company.

There is one additional structural recommendation, primarily for large companies for which the most senior executives are often removed from the day-to-day operational activities of the organization. The senior-laden steering committees are often not able to provide the level of detailed guidance that is often needed by the PI Department. For these kinds of companies, I recommend the introduction of an operational steering committee. This organization would be composed of director-level executives who have a more active role in the day-to-day operations of the company and are more familiar with the challenges that need to be addressed. The scope of discussion with this body would clearly be different from that of the executive steering committee, but would provide a valuable communication channel for the PI Department, both to receive and distribute information across the organization.

The operational steering committee would likely meet on a more frequent basis than the executive steering committee, and information and feedback between the two meetings would be communicated by the PI Department leadership team. The topics would tend to be more tactical in nature (often project specific) than those raised with the executive steering committee, but as strategic initiatives are discussed with the senior executives, it would be perfectly appropriate to socialize those issues (before and after) with the operational leadership team to gain insight and feedback. In this sense, the PI Department would continue its critical business function of bringing leaders together from across the enterprise to engage in dialogue about important issues facing the company. And the framework should remain the same. The details of the discussion should always be held in the context of Process Optimization, Information Optimization, and Total Cost Optimization. Since those are the goals at all levels of the organization, the Enterprise Optimization Framework should continue to guide the discussion for all levels of meetings.

Competitive Advantage

Before leaving the area of project justification, let's explore one area that is commonly mentioned as the reason to pursue a particular initiative; that is, to create *competitive advantage*. Sources of competitive advantage were discussed in Section I, including: (1) our ability to innovate and bring superior products and services to the marketplace and (2) our ability to optimize Processes and Information in the realm of lowest Total Cost. Neither of those sources mentions anything about information technology. Unfortunately, a common mistake made by present-day CIOs and their business constituents is to look for a silver bullet in some technology that all by itself will set them apart from the competition. People of this mindset tend to perpetuate the myth that somehow information technology will enable you to leapfrog the competition. I find this highly implausible. Technology alone can never make the difference. Only when the technology is viewed in the context of Process Optimization, Information Optimization, and Total Cost Optimization can advantages actually be created. It is how the technology is *configured, deployed, and utilized* that may yield the advantage. Put another way, systems by themselves do not yield competitive advantage. Rather, systems are an enabler for competitive advantage only to the degree that they are fashioned to support optimal processes and information management. The final component in this competitive advantage equation is the all-important execution of processes within these systems by the functional organizations throughout the company. All parties play a role in achieving competitive advantage, and the underlying systems are merely a tool that, if utilized in an optimal fashion, can help achieve that ultimate result (see Figure II-9).

Figure II-9: Fundamentals of Competitive Advantage

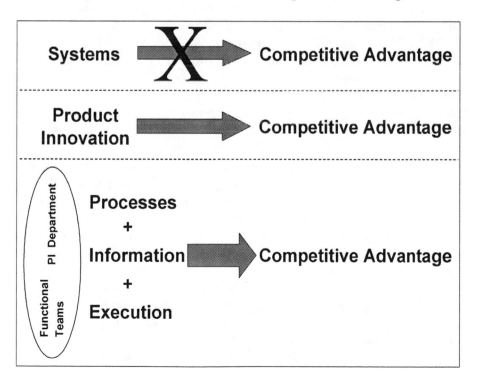

Contrary to this point of view, I have encountered a number of executives (both inside IT and in "the business") who refuse to approve an initiative until they are convinced they have found the *perfect* technology solution—possibly one that no one has ever used before. Since rarely does such a piece of technology exist, these executives find themselves doing one of two things:

1. Going on a never-ending search for this perfect solution that lands them in "analysis paralysis" when they can't find it, and, of course, nothing ever gets done, or
2. Insisting on building this perfect solution from scratch, which more than likely yields a highly complex, hard-to-scale, hard-to-integrate, hard-to-modify, extremely costly solution that results in a net negative result in the final analysis of the framework.

Do either of these approaches sound optimal? Remember, what is perceived as the *perfect* solution is by no means necessarily the *optimal* solution when viewed as a whole, especially if the process takes you down either of the two paths highlighted above in which the pursuit of the non-existent and unachievable simply results in disaster.

Take, for example, one company with which I am familiar that was so far behind the competition in terms of process and reporting capabilities for its Sales and Marketing organizations that almost *any* investment in an out-of-the-box solution and a commitment to the prescribed process execution would have yielded an improvement. This company had already implemented one of the top CRM software solutions for its Service organization. Yet the leadership in these functional areas refused to leverage that investment and move forward with its Sales and Marketing-related capabilities, despite the ability to identify numerous benefits that would result in quantifiable improvements. Why the reluctance? Because it wanted the silver bullet. The leaders wanted some *super technology* that would leapfrog them past their greatest competitors. It wasn't good enough to do what every leading company was already doing and simply try to execute better. No, they wanted to wait until they uncovered something that no one was doing yet. So what happened? The team spent *11 months* looking for a solution that simply didn't exist before finally agreeing to get back to the basics. The basics were as straightforward as they were 11 months previously: leverage the existing platform to maintain an optimal total cost level, and then optimize the process and information capabilities intrinsic to what is provided by the package. The result: 11 months wasted. I could even have understood the implementation of some other technology for Sales and Marketing that could have been integrated with the other systems. While the overall analysis likely would have indicated that this was not optimal (because of the impact on total cost), it certainly would have yielded *some* positive results given how far behind the company was in this area with respect to the competition. But this company did nothing but talk, look, and suffer. A framework for decision-making won't do a company any good if its leadership is unwilling to accept sound recommendations and insists instead on waiting for something better which may never come along. In this case, the delay generated by the implausible search simply created a competitive *dis*advantage for the company.

There is another company with which I spent some time, helping with the implementation of an ERP package for Financials, Distribution, and Manufacturing. This software company also had a professional services organization, so it required an application that would support the financial management of the projects performed by this team, including the processing of time and expenses and facilitating the timely billing of clients. The ERP vendor offered such a package, but the company executives felt that it was too cumbersome. Being a software company, it felt it could build its own solution that would provide much better flexibility and ease of use for its consultants in the field. So, that's what they did. They took some of their own engineers out of their day jobs (which was designing and building products for their customers) to come up with this *perfect* technology solution, designed exactly the way they did their business. The result? First, the development was late, so when the ERP system was ready to go-live, the company had to manually process all the project-related transactions for nearly three weeks. Then, the integration wasn't working very well, so additional teams had to assist in cleaning up the transactions for processing before they hit the ERP system for billing. It seems the company's consultants tended to make mistakes when entering their data, which was not something these software engineers were anticipating. Then, just when the system appeared to finally be up and operational, it was time for the first month end. This prompted the most time-consuming reconciliation process I have ever seen, as the engineers worked to match the data in the custom system to what was in the ERP system.

There is no question in my mind that the cost to develop this custom solution, plus the additional man hours required for the first month of support, far outweighed what it would have cost to implement the integrated solution provided by the ERP vendor. Now, one might argue that it would have been worth it in the long run if the custom solution was that much better for the team in the field, but we found that it wasn't for two reasons. Number one, the two-way integration was an absolute nightmare, frustrating the user community to no end, because the data going in either direction never seemed to match. The people in the field became so frustrated that they ultimately refused to use the new system, forcing all the administrators in the company to pick up the data-entry task. (This led to its own host of issues.) Second, about four months later, the company was feeling some market pressures and decided to make some structural changes in its professional services organization. As such, the processes needed to be adjusted. Unfortunately, all of the so-called *perfect* processes were hard coded into the workflow of the original solution, making it incredibly time-consuming to change them.

I maintained at the outset, and still maintain to this day, that the optimal solution would have been to implement the solution that came pre-integrated with the ERP system and provided flexibility for future alterations. Yes, the processes may not have been *perfect* in terms of the out-of-the-box solution. The consultants in the field may have had to click through a couple more screens each time when entering their data. But after a little training and regular usage, this would have all become second nature, and most of the other problems they encountered would never have materialized. In terms of the framework, the raw comparison between these two approaches may have yielded a slight preference for Process Optimization in the custom solution, but clear-cut advantages for Information and Total Cost Optimization for the out-of-the-box, fully integrated, packaged solution. In the end, even the process component clearly favored the package, since the custom solution was so poorly integrated and so hard to change that it ended up being much more complex and challenging for the users than if the company had gone with the package.

Almost every technology vendor claims the ability to deliver competitive advantage, but it's not the technology that provides the advantage—it's how the technology is *utilized* and how the processes are *executed* that makes the difference. From a configuration standpoint, this is often the value-add from the top business and systems consulting firms. The software companies specialize in writing the software, but the consultants specialize in maximizing the value out of the software. Sometimes it's worth the price, and sometimes it's not—but it's worth the analysis on how much benefit you can derive by doing it on your own vs. investing in some help. And this doesn't necessarily mean lots of customization here. This is talking about the appropriate level of insight into the company, its industry, and the particular solution to maximize this union for ultimate impact. Just investing in top-of-the-line software doesn't guarantee a positive return. For that you need to maximize what you get out of the software, and that may require outside help. This is the difference between *installing* enterprise software and *implementing* enterprise software. Anyone can install a system, but the benefit you receive will be limited if you aren't able to effectively utilize the capabilities of the tool based on the requirements of your business. Additional expenditure to unlock these capabilities may be necessary (and perfectly appropriate) in order to maximize your opportunity to achieve Process and Information Optimization.

This value would be measured in terms of how you set up the application based on industry best practices, as well as the attention paid to things such as knowledge transfer with detailed training and documentation that will greatly enhance the likelihood of high-caliber process execution for long after the system goes live.

In the Enterprise Resource Planning (ERP) boom of the nineties, claims were made left and right about the competitive advantages provided by these systems. Then, these claims were often refuted. Did they provide competitive advantage or did they not? Again, the context is the key. These systems certainly provided the *opportunity* for competitive advantage, but the depth of that advantage depended on the degree to which you were able to maximize the potential provided by the technology. Two direct competitors might invest in the ERP suite from SAP at exactly the same time and deploy it for exactly the same cost. Will one achieve competitive advantage in the process? Quite possibly. It all depends on the Process and Information Optimization achieved during the implementation, testing, training, and deployment processes. The rigor and energy invested in these areas will yield the advantage. A poorly run, costly implementation could easily turn sour and yield a negative result compared to the company's prior state. Sure, the software is the foundation. But the advantage comes from the process by which the software is configured, deployed, and ultimately utilized.

Some argue that the widespread adoption of these enterprise systems in and of itself has limited the ability to achieve competitive advantage because these "best practices" have now become commonplace across industries. This possibility exists, but is not altogether true, for the degree to which these practices have been deployed and are being executed by these competitive organizations tends to vary widely. Put another way, there are two distinct ways in which companies can achieve competitive advantage by way of Processes and Information. The first is to adopt industry best practices, which will likely leverage the capabilities provided by top-tier, enterprise-wide information systems, and then differentiate from the competition based on the ability to execute those processes far better than anyone else. The other way to differentiate and gain an edge is to identify unique processes that enhance customer or partner experience beyond the capabilities of the competition. The danger in this latter approach, of course, is the cost to deploy and maintain these unique solutions, relative to the benefit. Companies like Dell and Amazon.com have been able to differentiate with unique processes that have captured the attention of the marketplace, taking the capabilities of their organizations beyond previously known industry best practices. In the case of Dell, this approach has provided both a market share and profitability bonanza. For Amazon.com, market share has come, but the company has yet to figure out how to turn all these advantages into long-term profitability. There are certainly plenty of cases of breakthroughs for organizations along the line of unique processes. Just be wary of the cost and the challenges to support, maintain, and scale those processes. There may be just as many cases, if not more, where the uniqueness of the process is not the differentiator, but rather the flawless execution of those industry-standard processes that actually yields the competitive edge. In other words, you might not need to reinvent the wheel to gain competitive advantage. Perhaps having the best, longest running, most efficient and effective wheel in the marketplace may yield all the advantage you need, rather than chasing something new which may never materialize, or, if it does, may not yield profitable results because of the cost to obtain and produce it in the marketplace.

Even the most basic technology can provide a competitive advantage depending on how it is utilized. Electronic Data Interchange (EDI) still provides competitive advantage for some companies, both in terms of those who use it vs. those who don't, as well as in how the transactions are actually configured in any particular environment. It's the Process and Information Optimization levels achieved with EDI that can yield competitive advantage, not the technology itself. Which is better off, a company that has a robust EDI environment with multiple trading partners, or a competitor that decides not to implement EDI ("that's old technology") and searches for months for the second coming of trading partner technology? The answer is, you don't know. Maybe the Process and Information advantages yielded down the road by the trading partner technology will off-set the opportunities lost from the decision to skip EDI altogether. Maybe. But there's a good chance that the EDI investment is probably still paying reasonable dividends with low risk for the first company, and depending on how long it takes for the second company to get its environment up to speed, good old EDI may have been the foundation for advantage all along. Remember, there's a lot to be said for "keeping it simple," and then focusing on well-designed processes and flawless execution.

All of these scenarios need to be evaluated before knowing when to invest in new technology and the benefits that will likely be achieved vs. the status quo. The message is simple, and it is more than just semantics. New technology itself, no matter what the vendors tell you, won't yield a competitive advantage. It's how you *take advantage* of the technology in the context of your entire environment that yields the opportunity for competitive advantage. The degree to which you can optimize your processes and quality of information compared to your competitors, and the degree to which you can do so at a lower total cost compared to your competitors—that's what provides the opportunity for competitive advantage. And while due diligence is a critical component to getting this right, analysis paralysis is one of the worst enemies in your ability to create a competitive advantage. Harry Truman once said in the early days of his presidency, "I am here to make decisions, and whether they prove right or wrong I am going to make them."[37] Do your research, complete your analysis in the context of the Enterprise Optimization Framework, be confident in your results, make a decision, and manage aggressively in the context of that decision. The right answer may be to do nothing (i.e., maintain the status quo). That's perfectly fine, if the analysis indicates such a strategy. But not doing anything for fear of not yet uncovering the silver bullet of technology—that is certain to yield a competitive *dis*advantage in a marketplace that is already investing wisely in readily available solutions. In other words, it would be another source of disease that can lead to the long, slow, painful death of our companies.

Summary and Highlights

- The Enterprise Optimization Framework provides a focus for analyzing potential initiatives around the three components that merit consideration:
  - o Process Optimization
  - o Information Optimization
  - o Total Cost Optimization

- The framework is not only used by members of the PI Department for detailed opportunity analysis, but it also provides high-level guidance for all members of a company in terms of the areas of importance when seeking to optimize the overall organization.

- Quantifiable metrics in the areas of efficiency, effectiveness, and profitability drive the framework. The PI Department should be able to link these key metrics to direct impacts on standard financial statements, such as the balance sheet and income statement, as these are among the critical documents that are used to evaluate the performance of the company. Metrics such as "on time, on budget" are not indicative of true business success, and therefore should not be used as sole indicators of project success.

- **Enterprise Optimization** is defined as the never-ending pursuit of the ideal state whereby an organization achieves the optimal balance across its capabilities to (1) define and execute processes that maximize both efficiency and ultimate effectiveness, (2) provide the optimal amount of information required for timely and effective decision-making, and (3) to do so in the context of the lowest possible total cost, thereby yielding the maximum level of long-term profitability for the company.

- A conservative approach should guide the forecasted impact of each component of the framework, focusing on what is perceived as *reasonably likely* results. Multiple scenarios, including best-case, worst-case, assumed-case, and break-even case should all be modeled and considered in any analysis.

- Budget allocation for initiatives should be based on the metrics generated by the framework. Forecasted estimates should drive the initial budget, but ongoing measurements (continuing well past go-live) should yield adjustments based on actual results as necessary.

- The PI Department must work closely with line management for the appropriate staffing of individual initiatives. Resources need to receive input to their performance management evaluations based on their contribution to these cross-functional projects.

- PI steering committees provide essential leadership for enterprise-wide initiatives. Meetings that bring these executives together should allow for open discussion and debate and not be limited to superficial status updates. These meetings, and the decisions that result, should be grounded in a continual focus around the three components of the Enterprise Optimization Framework.

- One must be careful about falling into the trap of "analysis paralysis" based on the never-ending pursuit of the "perfect" solution that will automatically yield competitive advantage. The framework will often indicate that material improvements may be achieved and a degree of competitive advantage may be generated without satisfying 100 percent of your wish list. This result would certainly be preferred when compared to endlessly waiting for the ultimate solution that turns out not to exist.

Section III: Outsourcing

So far an organizational structure has been put into place that is part and parcel with "the business," that is consumed with a focus around processes and information, and that is focused on how to optimize those elements at the lowest total cost. A logical extension is to then determine who should really be doing all this work in order to obtain maximum benefits. In other words, are organizations themselves most capable of delivering in these areas, or should they be looking to change their models and look outside the enterprise for at least some of this expertise? *It is my belief that in the context of the Enterprise Optimization Framework any function or process that is not a core competency of a company or an essential of market differentiation should be strongly considered for outsourcing.* In fact, even some of those core and differentiated elements may be ripe for outsourcing as well. That doesn't necessarily mean that you're going to outsource it all, but the Process and Information Department should have as one of its main objectives to be constantly reviewing internal operations for areas where outsourcing makes sense. And the decision-making context remains the same:

- In what ways can a strategy of outsourcing yield lower overall total cost of a process or function and/or enable the achievement of Process and/or Information Optimization such that the overall impact on Enterprise Optimization is positive?

If outsourcing is identified as the most effective means to reach that end state, then it should be pursued aggressively. The service provider business for outsourcing functions and processes, both in "the business" and in IT, is maturing to a state where this should be one of the core avenues of pursuit for the PI Department. But beware: there are a multitude of outsourcing methods and solutions in the marketplace, all of which carry varying degrees of risk. I will outline the thought processes that will lead to optimal results in this area. There are plenty of alternatives, however, which could easily lead to disaster.

To that end, this analysis will be broken down into the following areas:

- Technology outsourcing, including:
  - o Core technology support (defined throughout this section primarily as software development, database administration, and system administration)
  - o Software vs. service
  - o Managed services
- Business process outsourcing, from business functions to end-to-end processes
- The essence of partnership

Technology Outsourcing

There was a time when technology developers were at a premium. The same went for database administrators (DBAs) and system administrators. In the consulting world, we found people who could work magic with the keyboard, and those people were gold to our projects and our practice. They were practically paid in gold as well. Many companies tried to find these people and pay them a fortune to come on board as full-time employees. That may have made sense at a time when many of the software packages were limited in functionality and required extensive customization, and where skilled development resources were few and far between. And while we're not completely past that state in the technology life cycle, we are certainly far along the curve. In fact, we're far along enough to state that core technology support has become a commodity, and as a commodity, it needs to be treated differently by corporations than it has been in the past.

For a long time, companies had full departments in their organizations related to telephone services. I remember spending time as an undergrad at Stanford University in the basement home of the campus radio station trying to understand a complex switching set of tools that routed telephone traffic all over the campus to lines dedicated to the radio station's infrastructure. I spent time in manholes with the station's chief engineer pulling and splicing cable to expand the communication infrastructure. Those are some of the war stories of my youth—it was not a pretty sight. Undoubtedly many companies did the same years ago, managing at least parts of their own telephone infrastructure, because no external entity was able to provide them with what they needed with high quality and at a reasonable cost. If you go back even further you can find departments responsible for distributing electricity for their companies. But we don't have a lot of Chief Electricity Officers anymore. And we don't have a lot of homegrown telephone switching systems encompassing entire data centers on company sites anymore, either. These technologies are commodities that are outsourced to vendors that can provide greater services at a lower cost than companies can provide for themselves.

Just as the technologies of electricity and telephone communications became outsourced commodities, we find ourselves on a similar path when it comes to functions surrounding core technology support. For some companies, that reality is in place today. For most others, they'll get there within the next few years. The biggest challenge will be for those companies that spent years and years building complex homegrown systems, which are held together by needle and thread based solely on the knowledge of the people who did the building in the first place. Those companies will be at a decided disadvantage in migrating away from those custom environments, compared to those that leveraged relatively vanilla applications and didn't stray too much from the original core. Eventually, though, most companies will find that the technology components required to build, maintain, and even integrate their systems will be outsourced, simply because various suppliers will be able to provide those services at a significantly lower cost and with equal or greater quality.

Technology outsourcing is not exactly a new phenomenon, but the current version is fundamentally different from the traditional offerings in this space. This new iteration of IT outsourcing goes beyond what the traditional players (EDS and IBM, for example) have done for years when they simply acquired the IT personnel and/or physical assets from a particular company. While this may have saved some incremental dollars and provided some leverage of the skills across those vast organizations, this is far different from going to a service provider and requesting a new set of skilled professionals to provide high-quality application support, including development, maintenance, and enhancements, across your end-to-end IT systems at a dramatically reduced cost. Many of the traditional IT outsourcing solutions have failed because the cost savings simply weren't sufficient to offset the management and communication challenges that can result from these kinds of arrangements. Now, quality in many areas is going up and costs are coming way down, all largely because a lot of work is going offshore.

As mentioned, it is clear that moving to this outsource model will occur much easier and much faster with some companies than with others. Companies that have standardized on a software infrastructure that is limited in scope (i.e., a small number of broad-based applications) will be ripe for immediate adoption of this movement. Moreover, global companies that have already positioned themselves for simplified global operations with as few instances of each software application as possible will also be well-positioned for adoption.

Unfortunately, most companies do not fall into these buckets. Most companies have a mix of homegrown and packaged solutions, tied together with a variety of integration tools. Most companies that have invested in the large packaged software solutions have heavily customized those solutions so that basic support functions are no longer viable except by the people who actually wrote the custom code. Most companies have such a mess on their hands that simply trying to explain the current state to a new set of developers may appear to be an insurmountable task. This mess is one of the reasons we have Information Technology Departments instead of Process and Information Departments. The mess is the *technology*. All those decisions made over the years to invest in custom solutions to meet the needs of one constituent or another are now coming back to haunt these organizations. There was a time when different organizations around the globe needed their own instances of each application because the lack of high-speed bandwidth was a limiting function. That's no longer the case. Inevitably when multiple instances pop up around the world, the solutions become out of synch, making it virtually impossible to have optimal global processes and manageable global reporting. Single instance should absolutely be the norm for global applications, and companies need to move in that direction. There are no longer constraints in either the applications or the communications technology to rationalize a multi-instance environment. (Technical architecture will be discussed in more detail in Section IV.)

Environment complexity aside, there are fundamentally two new elements to this equation that are driving this maturation process and are finally providing the impetus to make the cost component of these offerings virtually irresistible. These two things are:

- Widespread availability of high-speed, low-cost bandwidth, and
- Increasing availability of high-quality, low-cost application management and development resources across the globe.

Bandwidth brings everyone closer together. Multiple instances of software are no longer needed to support our needs in every region of the world. Enterprise software has all been Internet-enabled, providing for the ability for anyone to access these applications from across the globe and be productive. This goes for employees as well as system support organizations. You don't need that support organization sitting down the hall from you anymore. As long as you can contact that group in real-time, then what difference does it make where these people sit? The widespread availability of high-speed connectivity has fundamentally changed the needs of our technical infrastructure and the requirements around the physical location of support organizations.

That brings us to the second point, which is the availability of high-quality, low-cost resources for application management and development from remote centers of excellence around the world. This capability has enabled the outsource service providers to dramatically reduce the cost structure needed to support your applications. Real cost savings will finally be attainable, not just the incremental dollars that may have been trimmed in the past.

Current State of Technology Outsourcing: Going Offshore

Let's look at the marketplace today. India currently dominates the landscape for off-shore IT outsourcing services. India has invested heavily in IT skills development, providing a large and versatile labor pool. Government initiatives have resulted in relatively low telecommunications costs and incentives for foreign firms establishing operations in India. One such tax advantage is described as follows:

> Tax incentives provided to software firms under Indian tax laws presently include: (i) an exemption from payment of Indian corporate income taxes for a period of ten consecutive years of operation of software development facilities designated as "Software Technology Parks" (the "STP Tax Holiday"); and (ii) a tax deduction for profits derived from exporting computer software (the "Export Deduction").[38]

The investment in India has been extensive and the infrastructure is relatively mature, compared to other offshore locations. The capacity of fiber-optic lines connecting telephone systems into India increased almost sevenfold from 2001 to 2002, and the cost of telephone and data lines under the Pacific Ocean has fallen to about one-fourth the cost from between 2002 and 2004.[39] Finally, there is a high level of understanding of the English language in India, which is critical in the formative stages of any relationship with a U.S. entity.

For awhile, India would send its best and brightest to the United States to take advantage of the high rates companies paid for these services on-site. Trust was a major factor in gaining confidence as a service provider in this space, and that hurdle was usually overcome only when services were provided on-site, especially by individuals who had good skills in the English language. In addition, lack of pervasive high-speed bandwidth made offshore capabilities often impractical.

That paradigm is rapidly changing. The high fees are no longer available to these resources in the U.S., and high-speed bandwidth is plentiful. Plus, the desire to head to the U.S. is no longer as compelling. In a country where 25 percent of the country lives in poverty,[40] the per capita annual income is $500, and a two-bedroom flat goes for $125, developers who can make $10,000 a year right out of college have no reason to uproot to the U.S.[41] There is no question that communication and trust challenges persist in providing a comfort feeling for offshore development for U.S. companies, but this roadblock is evaporating as success stories become the norm in the marketplace. The cost takeout associated with offshore development is simply too compelling to ignore.

It is important to note that the offshore opportunities presented by these Indian firms are not simply about dramatic cost reduction (as if that wasn't enough motivation). These companies know what they're doing. Quality has been a hallmark of these Indian firms, and the rigorous commitment to world-class development processes and standards has been critical to their success. The global benchmark for software development is the Capability Maturity Model (CMM), which was developed by the Software Engineering Institute (SEI) at Carnegie-Mellon University. The CMM is to the software development community what ISO 9000 (from the International Organization for Standardization) and TL 9000 are for the manufacturing and telecommunications industries, respectively. It's all about adopting procedures that have been identified as best practices for a particular industry.

When SEI began the project to define these standards in the late 1980s, it came up with five levels in the CMM. (The objectives of the initiative and a summary of these levels can be found in **Appendix C**.) When the original model was published in 1993, the committee stated, "Maturity Levels 4 and 5 are relatively unknown territory for the software industry. There are only a few examples of Level 4 and 5 software projects and organizations....The characteristics of these levels have been defined by analogy with other industries and the few examples in the software industry exhibiting this level of process capability."[42] Eventually we started to find a few organizations that were able to achieve the illustrious Level 5 rating for at least parts of their organizations, including Motorola (India Electronics Division in 1994) and Boeing (Defense and Space Group, 1996).[43] In the last few years, we have seen a number of additions to the Level 5 status of the CMM.

While it is important to note that the SEI does not keep track of all organizations that subscribe to these guidelines and have achieved the various levels of certification, it does publish a listing of at least a representative sample of organizations that have been publicly identified at Levels 2, 3, 4, and 5. As of April 2003, there were 71 distinct organizations from around the world in this published list that had reached Level 5 status in CMM for software. What is interesting is that *two-thirds* of those organizations had one or more of their Level 5 certified locations based in India, *by far* more than any other country.[44] These Indian firms have recognized that a true commitment to quality is necessary for them to overcome any of the potentially negative perceptions about offshore software development (be it product development or information technology software). Cost savings is one thing, but these firms have had a high hurdle to overcome in getting Western companies to believe they are getting the same high quality for these low rates that they would be getting for the traditionally higher on-site rates. In many cases, at least in the area of core technology support (as defined at the outset of this section), they are accomplishing exactly that. This is what is so enticing for Western companies—to gain true advantages in the context of the Enterprise Optimization Framework, with positive results not just in Total Cost, but also with Process and Information Optimization as well.

Moreover, the pool of available resources will be increasing dramatically in the coming years, as the offshore trend moves well beyond the borders of India. The newest entry in this space is China. Technology development training is growing by leaps and bounds in China, and just as companies have been sending manufacturing chores to China to reap the advantages of low-cost labor, the trend will continue in the area of software development. In fact, Gartner predicts that by 2007, China will equal India in IT services revenue, with each projected to generated about $27 billion in this area.[45] Some of this growth in China is actually coming directly from India, as some of the larger Indian companies are taking some of their work offshore to even lower cost geographies. One example is Tata Consultancy Services (TCS), one of the largest Indian-based global IT services organizations, which has already begun to staff up in China. According to a report by the American Electronics Association, "By 2005, TCS plans to have 3,000 software engineers in China, or 15 percent of their global work force."[46]

China supports one of the world's fastest growing economies. IT spending in the country has increased 20 percent per year since 1999. Estimates put the number of professionals in the software exporting industry currently at around 200,000, with an additional 50,000 graduates entering the workforce each year. And the cost of labor is significantly less than the rates being paid in India, which already are significantly less than what it costs for U.S.-based resources. The Chinese government is also supportive of these ventures, offering tax breaks and rent-free office space in its attempts to attract foreign IT firms to China.[47] That being said, China will clearly also face roadblocks to fulfilling these predictions. The lack of English-language skills is one of those obstacles, along with the lack of professional project management and time-tested methodologies.[48] These barriers may impact the ability of the Chinese offerings to quickly expand beyond core application development and into the areas of systems analysis and full application management. That expansion in capabilities will likely occur, but it may take time, limiting the Chinese option to a partnership concept with other higher end solution providers, at least in the near term. All in all, though, the opportunities in China are way too promising not to be packaged into a viable solution offering in the near future, and possibly yield independent, end-to-end offerings down the road.

There have always been roadblocks with offshore development approaches, primarily around quality of service, ability to communicate effectively, and ultimate reliability. These barriers are breaking down, and breaking down quickly. This resource pool is a key ingredient that will enable managed services offerings to finally break some of the financial barriers that have prevented profitable offerings in the past. Cost savings are actually generated by two specific means that provide a powerful combination of savings. The first method is based on the direct cost of labor for these skilled resources in these particular pockets of the world. The labor rates are dramatically lower than U.S.-based rates, with little to no drop in quality across multiple areas of core technology support. Second, because of the high availability of resources, these offshore firms can staff their resources in large pools that can provide service across multiple accounts at the same time. This enables economies of scale based on resource sharing, whereby resource requirements are not driven by headcount needs of their clients, but rather by *service level* needs of their clients. Staffing models driven by Service Level Agreements (SLAs) reduce the cost of the service thanks in part to the leverage generated across accounts from the resource-sharing method. Thus, the cost savings stems not only from the low labor rate, but also from the ability to pool resources and leverage those teams across multiple accounts. In the past, U.S.-based managed services offerings struggled by primarily expecting to generate savings via the pooled-resource, service-level model. However, having to pay U.S. rates for resources, the savings from this method alone were insufficient to sustain the model. This was especially true given the wild swings in the economy and the challenges this presented for these companies to be able to scale their offerings relative to the market economics. With the offshore model, we're now looking at a large resource pool that consists of high-quality, extremely low cost resources, making a managed services solution that much more attractive.

Indian and Chinese companies are already providing outsourced development services that are taking market share from in-house IT shops and traditional U.S.-based consulting organizations. Other countries are sure to follow as they witness the economic possibilities of this high-tech export. Moreover, U.S. solution providers will undoubtedly drive this trend as well. The large software vendors are investing heavily in software development centers in low-cost labor markets that can only be found abroad. In addition, the major system implementation consulting organizations are also investing in offshore development capabilities, as a means to stay competitive in the cutthroat pricing wars prevalent in the consulting business today. The landscape for outsourced technology services has fundamentally shifted, and to have a chance at being a player in this space, high-quality, low-cost core technology support capabilities will need to be a component of the overall offering.

So what does this mean to an individual company? First, companies will be able to get out of the business of writing their own software code for information management and transaction systems. This specialized function is not part of the core competence of most organizations, so getting out of this business makes sense, especially with a high-quality, low-cost replacement readily available. People in these jobs currently should be reassigned or let go, either to provide more value to the company by some other means or as a straight cost reduction by the alleviation of some headcount. Second, one of the most important decisions to be made by the Process and Information Department will be in terms of partnership. Not all of these offshore solution providers will be the same in terms of cost, quality, service level, etc., especially in the ramp-up years directly in front of us. Competition is good, and will provide a real choice to CPIOs. There are dozens of firms entering this space, some big and some very small. While the Internet can bring the technologies close together, there are still vast distances in other areas between the U.S. and these offshore providers. With distance comes cultural differences, language barriers, and other challenges in making these relationships work smoothly. Thorough reference checks are strongly suggested for any organization you might consider as an offshore service provider. Investigate not only their technical capabilities, but also their maturity as an organization and their ability to work effectively with companies similar to yours. As mentioned in Section I, establishing partnerships with outsource solution providers requires a different kind of analysis and skill set from traditional IT procurement. The PI Department needs to understand these differences and embed these new skills in its Office of Program Management.

These relationships should start with a transition phase of limited scope, before complete development offloading occurs. Moreover, to overcome the trust and communication challenges, especially in the early stages of these relationships, the offshore supplier should commit to assigning individuals to be on-site to work hand-in-hand with the resources in the company's Process and Information Department. This practical step will prove to be an invaluable investment for both parties in gaining confidence in this new method of providing software development solutions. There will be individuals in the company who are nervous about losing the on-site presence of a development organization, and having on-site project management from the new partner will help ease those concerns. Managing the transition is one of the essential elements of any venture into offshore outsourcing. Skimping in this area of change management is an easy predictor of ultimate failure of an initiative of this kind.

It would be naïve to believe that there will never be political implications to these relationships. There is instability in many regions of the world, and there will certainly be some degree of risk for companies that invest heavily in solution providers in any of these unstable areas. Sending periodic development tasks implies only limited risk, but looking offshore for a complete line of technology and business process support services will yield additional risks that must also be considered. Alternate sites and emergency backup plans must be included in any long-term strategy tied to offshore capabilities in the event of sudden unforeseen political occurrences that may put your critical business assets at immediate risk.

There is tremendous opportunity presented by offshore outsourcing capabilities. In fact, there has never been a better time to invest heavily in this space. Companies pursuing this option have a clear opportunity to gain competitive advantage, but probably not for long because your competitors are sure to follow, and likely follow sooner than later. At the same time, things are not to the point where everyone can believe there won't be challenges and some element of risk in moving in this direction.

This evolutionary step in the cycle of offshore IT outsourcing is not the end point for service providers in establishing a successful end-to-end offering. Core technology support is the foundation, but it must be followed by high-quality and low-cost functional and technical support. Project management, proven methodologies, and effective communication must also be included in the solutions. The foundations are there for the taking, but the first providers to be able to extend the offerings to *full service solutions* will be the ones that will achieve huge advantages in this ever-changing marketplace. Core technology support is the starting point, but soon (if not already) that will simply be table stakes. These offshore service providers are also attempting to support companies with complete applications management, which requires high-caliber business analysts who understand business processes and how to map them effectively through these individual systems. The likelihood is that these skills will also be developed and offered at low cost by these offshore companies, but they are currently not as far along in these areas as they are with respect to the core development skills. The concern is that some organizations may get caught up in the hype associated with offshore outsourcing and simply expect too much from these low-cost providers. There are certain elements of these offerings that are absolutely real and incredibly compelling. But that doesn't mean that an offshore organization is capable of providing world-class program management and/or strategic business process guidance at 20 bucks an hour. At least not yet.

To assist companies in deciding what makes sense to send offshore and what to keep in-house, the following is an examination of the various levels of traditional IT functions and what is most viable for successful offshore outsourcing at this time.

- **Core Technology Support** (again, defined here to include software development, database administration, and system administration): This is the easiest area to analyze. Virtually all core technology support should be outsourced, taking advantage of the abundance of low-cost, high-quality resources located around the globe. Total Cost can receive a dramatic boost, while Process and Information Optimization can go anywhere from remaining neutral to being significantly advanced, depending on the capability of your partner(s). The only exception to this path would be the case where your environment is so complex (often through extensive customization and/or integration) that it would be virtually impossible to transfer the responsibility to a third party. If this is the case, then dramatic alterations should be made to your existing environment, followed immediately by proceeding on a path toward offshore outsourcing. These kinds of complex technical environments will be discussed further in Section IV.

- **Systems Analysis:** This is another area where outsourcing makes a lot of sense, although it may take slightly longer to transfer this responsibility than the core technology support functions. Systems analysis is defined here as the tasks related to the hands-on management of your applications. This includes setup, configuration, testing, and troubleshooting both existing and new functionality. Ideally, there is a strong business process focus to this role, but these resources typically know the system first, and therefore focus on system-enabled, out-of-the-box processes. Communication skills will be important for your service provider, as representatives from "the business" will be identifying requirements and working collaboratively with this organization for daily support and throughout project life cycles. Currently, India has the leg-up in terms of offshore capabilities in this space (over China, for example) based on experience with this skill set and broad English-language capabilities.

- **Functional and Technical Design:** It is one thing to move technical development and other elements of core technology support offshore, but it is a slightly different story when the tasks move to the design process. The design phase related to custom development requires tight communication between the business process owners and the design team. These activities tend to be highly iterative and are often very complex, getting down to very discrete levels of detail. The functional and technical designers must have knowledge of the systems from a functional point of view, and then be able to effectively translate requirements into their purely technical form. This requires business knowledge, excellent written and verbal communication skills, and an on-site presence to provide a high-quality result. Having two or three on-site functional and technical design personnel is precisely what makes having a large team of offshore technical folks viable. It is perfectly reasonable to outsource these roles to design specialists, but moving the functions offshore opens up considerable risk for the effectiveness of the overall outsource model.

- **Business Analysis:** As we continue to move up the food chain, away from the technology and closer to core business processes, it will be harder to find an outsource partner who can simply assume this role for you, especially in the mode of low-cost offshore resources. Business analysis is the ability to apply process knowledge related to your organization and your industry, and to translate those process requirements into system deployments. This function is more likely to remain as a core competence of your PI Department. Your ability to outsource your business functions (see the discussion on Business Process Outsourcing in the next part of this section) will also guide your ability to outsource the business analysis function. If you do expand your BPO initiatives, then some of the business analysis function may be appropriate for outsourcing as well. Even then, your PI Department will want to retain some of this capability in-house to ensure that you are constantly evaluating opportunities for Process and Information Optimization. There will certainly be times when you call on an outsource provider to lend assistance in this area (such as with the Big 5 consulting organizations), but that would likely be in conjunction with your own core team and be focused on relatively short-term initiatives.

- **Project Management:** This function should remain primarily in-house as a core competence of the PI Department. Success in project management relies on the ability to communicate effectively up and down the value chain within your organization (and with partner organizations), and to identify and resolve issues in a timely fashion. There is a cultural component to project management that is very difficult to outsource. Again, as with business analysis, there will likely be times when you partner with a service organization that provides project management as a component of its service offering, but this should be complementary to in-house project management, and not a replacement. In addition, many companies rely on their project management structure to assume responsibility for the all-important risk management and change management components that are fundamental to the success of any initiative. Projects that ignore these core activities are destined to fail, as it is incredibly naïve to assume that all will simply go well and everyone will be quick to get on board and prepare to transition to the end state of a project. Consulting organizations can certainly offer guidance and hands-on assistance in these areas, but outsourcing these entire functions will be a risky proposition.

For these last three areas, take heed of the following warning: "Buyer beware" when outsourcing these roles to an offshore provider. While the tremendous cost savings that are achievable with offshore outsourcing have been emphasized for the functions of core technology support and systems analysis, as you move into functional and technical design, business analysis, and project management, you have to realize that these are more sophisticated skills that require broader experiences than those that are often available from offshore service providers. For these skills, you're more likely to fall into the category of "you get what you pay for." Bandwidth brings us closer from a technology perspective, helping to make the offshore solution viable for the core technology support and systems analysis functions. But bandwidth doesn't help much with these other more sophisticated roles. Just as it is no longer reasonable for U.S.-based consulting organizations to expect you to pay premium prices for core technology support and systems analysis given the availability of the high-quality, low-cost offshore alternative, it is also unreasonable to expect that the offshore providers will be able to provide these higher caliber business skills at the same high-quality, low-price combination (again, at least *not yet*).

There are extremely compelling reasons to go offshore for certain skills that have become commoditized, but be careful about assuming what falls into the category of a commodity and what still requires enhanced skills for which a premium price may be appropriately attached. Companies can't simply assume that they can just throw *all* of their IT requirements offshore and still be successful. Remember, these are *business* systems, not *technology* systems. Successful deployments will continue to require business (i.e., process and information) expertise in order to achieve optimal configurations and effective buy-in from the user community. Pure technology projects that lack business participation (implementations or upgrades) have always been a bad idea. Don't let the low-cost opportunities presented by offshore organizations lull you into believing that all of a sudden pure technology focused projects are now all of a sudden viable. Forget it. The PI Department needs to find a *balance* when pursuing projects. The PI Department needs to fulfill its obligations in having the appropriate program management infrastructure in place to facilitate internal alignment around Strategy, Controls, People, Process, and Technology, and how that alignment will be extended to any outsource service providers. The PI Department needs to understand both the internal capabilities and availability of resources within its company, as well as those that are available from qualified partners, with respect to the entire lifecycle of the initiative. The PI Department needs to understand that success will depend as much on these structural components as on the technical capabilities of the individual contributors to the initiative. Just because a company chooses to outsource an initiative, doesn't change this imperative, and doesn't mitigate the requirement that the company understands what is truly viable from an internal perspective, as well as what is viable from the technology outsourcing community. You can now gain tremendous advantages from offshore outsourced capabilities in well-defined areas (primarily core technology support and systems analysis), but you will still have to dig a little deeper into your pocket if you need to obtain business-focused process expertise that will provide high quality assistance that leads to ultimate success. This is why the bundled services of consulting organizations that combine on-site process expertise with offshore development and assorted technical skills may yield the optimal balanced approach. Even if the ratio of resources is 20 to 1 (with 20 offshore to 1 on-site), that one highly-skilled on-site resource can make all the difference between the success or failure of the initiative.

Offshore outsourcing presents logistical, communication, and coordination challenges that require experienced on-site program management. You need an on-site presence to provide direct communication to the client on whatever issues may arise and to be able to effectively communicate with client staff in business-focused terms. You also need an on-site presence to effectively translate user requirements into clear and direct technical specifications that can then be communicated to the offshore team. Close, iterative communication with the functional users is essential in the design process, and will be difficult if sent completely offshore. In fact, precision with technical design will be more important than ever as offshore developers will need to rely heavily on these written documents for their specific development guidance. The preponderance of the resource pool may be offshore, but an on-site, hands-on management presence is critical to the success of these overall programs. In the service provider market, the ultimate race is for which of these organizations can bundle as much of the whole package into an offering that continues to stress both low total cost and high quality (yielding Process and Information Optimization) throughout the entire service offering. Those are the providers that are going to win in this new landscape of information technology services.

Fortunately, we now have a framework in place that can guide our decision-making in each of these areas. For business leaders, the framework may be mostly conceptual, but it reminds us to always consider all three major components when making a decision such as what to outsource and what to keep in house. All three of the following questions must be asked:

- What will be the impact on my capabilities with respect to end-to-end processes?
- What will be the impact on my capabilities with respect to the quality, accessibility, and security of information?
- What will be the impact on my total cost of ownership of what is being considered for outsourcing?

As with any initiative, just lowering hard dollar costs is insufficient justification for the project in that if it corresponds with an overriding drop in capabilities with respect to processes and/or information, then you'll end up hurting the company, not helping it. The concept of outsourcing needs to be analyzed by the PI Department, and then the specific components that are being considered for outsourcing need to be analyzed at an even more detailed level. I am a major proponent of outsourcing in general as a means of achieving Enterprise Optimization. However, there is no one-size-fits-all approach, so due diligence is warranted in every opportunity under consideration.

Software vs. Service

As has been identified, there are many potential advantages for companies to outsource some or all of their core technology support requirements, taking advantage of an emerging pool of high-quality, low-cost resources. The availability of these services also provides opportunities to the companies that are developing technical solutions, including many of the software companies that are looking to find ways to expand their offerings (and market share) at a reduced cost of service. It is now time to explore some of the changes in the software market space that factor in the desire for outsource services and the cost-saving opportunities presented by offshore capabilities.

We are now in the early stages of adapting to this newly connected world of the high-speed Internet. What does that mean for the way we're going to use software and technology as a means by which to run our companies? How have the software and services worlds changed, or how will they change with this new technological architecture available to us? There are multiple schools of thought, probably as many as there are companies trying to pick up some market share in this space. From an enterprise software perspective, there are two primary camps vying for your investment dollars. On the one hand, you've got the traditional software companies, which sell clients a license (and ongoing maintenance) to use the software as an internal tool. On the other hand, you have various forms of application service providers (ASPs), which sell software as a service, allowing customers to get up and running quickly and then rent the solution on a periodic basis (usually monthly). There are also examples in the marketplace where these models have converged, as in the case where some traditional software companies are also trying to provide ASP offerings, either as a complementary service to their traditional offerings, or as a long-term replacement strategy for the status quo. Let's take a look at these approaches and try to draw some conclusions in the context of the Enterprise Optimization Framework.

Let's start with the traditional software companies, whose model has been to sell licenses of software to individual companies and to provide technical support for a yearly maintenance fee. With this approach, the cost paid out to the software vendor often represents only a portion of the overall total cost. Most of these packages require assistance from system implementation vendors, which install the software and train users over some extended period of time. Then there's the ongoing support staff and training and maintenance costs over the useful life of the software. And while the software cost of major and minor upgrades is usually included in your annual maintenance fee from the software vendor, these upgrades often entail significant implementation investments with third-party consultants as well.

There is now huge infrastructure associated with this architecture, one that will be very difficult to unravel even if an alternative is identified that provides significant advantages. But there are significant downsides to this long-standing approach to business systems. Total Cost Optimization is clearly out of control, and it is inconceivable that this is the only way to process transactions and manage information. It also continues to fly in the face of sticking with what is core to a company's business and outsourcing the rest. Systems development and support is not core to most companies, yet they are forced to hire numerous professionals to keep these environments going, customizing and integrating them based on the needs of the day. Companies, *at their best*, may be able to create a competitive advantage with these systems based on Process and Information Optimization, but the Total Cost associated with this approach will never be optimal.

That being said, clearly one of the challenges in moving this kind of infrastructure to a service-based model is that while all companies may start out with the same application code, the minute the installation begins, the solution becomes tailored to the needs of that company. And even if customizations are kept at an absolute minimum, the mere complexity of these enterprise packages has resulted in a myriad of bug fixes being inserted to resolve the problems encountered by each individual company. Functionality requirements have expanded capabilities but often at the expense of stability (and, ultimately, customer satisfaction). While the software companies have tried to standardize their patch releases, this effort has been only mildly successful. The fact is, there are no two systems alike in the marketplace in terms of configuration, integration, degree of customization, and release level. With this much diversity, how can service providers have any chance of providing *standard* levels of service when there is no such thing as a *standard* deployment in the marketplace? In other words, the very complexity of the software, which is pitched as a positive differentiator in terms of functionality and benefits to customers, can also be the greatest detriment to these solutions, as they become virtually impossible (and extremely costly) to support and maintain.

One attempt to address some of the fundamental problems has been to start fresh from the ground up with an entirely new model. In an attempt to overcome many of these challenges there has been the birth of the application service provider (ASP) market space. In this service offering, you have solution providers that are renting out software over the Internet, thus far mostly to small and medium-sized companies. The solutions have been designed from scratch to be accessed over the Internet and with the intent of maintaining consistent and stable versions across the customer base. The offerings are usually fairly clean and simple. The feature set is often rich in functionality and highly configurable, but actual customization is usually out of the question. Configurations may change from one customer to the next, but the software release levels are kept consistent, enabling a standard level of support. This is a completely different model from traditional software vendors, and it is in large part this architectural design and its successful execution that is making the solution viable as an outsourced, hosted service.

One company that has found a path in this market space is salesforce.com, with which you have the ability to receive Customer Relationship Management (CRM) capabilities for your organization for as little as $65 per month per employee.[49] You have no additional software or hardware costs. You just need a browser and access to the Internet. There is no upfront cost for software and no cost for upgrades. The motto for salesforce.com is "The End of Software" (see Figure III-1), as you no longer need to install or maintain anything. You just access a solution over the Web. Now, there is still some degree of implementation work to be done as the solution is tailored to your needs (process design and configuration, though, not customization), but there is nothing physical for you to install or technically maintain and the implementation timeline is considerably shorter than with typical CRM solutions.

Figure III-1: Logo for salesforce.com

Source: salesforce.com, March 2003

Simplicity represents a significant portion of the value proposition for salesfore.com, especially when compared to traditional enterprise software, and this simplicity comes in the way the company has constructed its solution. Salesforce.com uses the so-called "multi-tenant" model, whereby all customers are actually sharing the same system of software. This makes the patching and upgrade process completely standardized and much more straightforward than with traditional enterprise software. It also makes it much easier to scale compared to traditional ASP offerings. When salesforce.com adds a customer, there is no additional infrastructure that needs to be procured and deployed in the data center—no extra hardware or software is needed. The customer is just added to the existing infrastructure, with internal security managing the separation of the data. This "simple" approach solves the scalability problem that has long troubled ASPs, thereby contributing to the incredibly low cost for this solution.

Marc Benioff is the founder, chairman, and CEO of salesforce.com. Benioff speaks passionately not only about his company, but also about the entire model for application service providers:

If you think that SAP is going to be the future, well the past never equals the future. And certainly the present never equals the future. SAP is partly the past and partly the present, but SAP is certainly not the future. And Siebel is certainly not the future. It's a big, monolithic, client-server application. It's not what people are going to use as the Internet matures and grows and evolves....Our fundamental competition is ignorance. That is, people do not realize that they just don't have to buy this stuff and they don't have to be held hostage by the CRM and ERP vendors. They think that there's only one path and there isn't. There's another path and there's a better path and a higher path and that path requires no software.[50]

There are other ASPs in the CRM space as well, including Salesnet and UpShot; the latter having been acquired by Siebel Systems in October 2003.[51] Then there's NetSuite (formerly called NetLedger), which entered the ASP space with offerings centered on finance and accounting functions, and has now expanded its footprint to also include competitive functionality within CRM. In fact, NetSuite is one of the first ASPs to make some legitimate strides in providing a complete end-to-end business solution with products that combine much of the functionality offered by the traditional ERP and CRM vendors in an integrated solution.[52] Salesforce.com has also extended its offering beyond core CRM to now include some of the traditional finance functions, such as billing and invoicing, electronic bill presentation, contract management, order management, and order entry.[53] For these companies, this is pure software as a service with an incredibly low total cost, in large part because of the standardization of the offering in terms of the software, functionality, support, and even infrastructure. All that sounds pretty good, but skepticism has remained in the marketplace about ASPs and has limited their ability to move toward widespread acceptance and a general state of profitability.

Back in 2002, Craig Conway, the CEO and president of PeopleSoft, one of the world's largest enterprise software companies, said, "The biggest flaw in outsourced solutions is lack of integration. Is there a major company that doesn't want to integrate their customer-management systems with their financial systems? Or their supply-chain systems? Or their human-resource systems? Companies today want seamless, transparent, real-time business processes. You can't achieve that with a single-solution outsourced approach."[54]

From this perspective, many of the original ASPs failed in the areas of Process and Information Optimization, as they tended to operate as remote islands in the overall technology landscape. However, some of the remaining ASPs are taking this issue to heart and beginning to design integration capabilities into their solutions, especially as they begin to move beyond small market customers and try to compete in the enterprise market space. Salesforce.com is one such organization, having introduced its Enterprise Edition in 2003 with integration capabilities and extensions built into the solution, thereby providing opportunities to target larger customers than in the past. Salesforce.com CIO Jim Cavalieri says his company's product integrates with enterprise applications by offering an XML API.[55] The company has also established partnerships with some of the leading integration vendors, including Informatica, Tibco, Grand Central, and Data Junction for what Cavalieri calls "prepackaged solutions" to enable integration to back-office systems.[56] One salesforce.com customer is Dow Jones Newswires. Diane Driscoll, the Newswire group's customer service manager, said, "Salesforce.com S3 has solved the serious software, synching, and user issues of many CRM solutions and delivers what we need in a CRM application: accessibility, flexibility, ease of use, and integration with back-end systems."[57] The last part of that statement is awfully compelling, given the objections raised by PeopleSoft's Conway. If these ASPs are beginning to conquer the problem of back-office integration, then one of the major obstacles for their business models may become a thing of the past. Beyond this example, you've got UpShot's CRM application, which is built using Microsoft's .NET technologies, and which also claims support for integration needs. Its founder and chairman, Keith Raffel, points to Xerox and Hewlett-Packard as among the customers taking advantage of UpShot's integration capabilities.[58]

NetSuite may have the most compelling story in this space, as it not only provides integration capabilities to other applications, it also offers the most complete end-to-end solution in the ASP market space with ERP *and* CRM functionality,[59] lessening the need for integration capabilities outside the ASP environment. Now we're really talking about breaking down the barriers of the ASP solution set and helping small- to medium-sized companies optimize their overall environments! Many of the ASPs that went belly-up certainly struggled with the concept of integration, as Conway described, but the survivors are beginning to demonstrate the means to overcome some of these hurdles. Plus, the fact remains that integration is a major challenge regardless of whether application hosting and management is done in-house or outsourced. In fact, it is such a significant issue that it won't be covered in detail here. Rather, that hot topic will be discussed in Section IV. Stay tuned.

Back to the concept of the pure ASPs. Many of the leaders in the software industry were not convinced that software as a pay-as-you-go commodity would ever evolve into a viable solution in the overall software industry. Conway, for one, stated, "Many industries today are fundamentally information-processing businesses—banks, brokerage firms, insurance companies, telecommunications, etc. The core of these companies is their ability to manage data more efficiently than their competitors. They will not outsource or depend on commodity software because it is too critical to their business. They certainly won't trust critical business processes to an outsourced provider with 100 venture-backed employees working out of a garage in Silicon Valley."[60] Siebel Systems CEO Tom Siebel has also been outspoken against the prospects for salesforce.com. He proclaimed in April 2001, "There is no way that company exists in a year."[61] In October 2002, he stated, "There is not one example of this outsourcing application business model being successful. I just don't think it is a viable business model."[62] Leaders such as Conway and Siebel did raise once-legitimate concerns about the willingness for companies to adopt these hosted solutions that may appear to be beyond the client's control, and enterprise vendors have tended to exploit this perception for their benefit to promote the more traditional packaged software solutions. But those perceptions are rapidly changing as companies such as salesforce.com and NetSuite overcome these previous obstacles and build a consistent and expanding track record of success. As a result, the software industry has actually begun to recognize the viability of the ASP solution and, rather than yielding market share to the successful ASPs, some traditional software companies have actually begun adopting a similar model. In October 2003, Siebel Systems announced that it was re-entering the ASP space for CRM solutions, partnering with IBM to offer "Siebel CRM OnDemand" with a solution footprint that sounds a whole lot like what is being offered today by salesforce.com. Mr. Siebel's statement at the time of the launch of this new offering demonstrates a clear change of heart echoed throughout the industry: "This is the way software is going to be delivered in the future."[63] That's a pretty dramatic shift in a very short period of time. We now have some of the traditional software companies preparing to leverage their large install bases to take on these surviving ASPs head-to-head, rather than waiting for their demise. It should make for interesting competition in the marketplace!

Many of the original ASPs did fail. But, as mentioned, NetSuite continues to thrive in its niche, and privately held salesforce.com broke even in February 2003, after more than 100 percent annual growth and sales of $52 million in FY02. It further states that it is looking for increased profitability with another year of 100 percent growth, anticipating more than $100 million in revenue for FY03.[64] These kinds of numbers are making people in the marketplace take notice. Salesforce.com boasts customers of the likes of General Electric, Honeywell, AOL Time Warner, Cigna, Avis, and Cable & Wireless—and hosts nearly 7,000 customers in all.[65] And just to emphasize the point in terms of increased market adoption, take a look at what the customers are saying about their satisfaction with what they're getting from this ASP: [66]

- "Salesforce.com has enhanced our healthy sales pipeline. The system is robust and intuitive yet requires no outside IT support. New users have been extremely satisfied with salesforce.com. In less than a year we have tripled the user base and currently have employees in sales, marketing, finance, and management using the application."

  Ken Mason, Vice-President of Marketing
  Fujitsu Technology Solutions, Inc.

- "The salesforce.com S3 on-demand delivery model, intuitive interface, and flexibility was a good match for our needs. The solution is helping us to achieve the organization-wide visibility and coordination that is critical to our success."

  Lon Otremba, Executive Vice-President, AOL Interactive Marketing
  AOL

- "Salesforce.com S3 delivers internal transparency and enhanced client service without requiring the resources to implement, integrate, and maintain a complex conventional system. The bottom line is that the system works, it is easy to use, and we have it at an affordable price."

  Graeme Muirhead, Executive Director
  Daiwa Securities

- "We needed a CRM application that could integrate valuable client information from customer call centers and legacy financial systems into daily customer care activities. Salesforce.com S3 provides us with a cost-effective and user-friendly solution, at a fraction of the cost of client-server CRM systems."

  Eddie Myers, Group Manager
  Paymentech

- "We focused on three major issues: cost, time to implement, and flexibility. Salesforce.com S3 came out on top in each category."

  Dave Janssen, Regional Inside Sales Manager
  F5 Networks

- "With the old system, we literally had to have programmers go in and change any type of existing report. With salesforce.com S3, we have redesigned our sales forecasting and all of our sales reporting, and we are able to do any type of online ad hoc reporting that we need."

> John Shope, Senior Vice President and National Director
> Wachovia

All vendors have great quotes from customers on their Web sites, so salesforce.com is not unique in that regard. However, these are particularly noteworthy in that they certainly paint a vastly different picture from what you would expect based on the naysayers in the world of traditional enterprise software and in much of the analyst community. These are real customers, some of which are rather big companies, all of which appear thrilled with this ASP solution, and all of which appear to be receiving benefits in all three areas of the Enterprise Optimization Framework. In other words, it's not just about low cost. Process and Information effectiveness are vital components to this solution. You'll also note that all of these quotes are from *business* leaders, and not from IT resources. These folks clearly like the cost savings, but would not be satisfied unless their business performance was enhanced as well. In these cases (and more), it clearly is. One wonders if all these predictions of demise from the software establishment about the ASPs are being made out of confidence or out of fear.

There is another fundamental level in which ASP offerings such as salesforce.com are finding acceptance in the marketplace, and this gets back to one of the ongoing themes of Enterprise Optimization—keep it simple. Salesforce.com currently estimates that the adoption rate of its solution in its customer base is greater than 90 percent with a customer retention rate of greater than 97 percent. These percentages, which are simply unheard of for traditional deployments of CRM solutions, are due in large part to the simplicity of the solution. Jim Steele, who spent more than 20 years of his career at IBM, is now President of salesforce.com. I spoke with Steele about his company's approach compared to that of Siebel. He told me:

> On paper, when you see Siebel, it is everything you could ever want, so the management loved it. The problem is that they made it so complex that the people who were actually using it day-to-day couldn't figure out how to make it work....Siebel stands for highly complex, not intuitive, not easy to use, long implementation cycles, and very expensive. We stand for the exact opposite: an order of magnitude less costly, very intuitive, the sales guys love it so they actually use it...it's simple, fast, and flexible, and that's why we're winning in the marketplace.[67]

Once again we find the "simple" path generating significant benefits, this time in terms of user adoption, which in the past has been the biggest inhibitor to success in the CRM space, where typically authoritative mandates with punitive consequences have been the only sure method of gaining adoption with CRM software. Imagine if your sales force actually didn't mind using a CRM solution! Imagine the difference that would make toward the solution having a chance to positively impact overall Enterprise Optimization. Plus, this concept of simplicity extends far beyond the sales organization and the hands-on user community. It's the ease of configuration, deployment, and maintenance for your IT organization. It's the flexibility of the solution to make functional and process changes quickly and without complex programming. It's the ease of generating reports to optimize the information flow throughout the organization. These benefits are the results of a robust but simple model that permeates the entire solution. Now, a key question remains in terms of the company's ability to scale this approach and keep things simple as the solution is extended into larger, more complex organizations, including integration to multiple other systems. This expanse is just now gaining momentum, and it's too soon to tell if the company will be able to continue to maintain its "simplistic" roots in these more complex environments, but that is the plan, and so far the plan seems to be working.

Just because this type of offering underachieved in its initial incarnations does not make it reasonable to reject this business and technical approach out of hand. The fact that many of the initial attempts failed and that market acceptance has been rather slow doesn't mean the concept doesn't have merit. As Benioff from salesforce.com states, "Like all new models, it has to have slow incremental gains. Things don't happen overnight."[68] As with most new business models, there will be a natural string of starts and stops. As Figure III-2 shows, Gartner offers a view of what it calls the "ASP Hype Cycle," which depicts the arrival of a hard fought positive trend.

Figure III-2: ASP Hype Cycle

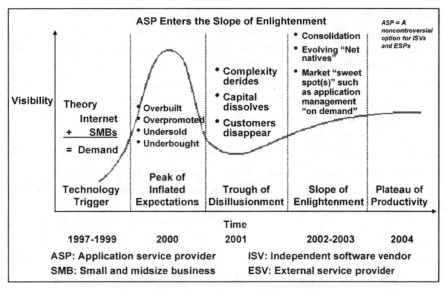

Source: Gartner Group, "2003 ASP Hype Cycle: Hype? What Hype?" May 16, 2003

There appears to be a lot of validity in this chart. We've progressed through the initial, out-of-control hype, have witnessed a number of failures, and are now moving toward a reasonable maturation curve on which the industry will grow. The desire is still there, driven by the ever-present need to drive down costs of operations while still receiving a high-quality solution. It is that customer demand which will continue to drive suppliers to look to provide viable offerings to satisfy that demand. We're starting to see ASPs emerge that are addressing the concerns of the marketplace, and customers are beginning to take notice, especially in the mid-market, where this kind of offering has begun to gain noticeable traction. And, as Benioff points out, this may be just the beginning as these models continue to expand and adapt to the marketplace. Finally, don't forget about the opportunities that widespread high-speed bandwidth and the availability of high-quality, low-cost offshore technical resources may yield in terms of making the ASP model that much more attractive in terms of the components of the Enterprise Optimization Framework for decision-making. Who's to say that some of the technology development and support roles can't be moved offshore over some period of time? This could lower the cost of these solutions even further, making them even more attractive in the marketplace.

In addition to those companies that began as ASPs from the ground up, many of the traditional software companies have tried to hop onto the bandwagon as well. Most of these efforts have been full of nothing but struggles. Conway mentions his own lack of profitability at PeopleSoft with this model.[69] Siebel shut down its original ASP spin-off (Sales.com)[70] but is now going to give it another try. Oracle has tried multiple versions of its ASP offering, fading in and out with various brand names, including Business On-Line, Oracle.com, Oracle Outsourcing, and, most recently, Oracle All-In-One. While Oracle has seen some growth in these offerings, none has yet won widespread acceptance in the marketplace. A major part of the problem has been the technical design and complexity of the products themselves. Stable and consistent releases are an absolute must before this model can become viable for traditional enterprise software vendors.

More importantly, ASPs are not selling software. They are selling a service. And service companies are very different from software companies. Despite what the software vendors will tell you, these are not companies that have made their reputations based on their service offerings. They write complex code that typically is differentiated based on functionality, integration, and price. Service is something that comes with your maintenance contract, but is rarely factored into decision-making around a purchase. It almost becomes a necessary evil around which you hope for the best when it comes time for the need. This ridiculous concept of having to apply software patches all the time and perform major upgrades (which can shut down a business if not done right) flies in the face of a service-oriented business model. This problem stems partly from where the software industry has evolved in terms of code complexity and its inability to maintain effective quality control. According to a study published by the National Institute of Standards and Technology:

> The complexity of the underlying software needed to support the U.S.'s computerized economy is increasing at an alarming rate....This increasing complexity along with a decreasing average market life expectancy for many software products has heightened concerns over software quality....Estimates of the economic costs of faulty software in the U.S. range in the tens of billions of dollars per year [estimated in this study between $22 billion and $59 billion, with the costs shared by software providers and their customers] and have been estimated to represent approximately just under 1 percent of the nation's gross domestic product.[71]

There is not only a hard dollar cost associated with these traditional methods of software development and deployment, but also an ongoing cost in terms of the frustration that the user community experiences related to these never-ending patch and upgrade projects. Because these solutions have become so complex, it is not uncommon for a patch that fixes an identified problem actually causes other problems. The testing cycles never seem to end. Try as it might, service has never been a core competence of the software industry, and its own complex technical model contributes to struggles in this area. Maybe the surviving ASPs, which have gained momentum with leadership around robust, simple, reliable, and standardized solutions, have found an answer to the mess in which we find ourselves related to the total cost of ownership and customer reliability for most of our traditional enterprise software offerings.

The other area where software companies have fallen flat in terms of customer service with their ASP offerings has been custom development and integration. Let me first state that I categorically support the approach of utilizing vanilla, out-of-the-box systems as much as humanly possible. That being said, the software companies hosting their own applications have made it very difficult for their clients to pursue *any* customizations. After all, their leverage is to provide support via their traditional support organizations, and that's hard to do when the software has been customized. But that's looking at things from what makes sense to the software companies. That's not the customer service perspective necessary to gain acceptance from actual customers.

The configurable components in the enterprise software packages have tended not to be robust enough to satisfy customer needs, even with the advances in technologies such as workflow engines. The result has been that more requirements for customization have tended to creep into these environments, but the traditional software companies that are trying to rent their solutions over the Internet are loath to allow any customizations whatsoever. Some of the new ASPs have designed robust configuration capabilities into their solutions, knowing how important this element is to their customers, especially when customization is not a practical alternative because of their technical architecture and business model. Customer service demands require the traditional enterprise software vendors to provide these configurable capabilities as well if they expect to expand their footprint in the ASP space.

This same conversation translates to the software companies' willingness to allow other competitors' products into their own data centers, and supporting integration with other packages. How will Oracle feel about having PeopleSoft or Siebel applications sitting on top of a Sybase database integrated with Oracle ERP on the back end in an Oracle-owned data center? This type of co-location of assets has been a stumbling block for the software companies moving into the overall managed services space. From a software standpoint, it doesn't make a lot of sense. The vendor's expertise is in its own software, and supporting a competitor has not been a very popular notion for these companies. But from a *service* perspective, these kind of robust offerings are essential to making managed services solutions work for customers. Life would be so much easier for those companies that grew their infrastructure on a single platform and are content to stay within those confines. And while there are some cases where this model applies, and there are definite merits to this approach, the reality is that most companies are not vanilla with their applications and most are not limited to just one or two application platforms. The complexity is a reality, and these ASP vendors are going to need to support that complexity, or their offerings will simply not be compelling for the vast majority of the marketplace.

Despite many of the significant challenges presented to the ASP providers, some organizations, such as salesforce.com and NetSuite, are beginning to overcome these obstacles, trying to grow into leadership roles while the established software vendors struggle to adapt to this new software-as-a-service model. Things that seemed insurmountable just a couple of years ago in terms of ASPs providing integration, flexible process solutions, and robust reporting engines are now beginning to become reality with at least some of the ASP solutions. These solutions will become even more attractive as they grow in depth and breadth, as long as they maintain the focus around simple, stable, highly configurable platforms, all at a low price point. And while enterprise vendors have struggled to adapt their solutions to the ASP model, this is not to say that further efforts along the lines identified in this section will not reap rewards for them down the road as well. These solutions already are differentiated based on functionality, integration, and vertical alignment. They need to improve on stability and flexibility, as well as settle on a competitive pricing structure, but those enterprise vendors that choose to pursue this business model may yet find the right balance where they can provide a viable offering. They need to offer the whole package. Some ASPs are growing into this complete package, while some enterprise vendors remain committed to adapting to this model. Those that get it right will have a compelling offering that will certainly play in the mid-market space, and may, over time, become viable in the large enterprise sector as well. Who wouldn't want a fully-functional, integrated suite of front and back office business applications that requires no internal infrastructure or support and maintains a low and predictable price point? That kind of solution has Enterprise Optimization written all over it.

Managed Services

At this point, let's take a moment to draw a distinction between what I refer to as application service providers (ASPs) and what I label managed services offerings. The main difference between the two is that ASPs are running software as a service whose foundation is code written and maintained by the company itself—the entire service operates under a single brand. With salesforce.com, for example, the company writes the code, hosts the solution, provides all the support, etc. Similar offerings from traditional software companies that have been mentioned (Sales.com from Siebel and Oracle.com from Oracle, for example) also fall into this definition, as the solution is all geared around code written by the same company. The broader concept in the technology outsourcing space is that of managed services. With these offerings, the service provider will host and support any number of your business applications, often including the complex integration that goes along with those kinds of environments. During the initial hype of outsourced technology in the 1990s, a number of companies started from scratch with a business model of hosting services and application support expertise across a variety of platforms, with the intent of taking over entire IT application departments. Some of these examples include Corio, Qwest CyberSolutions, and Exodus. While the results of these stand-alone, start-up efforts have proven to be rather dismal, we can still be the beneficiaries of the knowledge gained from each of their struggles.

One of the core challenges for the original pure play managed services providers was that they found that scaling the business was extremely challenging. From a technical perspective, these service providers were essentially replicating the data centers of their customers in their own technical environments, but there were very few economies of scale provided by the technical components of this kind of solution. Whenever a new customer came into the mix, a complete new set of hardware, software, networking, etc., needed to be procured, configured, and maintained. Yes, these companies could provide incremental savings to their customers, but there was still a significant infrastructure investment involved. Moreover, from a personnel standpoint, scaling the business from a human resource perspective was equally challenging. Once these service providers landed a big account, they often needed to add significant resources in a short period of time. This put the companies in a position to pay a premium for those resources, cutting the already low profit margins. Simply finding qualified resources was a challenge in that high-demand market. And while scaling up was hard, scaling down may have been even harder. As customers would go out of business or downsize, matching that scale was equally challenging for these managed services providers. This lack of market flexibility and reliance on expensive U.S.-based resources were fundamental to the financial difficulties that came crashing down on these companies. (Imagine how this might have played out differently if the resource pool consisted of high-quality, low-cost functional and technical resources staffed in India, or elsewhere around the world. Scaling and financial viability would not have been much of an issue at all. Those skills weren't available in the late 1990s, but they are definitely available today and are helping to resurrect the managed services marketplace.)

The other area in which many of these early entrants into the managed services business struggled was in forming and maintaining close relationships with their clients. When the implementations were completed and the application management and support responsibilities moved to these companies, there was often very little in the way of on-site transition. Companies that had been used to walking down the hallway for IT support now called an 800-number with the hope of getting a competent analyst to call them back. These service providers often failed to forecast the need for a burn-in period of on-site transition, to ease their customers into this new model. Yes, there would have been an expense associated with this effort, but it would have been an infinitely more personal approach, and would have gone a long way to establishing a working partnership with these clients, rather than the cold awakening of the 800-number.

These were some of the causes for early failures in the managed services space—failures both for the service providers and for their clients. As the struggles mounted, so did the diminishing reputations of these providers and the entire business model. But, as you would expect, we have learned from these early failures, and are now starting to see providers make dramatic improvements in these offerings, especially some of the new entrants in the space that have sufficient capital to invest in a world-class solution. Moreover, as mentioned earlier, the widespread availability of high-speed, low cost bandwidth, along with the emergence of high-quality, low-cost application management and development resources across the globe are changing the game in the outsourcing business. This phenomenon has heralded a new core offering for many of the top tier global consulting organizations.

These consulting firms represent an element of the technology sector that features customer service at its essential core. They may not write the code, but they understand the systems to the nth degree, and service is the lifeblood of their business. Virtually all of the large consulting organizations are moving aggressively into the managed services business, whereby they will assume responsibility for your IT infrastructure from design through implementation and then on to support. They will implement your solutions, build integration to other systems, host the hardware, arrange for the network infrastructure, and provide ongoing applications management support—basically everything except writing the application software itself. There are certainly advantages with these organizations in that they offer highly skilled practitioners who understand both business process and technology (including a growing pool of high-quality, low cost offshore technical resources), and for whom customer service is a high priority from the top of the org chart to the bottom. The concept here is to leverage those skills to provide a single-stop offering to enable improvements in Process Optimization and Information Optimization, and do so for a lower overall Total Cost.

There has been a mixed track record of results for a number of these consulting organizations. Among the challenges that many have faced is that, like their software counterparts, they don't own all the components of the solution (such as data centers, network connectivity, hardware, etc.) so their success is sometimes dependent on their ability to create strong partnering arrangements with other organizations in order to yield a seamless, single solution to their clients, but which tend to be rather complex on the back-end. The challenge for the consulting organization is that if the partner fails to live up to its commitments, it is the consulting organization that typically faces the direct consequences (a true "One Throat to Choke"). These partnerships are maturing, but will always require a true commitment to that partnership from both sides, as well as excellent program management across all of these service delivery organizations. Competing software companies will take every opportunity to make the case that they have an advantage over the consulting organizations in that they're the ones who write the code, so they're the best ones to fix the code when there are problems. In some cases, that is true, particularly when the underlying problem lies with the software itself. But that advantage typically ends when clients require support for multiple applications made by different vendors, or when other process-related factors come into play. The consulting organizations may not have access to modify source code, but they do tend to have much broader portfolios of skills compared to the software companies, spanning across most of the major application platforms. The complexity of your environment may become an important factor in determining the optimal kind of partner to engage for your outsourcing support.

Let's take a look at a couple of examples from the Big 5 (or, more accurately, former Big 5 consulting organizations). Accenture has seen a dramatic shift in its overall business model with its push toward the outsourcing business. The company's outsourcing business accounted for only 17 percent of its total revenue in 2001, but that percentage has increased steadily ever since (see Figure III-3). In fact, the total income from outsourcing has jumped more than 30 percent for each of the last three years, while total income for the rest of the company's business has actually gone down (year-over-year) over the last two years.[72] One interesting impact on this shift is the decrease in gross margins for the company. "The total gross margin for fiscal year 2003 was 36.5 percent of net revenues, compared with 40.4 percent of net revenues for fiscal year 2002. This change resulted from the shift in the company's mix of business toward outsourcing, which has lower gross margins, particularly during the first year of new contracts, and from continuing pricing pressures."[73] Demonstrating its commitment to this model, Accenture tripled the size of its resource base in India to around 4300 between 2001 and 2003, and plans to more than double that to 10,000 people in 2004.[74]

Figure III-3: Accenture's Evolving Services Mix

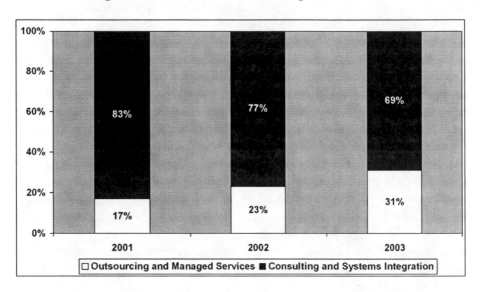

Date Source: Accenture, 2002 and 2003 Annual Reports

Another example is BearingPoint, which initially entered the offshore outsourcing market on a large scale by moving toward direct investment in the low cost opportunities available in China. This effort was formally launched with the opening of the company's 48,000-square-foot Global Development Center (GDC) in Shanghai in the spring of 2003. The company is currently the largest employer in the Shanghai PuDong Software Park, one of 11 software parks supported by the Chinese Government with tax and rent breaks for organizations entering the services export market.[75] By being an early mover to the China market, BearingPoint has an opportunity to undercut the cost structure of those companies that have invested heavily in India, but it will need to do so quickly in order to take advantage of this small window of opportunity. As with other new entrants into this market space, BearingPoint is looking to demonstrate to its potential clients that it can deliver on all cylinders with its offerings, leveraging its success in the systems integration business as the natural transition to maintenance and support offerings (see Figure III-4 for where BearingPoint is positioning itself with the emergence of Managed Services as part of its overall portfolio of offerings). The company has demonstrated a strong top-down commitment from management to making this happen, and the initial results have been very promising. The company has grown its Shanghai center from zero to 59 client engagements in a little more than a year. The GDC now employs more than

300 high-quality, low-cost resources, and continues to hire at a rate of 40-50 resources per month. This rapid growth has the company positioned to open its second China facility in Dalian in April 2004, where it expects to be able to take advantage of the multiple Asian language skills that are available in that region.[76]

Figure III-4: BearingPoint's Managed Services Offerings

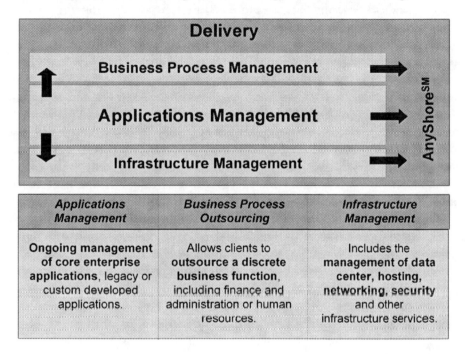

Applications Management	Business Process Outsourcing	Infrastructure Management
Ongoing management of core enterprise applications, legacy or custom developed applications.	Allows clients to **outsource a discrete business function**, including finance and administration or human resources.	Includes the **management of data center, hosting, networking, security** and other infrastructure services.

Source: BearingPoint, 2004

As mentioned earlier, the primary drawback in utilizing a resource base in China is that English language skills are neither as mature nor as pervasive as in other low-cost geographies, such as India, limiting some of the opportunities in the U.S. and European markets. BearingPoint has responded to this reality by enhancing its set of its so-called AnyShore[SM] services, by introducing a business arrangement with Covansys, a CMM Level 5 certified company based in Chennai, India. This relationship provides BearingPoint with up to 2000 resources for high-quality, low cost technical development, system analysis, application support, and BPO resources.[77] Where English becomes a broad and critical component to the client's needs, India will be the likely destination for the origination of the services. Where direct communication in English is not as needed, or when Asian languages actually represent the requirement for communication, then China will continue to be the destination of choice.

One other important point needs to be made with respect to the changing nature of the Big 5 and the increasing focus on offshore development and support. One can never forget the importance of the value-add that has typically differentiated the Big 5 from its competitors; that is, the leading offerings with respect to industry-specific business processes, strategic advice, program management, and overall project methodologies. Do not mistake the emphasis on outsourcing as a replacement for tried and true methodologies that focus on optimizing business processes, using technology as one of its solution components. The offshore managed services offerings most prevalent today remain technology-centric, and as such may not yet provide viable end-to-end solutions. They are maturing in this regard, but the maturation curve is wildly differentiated in the marketplace, and in general, is still early in its life cycle. Business processes and business benefits must come first, and must remain the focus throughout the life of any business initiative. You can't simply jump to the end of the equation with a technology slam using low-cost resources and expect dramatic improvements relative to Process and Information Optimization. This will end in disaster. Either the Process and Information Department of your company needs to provide this knowledge and perspective, or it needs to come from somewhere else (such as the Big 5). This is the compelling message that the Big 5 still holds in the consulting marketplace. These organizations will continue to prosper by offering the *combination* of U.S.-based industry and process experts coupled with their high-quality, low-cost brethren overseas to provide a comprehensive solution at a competitive price point. If that's not their vision, it should be—both for implementation projects and for managed services offerings.

The Big 5 firms need to realize that the opportunity to win large system implementation projects with fat margins staffed entirely by U.S.-based resources is a thing of the past. That being said, nor should the Big 5 send everything overseas at a time when India, China, etc., cannot provide the process and project leadership expected from those organizations. The market differentiation for the Big 5 should be the appropriate *combination* of these skill sets, leveraging their global assets in providing a cost-effective and high-value set of solutions. The costs and benefits of this combination of offerings need to be carefully weighed by the marketplace against the lower cost/potential lower overall quality for complete end-to-end solutions from the competition. *All* components of the Enterprise Optimization Framework should be utilized in the evaluation of which partner(s), and which tier of partner(s), makes the most sense for individual organizations.

One of the dangers of this push to outsourcing and overseas development is the expectation that you can just throw a project over the wall (or overseas, in this case) and expect it to come back 100 percent complete, with very little action required by the U.S.-based company resources. The result may be a system that is bug free and functions based on known specifications, but it will likely fall far short in meeting the overall objectives of the people who will end up using the system. The process-focused business community must remain involved throughout these implementation projects to ensure that company-specific Process and Information Optimization objectives remain at the core of any technology project. This is no different from those companies that have selected small boutique firms (technology shops) to handle their implementations in years past. Typically, they would "get what they paid for"—a working system that no one would willingly use because process and information requirements were simply ignored in order to get the technology up and running. This even gets us back to that nonsense about "on time, on budget," where the IT director can be proud of achieving this meaningless metric and producing a "technological success" that doesn't address the company's real needs. In other words, a failure. Nothing about utilizing the advantages provided by offshore development implies that any drop in attention to the business focus of an initiative is at all warranted. Eventually, the offshore offerings may include this skill set, but you should be leery about them having reached that state thus far. You must either provide this component yourself, through the PI Department, or still retain contacts with the Big 5 or other consulting organizations that focus on project management, proven methodologies, and business process expertise. If you scrimp in this area, your entire initiative may be very much at risk.

What has also been interesting related to the former Big 5 consulting organizations is the trend for them and the other global IT services firms—such as IBM, Electronic Data Systems (EDS), Computer Sciences Corporation (CSC), Hewlett-Packard (HP) and others—to be increasingly encroaching on each other's traditional territories. The Big 5 firms have moved beyond their traditional set of offerings to provide solutions in the outsourcing, infrastructure, and BPO spaces, while these other firms have equally moved toward robust offerings in systems integration and IT consulting. Everyone is looking for opportunities for growth in these difficult economic times, and they are all trying to cannibalize each other's businesses. U.S. and Indian firms are included in this aggressive approach. The Big 5 have basically disappeared either by splitting from their accounting and audit partners or by being sold to other entities. This change appears to be occurring at the same time that the distinctions between the Big 5 and the other global IT services firms is much less obvious. While circumstances for the Big 5 were rosy during the 1990s, struggles have set in as the economy has soured and large system integration projects have been put on hold. In order to remain competitive and viable, the Big 5 have been forced into the realization that they need to be able to develop predictable revenue streams, to insulate them from the ups and downs of the economy. The margins with outsourcing and managed services are nowhere near what these firms are used to, but revenue sustainability, along with consistent evidence of profitability, have been critical for these organizations, especially as most have moved from the partnership model to become publicly owned companies. A path toward consistency in earnings is represented by these outsource solution offerings, which often entail large, long-term, low-margin contracts.

As for the global IT firms, they have also seen opportunities outside their traditional space, and have begun to pursue those openings. They have tried to leverage their traditional skills and assets into expanding opportunities in the traditionally higher margin systems integration and consulting engagements. The skills in these areas are more specialized than those in the outsource offerings, so the barrier to entry here is slightly higher, but has certainly not been insurmountable. Acquisition is, of course, the easiest way to break down these barriers. For example, IBM's acquisition of PwC Consulting was intended to provide IBM with the complete end-to-end solution offerings. While this acquisition has improved the depth of offerings in the IBM portfolio, it has not stopped Hewlett-Packard from taking on the industry giant. In one week in alone in April 2003, HP came to agreement on three of its largest outsourcing deals to date— one with Proctor & Gamble ($3 billion over ten years),[78] one with the Bank of Ireland ($600 million over seven years),[79] and one with Ericcson (identified by analysts as being worth "billions of dollars").[80] Interestingly enough, HP beat IBM in all three of these deals.[81] These actions signal a clear move by HP to get in the game in a big way in the services and outsourcing spaces, which happens to be an area in which HP has already proved a high degree of excellence.

An *InformationWeek* study surveyed 700 business-technology professionals in November 2002, covering a variety of categories related to managed services offerings. HP finished first in the overall study, ahead of several of the organizations that have already been mentioned. (Survey results can be seen in Figure III-5.) [82]

Figure III-5: Analyzing the Outsourcers: Rankings from *InformationWeek* Research

	Overall	Range of services	Reliability	Cost and value	Technical skill	Industry knowledge	SLAs	Strategic advice	Trust	Innovation	Reputation
HEWLETT-PACKARD	1	7	1	2	2	3	1	6	2	3	3
SPRINT	2	3	2	1	1	1	2	7	4	2	6
ACCENTURE	3	5	3	8	3	2	7	1	1	1	5
CSC	4	6	5	3	6	5	2	3	3	5	4
AT&T	5	2	6	5	5	4	8	5	7	4	2
EDS	6	4	4	4	4	8	4	8	7	7	8
IBM	7	1	7	9	6	6	5	4	4	8	1
PRICEWATERHOUSECOOPERS	8	8	8	6	8	7	5	2	6	6	7
WORLDCOM	9	9	9	7	9	9	9	9	9	9	9

How They Rank

Data: *InformationWeek Research Analyzing The Outsourcers* study of 700 business — technology professionals, November 2002

While all of the categories explored in the *Information Week* survey are critical to the overall success of these offerings, the companies that can stand above the rest in terms of trust, reliability, and overall relationships are the best positioned to win in this market space. Competence is required in the core deliverable areas if the company is to be considered a viable player in this space, but it is these less tangible areas where true differentiation begins to emerge. The very essence of these long-term outsourcing relationships is such that you are putting your company at risk with the intent that a mutually beneficial relationship will result in a win-win for both organizations. The key differentiator here will be quality of customer service, and the ability to move from just being another vendor to becoming a trusted business partner. Partnership, in the end, is the human element that binds organizations that have committed to providing each other products and services for mutual benefit. Before we extend this outsourcing concept beyond IT and into end-to-end business processes, let's take a look at one example of the human element of outsourcing.

The Face of Outsourcing: India

Anant Soni has come full circle in the ever-expanding world of global IT services, and he provides an example of the kinds of opportunities that have been created in the last decade for the best and brightest in the world's second most populous nation. After graduating from AG College in Pune, India, in 1993 with a bachelor's degree in computer science, Anant gained his initial professional experience supporting the relatively new set of business applications from Oracle Corporation. This work brought him to Singapore, which quickly opened his eyes to the possibilities for work in the United States, where his opportunities expanded significantly.

A referral from a friend brought Anant in touch with Intelligroup, a company based in New Jersey, which primarily consisted of transplanted Indians who had developed skills in Oracle Applications and other information systems. The company took care of the paperwork, including sponsoring him for an H1B visa, and started him on a two-year journey that took him to projects in New York, Southern California, and Wichita, KS. "I was 24 years old and wanted to experience world cultures, to see societies that were different from what I had grown up with in India," Anant told me. "Plus, I wanted to make money, which I could do in the U.S., not only with salary, but also the attractive exchange rate against the rupee." Based on his individual skills, opportunities within the company, and the booming market for Oracle Applications experts, within four months he had a near six-figure (USD) salary, light years away from anything he would have had a chance to make in his home country.

After two years with Intelligroup, Anant joined KPMG Consulting (now BearingPoint), entering as a Senior Consultant in the Oracle Applications team, followed by a quick promotion to Manager based on his individual and team success. According to Anant, "The best opportunities I had in the U.S. were with KPMG Consulting. I had wanted to get into the Big Leagues of consulting, and I got that with great assignments in my time with KPMG. I was able to experience challenging work, both functionally and technically, and was allowed to grow from a business perspective, working hand-in-hand with other consultants and with business leaders from top companies from around the United States. I couldn't have asked for more."

After nearly five years with KPMG Consulting/BearingPoint, Anant decided the time was right to make a change. He had never intended to stay in the U.S. forever, and he felt that he had accomplished most of what he had sought to do when he first came to the United States. He had gained tremendous professional experience, had provided value-added services to his clients, had seen much of the U.S., and had saved the kind of money that when he returned to India he would no longer need to worry about his savings for the future. That nest egg was already in the bank. Plus, returning to India at a time when the Indian-based offshore IT services market was booming with a resume that included seven years in the U.S. (including five with a Big 5 firm), made Anant a very hot property back home.

Eventually, Anant settled on Zensar, a company with which he was familiar based on his contacts in the U.S., and was, "big enough to play with the big boys, but small enough that I could go into a great position right away. If I had joined one of the larger firms, they would have already had a number of people with my background and experience, but here at Zensar, my experience was in the minority, so I could take on a leadership position right away." That leadership position is the head of the company's CRM practice, specializing in the offshore delivery of Oracle Applications CRM projects for clients in the U.S. Zensar offers solutions which combine on-site and offshore resources, as well as pure offshore services, and Anant's hands-on implementation experience with U.S. clients has been incredibly valuable in gaining the confidence of U.S. clients to entrust their projects with the company.

"The Indian industry has changed dramatically in the last eight years, since I first left the country," Anant told me. "The local economy now offers salaries which provide tremendous purchasing power here in India, so the financial incentive is not as strong to go abroad as it used to be. My experience in the U.S. was invaluable in so many ways, but it's also good to be home, and I now see a lot of my colleagues returning from the U.S. as well, bringing their experiences back home where they can find great leadership opportunities right here in India."

Anant Soni has seen the global IT services business from just about every angle over the last ten years. He has grown his skills from technical support, to functional and process leadership, and now to a management position back home in India. He has done well financially, able to afford a very comfortable lifestyle both abroad and at home, where he now lives in a very nice apartment and has a chauffer to drive him around during the day. This is in addition to the long-term financial security he's established for his family based on the opportunities he's pursued and the work he has performed. Plus he has seen the world, which was one of his other important goals for the decade of his '20s.

But this journey has not just been about Anant Soni. His U.S. clients benefited for years from his exceptional skills and personal commitment; his colleagues benefited from having him as a trusted teammate who would consistently deliver in the clutch during very challenging engagements; and his industry is benefiting as he brings back skills and experiences to his colleagues in India that will help provide the necessary foundation for long-term success in the global IT services business. As people such as Anant bridge the U.S. and Indian business and cultural environments, this industry will continue to fill in some of the gaps that exist today. That component of the industry's maturity will be critical to enable the further viability of the on-site/offshore outsourcing services model.

Business Process Outsourcing

Just as IT operations are typically not core to a company's business, neither are many other processes. One of the most common processes companies outsource is payroll. This function tends to be very complex on a global scale, but there are a handful of well-respected outsource providers (including ADP, Ceridian, and Paychex) that have the expertise to handle the details of this set of activities. All that is really required is a simple data flow going from the company to the service provider and back. The service provider takes care of the rest, including individual transactions as well as management of the complex set of content and business logic. Why do it yourself if someone else can do it for you at higher quality and lower cost? Just as with IT outsourcing, the same compelling case exists in many areas of BPO, with offshore solutions representing increasingly more attractive alternatives, and the marketplace is responding. BPO is growing faster than any other segment offered by IT service providers. The global market size for BPO was about $110 billion in 2002, with Gartner and Aberdeen Group predicting 10%–13% annual growth through 2005.[83] All this at a time when many other service areas are flat or even seeing negative growth. Further, BPO is expanding in form as well, as offshore providers have entered the mix in terms of providing an intriguing alternative to the traditional U.S. service providers.

Payroll outsourcing may be one of the most common forms of BPO, but it really is just one component of an ever-growing landscape of outsource offerings. Just about any of the processes and sub-processes identified in Figure I-3 (Sample Business Processes) in Section I are fare game for BPO. The hottest growth areas are in call center/customer interaction services, finance and administration, and procurement, along with a myriad of industry specific solutions. Some business processes/components are absolutely core to the business of some companies, and it would not make sense to outsource them. However, for many companies, outsourcing will make perfect sense across the entire spectrum of enterprise processes. Many of these functions are simply staffed internally because up until now there has not been a quality cost-effective alternative. That limiting factor is rapidly changing.

Just as with any initiative, with BPO a company is looking to lower its total cost of ownership with respect to these functions/services, while also attempting to enhance capabilities with respect to the management of processes and information. As part of that effort, the impact on IT can also be significant. Companies that outsource payroll don't require a payroll system. Companies that outsource billing and collections don't need a billing and collections system. Yes, you still need to be able to send data to your service providers, and likely receive some kind of automated journal entry on the back end, but, depending on the process, this will likely require significantly less support from the IT Department than if these processes were supported by in-house systems.

A broader trend in BPO is for companies to develop shared service centers for many of their global operations, and then outsource those service centers to multi-process outsource providers. According to Lehman Brothers, the next phase in the BPO market is the sale of large shared service centers (centralized back-office operations for HR, Finance and Accounting, or Procurement functions) by Fortune 100 companies to external service firms. Most very large U.S. firms have already centralized G&A functions, but the next step will be to sell them to an outsourcing firm to drive further cost savings and to effectively commercialize these assets via contract awards from third parties.[84] This could be entire Finance organizations, including Accounts Payable, Accounts Receivable, Fixed Assets, and even the General Ledger, along with HR and Purchasing. Many companies are rapidly consolidating operations in some of these non-core areas as a means of cost reduction, especially global companies that have been duplicating many of these efforts in multiple places around the globe. Consolidation of these functions contributes to lower the total cost of ownership of these processes, and outsourcing would just be an extension to lower these costs even further.

The movement of IT services from U.S.-based resources to offshore providers has already been highlighted, with India leading the way to date. While not as mature as an offering, India is trying to take market share from U.S.-based companies with offshore BPO services as well. BPO services in India started with call centers and CRM services, but now range from Accounting to HR functions such as payroll management and transaction processing. India's BPO market grew to $825 million and 35,000 people in 2001, and then to approximately $1.4 billion in 2002.[85] Dramatic cost savings is the lead reason the growth trend is beginning to unfold, much as it did in the early days of the IT offshore outsourcing phenomenon. I have seen the labor savings for offshore BPO services to be as much as 75% in some cases when compared with U.S.-based resources. So even when you factor in the 25%–35% additional overhead costs for management and infrastructure necessary to complete a successful offshore BPO model, you're still looking at net savings of *40 to 50 percent*! In other words, the Total Cost Optimization is extremely compelling. However, Process and Information Optimization *must* remain critical components of any outsourcing decision. If the company suffers too much in either of these areas as a result of BPO, then the overall impact on Enterprise Optimization may be negative. In other words, the *cheapest* solution may not represent the *optimal* solution.

Driving down costs, allowing companies to focus on their core competencies, and improving processes and service levels are all factors in this growing trend toward BPO—just as they are in outsourcing strictly technology-based services. Companies need to ask themselves: What is core to our business? What sets us apart? Typically, this list may include engineering (R&D), product marketing, general management, and possibly sales, but maybe not a lot more. And even some of these may be prime for an outsourcing strategy. Many companies have outsourced core components of their Sales organization for years, using a variety of distributors, resellers, and other channel partners to sell product to the end user community. As with any BPO strategy, picking the right (or wrong!) channel partner(s) in terms of Sales execution can have a big impact on your degree of success with this approach. Moreover, one of the growing trends in BPO is in the area of product development. India, China, and a number of other countries are bursting with highly skilled engineers (hardware, software, electrical, and mechanical engineers), many with advanced degrees. In each of these disciplines there may be an extensive amount of coding, prototyping, and testing, all of which are well-suited to taking advantage of these highly skilled, low-cost offshore resources. Many companies have been reluctant to turn over their intellectual property to external partners, especially during the highly secretive stages of product development, so once again partner selection needs to focus not only on skill and cost but also on trust. Here are a couple of guiding principles to consider in the context of BPO:

- If a process is not core to a business or to its differentiation in the market-place, it should at least be considered for outsourcing, and those consider-ations should take into account all three components of the Enterprise Optimization Framework.
- From the service provider's side, those that can offer superior customer service, process expertise, vertical industry knowledge, proven BPO methodology, operational excellence, financial stability (important these days!), and low cost per transactions are the ones that have the opportunity to take big gains in market share in this space.

One thing to keep in mind is that the ability to succeed in BPO is highly con-tingent on the current state of your company, regardless of the capabilities of the provider. It is completely unrealistic to assume that you will be able to hand over a mess to an external provider and expect to receive immediate process and infor-mation improvements. It *is* possible to immediately receive significant *labor* cost reductions by taking this approach, but a mess is a mess, and you need to antici-pate extensive time, cost, and effort to unwind that mess before an optimal solu-tion will be realized. This is yet another example on the importance of an internal Process and Information Department to initiate internal optimization projects, to standardize and improve internal operations, thereby making initiatives such as BPO that much more viable. If you're hurting financially, you may decide that cost reduction is the single most important objective of your organization, and you may want to pursue immediate BPO for the labor savings, but you shouldn't stop there. You need to continue the commitment for Process and Information Optimization, and your internal team of process-focused professionals will need to be intimately involved in this effort. Moreover, this is a reminder that any ini-tiative that is expected to yield transformational benefits must be pursued in the context of organizational alignment around all five areas of Strategy, Controls, People, Process, and Technology. In the case of BPO, this alignment needs to per-meate the company, as well as extend into the overall makeup of the outsource service provider. That's the kind of relationship that will truly drive the desired benefits. From the standpoint of the service provider, this goes far beyond low-cost transaction processing, and includes process and vertical industry expertise, along with program and change management, to be able to effectively drive con-tinuous improvement. You don't get these improvements just by sending these processes over the wall to a third party. That takes work, and it takes ongoing col-laboration between your PI Department and your external solution provider.

So who are the dominant players in the BPO space? While IT outsourcing is beginning to establish a reasonably well defined landscape for leaders and follow-ers, BPO is much more wide open. According to a Gartner study from August

2003, ADP, the payroll processing company, leads the way with a 7.7% market share among global process management vendors. First Data, which processes transactions such as credit cards and wire transfers, is next with a 4.9% market share. After that, there's no one with more than 3%. (EDS, ACS, and Convergys Corp. are next with 2.9%, 2.8%, and 2.5% market share, respectively.)[86] One reason is the overall breadth of service offerings in this space, and the lack of a one-stop shop focus for any of the leading providers. Nevertheless, this highlights ample opportunity to gain market share. It also begs the question to what degree service providers can combine BPO offerings with IT outsource offerings to provide broader packages for their clients. Properly executed, synergies and leverage in the marketplace could be significant. But remember, BPO has not matured to the commodity status of core technology IT support, so buyers need to be careful of vendors which equate the two in their marketing presentations. Leverage may exist for IT outsourcers venturing into BPO, but they are not the same, with different skill sets required up and down the value chain.

While cost has been identified as a key driver for companies looking to outsource business processes, it is clearly not the only factor that needs to be considered in such decisions. Companies need to be looking for partners that can optimize their processes based on the industry and functional experience of that partner. The key is to find the experts in BPO in a given area, and leverage that expertise to ensure that you're performing at the optimal level. Ideally, your BPO partner will be able to leverage its own industry and process knowledge to *improve* your capabilities and overall effectiveness, expanding the benefit beyond Total Cost Optimization and into the areas of Process and/or Information Optimization. A prerequisite step to this analysis, of course, is to understand what your capabilities are prior to making the jump to outsourcing. According to Stan Lepeak, a vice-president at the Stamford, CT-based consulting firm Meta Group, "Many companies fail to benchmark process performance. [But] if you don't have current process performance metrics, how do you know outsourcing will improve upon what you already do?"[87] Exactly my point! You can't just play follow the leader and leap at BPO without an understanding of the pros, cons, and expected return, and for that we need to rely on the PI Department and the Enterprise Optimization Framework to provide this benchmark and ongoing metric-based analysis.

As mentioned, the leaders in this space are still not well defined, so due diligence is essential in the selection process. Picking the right partner again becomes the critical step in this decision-making process and is a central responsibility of the PI Department, which must decide whether or not you're prepared to send your transaction processing or call center to an offshore facility. The challenge is making an apples-to-apples comparison among the plethora of contending solution providers since there are few standards for comparison in the marketplace today, and because a lot of these vendors are providing specific offshore BPO services for the very first time. This is why existing client references often become the most important factor in gaining the trust that the provider will be able to deliver as promised. Companies must remain aware that many end-to-end BPO services are not a commodity. These solutions are certainly viable, but if you don't make a wise partner selection, process degradation can occur, and the resulting decrease in capabilities can more than offset the initial cost savings. Put another way, proper partner selection in the area of off-shore outsourcing can mean the difference between optimizing the enterprise and killing it.

From what I have seen, the Indian firms are staffing extremely well trained, highly educated individuals for these transaction processing roles. I have no hesi-tation tapping into this resource pool for high-quality, low-cost transaction pro-cessing services. Indeed, an IBM survey conducted in October 2002 found that *68 percent* of companies that had gone offshore for some element of BPO had achieved service quality improvement (along with the tremendous cost savings). That same survey reported a *94 percent* level of satisfaction for companies that had pursued offshore BPO.[88] You don't get survey results like that just based on cost savings. Clearly many of these offshore solution providers know what they're doing, and have actually been improving levels of process performance for their customers as well as dramatically decreasing their total cost of operation. But, as with IT outsourcing, companies need to be careful about which roles are out-sourced to which partners.

Even though BPO continues to grow, it is starting from a very small base, and many U.S. executives remain skeptical, especially with the offshore component of these solutions. IT communities in the U.S. have been working with highly skilled Indian resources for years, but sending transaction processing offshore is a relatively new concept for functional business owners in the U.S., and they are proceeding cautiously. At the core, this caution is based on the fact that offshore BPO is still a relatively new set of offerings, it is unfamiliar territory to these executives, and it is something that may sound just a little too good to be true. In addition, while the U.S. decision-makers may have a general appreciation for some of the skills of the offshore teams, they remain unconvinced of offshore capabilities to provide the *total* solution. This brings us back to the same issue we saw with technology outsourcing, where the further away you got from the core technology and the higher up the chain in process and project management skills, the harder it was for the Indian firms to gain the confidence of the American consumer. At this early stage in the BPO life cycle, companies must be aware that there may not be a single partner capable of providing the optimal outsource solution for your particular set of business processes. As we saw with IT offshore outsourcing, Indian firms are investing heavily and growing their capabilities in the BPO space while the U.S. service providers are trying to build their own organizations in low-cost offshore geographies.

The critical question remains: Is anyone ready to "do it all" on your behalf? The analysts, at this point, remain skeptical. Forrester came out with the following conclusions in its Research Note, *BPO's Fragmented Future*: "The promise of business process outsourcing as a one-stop, lower-cost answer for complex core business processes is a myth....No single vendor is equipped to handle the range of end-to-end complexities that accompany the largest BPO requests, including human resources, finance, and administration."[89] Process leadership and program management leadership are essential to the success of any BPO initiative. The offshore teams are perfectly well-suited for the high-quality, low-cost transaction portion of ongoing BPO services, but are they the right answer for the overall process definition and transition management components of the total solution? While the U.S. providers have the expertise in this latter area, are they truly able to quickly scale to provide the requisite skills for ongoing transaction processing with a talent pool based in one of the low-cost geographies? This is a quickly maturing marketplace, but that doesn't mean that single firms have yet mastered all the requisite skills and price points to be able to compete on all facets of a BPO solution. As I suggested with IT outsourcing, the combination of the best of each offering is what the marketplace desires, and if you can't find all of those capabilities under one roof at this time, then you need to look at different types of offerings in which to receive the optimal level of services. That objective brings us to the situation depicted in the following case study.

Case Study: "The Best of Both Worlds" for Business Process Outsourcing [90]

One of my noteworthy experiences in a BPO opportunity involved a case where I originally opted not to pursue the business but ended up winning the selection process based on a solution I called "The Best of Both Worlds." Here's what happened. A global manufacturing company had already consolidated its North American Finance organization into a centralized shared services unit, spanning the functions of Accounts Receivable (Billing and Collections), Accounts Payable, and General Ledger/Intercompany Accounting. While this standardization and centralization effort helped improve the organization with respect to Process, Information, and Total Cost Optimization, financial pressures throughout the company demanded further efforts to lower operating costs. This company decided to look into a BPO solution, to see if it could achieve two fundamental goals:

- Reduce labor costs for the Finance shared services organization by 40 percent, and
- At a minimum, maintain internal service level agreements that had already been established with the rest of the business.

BearingPoint was one of six vendors that received the RFP for this opportunity, three of which were based in the U.S. and three of which were based in India. Despite our deep interest in this opportunity, I quickly decided not to bid. It was clear that we could not satisfy *both* of the fundamental goals identified in the RFP. In fact, I was skeptical that *any* of the companies responding to the RFP would be able to satisfy both requirements. It turns out I was not alone with my skepticism.

Early in the selection process I received a call from Raghu Kidambi, the VP in charge of the pursuit from one of the Indian firms, HCL Technologies (HCLT). HCLT is one of India's leading offshore services providers, with nearly 9,000 employees driving annual revenue of $750 million. The company operates 16 state-of-the-art development centers in India, each of which has been assessed at CMM level 4 or 5 for software development. Its client list includes the likes of Cisco, Deutsche Bank, American General, KLA Tencor, Sony, NCR, Johnson & Johnson, General Motors, Hewlett-Packard, Hitachi, Toshiba, and NEC.[91] The company has four main solution areas, which are available across numerous industry verticals (see Figure III-6).

Figure III-6: Solution Set for HCL Technologies

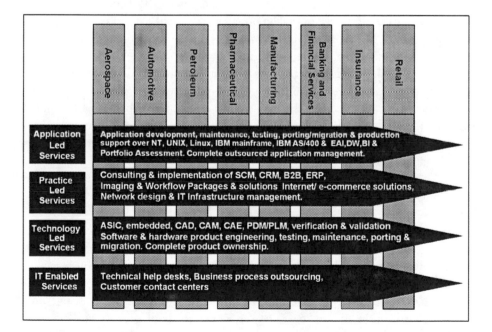

Source: HCL Technologies, July 2003

As with many Indian firms, you've got the core technology solutions leading the mix, but the company has been expanding rapidly in the Help Desk, Contact Center, and overall BPO service areas since 2001. The BPO services incorporate extensive offerings in the following four areas:

- Finance
- Order Management
- Procurement
- Human Resources[92]

Impressively, the company has gone from a scratch start in 2001 to 24 BPO clients in about 20 months, delivering 45 discrete processes. Some of the company's BPO clients include Deutsche Bank, British Telecom, Federated Stores, Dunn & Bradstreet, and SBC Communications. This is still a small and growing business, but the ramp up has been fast compared to the rest of the marketplace, and the client feedback has been consistently very positive.[93]

The HCLT VP who was calling happened to be someone who had worked for me previously at BearingPoint. This was just as important to me as were the qualifications and references from the existing client base. Just as BPO clients need to pick their service providers wisely, so do the providers themselves when choosing a partnership approach. Solutions are only as strong as the weakest link, and mutual trust and respect are essential in having any chance at success in these kinds of long-term, complex relationships. Kidambi told me that he was concerned that the client was not going to go for a pure Indian solution, given that some of the client executives who would be making the final decision had no experience with an offshore model. I told him that I had already decided not to bid because I couldn't meet the client's financial objectives with the pure U.S.-based solution that I could offer. Two things became immediately obvious. Number one, our U.S. and India-based competitors had to be struggling with the same problems, and number two, the ultimate answer for us *and* the client would be a joint solution from BearingPoint and HCLT. That realization spawned the effort to create our joint "Best of Both Worlds" proposal.

We realized that the client was going to need a comfort level with its partner, so BearingPoint took the lead in the proposal, as we had a long history of success and established trust in the account. Overall credibility was going to be crucial, as this operating model was foreign to many of these executives. Having an established relationship certainly gave us a leg up on the competition. BearingPoint's specific contribution to the solution was in the form of process and program management, which was embodied in extremely strong resources who had extensive finance and systems backgrounds and who had spent significant time working on a variety of projects in the account. We then coupled this leadership component, which would be staffed full-time at the client site, with a team of well-educated, highly-trained offshore resources, all of whom had finance backgrounds and had gone through training in each of the following areas: corporate induction, customer skills (including voice neutralization), and behavioral training (including leadership skills and stress management).

Our partnership gave us the ability to compete across all the components in play (including cost, quality, and program leadership) in a way that our "single world" competitors could not. We were confident that our approach would provide the comfort, trust, and process and program management skills that were viewed as stronger in the U.S.-based providers, as well as the high-quality, low-cost component that was the strength of the India-based providers. If we had a roadblock to overcome, it was our ability to demonstrate that we could work as a single unit ("one throat to choke"), which we felt would be very manageable in that we had worked well together in the past, and we were confident that we could keep the dual nature of our solution transparent to the client. When we pitched the solution, we were completely up front with the partnership model we were proposing, highlighting the fact that the client would be getting the best that both worlds had to offer, yet BearingPoint would provide a solution under one brand, with one organization held accountable for ultimate delivery.

After all the vendors made their initial pitches, the results were as we anticipated. From a cost standpoint, the highest bid was nearly 250% greater than the lowest bid—an unbelievable disparity. One of the U.S. solutions, in fact, would have been more costly to the client than if it continued to run the operation in-house! That company was immediately eliminated from the competition, as were the two pure-play Indian solutions. While the Indian companies offered the best proposition from a cost standpoint, the client was simply not convinced that it would receive the level of service it required (goal number two from the original RFP). Those companies *may* have been able to deliver at that level, but the important lesson was that this U.S. company wasn't convinced, and in this case perception defined reality. Again, U.S. business professionals haven't had a lot of exposure to the offshore model, and this is one of many cases where they were simply uncomfortable with making the leap of faith that the pure-play offshore organizations could meet their expectations.

Two of us were now left in the bidding process: one of the U.S. firms and the joint bid from BearingPoint and HCLT. The client's senior management was clearly very *comfortable* with the single U.S. provider, and gave it every opportunity to win the business. The problem was that the competitor's bid was about 75 percent more than our bid, and not close to the company's financial goal. Three times this company was coached into cutting the cost of its U.S.-based solution, but without an offshore option, it simply couldn't get to an acceptable price to make the offering make sense. This is exactly where I would have been if I had bid this effort on my own—with a quality solution but non-competitive on price.

The client was telling us exactly what it needed. It needed to be able to cut costs dramatically (40 percent in this case) while maintaining existing service levels (at a minimum), and to do so with a partner with whom it had a trusting relationship. In the end, we were the only bid that met the financial target and inspired confidence in the quality of the solution. As such, we were selected. Without the trust associated with BearingPoint's relationships in the account, the specific individuals we included in the key leadership roles in the solution, and our track record for high-quality process and program management, our bid would not have been accepted. Just as important, without the availability of high-quality, low-cost resources from HCLT and a strong reputation for BPO services within its client base, our bid would not have been accepted. And none of the individual bidders were able to offer all of these components under a single branded solution. The client wanted "The Best of Both Worlds," and it took our partnership approach to provide it.

At some point in the not too distant future, there will be companies that will be able to provide all of these services under a single brand. That's the goal of both the U.S. and offshore firms—to expand their solution sets to capture the best of each other's offerings to complement what they already have. We're just not there yet, and you must be cautious about claims to the contrary. Don't mistake success in IT outsourcing as a comparable capability with BPO, and don't mistake success in U.S.-based BPO for a comparable capability with offshore BPO. The differences in both of these cases are vast, and your PI Department must be discerning in its analysis. Whoever gets to this point first will certainly have a tremendous advantage, both for itself and for its clients. In the meantime, look for partners you can trust to put together the complete package for what you're looking for, and to operate that partnership as a seamlessly integrated single entity. That's the best bet ("The Best of Both Worlds") in the short run while the marketplace figures out how to provide these complete end-to-end services in an optimal fashion under a single brand.

The Face of Outsourcing: China

At the age of 30, Dennis Liu has been in the offshore services business for nearly three years, working as an operations manager on the finance team for General Electric at the company's facility in Dalian, China. Dennis received his Bachelor's degree in Industrial Administration from Jiaotong University in 1997, then went into industry for a year before returning to school to complete his Master's in Economics at the Dalian University of Technology in 2000. In 2004, Dennis left GE for broader challenges in the BPO marketplace, joining BearingPoint at its new facility in Dalian.

Dennis is extremely excited about the opportunities presented to his colleagues in China in providing high quality services to companies around the globe. While companies may be looking primarily for labor arbitrage in these deals, the focus is much broader than that for people like Dennis. "BPO is a new field for China," Dennis told me during our meeting in Shanghai. "This is not just about cost, but service improvement as well. We must solve problems, and keep going with continuous improvement. I believe that improved operations will be more important to our customers than just labor cost reduction in the long-run, as we continue to add value to those operations."

Getting into the BPO field at this stage in its development in China presents tremendous opportunity for people like Dennis, who is already certified as a Six Sigma Green Belt and is well on his way in the extensive requirements needed to achieve Black Belt status. "BPO can be the most important part of my life. It gives me the opportunity to improve my capabilities and grow. I have the opportunity to develop myself into an expert in this field, for a variety of business processes. People in Dalian have tremendous energy right now to develop this field for their career path.

"People choose their career based on the opportunities for development, salary is second. We have that opportunity now in BPO in China. This is not a short-term activity for us; it is a long-term career. Some people may find these jobs boring, but not to us. We're developing new skills with opportunities to grow. Plus, we have the chance to provide services to some of the greatest companies in the world. That's very challenging and exciting to us."

Dennis told me that fundamental changes in China are opening the doors to opportunities such as outsourcing. "When the Chinese government decides to grow in a field, it shows strong support, and it's doing that today for the services field." Moreover, cultural changes continue to take place. "Change is occurring socially, and in people's minds. People can take bigger risks today, and move into new areas….Even my parents have surprised me by their excitement about my new opportunities. My parents' generation usually avoids risks, but my father has surprised me with his support and excitement for this new career path."

China is indeed changing. People like Dennis are putting a face to that change, with their pride and enthusiasm about growing their own careers while providing high quality services to companies around the globe.

At this point it's still too early to tell which company or group of companies will be able to establish dominance in the outsourcing arena, in terms of both technology outsourcing and business process outsourcing. Given the evolving state of affairs, any predictions made today may be out of date in just a matter of months. However, there are patterns that indicate the possibility for some organizations of building a comprehensive set of offerings that would provide distinct advantages over the rest of the field.

The ideal scenario for a company that decides to outsource its processes and technology is to find a partner on which it can rely for a complete solution offering. Just as system and instance consolidation are integral components of the approach to Enterprise Optimization, so is the ideal of consolidation of outsource suppliers whenever it is practical. When it's not practical, as often may be the case with BPO, make sure you understand how your optimal set of partners will be able to deliver the complete solution in a seamless, unified manner.

A complete solution offering for outsourcing is defined as including the following components:

- Software: Applications
- Software: Database
- Software: Tools
- Consulting Services: Project/Program management
- Consulting Services: Business process expertise (including advice, management, and execution of the business processes)
- Consulting Services: Systems integration (functional and technical)
- Consulting Services: Technical development
- Operations: Data center
- Operations: Help desk
- Operations: Network services
- Operations: Hardware
- Operations: Functional support/application management
- Operations: Technical support

That's the "stack" of offerings that companies typically need in a complete outsource partnership. There are certainly advantages if these services can be procured from a single, trusted partner, specifically related to cost, management, and accountability. While there isn't anyone in the marketplace who can claim complete capabilities in each and every one of those solution areas, there are some models that offer intriguing approaches that merit attention. Some of these organizations, such as salesforce.com, Accenture, BearingPoint, and HCL Technologies, have already been highlighted earlier in this section in this regard. **Appendix D** provides profiles, analysis, and case studies of some of the other vendors that have penetrated this market space with different, but compelling, offerings. The highlighted vendors represent different approaches to end-to-end outsource solutions, including a couple of the leading U.S. multinational organizations, as well as some of the well-established India-based firms. But even with these organizations featured in the profiles, as well as any other organization that ventures into this space, it is not sufficient merely to be strong in the areas identified in the "stack." Competence and depth of offering is important, as is total cost, but the success of these offerings is increasingly dependent on the *relationship* between the service provider and the customer. This two-way relationship requires a particular kind of commitment in order to achieve optimal results. This relationship is what I call the Essence of Partnership.

The Essence of Partnership

Around my company we often talk about avoiding at all costs the possibility of getting stuck in a place we call "Vendorville." Vendorville is where no service provider wants to reside, because there you will simply be viewed as a tactical implementer who will likely go away once the specific project is done. Service providers looking for long-term partnerships with recurring opportunities for projects need to escape Vendorville and move to the exalted status of "Partner." Having been in the service provider business for a number of years, I can state unequivocally that there is a world of difference between being perceived as stuck in Vendorville and having made it to Partner. And the benefit goes both ways. Just as vendors are limited in the depth to which they can penetrate an account for long-term opportunities, if the client doesn't trust the service provider enough to let it out of Vendorville then the service provider will never be able to reach its full potential in providing the highest quality of services.

This all comes down to trust. An *InformationWeek* research report of 700 business-technology professionals identified *reliability* and *trust* as the top two criteria in what mattered most when selecting an outsourcing vendor.[94] For the relationship to work, service providers need to earn the trust of their clients. It's fundamentally as simple as that. But it's also one of the hardest things to achieve. There is an innate lack of trust built into the client—service provider relationship. The client believes the service provider is just in it for the money, and will soak the client for his last dime, if possible. After all, the common perception is that the bottom line in the service provider business is that for individuals to get ahead, they need to sign the big deals over and over again (and to a great degree, that perception is true). So the natural tendency is to mistrust the service provider, because his motivation for selling you services may be misplaced given his own metrics of success. Similarly, the service providers are naturally wary of their clients. All too often service providers are "used and abused" in a body shop approach where consultants are worked to death with no real appreciation for their time, effort, or accomplishments. "You guys make the big bucks, so stop your complaining," is a common sentiment in client environments. It may not be stated that openly, but consultants often get the distinct feeling that that's how they are perceived by the client—not exactly a sentiment that would foster a trusting relationship.

The fact of the matter is that for *either* side to be successful in any endeavor, *both* sides need to be successful, and that can't happen unless both sides are mutually aligned toward a common cause and are working collaboratively to achieve that end. In the environment described throughout this section, where a significant portion of project work is outsourced to one or more partners, the only way to be successful is to adopt this concept of mutual trust and collaboration between companies and their service providers. If companies treat their service providers as pieces of meat, this whole outsource model will not work. The same goes for service providers who see each client solely as the gravy train to the top. That mindset will result in disaster in an outsourcing relationship as well. More than anything it's a mindset that needs changing, and it won't happen by itself. CPIOs and their leadership teams need to bring the concept of partnership to the table with all constituents who interact with these outsource service providers. It needs to become part of the culture that these folks are "part of the team." Similarly, the service providers need to get out of the mode of always trying to make the next deal. Nothing puts off clients more than "aggressive partners." In fact, those two words are simply incompatible. These providers need to stop forcing what I refer to as "unnatural events" in the business development cycle. Partners work together on long-term planning and put programs in place to address the needs of the organization. In the world of true partners, those are "natural events" that occur without pressure and under the common understanding that working together on a long-term basis is mutually beneficial, and therefore easy to pursue. Unnatural events are when the service provider is constantly pushing its latest and greatest offering, regardless of whether the customer really needs it or not. That's the act of a vendor who is probably not long for the account. Service providers need to demonstrate in their words and their actions that they have the best interest of the client at heart. And that's not just for the executives making the deals, but all the way down to the consultants on the floor working hand-in-hand with the client.

In my practice I often hold sessions with my consulting teams to emphasize the importance of this very point. And I do so especially at those difficult phases of a project when everyone may be struggling and people are a bit on edge. These aren't just "rah-rah" sessions. They are to remind everyone on the team of the importance of what they're doing and why they're the ones doing it. The fact is that for some of this work, every one of us on the payroll may represent one or two employees who no longer have jobs. There will be some resentment around that. We have to overcome it. We need to go beyond what's in our Statements of Work. So help me, I would come down so hard on any of my people who would quote a Statement of Work to a client in terms of scope or approach. If it comes to that, then we've failed in building the necessary relationships for long-term mutual benefit. Even in my executive relationships I avoid reference to Statements of Work at almost all costs. I don't disagree in the importance of having these documents, and working rigorously to define the detailed contexts of each engagement in writing prior to beginning. There is a legal and financial responsibility that must be addressed in executing appropriate contracts. These documents also force the effort to achieve buy-in on scope, approach, timelines, etc. But if the contracts define the relationship, then Vendorville is where the service providers will remain, and the optimal benefits for both organizations will not be achieved. The documents are our guides, but as partners we need to work together to get through tough issues and come through in the end united as a team. If you start quoting legal documents, then your attempt at partnership has failed.

One of the other things I often ask my teams is to put themselves in the shoes of their counterparts. Ask yourself, "What's keeping my counterpart up at night?" Ask yourself that question driving to work in the morning or back home at night. And then ask yourself what you can do to help ease whatever burden may be on the person's mind. The point of this is not to get inside someone's head, but to demonstrate that you care, and that you're in this together, whatever "this" might be. And "this" might be related to your project, or it might not, but you still may be able to help. Believe it or not, it will be the most satisfying personal accomplishment of the entire project for those of you who can get close enough to help your counterparts through his or her trials of the day. Talk about something you will feel good about when *you* go home at night. That's what is meant by partnership at all levels of the organization. It's one thing for senior management to share this mindset at the executive level. But true partnership from the service provider side is born when all members of the team take this approach to the job on a day-to-day basis. And these concepts apply whether you're an on-site resource or sitting in a call center or data center offshore. Global service providers need to extend this mindset to all facets of their service offerings.

So what about the companies? What's their obligation in this context? First, they have to be open to the concept of a trusted partnership. This will be relatively easy for some, and seem like climbing Mount Everest for others. But if you're not open to the idea, then the outsource model will never work. You can't have a long-term, successful outsource arrangement, the kind being discussed here, with your service provider(s) stuck in Vendorville. You will never be successful. Get over the "high-priced consultant" mindset and the negative connotations that come with it. Usually if these folks are making a little more money it's because they're willing to travel all the time and live in hotels instead of with their families. You should appreciate their sacrifice, not resent them for the extra compensation they may receive for it. If you're willing to take some of those first steps in letting your service provider past that invisible wall dividing "us" and "them"—bringing them on the inside to your real underlying issues and seeking out their assistance—this will go a long way in terms of starting the relationship down the path of trusted partnership. Just as IT wants to be part of "the business," consultants want to be included as part of the team. They spend way too many hours struggling through really challenging assignments to not want to be considered "one of us." It's hard to express the glee that can be seen in the eyes of my consultants when I get direct praise from a client about their work. That means a tremendous amount. More importantly, it means that much more when they're brought into the "inside" issues in the first place. Nothing motivates them to work harder than feeling like you're all in this together. If your company extends a sense of trust to the consultants, you will get that trust returned in spades.

Here's another tactical way in which companies can contribute to the partnership status of the relationship. Companies need to consider what the service provider goes through in trying to provide the highest quality of service through all aspects of the relationship. Service providers need to manage their inventory just like any company. In this case that inventory is typically in the form of people. Clients seem to think it's natural to wait until the last second to decide whether or not to extend existing resources. Often these customers will dangle future business so the service provider will not want to pull a resource, even though this may cost the company business opportunities elsewhere in the practice. What selfish companies like this need to realize is that this will never be an optimal approach because what goes around comes around. If everyone takes this approach, then everyone ends up getting burned at one time or another (companies and service providers alike). More than anything else, the one thing customers can provide as part of the partnership approach is assistance in the long-term forecasting of resource needs. Honesty and a willingness to participate in these discussions without forcing the service provider to literally beg for this insight will be gratefully received on the other side. That's treating someone like a partner, not like a vendor, and that vaulted status can only be achieved by means of a two-way street. That's the path to optimization.

Partnerships cannot be based solely on financial transactions. You can't just *buy* a partner in the context of what I'm describing as this optimal, mutually beneficial relationship. You can buy (or rent!) a vendor relationship, but you can't buy a true partnership. Many organizations enter into financial transactions where one organization agrees to purchase goods from another, which in turn will supply goods or services to the other. These kinds of relationships may be a positive experience for the executives who put the deals together, and may in fact prove to be economically beneficial as well, but they will often never achieve the optimal status of partnership. That's because partnerships are based on people, and on trust, respect, and the genuine understanding that the whole can be greater than the sum of the parts. Partnership is a mindset in which two organizations rally around a common set of objectives, and not just a financial transaction based on reciprocal purchasing or reselling arrangements. In the context of the service provider business, and specifically in the outsourcing space, these financial arrangements tend to be short-lived and end up forcing solutions on the people who need to perform the actual work and where the fit is often unnatural. It then puts a strain on the primary relationship that evolved around outsourcing, or any other offering from the service provider, for that matter. The end result is that both sides of the relationship treat each other as vendors, and they reluctantly live up to the terms of the deal but not in the spirit of what was envisioned. These relationships may yet be profitable for the organizations and may be worth pursuing in some circumstances, but they will rarely yield the optimal results that can be achieved when two or more organizations rally around the essence of partnership.

Along these same lines, true partnership is not based on friendship or on fringe benefits. Golf outings, expensive lunches, and tickets to special events may be attractive, and may in fact influence the outcome of deals, but don't confuse these "good times" with business partnership. It's only a matter of time until the benefits of these events wear off (or the funds go dry), and if this represents the foundation of your relationship, it won't take you very far when issues start to rise and things begin to go sour. The same thing goes for friendship. Yes, it's awfully nice when you can achieve a level of friendship in these client/service provider relationships, but I maintain that trust and respect are more important characteristics than friendship. Partnership doesn't mean going out together after work or getting together on weekends. Partnership means a singular motivation around a common set of objectives, and a mutual commitment to collaborating on doing whatever it takes to achieve those goals. You can probably get by without it, but not if Enterprise Optimization is your ultimate goal in these sorts of joint relationships.

Undoubtedly the hardest part in venturing into this kind of partnership is taking the first step. As has been stated, the natural state is one that is at least leaning toward distrust, and not the other way around. Vendorville is the natural state. But executives on both sides of these relationships have to realize that Vendorville is a suboptimal state in the context of the outsource arrangement being advocated here. This environment can only succeed in the context of a trusted partnership. This makes it all the more important to pick the right partner. Clearly not all service providers are the same. Check references beyond technical capabilities. What are they like to work with? How do they handle adversity? Ask tough questions. Get concrete examples. The ability to establish a trusting relationship should be at the top of the list of criteria when choosing such a partner, and you should be able to learn from others who have gone before you. Ultimately, that may be a leap of faith, but it needs to be right there on the table as part of the critical selection criteria. It is incumbent upon the leaders on both sides of the relationship to recognize the criticality of this component to success and be willing to take that leap of faith. It has to start at the top. And, again, your chance of success is extremely limited in this outsource model if you don't consciously take these steps toward partnership.

Long-Term Relationships

Another component of the relationships between companies and their outsource suppliers is that they are typically long-term arrangements, ranging from three to five or even seven years (or longer). While you can attempt to capture as much detail of the agreement as possible in that initial contract, and to build in at least some flexibility, there will inevitably be things that evolve over time that need to be addressed as part of the working relationship. It is both an art and a science to create service level agreements (SLAs) that are flexible enough to be effective while not straining the relationship beyond the breaking point. Just as the Founding Fathers were wise enough to build in the opportunity to amend the Constitution, companies and outsource service providers need to look to the possibilities of the future when venturing out on a new agreement. They need to be able to anticipate how to handle fundamental economic shifts, be it sudden growth or rapid demise. The outsource agreement needs to contain provisions that make economic sense for *both* parties as the entities undergo change. When companies enter into these long-term partnerships, both organizations are significantly invested in the success of the other. As such, they need to be able to adapt together in order to keep the arrangement viable. The bottom line is that *both* entities must be successful when tied at the hip in these kinds of arrangements, so flexibility needs to be a foundational tenet of long-term partnerships.

The long-term relationship also needs to be supported by the appropriate incentives for all parties to continue to vigorously live up to their commitments. Performance evaluation, which has a tangible impact on both organizations and their teams, needs to be an ongoing activity. This implies that there will be an appropriate set of rewards and penalties based on performance. As such, a scorecard with quantitative and qualitative components should be generated on a regular basis throughout the lifecycle of the relationship. In the first year, a quarterly review is recommended. In subsequent years, semi-annual reviews may be sufficient, but quarterly reviews may be merited as well. These should not just be cursory reviews or simple data snapshots in terms of up-time and cycle-time of trouble tickets, although those would be among the elements to include. Machines can provide those metrics. While they should factor into the overall evaluation, they represent only one component. Detailed surveys should be created and agreed upon by both sides, representing the most salient qualitative areas that are fundamental to the ongoing relationship. Respondents should be asked to rate their individual counterparts and counterpart organizations in terms of overall satisfaction, attitude, approach, willingness to assist, sense of urgency, etc.—all the things that would be expected if these were your own employees. Individuals should be rated in terms of technical competence, client management, fiscal/budgetary management, etc. And just as rewards and penalties should be written into the SLAs for the purely quantitative metrics, similar rewards and penalties should be applied based on these relationship-oriented metrics.

Most often when rewards and penalties are outlined in these relationships, the risk is (a) always on the side of the outsource service provider, and (b) geared entirely to an impact on the provider as a company, and rarely tied to the individuals on the team. Both of these approaches are suboptimal. First, these relationships are a two-way street. There are responsibilities on the client side that often impact the ability of the service provider to meet its commitments. In a true partnership, the customer should also be subject to review on a quarterly or annual basis by way of a similar survey, and should be held accountable for its actions. The customer is *not* always right, and if we're really talking partnership, then *both* sides should have contractually bound risks and rewards. Note that I say risks and *rewards*. Service providers should have upside potential built into their SLAs for when they exceed a target by a predetermined amount, particularly when this upside is able to drive quantifiable benefits in terms of Process and/or Information Optimization. Outsource service providers should be measured beyond transaction processing metrics. They should be motivated to improve the capabilities of their clients, and they should share in the benefits when they do.

That being said, it is often the case that the upside for companies in these "funds at risk" relationships is geared toward the bottom line of the companies, and not directly toward the people involved in the service delivery itself. But this is a service business, and people drive the results. The people should be involved in the risks and rewards. If rewards are won by an organization in one of these partnerships, then some percentage of those rewards should be earmarked for the people who made it happen. All too often, these rewards just go to the bottom line and may never benefit the people who brought about the outcome. The team members need to be given incentives to continuously provide superior customer service, and tying rewards to this performance management review process is an excellent way to get everyone focused on exactly the right things and to drive the highest level of service. Experience indicates that even small degrees of incentives related to the risk/reward model for individual participants can yield dramatic improvements in performance.

Single Face to the Customer

Long-term observation has indicated that over time one of the hardest things to achieve for a business, especially a global business that supports multiple products or solutions, is to provide a single face to its customers. In service businesses, practitioners tend to focus on what they have been specifically tasked to do and pay little regard to the other solutions being delivered by the same company. Outsource service providers need to ask themselves questions such as:

- How well integrated and motivated are the individuals in your various solution groups to work collaboratively across the entire value chain: help desk vs. application support vs. network support vs. database support, etc.?
- How well is database or instance management coordinated amongst the implementation teams and application support teams?
- How well is the help desk kept up to speed in terms of changes in the call center procedures and responsibilities?
- How well is the implementation team coordinating with the support organization that requires effective transition in order to perform at peak levels at go-live and beyond?
- How well is the implementation team coordinating with the BPO team that will be responsible for executing the processes being deployed?

Having lived through the challenges of all these scenarios and more, it has become apparent that those organizations that wish to play in the end-to-end outsourcing space need to be able to align their companies around this "one face" model. If any global service provider tries to differentiate itself as the "one throat to choke," then it needs to be able to rethink its own internal operations to support this model. Remember, for most of these organizations, this is a new business. They may have the appropriate assets in which to provide end-to-end solutions, but if they are not aligned internally, they will provide no competitive advantage over a contract house cobbling together the solution from multiple service providers. Typically, different functions within companies report to different leaders who are motivated by their own personal metrics. All too often, when you start venturing into multi-solution offerings such as the ones being discussed, these metrics do not apply in their original form to encourage cross-organizational sharing of resources. These outsource providers need to be able to tap into the right resource pools to address the needs of their clients. To be successful, they need to have access to the best resources for the job at hand, even if they are housed in organizations outside their immediate domain. This will happen naturally only if upper management identifies that a conflict may exist and realigns goals and associated metrics around this cross-organizational need. You can't just tell someone to "do the right thing" if you're not prepared to step up with the right set of objectives and measurements. Senior management needs to be proactive in recognizing the potential conflicts of interest that may exist within a multi-solution service provider organization and address them prior to venturing into these types of agreements. This will enable the team's program leadership to be able to effectively meet its needs without having to break down barriers each and every time requests are made.

Back in Section I, a lengthy discussion unveiled the appropriate organization structure for the Process and Information Department within a company. That structure has critical connection points across the organization. You have similar organizational needs with end-to-end outsource service providers. To be able to provide end-to-end solutions, service providers need to be aligned around a model that supports that kind of solution. Providers in this space are coming at this business opportunity from a variety of backgrounds, many of which have different organization structures. You have software companies, pure ASPs, consulting organizations, etc., all venturing into the outsource managed services and BPO spaces. For those entities that are trying to differentiate themselves in the marketplace as a one-stop shop, pay heed: promising one face to the customer and failing to execute can yield a complete disaster.

Software companies need to understand that there is a challenge here and proactively address this potential barrier to success. For example, if Oracle's market differentiation is based on its ownership of the complete solution (software, services, and operations/support), then it needs to be able to deliver on all cylinders. Oracle will suffer as a whole if the software is unstable, regardless of the efforts of the services or support organizations—or any other combination on the theme. Software companies and consulting organizations tend to have strong divisional lines built around strong leaders who work toward personal metrics. One-stop shop offerings need to break down those barriers or ultimate success will likely be elusive. My role in account management at BearingPoint has often required me to represent all of BearingPoint, even though I have direct control over only a limited number of resources. I believe that my ability to work the internal organization structure to identify and procure the services of the right solution-focused talent has been a key to my success with being a one-stop solution partner. This applies to partner-based solutions as well. When BearingPoint signed up as the "one throat to choke" in the BPO case study from earlier in this section, we were assuming complete responsibility for the entire service offering and SLAs, even though we had only a fraction of the resources on the team. Making the solution work was our responsibility, and success hinged on our ability to seamlessly integrate the India-based team from HCLT into our processes and methodologies, as well as our ability to adopt the best-practice processes that made up the core of the successful HCLT methodologies. It worked both ways, and we had to be prepared to work together to provide the ultimate solution for the client. It takes true partnerships to do that, and a complete commitment to a common set of goals. Was it risky? Sure. But we were confident that it represented the optimal path available to achieve the "Best of Both Worlds" for our client.

All too often for organizations venturing into new solution areas, the critical component of structural alignment is treated in the context of the chicken and the egg. As companies move into new areas, such as the managed services business, it often takes the first few sales to drive home the point of these pending conflicts, and only when the conflicts arise do these organizations react. It is a painful process for these companies and even more painful for their customers. History need not repeat itself. There have been plenty of examples in which organizations refuse to act on these internal changes until pushed against the wall by customers and deals. This is a direct path to customer dissatisfaction and the loss of customer references—crucial for growing a new business. It is strongly suggested that these conflict areas be addressed *in advance*, from the top down, with clear direction on how managed services and BPO offerings will be accounted for in terms of metrics, personnel, compensation, etc. Some companies that are already far down this path have already suffered from this disconnect. For others venturing into adding managed services to existing offerings (or any other significant new programs, for that matter), the advice is offered to plan ahead regarding the topics just highlighted.

Further, along these lines, is the effective program management of the service providers in delivering a coordinated set of services to their customers. The importance of program management within the PI organization for internal management of communication and activities has already been discussed. The service providers have the same requirement. Again, the norm is for different solution teams to focus on their own solutions, with little regard or even knowledge of what their brethren may be doing for the same client. This should be on the list of the top scenarios that are to be avoided at all costs for service providers. In fact, this is an area where metrics should be derived in the quarterly surveys in terms of how effective these organizations are in providing a single, integrated face to its customer. Service provider program management should have as one of its highest priorities the need to provide internal coordination and communication to ensure adherence to this goal. Failure in this area is not the responsibility of the team. Failure in this area is the responsibility of the team's leadership, and should not be tolerated. This point is emphasized because it is a common failing in large service organizations that attempt to provide multiple services to other large companies. The disconnects appear all the time. They are embarrassing and counter productive, and avoidable with the right level of management commitment. A true partner takes those extra steps in order to ensure that the teams are working together and not against each other. This should be a requirement for all multi-solution service providers, and satisfaction in this area should be subject to reward or punishment.

No matter what structure a service provider puts into place, it needs to be flexible and collaborative if the organization is going to be able to deliver on any end-to-end solution offering. The common requirement is the ability to effectively tap into any component of the overall structure whenever it is needed by a client, and to expect collaborative participation on very short notice. Unfortunately, many large service providers (consulting organizations, software companies, etc.) are *not* structured around such an environment, or, at least have tremendous difficulty executing on that vision. Many have been forced to learn the hard way that failure in this regard can be deadly to a client relationship. Service providers and potential customers, take heed: Do not underestimate the importance of being able to operate on all cylinders in providing your end-to-end solutions. If you can't coordinate and collaborate, then your value proposition as a single source supplier is really not worth anything at all, and it won't take long for the market to figure that out.

Case Study: Oracle All-In-One for JDS Uniphase [95]

Oracle has always tried to be the complete software provider for its customers, including database, applications, tools, etc. in its offerings. Its outsourcing solution has been around for a few years, but up until recently it mainly targeted small companies with a pure out-of-the-box solution. The strategic move toward complete end-to-end solution offerings, including managed services, for medium- to large-sized companies is a relatively new undertaking. This case study will take you inside the experience of one of the early adopters of this approach in making Oracle this company's end-to-end outsource application service provider, otherwise known as its "one throat to choke."

JDS Uniphase (JDSU) is a worldwide leader in optical technology. The company designs and manufactures products for fiber optic communications, as well as for markets where its core optics competency provides innovative solutions for industrial, commercial, and consumer applications. JDSU's fiber optic components and modules are deployed by system manufacturers for the telecommunications, data communications, and cable television industries, as well as for display, security, medical/environmental instrumentation, decorative, aerospace, and defense applications.[96]

The relationship between JDSU and Oracle Corporation began with an investment in and implementation of Oracle Applications as JDSU's sole ERP system during the company's rapid build-up from 1999 to 2001. This was at a time when JDSU acquired more than 15 companies and was on a $4-billion annual revenue run rate. The complete suite of Oracle Applications was implemented, with the assistance of BearingPoint (then called KPMG Consulting), as a single, enterprise-wide instance of business software for 27 factories in 9 countries across the globe. The scope included Oracle modules to support Finance, Distribution, Customer Service, Manufacturing, Procurement, and Human Resources. JDSU leveraged the rapid, process-driven approach from BearingPoint to replace all existing legacy systems for transaction processing and management. Information reporting was available in real-time using Oracle's Discoverer tool, as well as via a data warehouse, which leveraged the following toolset: Decision Point, Brio, and Essbase. As a strong advocate of outsourcing IT services, JDSU retained Qwest Cyber Solutions (QCS) as its managed services provider. QCS was responsible for hosting the application environment, providing production application support, and all network operations. BearingPoint provided ongoing development services with an on-site staff of highly skilled technical developers. Figure III-7 represents the IT infrastructure at JDSU in terms of roles and responsibilities during the ramp-up time of the rapid, global deployment.

Figure III-7: Initial IT Infrastructure Roles and Responsibilities at JDS Uniphase

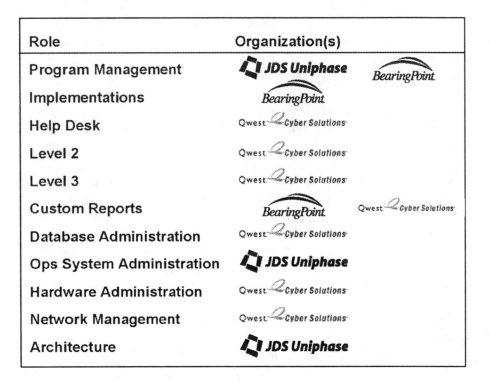

Source: JDS Uniphase

This environment was anything but stagnant. Quality of service and economic realities played into the reshaping of this IT structure from 2001 through 2002. From a quality of service perspective, QCS proved time and again that it could not support a company of the scale and complexity of JDSU. Its network services were woefully inadequate in meeting customer demand, and several portions of its application support proved to be substandard as well. One of the first changes JDSU made in the environment was to reassign database administration duties from QCS to a group of DBA specialists from Oracle Consulting.

As the economy tanked, JDSU needed to find ways to cut costs. While the quality of service from BearingPoint remained excellent, the on-site development resources were simply too expensive to justify the cost. As a result, ongoing technical development was handed to Infosys, an India-based company, and Montage, a Canada-based company, which began providing these services at a fraction of the cost, using an on-site management model, but an offshore development model. In addition, QCS began to struggle to fulfill its support obligations, so JDSU began supplying its own resources to supplement the outsource support team. BearingPoint was still utilized extensively for project implementations and overall program management. Figure III-8 represents the IT infrastructure in terms of roles and responsibilities at this point in the company's evolution.

Figure III-8: "Midway" IT Infrastructure Roles and Responsibilities at JDS Uniphase

Role	Organization(s)	
Program Management	JDS Uniphase	BearingPoint
Implementations	BearingPoint	
Help Desk	Qwest Cyber Solutions	
Level 2	Qwest Cyber Solutions	
Level 3	Qwest Cyber Solutions	
Custom Reports	Infosys	MONTAGE Integration
Database Administration	ORACLE	Qwest Cyber Solutions
Ops System Administration	JDS Uniphase	Qwest Cyber Solutions
Hardware Administration	JDS Uniphase	Qwest Cyber Solutions
Network Management	AT&T	JDS Uniphase
Architecture	ORACLE	JDS Uniphase

Source: JDS Uniphase

As you can see, this model began to stretch across multiple partners, making the overall management of the outsource environment significantly more challenging for JDSU. The original partner landscape had become much more complex and often problematic as a result. (Remember, keep it simple!) Nevertheless, this structure remained in place as the core implementations wound down and a handful of business consolidation projects took place, reflecting the economic conditions of the company. However, the economic conditions continued to worsen beyond the company's ability to react, and dramatic cost reductions were further necessitated as the company struggled to return to a level of overall profitability. Paul Brinkley became the CIO of JDSU around this time. Brinkley had just completed a year as the company's Vice-President of Customer Service (in "the business"), which had followed a two-year stint in his role as VP of Business Applications (in IT). Given the dire economic conditions, Brinkley's first charge was to find some way to significantly reduce the cost structure of IT. This is where Oracle came in with its pitch for Oracle All-In-One, which included the full gamut of Oracle offerings (licensing, consulting, support, and outsourcing).

Since Oracle owned the software license to which JDSU was obligated in terms of long-term depreciation and hefty maintenance fees (negotiated at a time when the company was several times larger than its current state), Oracle had by far the most leverage in terms of being able to assist JDSU with its IT cost structure. In return, Oracle wanted to showcase JDSU as the poster child for its one-stop shop offerings, including outsourced managed services. The result of this win-win scenario was that JDSU agreed to use Oracle Consulting Services for a major software upgrade, and agreed to engage Oracle Managed Services to host, manage, and support its application environment at its brand new data center for the next five years. Oracle could make the offer attractive by leveraging the entirety of its solutions offerings, as well as by using a resource mix that would include on-site, off-site, and offshore functional and technical resources. Software, consulting services, and operations. One throat to choke.

From the outset, JDSU was a bit skeptical of the offering, as this was new territory for Oracle. Oracle had provided high-quality service in terms of its limited role of database administration, but putting all its eggs in this one basket felt very risky to Brinkley and his leadership team. But the economics could not be ignored. From a total cost standpoint, the offer was too compelling, despite some of the risks (or at least unknowns) in the realm of Process and Information Optimization. Oracle owned the software, which gave it unique leverage to assist JDSU in its economic nightmare—no other partner could match the savings Oracle could provide. As such, JDSU agreed to the proposal. Figure III-9 represents the IT infrastructure in terms of roles and responsibilities after this strategic decision.

Figure III-9: Current IT Infrastructure Roles and Responsibilities at JDS Uniphase

Role	Organization(s)	
Program Management	**JDS Uniphase**	
Implementations	ORACLE	*BearingPoint.*
Help Desk	ORACLE	
Level 2	ORACLE	
Level 3	ORACLE	
Custom Reports	ORACLE	
Database Administration	ORACLE	
Ops System Administration	ORACLE	
Hardware Administration	ORACLE	
Network Management	ORACLE	
Architecture	ORACLE	

Source: JDS Uniphase

From a management perspective, now that's keeping it simple!

The upgrade project went live at the end of January 2003, corresponding with all the new services going into effect. The economic benefits began hitting the bottom line almost immediately, with JDSU estimating a *60 percent* reduction in its annual IT budget as a result of this makeover.[97] That's what I call Total Cost Optimization! But what about Oracle's performance in this new "one throat to choke" role?

On the whole, JDSU was pleased with Oracle's overall implementation performance, primarily with discrete groups providing a solid level of service. That being said, the one area of complaint heard throughout the software upgrade was the continuing challenge for Oracle to perform as a single entity. As was discussed earlier, large companies such as Oracle that go to market with multiple solutions for a single customer, need to learn to break down those internal barriers to achieve the true benefits of "one throat to choke." If you can't provide that single face to the customer, then the heralded leverage doesn't really exist, and you're no more optimal to the customer than a best of breed mix of providers. This concept is similar to the purported strength of Oracle's integrated suite of business applications. If the integration isn't completely seamless, then the value proposition vs. best of breed software falls off considerably. If the integration of all of the solution providers within Oracle's overall managed services offering is not equally seamless, then its value proposition also falls by the wayside. JDSU suffered through many of these challenges in terms of the inability of one part of Oracle to influence or assist the others. Instead of the implementation team being able to work closely with support or development in resolving problems, it would often take one of those organizations to voice complaints up its own management chain, which would then drive resolution down the counterpart's management chain. The result was often tremendous frustration for the practitioners on the ground (both JDSU and Oracle Consulting). That was supposed to be the *old* way of getting things done with Oracle, but JDSU continued to experience it all too often during its upgrade project. That needs to change if the one-stop offering approach is going to be viable.

The concept of software as a service was discussed earlier in the context of the challenges faced by software companies as they attempt to move into offering end-to-end solutions. This is clearly in play in the case of Oracle and its relationship with JDSU, and was one of the primary concerns for Brinkley and his organization as they entered into the partnership. This is how Brinkley views Oracle's progress in this area, after having gone through the upgrade project and the first few months of production support:

> Oracle is undergoing the transformation to a service mindset today, working with companies like JDSU as a turnkey support provider. Its culture has traditionally been one of technical innovation, rapid delivery of capability to market, with a lot of subsequent patch application and tuning to ensure robustness once their applications are live. It has been over a year since we went live on the Oracle support business, and we have been very pleased with their performance. The costs of their own rapid software delivery philosophy when quality problems occur are borne by Oracle, not the customer. I believe this will result in further improvements in the company's overall software release process in the future. It is early today, having only been live on the Oracle support business for one financial quarter, but so far so good. [98]

Further consideration of this case brings us to the concept of "the Essence of Partnership." The case demonstrates that both organizations are still figuring out how to work as true partners. On the Oracle side, all too often its team of consultants focused on its contractual obligations as a vendor. The norm for them was to treat the issues that came their way not as their own issues, but rather just those of their customer. Many of the Oracle resources would revert back to quoting Service Level Agreements and roles and responsibilities whenever times would get tense over upcoming deliverables. The mode was to hunker down amongst themselves and enforce painfully detailed activities for the JDSU team, which usually served only to annoy and inconvenience the client. As for the JDSU team, some of its members were often too quick to jump on the Oracle team whenever anything was missed in its processes. This kind of scrutiny, which was evident primarily in the early stages of the relationship, only caused the Oracle team to circle the wagons and move further toward the minimalist approach to its services (i.e., those based on the SLAs).

You may say, "So what?" After all, this kind of relationship is actually basic and natural when organizations are engaged in these kinds of projects. Natural, yes; common, yes; but optimal, no. Both sides become resentful of each other, and end up focusing on the *safest* level of service within the confines of the contracts. This *safe* level is far from optimal for either organization. The fact is that these relationships will always be under positions of stress, just as traditional IT shops face that kind of stress from "the business" all the time. If these relationships focus on finger pointing and finding fault, then they will never achieve trust and will likely never be considered successful. Organizations that adopt true service mentalities understand that sometimes you need to go beyond the specifics of the written agreements and just do what it takes to complete the project that both sides agreed to up front. You can't make concessions all the time, but when you adopt a flexible attitude at appropriate moments, it is an excellent way for you to build the kind of trust that gets you through the really tough times, and it establishes the basis for you to collectively achieve great things.

This is not to say that these organizations don't have specific responsibilities that must be met, but the ideal scenario is when these expectations are *exceeded*. That won't happen unless trust is established on both sides. The service provider needs to be reasonable and responsive to the requests of the client, even if sometimes those requests exceed what is defined in the legal contracts. It is the client's obligation to push the envelope only when necessary and not to take advantage of the generosity and time commitments of the service provider. The client also needs to be willing to trust the service provider, even if it makes mistakes once in awhile. This stuff is very complex, and mistakes will happen. It's one thing if the mistakes turn into a pattern, but you can't make a federal case out of every error, or you're back to the safe (i.e., suboptimal) approach to service delivery.

Oracle and JDSU are still figuring all this out, but the relationship is still in its infancy. Fortunately, the leadership on both sides is completely committed to the true partnership approach. The leaders are working continuously with their teams to convey the importance of this kind of mutually beneficial relationship. The real tests will always occur during crunch time. How both teams respond to the stress of these intense periods of engagement will determine a lot about how successful the overall relationship is going to be.

The partnership between Oracle and JDSU is off to a good start. Have there been bumps in the road? Sure. Will there me more? Undoubtedly. That's the nature of the business. But a tremendous number of positives have been achieved in a very short period of time. Oracle has clearly committed itself as an organization to making JDSU a success story. Not only has this arrangement worked out well economically for JDSU, but Oracle's commitment to quality has also enabled process and information improvements for the company as well. JDSU anticipates that having its software and support providers as one and the same will pay further dividends in all of these areas throughout the relationship. As Brinkley told me, in addition to the immediate economic benefit that JDSU received, "The most significant benefit is the total accountability that Oracle has for system performance. In the past, other service providers faced with a technical problem would have to log a service request with Oracle or another vendor for support. Today, Oracle is completely accountable for its own software, and the speed with which we see issues resolved compared to the past model with a third-party outsource provider in the mix is remarkable."[99]

Finally, it is worth mentioning again that the simple, single-instance, common infrastructure that utilizes out-of-the-box software has clearly provided JDSU with a scaleable platform that has been critical for the company in riding the economic roller coaster over the past few years, and also enabled a smooth transition to Oracle Managed Services. (This architectural component of the JDSU model will be explored in more detail in Section IV.) It also leaves JDSU extremely well positioned for the time when the economy gains momentum and the company will be able to scale upward again with very little increase to its cost structure. By all angles of analysis this has been a successful arrangement for both companies. Is it the *essence* of partnership? Well, maybe not all the way there yet. But the potential is there, which bodes well for a successful, long-term, mutually beneficial relationship.

Summary and Highlights

- Any function or process that is not a core competency of a company should be considered for outsourcing. The Process and Information Department should analyze outsourcing opportunities across all three components of the Enterprise Optimization Framework.

- Core technology support (defined in this context as including software development, database administration, and system administration) is a commodity that can be best provided by low-cost, high-quality offshore resources that are globally connected by high speeds over the Internet. India is the dominant player in offshore IT services, but China represents a fast-rising challenger.

- One must be careful about what roles are appropriate for offshore technology outsourcing. While core technology support and systems analysis are currently well-suited for this model, the more business and process-focused skills of functional and technical design, business analysis, and project management are much more suspect for the low-cost offshore approach.

- The software industry has struggled to provide a compelling model for its solutions as a pay-as-you-go service, although there are a handful of cases of application service providers (ASPs) that are finally beginning to break through and successfully overcome some of the initial roadblocks to success.

- Managed services organizations have also struggled to date, but the low-cost, high-quality offshore offerings are becoming a core component of these solutions, making them immediately more compelling.

- The major consulting organizations are quickly moving into managed services, coupling their traditional offerings with offshore capabilities. Intense price pressure in the marketplace is driving this evolution in order to stay competitive.

- Non-core business processes should be reviewed by the PI Department for outsourcing opportunities. It should also look to leverage low-cost, high-quality offshore services where applicable. As with offshore IT outsourcing, however, the PI professionals need to be aware of the limitations of which skills are appropriate for offshore (such as high-volume transaction processing) and which ones should remain on-site (such as program management and business process expertise).

- Long-term managed services relationships will only be optimal when viewed by both parties as true partnerships, and not as vendor-customer relationships. *Both* sides must work collaboratively in the spirit of each other's well-being, rather than fall into the typical trap of a "safe" relationship that is dictated by contracts and Service Level Agreements. Proper partner selection, in terms of competencies and relationships, is a fundamental harbinger of the success of any outsource arrangement.

- Service providers in the managed services space must break down their internal barriers (which is no small feat) to provide a true "one face" to its customers. All the assets in the world for these large service provider organizations won't do any good if the client-facing team cannot seamlessly leverage those assets in consistently providing the highest quality of service across all facets of the complete solution offering.

Section IV: Information Technology

Our Current Mess

At this point, most of the blueprint for CPIOs and their Process and Information Departments has been explored. Organization structure, a framework for analysis and decision-making, and the key opportunities available from outsourcing and managed services have all been discussed. The next question to address is to what extent this is a one-size-fits-all approach. Will all companies of all sizes and complexities be equally able to adopt the concepts that are being espoused? The *ultimate* answer is "yes." There is no structural inhibitor to *eventually* achieving the state described here. But that is not to say the path will be smooth for all companies. In fact, the path may be considerably more difficult for some given their current situations. The *technical infrastructure* in place for any particular organization will play a major role in the speed at which these kinds of opportunities can practically be pursued.

The unfortunate reality is that technical infrastructure will be an impediment to most companies in this regard, as opposed to an asset that could yield near-term optimization opportunities. As stated in Section II, systems cannot, in and of themselves, yield competitive advantage. Systems can be a valuable enabler of differentiation, but it takes optimization efforts around processes, information, and execution to yield the desired results of competitive advantage. However, systems and their associated architectures can, in and of themselves, *impede* the pursuit of competitive advantage. Technological environment complexity can represent extraordinary challenges for organizations, and the proliferation of integration challenges just seems to grow more and more each day as corporate application footprints continue to expand.

Given the fact that most companies today run their organizations on anywhere from dozens to hundreds or even thousands of software applications, the following questions must be asked:

- How do these complex environments address the challenges of Total Cost Optimization given the costs of integration and support for each of these discrete applications?

- What about Process Optimization and the challenges of seamlessly integrating end-to-end processes across all these disparate platforms?
- What about Information Optimization and the challenges resident in an environment where the company's information assets are stored in so many different locations?
- How can companies effectively use outsourcing as a strategy in which to achieve dramatic improvements in each of these three areas of the framework given this level of environmental complexity?
- How can Enterprise Optimization be achieved in such diverse and complex environments, where efficiency and effectiveness must struggle against the challenges inherent with these architectures?

A Morgan Stanley survey of 225 CIOs (October 2002) stated that "software simplification is the corporate tech boss's greatest challenge."[100] There is absolutely no question that in the area of application architecture, simplicity is our ally and complexity is our enemy. *CIO* magazine asked the following question in a survey (September 2002): "What will be the top three strategic, IT-driven priorities as we emerge from the recession?"[101] You can see the results in Figure IV-1. "Integrated Systems and Processes" easily tops the list. This complexity is overwhelming companies these days. Simplification and consolidation represent the optimal way to get out of this mess.

Figure IV-1: Top IT-Driven Priorities as We Emerge from the Recession

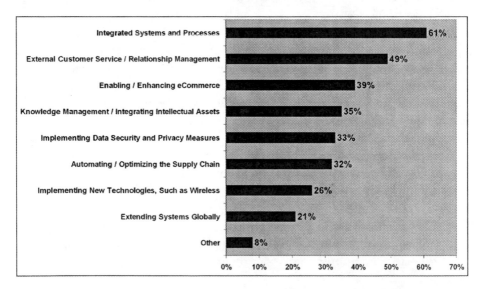

Source: *CIO* magazine, September 2002

Integration is a nightmare. There's no other word to describe it. Even with the most sophisticated (and expensive) integration tools, it's still a crap shoot trying to get all these systems to remain in synch. And forget about upgrading or making any significant changes. You're just asking for trouble. Any analysis with respect to total cost of ownership needs to account for *all* the elements associated with the integration required to support any system or process. You may choose a fantastic point solution to solve some particular business problem, and you may achieve increases in Process and/or Information Optimization, but if technical integration is required, then the total cost associated with that point solution, over the life of the solution, may in fact degrade the overall benefit such that the project doesn't even pay for itself.

Enterprise-wide Process and Information Optimization are also highly unlikely in these complex, integrated environments. From a process standpoint, you're subjecting yourself to mapping decisions at each and every integration point, often having to make concessions in order for the data to flow effectively from one piece of technology to the next. Systems were not designed to work with other systems, and it is commonplace to find that the concessions made in order to further the transactions through the processes often degrade overall effectiveness. Moreover, Information Optimization is nearly impossible in a highly integrated environment. This concept reminds me of the game "Telephone," which many of us played as kids. The object of the game is to whisper some phrase from one person to the next, and by the time it gets to the end of the line, the phrase typically has no resemblance to what it was at the beginning. Distortion naturally occurs from one person to the next; i.e., from one integration point to the next. I don't care how good your integration tools are, or how much energy you invest in data mapping, the common result is a powerful negative correlation between data integrity and the number of integration points in which the data is passed from system to system. In the context of the Enterprise Optimization Framework, each and every solution that is integrated into your core infrastructure must represent an *overwhelming* functional asset in order to justify its existence. Each additional integration point in your environment needs to be evaluated in terms of Process, Information, and Total Cost Optimization and its impact on each of these areas for the company as a whole.

While integrated point solutions may provide improvements for a particular function, inevitably one must ask the question if *overall* processes are truly enhanced. Let's take a look at this issue in the context of a CRM service solution. One can certainly make the case that the service functionality provided by the software from Siebel Systems outdistances the functionality provided by traditional ERP vendors, such as SAP or Oracle. But let's review what it means for a company to have SAP or Oracle as its ERP solution, and Siebel as its service solution. You're now looking at designing, building, and maintaining over the life of the solution the integration necessary to keep these systems in synch and able to support end-to-end business processes. You'll need to determine which of these systems will serve as your system of record for things such as customers, contacts, items, and price lists, and then facilitate keeping these systems in synch with respect to those master data elements. And if you decide it's okay to enter updates for master data in either system, then this becomes two-way integration, and much more complex to build and maintain. Of course you also have to resolve the differences between the very structures of these master data elements. A "customer" in SAP or Oracle is by no means represented by identical data elements as a "customer" in Siebel. You need to make decisions (and often concessions) about how these data elements will map. And as your business evolves, you'll need to make sure that evolution is correctly reflected in these mapping decisions relative to both systems.

From here, let's move forward, beyond the master data to the transactions themselves. In order for Siebel to support the customer service processes, it needs to have all the transactional data relative to sales orders that contain both products and service items. It needs to track serial numbers and the logic associated with service entitlements. This logic may be imbedded in part numbers, such as service duration and/or service level, and therefore needs to be effectively translated into something meaningful in the service system. And, of course, it can never fail. Anything that gets stuck in the integration (and, believe me, things will get stuck) must be resolved immediately, or as sure as Murphy's Law is alive and well, the transaction that gets stuck will be the one that requires service that very same day.

Of course that's not all. As much as you'd like to never have your customers return products, we know it happens all the time. Return Material Authorizations (RMAs) need to be initiated, and you need to decide in which system you're going to begin these transactions. Then you need to figure out what needs to get updated in which system (asset tracking, inventory management, shipping and receiving, and credit transactions all need to be completed). Again, any break in the chain, from an irregular procedure to a simple typo, and customer satisfaction may be at risk, especially since transactions such as these are all customer related. Furthermore, any time you need to patch or upgrade one system, your commitment to test the end-to-end process becomes much more complicated as these changes to the initial system may break components of the solution in one or more of the integrated systems. The cost for these upgrades is always much higher when integrated systems are involved, and, unfortunately, patching is a fairly common occurrence with these enterprise systems. Finally, look out for any changes in these processes. You may try to convert your service organization from a cost center to a profit center, looking to aggressively sell additional service to people who contact the support team. How will that affect the relationships between these systems? If someone on the line with the service center wants to order additional product, what's the process, who enters the data, and into which system does it go?

All this just for a couple of reasonably straightforward processes that are linked between just two systems—a rather simplistic integration environment compared to the norm. For this particular case, here are a just few of the questions that must be addressed in making the decision about implementing an all-in-one solution from a single software vendor vs. pursuing a best of breed approach with custom integration:

- Is the Siebel functionality superior enough to the SAP or Oracle Service CRM functionality to provide sufficient Process and/or Information Optimization to overcome the additional total cost associated with this type of environment? (Don't forget that you also have to calculate the cost of your middleware solution in terms of software, additional hardware, training, and maintenance into the total cost of this type of solution.)
- Will the processes achieve their optimal state if decisions (and concessions) around data mapping between the systems needs to take place?
- What is the impact on the accuracy and credibility of the information generated by these systems given that decisions (and concessions) have been made in terms of data mapping, timing of synchronization, and that the data now needs to be pulled from multiple sources to provide a single view of the entire process? What is the impact if someone tries to audit the information and finds discrepancies, thereby yielding a lack of trust in the reporting system? A common finding is that this inevitable lack of trust in information, based on discrepancies that have resulted from data moving across systems, represents one of the biggest drawbacks of integrated environments.
- What impact do transactions that get stuck in the integration have on your ability to achieve Process and/or Information Optimization?
- What are the future expectations around functionality within the SAP or Oracle Suites? If one of these vendors can achieve an equal playing field within six months or a year, does that change your decision?
- Are you better off by effectively outsourcing your integration requirements to the software suite vendors, making the design, development, quality, and support their responsibility, or are you better off building and supporting this integration on your own using a tools-based solution with in-house resources? Can the potential functional benefits of the integrated point solution outweigh these other costs and risks that result from integrated solutions?

- How does this integrated environment affect your company's agility in terms of adapting quickly to an ever-changing business environment? What is the impact of this question relative to the optimization components of the framework?
- On the other hand, what other processes can be optimized within the rest of the Siebel system based on the integration that has been prepared for the service transactions highlighted above? In other words, if it were shown that the integrated service processes are suboptimal, but other processes for the sales, marketing, or service functions are optimized by the *overall* capabilities of Siebel, would that justify the integrated approach to these systems and processes?

While these may appear to be leading questions, it cannot be stated outright that the answers are obvious and will be the same for all organizations. Each case must be analyzed independently in terms of the impact on Processes, Information, and Total Cost. Further, answers that may have been correct two years ago may have changed since then, and may change again in another year or two. The time element will often sway the outcome, as technology is far from a static component in the overall equation. Plus, these questions apply whether it's a single process, dual-system integrated environment, or if you're tasked with evaluating something significantly more complex. The point is to ask the questions and address all the appropriate angles in the context of the Enterprise Optimization Framework in order to determine the optimal strategic approach for your particular organization.

Let's take this scenario one step further. More typical for a global organization is an environment with *multiple* ERP (Enterprise Resource Planning) systems, *multiple* CRM (Customer Relationship Management) systems, *multiple* PDM (Product Data Management) systems, and *multiple* reporting environments. These environments may include a combination of (a) the same software platform but multiple instances, and/or (b) different platforms and multiple instances. In either case, you can take the "simple" integration challenges highlighted in the questions above and multiply them several-fold in terms of complexity and risk. These global entities that support environments such as this need to consider the integration requirements from system to system and site to site, with the data undergoing multiple integration links all along the way. This often requires translation from one system to the next, as well as delays in consolidation of data for reporting purposes. An example of such a scenario can be seen in Figure IV-2. This representation is a global company that has a dozen locations around the world, and a mix of systems supporting various regional entities.

Figure IV-2: Representative Technical Architecture for a Global Company

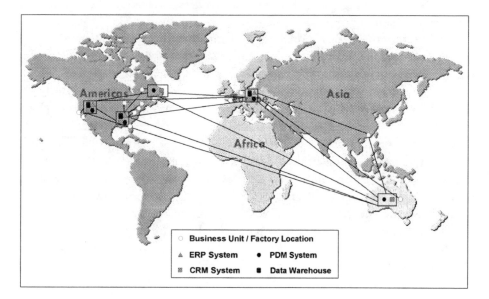

Let's examine this environment in light of the framework. From a total cost standpoint, you're supporting infrastructure and personnel in multiple locations to deploy and maintain each of these systems. This requires redundant headcount throughout the global entity with very little ability to leverage those teams throughout the organization. Network costs, hardware costs, and software costs are all significantly greater than if the environment were consolidated into a single location or on a single platform.

From a process standpoint, there is no true end-to-end process in this kind of structure. Even if all of these systems are integrated, the different platforms make it incredibly challenging to gain true process integration in a seamless manner. Plus, process flexibility is severely restricted in that the time and cost to deploy any changes (even relatively small ones) are compounded due to all the connections between systems. Along these lines, global organizations find it virtually impossible to provide a single face to their customers. Each region inevitably becomes an entity unto itself, and customers are often required to contact multiple locations within the organization to receive end-to-end satisfaction for product demand and service. Since the systems are often disconnected, you end up with Asia sending faxes to Europe to order products (or vice versa), and then trying to consolidate the documentation to keep this ugly back office transparent to the customer, who thinks he is actually dealing with a single entity. Even if these kinds of transactions are automated, it is an expensive proposition, and again, very difficult to change, as one alteration requires adaptation throughout the entire value chain.

Finally, we have enough problems with information management in single-system environments given the problems of data quality so pervasive today. This kind of integrated environment compounds that problem with multiple systems providing different treatment and understanding of what should be the same data elements. The problem of keeping things in synch mounts with each new system added to the environment, and providing global reporting for a particular slice in time becomes nearly impossible. As mentioned earlier in terms of the decentralization and fragmentation of process controls within a company, this approach may yield some degree of improved responsiveness to customers at the local level, which may appear to generate an optimal impact for the company. The problem is that these so-called optimal local processes, supported by these disconnected, often highly customized information systems, inhibit the efficiency and effectiveness for the company as a whole. If local responsiveness is the hallmark for differentiation for these companies, then why aren't they spun off and operated independently? Too many companies are killing themselves by continuing to support these inefficient, ineffective, and costly environments. The world of technological capabilities has evolved, and our decisions from the past must be reconsidered. It's yet another example where additional complexity has become an inhibitor to achieving an optimal result.

It is important to remember, especially for the Process and Information Department, that the framework must be considered in terms of the *entire company*, not just one functional or geographic unit or another. If you were only looking at these questions in terms of one unit, then your ultimate decision might be very different than if you were looking at the overall impact on the entire company. This isolated perspective is one of the reasons we have so many interconnected (and disconnected!) systems in our environments today. Individual functions and business units that have had the autonomy to make their own decisions about processes and systems invariably make those decisions based on their own best interest. However, what may be optimal for one unit may be suboptimal for other units or the company as a whole. This is why we need CPIOs and PI Departments. We need a group of business-savvy professionals providing the appropriate context for these types of decisions and the budgetary control to authorize spending in the context of the needs of the company. We need a framework that supports identifying appropriate metrics on which to base company-wide decisions. Most companies don't go through this kind of analysis, and what looks good in the beginning tends to cause headaches down the road.

When the environmental complexity grows out of control (which it often does), processes degrade, no one trusts the information because it's maintained across multiple systems with slightly different logic and different timings for synchronization, and the total cost spirals well beyond anyone's initial projections.

How did we get ourselves into messes like this? The fact is the environment depicted in Figure IV-2 may have been considered optimal just three to five years ago, as at least it was deployed with a regionalized infrastructure instead of separate systems for each and every location. In the mid-to-late nineties we still did not have the technology (software, hardware, and network) available to deploy viable single instance global environments. We had no choice but to regionalize. Further, the suite vendors were not nearly as mature as they are today in terms of providing world-class end-to-end functionality. This lack of robust capability is what pushed many companies to deploy best of breed solutions in the first place. In those days, we had no choice, and while it may no longer represent an optimal architecture, these decisions may have been perfectly justified not that long ago. But things have changed, and our decision-making needs to change with the times.

This whole topic begs the age-old questions about the philosophical approaches to IT systems: single-vendor suite vs. best of breed, and multi-instance vs. single, global instance of software. Are you better off investing in a single environment backed by a single vendor that is your sole supplier of both functionality and integration (within the suite), or are you better off looking at discrete functional needs and investing in a variety of technical solutions that are then integrated into a collective environment? After extensive observation in the marketplace with respect to this question, and as addressed in the context of the Enterprise Optimization Framework, I must advocate, *to the degree that it is practical,* the consolidated approach; i.e., suite over best of breed, and single vs. multi-instance of software. That is not to say that one set of applications from a single supplier can support your entire company. When you look at the complete list of functionality required to support a company, there is no one vendor that can do it all. But I am absolutely convinced that your ability to achieve Enterprise Optimization, as viewed through the framework, is greatly enhanced by the "simple" approach, which advocates the maximum consolidation of systems and instances of systems.

Benefits of a Single-Instance, Common Infrastructure

CIO magazine commented that "In the Go-Go '90s, large companies everywhere decentralized and customized their ERP systems. Now that the party's over, it's time to clean up and work on the difficult task of integrating many systems into one. This kind of systems rollup will be the predominant type of ERP project CIOs at large companies will face during the next half-decade."[102] I agree, and for most companies there's a lot of work that must be done in this regard in pursuit of Enterprise Optimization.

The benefits of instance consolidation are far-reaching. In a March 2003 report, AMR Research identified a number of the goals and potential benefits of a strategy of instance consolidation (see Figure IV-3).

Figure IV-3: Potential Business Goals and Savings via Instance Consolidation

Business Goal	Technique or Performance Indicator	Potential Benefit
Standardize business processes worldwide	Implement shared services Common suitable processes Experience moving many groups to global instance	Reduce financial headcount up to 30% Reduce Sarbanes-Oxley Act compliance costs Reduce time to integrate acquired companies by 2/3
Single face to global customer	Consolidated order management	Reduce order management costs
Change from regional organization	Real-time operations view of all countries Real-time financial view	Reduce reaction time from months to days Reduce closing time by up to 90%
Reduce IT costs	ERP instance consolidation	Reduce ERP-related IT costs up to 20% to 45%
Coordinate supply chain globally	Visibility of materials across factories Global view of finished goods availability Global coordination of sourcing and suppliers	Reduce raw materials inventory up to 50% Reduce stockouts at distribution centers Reduce purchasing staff up to 25%

Source: The AMR Research Report, *Justifying ERP Instance Consolidation Requires a Strategic Business Goal*, March 2003

As you can see, the benefits go far beyond IT organizations and cost reduction. In fact, the AMR Research Report summarized its findings with, "The Bottom Line: ERP Instance Consolidation cannot be justified solely on the approximately 25% IT savings and requires estimating the value of better global visibility and business process coordination."[103] In other words, instance consolidation will be appropriate when measured against the expected return across all three components of the Enterprise Optimization Framework. From my perspective, the justification *will* be likely for most organizations based on all three of these components.

The only scenario where instance consolidation would *not* be appropriate would be in the case of conglomerates that represent a collection of completely separate businesses. If there is indeed no overlap in customers, partners, or fundamental business processes, then putting everything within one environment may not yield any advantages. While there are certainly occurrences of this type of business model, it is not the norm. There is also probably some ceiling in which transaction volume still reaches a point where the technology can't keep up with the requirements for processing above that level, but companies probably need to be above $10 billion in revenue to even start feeling this limitation. For everyone else out there, single-instance, common infrastructure is absolutely the way to go, and the technological advances no longer allow companies to point to technology inadequacies as their justification for going with distributed, disconnected infrastructure. Let's take a look at one company that has used the strategy of the single-instance, common infrastructure from its earliest days, and see the benefits that have been realized as a result of this approach.

JDS Uniphase (JDSU) was discussed at length in Section III in terms of its organization structure, systems environment, and approach to managed services. When JDS Fitel and Uniphase merged in the summer of 1999, senior leadership initiated the efforts to build the dominant player in the rapidly rising industry of fiber optic components. Even before this merger, growth by acquisition had been the corporate strategy of Uniphase, under the direction of then-CEO Kevin Kalkhoven. As the company ramped up aggressively to meet increasing demand, that acquisition approach continued for another year and a half under Kalkhoven and Jozef Straus, who took the reigns of the company in mid-2000. While all this was occurring, and while customer demand was still increasing more than 100 percent quarter over quarter, the company had to try to integrate all these disparate organizations into a single entity. A key component of the strategy, formulated by CFO Tony Muller and CIO Joe Riera, was a single, unified IT infrastructure. JDSU would not try to tie together its legacy companies, all of which had different legacy information systems, via integration tools, and keep those legacy systems in place. No, the strategy was very much the opposite. All legacy systems would go, and go immediately upon acquisition. Oracle Applications would be implemented on a worldwide basis as quickly as possible as the sole system of use for Finance, Manufacturing, Customer Service, Distribution, Procurement, and Human Resources. All business units would begin using the single, global instance of Oracle Applications as soon as the implementation phases could be completed. In all, with the assistance of BearingPoint, 27 sites in 9 countries went live on this single instance of Oracle in a phased approach over an 18-month period of time. This coincided with a single instance, global implementation of product data management (PDM) software from MatrixOne. The PDM deployment leveraged a single interface to Oracle for the transfer of new and updated items and bills of material. On top of this environment sat a single data warehouse that serviced the needs of the entire company. All legacy ERP, PDM, data warehouse, and assorted other systems (including hundreds of Lotus Notes databases and applications) were decommissioned. Only the site-specific shop floor systems remained, although most of them were migrated to a single platform (Camstar) over time as well. The net result was a global IT infrastructure consisting of a single instance of Oracle Applications (ERP), a single instance of MatrixOne (PDM), and a single data warehouse to support the core business process and reporting requirements of the entire company.

The strategic decisions made in 1999 set the stage for a single systems infrastructure for the entire company that is almost unheard for a company of this scale. This common infrastructure approach has been additionally instrumental as JDSU has dramatically consolidated its environment in reaction to the tremendous slowdown in telecommunications spending in the last couple of years. A principle benefit of a common infrastructure such as this one is that scaling the business (up or down!) is infinitely easier than for a company that is tied together by a complicated set of point solutions and interfaces. In addition, the common environment made the transition to an end-to-end managed services solution very straightforward. As part of the Oracle upgrade to version 11i, the entire Oracle environment was re-established with new hardware in the new Oracle-owned data center in Austin, Texas. The PDM and data warehouse environments were also transferred to this data center. Oracle became the "one throat to choke," hosting the production and development environments, providing system administration, database administration, technical development, and applications support on a worldwide basis. The company's entire corporate infrastructure was relocated in a single shot, and the company never missed a beat. Try doing that with a multi-instance, multi-platform architecture! (Figure IV-4 depicts the current application architecture at JDSU. Compare this to the more typical structure in Figure IV-2.)

Figure IV-4: Technical Architecture for JDS Uniphase (January 2003)

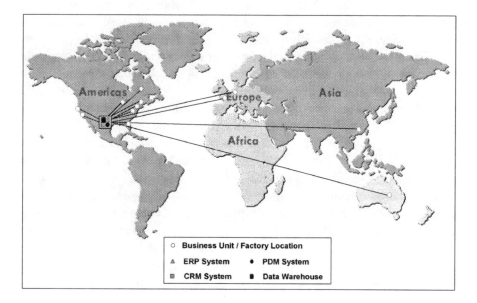

Given the volatility in JDS Uniphase's business, it is rather fortunate that the company never went down the typical path of a multi-instance, highly customized ("complex") ERP environment. The single-instance, common ("simple") infrastructure at JDSU proved to be a critical element in the company's ability to rapidly scale its business, both during the hyper-growth period of 1999 to 2001, and then again during the dramatic decline over the subsequent two years. Agility becomes one of the essential corporate traits during economic swings on this sort of scale, and the technology environment at JDSU played an important role in the company's ability to alter its fundamental business structure to respond to these wide swings in the economic landscape. During the growth period, a key corporate driver was not only to get the entire company onto a single system as quickly as possibly, but also to allow maximum flexibility to the local business units, whose sole purpose was to continue running full bore in order to meet customer demand. The best of breed, multi-instance advocates would likely say that these objectives are incompatible with the single-instance, single-platform approach. Nevertheless, JDSU was able to leverage the flexibility in the Oracle system to satisfy the majority of its needs, while at the same time providing a repeatable, rapid approach to on-boarding the recently acquired business units.

Did this approach provide each of the business units and functional teams each and every feature desired? Absolutely not. The company realized that tailoring the solution to the wants and desires of every constituency in the organization would never yield an optimal result for the company as a whole. One entity may receive some benefit, but what good is that if the organization as a whole suffers? As a result, there were plenty of issues where conflicting objectives needed to be addressed. These were raised and resolved based on a set of guiding principles that emphasized commonality whenever possible, flexibility when practical, and an intense focus on rapid deployment in order to expedite the onset of benefits. Was this optimal for every individual unit in the company? That answer is no. Was it deemed optimal for the company as a whole? That answer is a resounding yes.

With BearingPoint's assistance, JDSU was able to on-board a new company into the JDSU technical environment on average within 90 to 120 days, based on the size and scale of the acquired entity. At the time, local process control was critical, and the overriding guidance was to ensure that in any transition these new entities continued to be able to support their customers without missing a beat. The Oracle system was flexible enough to support local processes, but still in an environment where master data was standardized, and access to data for reporting purposes all came out of the single, enterprise-wide system. Speed to deploy and process flexibility were the drivers at the time, but all within the long-term vision of "one face to the customer" and one system on which to base information reporting.

The single instance, common infrastructure was as important, if not more so, when the company faced the reality of the dramatic meltdown in the telecommunications market space. Changing business conditions required a rapid response in terms of business strategy, and the agility provided by the technology framework was critical to achieving these changes in very short time periods. Working with BearingPoint, JDSU was able to collapse all of its U.S.-based business units into a single transactional entity (called an *operating unit* in Oracle) in a matter of weeks instead of months (or longer). While this technology shift occurred, the business reacted by standardizing all Customer Service/Order Management processes throughout North America, and gained significant economies of scale by creating a shared services organization for Customer Service. This group was based out of the company's Ottawa location, which provided the lowest cost option while still retaining high quality of service. Similarly, the Finance organization also rallied around shared services for North America, centralizing the functions for Accounts Receivable, Accounts Payable, Payroll, Fixed Assets, and the General Ledger.

The fact that the global data and the global transactions all occurred in a single instance of Oracle Applications software was absolutely essential to making this kind of business reorganization possible in such a short time frame, and the results speak for themselves:

- 40% process efficiency improvement after just one quarter after the introduction of standardized processes and centralization of the Customer Service team;
- Nearly 56% process efficiency improvement after just two quarters after the introduction of standardized processes and centralization of the Accounts Receivable team;
- Reduced Day Sales Outstanding (DSO) by 36% over those same two quarters;
- Also within two quarters, the Accounts Payable department was able to support a 32% increase in invoices processed, despite a headcount decrease of more than 50%.[104]

A key element that enabled JDSU to implement these process changes so quickly was an IT infrastructure that was well-suited for rapid changes. As Paul Brinkley, the company's CIO and Sr. VP of Supply Chain Management, told me, "For JDSU, moving factories or consolidating operations involved resetting pointers in the database—no systems conversions or major data migration activity was needed for any of our finance, HR, product development, operations, or customer information. This level of organizational flexibility was built upon Joe Riera's vision of IT at JDS Uniphase. It had a major impact on our ability to reduce the size of our company quickly and maintain a very low cash burn rate as we faced an ongoing dramatic decline in revenue. As we begin to grow, we have tremendous upside scalability with minimal additional cost or investment in systems."[105] Imagine the cost and time it would have taken to complete each of these dramatic changes if each of these units were on different systems, with different master data controls, and different integration points going in all directions. Could your company have scaled to a centralized, shared services model as rapidly as this? JDSU received benefits thanks to both components of its architecture having chosen a single platform (suite) solution and then deploying it globally on a single instance of the software. Consolidation along *both* paths yielded positive results for the company, and avoided the pain so many other organizations have had to deal with these past few years. At a time when economic survival was at stake in the telecommunications industry, JDSU was able to rapidly scale its business (first up, and then almost immediately back down) with dramatic organizational changes, thanks in large part to the agility inherent in its strategic approach to information technology.

Another thing to consider in terms of this suite vs. best of breed and multi-instance vs. single-instance analysis is the impact on your ability to staff the support team for your overall environment, including your ability to outsource that support to take advantage of some of the significant cost savings that may be available. The single-instance, common infrastructure was certainly a major reason why JDSU was able to upgrade and outsource its global technology infrastructure so quickly and with such little interruption to the business. If, on the other hand, you retain core technical support as an in-house responsibility, unless you are fortunate to have individuals who are cross-trained in multiple applications, you lose the ability to maximize the leverage of your support team in a best of breed environment. This results in higher support costs with the addition of individual support personnel for each application, which may not require full-time heads, but in an in-house environment you can't exactly staff half a person. Fewer applications mean fewer skill sets required for your support organization, and this can translate into bottom line savings. In the case of JDSU, Brinkley noted that, "JDSU never exceeded 250 total IT headcount, even when we were a company with over 25,000 employees worldwide. That number included desktop support, shop floor systems, and other site-specific resources, as well as the central core systems group. That core group was very small and scalable, as it only had to work with one application that was operating under outsourced support."[106] That's a pretty compelling environment for global organizations looking for Total Cost Optimization, regardless of whether they decide on an in-house or outsourced support model.

JDSU has clearly benefited in the total cost component of the Enterprise Optimization Framework thanks to its strategic decisions around global instances for its application infrastructure. But that's just as clearly only the beginning to the benefits of this approach. As the company has evolved, its needs from a process and information perspective have changed rapidly over the last four years. The company went from a hyper-growth mode, where getting product out the door was the driving factor for all processes, to a dramatic downturn in which efficiency and cost takeout were the primary motivators. As the company itself scaled (up and down) due to market conditions, so did its ability to build and execute appropriate processes given any stage in that volatile cycle. It could move from decentralized process management to a more centralized approach in short, smooth transition cycles, rather than via massive transformation projects.

The key element for JDSU was to be able to alter its processes rapidly to meet the ever-changing demands of the marketplace. The company was able to take advantage of some of the best practices already in use in some parts of the company and quickly standardize on those approaches across the organization. The company was able to quickly deploy shared services infrastructure for Finance and Customer Service as the business conditions required. Since the same software infrastructure existed throughout the company, these changes were far easier to implement than if all the business units were operating on separate and distinct software platforms. In the midst of the marketplace meltdown, the company didn't have time for extensive, time-consuming business process redesign. It had to happen right away or it would be too late. The company found that it didn't really need all the variations in business processes that existed throughout the company, and that it could operate more efficiently and effectively with a standard set of enterprise-wide processes. The single-instance, common platform was essential in being able to make moves along these lines in such a short period of time.

JDSU also benefited from its architecture in the form of Information Optimization. Prior to the implementation of this single-instance, common architecture, it was virtually impossible for the company to perform any meaningful analysis on its global data. For example:

- The company was sourcing the same supplies from numerous vendors, thereby not supporting any leverage for negotiating better contracts with key suppliers.
- There was no ability to manage the supplier quality, as separate systems stored the relevant data for the different business units.
- There was no ability to manage customer credit on a global basis as the exposure was identified solely at the business unit level.
- The company had no means in which to present "one face to the customer," as the multiple legacy systems operated individually with many of the same customers. As a result, when customers called with questions related to their global activity with JDSU, the customer service representatives had to then get on the phone with many of their colleagues in order to finally pull together what was believed to be an accurate representation of the truth.
- The company maintained multiple charts of accounts, making it extremely difficult for consolidated financial reports to be prepared in a timely fashion.
- The company couldn't even provide an accurate global headcount report without taking a couple of days to manually gather and combine the data.

All of these information management limitations went away with the global implementation of this single-instance, common infrastructure. They were optimized even further with the deployment of standardized processes and single points of contact for the Customer Service and Finance organizations, leading to a significant up-tick in customer satisfaction. And these global views didn't require extensive customization or data-mapping exercises. All of that complexity was outsourced to the folks at Oracle who wrote the software. Decisions at JDSU could now be made in minutes instead of days, because the relevant information was available for global analysis in real time.

There were two primary reasons for these information-related benefits. First, because there was no integration to other systems for core transaction processing, there was only one system of record for management analysis. All of the integration was bundled within the Oracle suite of applications, so there was never a case where concessions needed to be made as data moved from one system to the next. Whether the reporting requirements came from the executive staff or from the local business operations team, the data originated from a single source in a single system, providing consistency for all reporting beneficiaries. Second, for those who relied on the analytical reporting stemming from the data warehouse, again, the data was all extracted from a single source, making it very straightforward to tie the information back to the single system of record. A data warehouse team of less than five people was able to support the needs of the entire company largely because of the simple, consolidated enterprise architecture.

The JDSU example demonstrates the incredible advantages that can be achieved via a single-instance, consolidated technical architecture. That being said, it would be inappropriate to categorically condemn all facets of the best of breed approach. While system consolidation is likely to yield optimal results, that does not mean that in order to achieve an optimal environment you must run your entire company on just one or two systems. No one is suggesting that we've reached the point where a single system can satisfy 100 percent of a company's requirements. But, in this day and age, it is advisable to rethink best of breed decisions from the past and consider the opportunities for overall optimization presented by the suites.

These decisions need to be made from a company-wide perspective and in terms of the long-term approach to Process Optimization, Information Optimization, and Total Cost Optimization. In honest and objective analysis, ask yourself: What's the upside of best of breed in these areas and what's the downside? What's the impact in the short term, and what's the likely impact in the long term? In some cases, short-term realities may, in fact, override your analysis and appropriately drive a short-term decision. You may have a customer that requires some type of automated interface for order placement or invoicing, and a quick and dirty best of breed approach may be the only answer to meet immediate demand. It may fail the analysis of the framework, but it still may be the right decision in the short term given the realities of the situation. All of this needs to be taken into consideration and analyzed in terms of the overall impact to the company, and then a decision needs to be made. And, don't forget, it's part of the PI Department's responsibility to revisit these decisions over time. What was a good decision two years ago may no longer make sense. Best of breed may have been the only option to obtain the required functionality when your systems were initially installed, and it may have been absolutely the correct decision given the information and capabilities available at the time. But technology evolves rapidly, and your ERP vendor may have improved its CRM, supply chain, or human resources functionality now to the point that updated analysis is required to see if replacing the old integrated solution may now be the optimal approach based on this analytical framework.

This may all be well and good if you are starting anew, but what about the majority of companies, which have already invested in complex technological architectures and have multiple instances of best of breed software being operated around the world? What are these companies supposed to do? First, to reiterate, in the context of the Enterprise Optimization Framework, system consolidation and instance consolidation within individual systems is the appropriate path to pursue. It may have been the absolute correct decision two or three or ten years ago to go multi-instance and best of breed, but those decisions are ancient history and, frankly, are no longer relevant. Those investments are sunk costs. If they're no longer optimal, then they need to be revisited. If it is cost prohibitive to change course, or if certain processes would be materially damaged, then maintaining some portions of your best of breed environment may still represent the optimal solution. But your investment decisions from the past are no longer relevant, and the *emotions* invested in those decisions need to be put aside as well when determining the most appropriate path moving forward.

The first recommendation for companies in this complex state is regarding instance consolidation. As was discussed earlier, there is no longer any reason to have different instances of the same software running to support different functional units or different geographical units within the same company. Multi-instance fails the framework on all three counts, and the technological advances that have been made relative to software and high-speed networks cry out for consolidation into single, global instances. The viability of such a move should be reviewed immediately by any company still operating under a multi-instance architecture.

Oracle Corporation provides a classic example of a company that has received the benefits of instance consolidation. Whether or not the company actually saved a full $1 billion a year (as advertised) with its instance consolidation initiative may be debatable, but whatever the actual results, the story is certainly compelling. Take a look at the following data points:

- In 1999, Oracle had built out its internal client/server architecture to support 32 servers with 60 disparate financial databases. The company was spending approximately $600 million annually on global IT operating costs and supporting a team of 1,500 IT employees.
- By 2001, Oracle had decreased its back-office infrastructure to just two servers running four databases. The company also consolidated its 27 support applications into one worldwide instance. The cost to support IT had dropped by approximately $200 million annually (to $400 million) and the IT staff was reduced from 1,500 employees to approximately 900. This all occurred while the company was adding approximately 10,000 employees to the payroll.[107]

The success of this initiative is nothing short of astounding. It's astounding in how complex and costly the original environment had become, and all the more impressive that the changes could be made in such a short period of time while the company was actually in a mode of rapid growth. This kind of transformation can only occur with complete buy-in from top management, which Oracle had throughout this endeavor. It also demonstrates that even the most complex, robust enterprises that are living in distributed, integrated, multi-instance environments have just as much opportunity to rethink those strategies and optimize their environments as the smaller, more centralized companies. Finally, it should also be noted that you don't need to take on everything at once. Gary Roberts, a senior vice-president at Oracle, stated, "Remember that any small change toward that end [i.e., instance consolidation and an Internet-enabled approach to e-business] can be very profitable. What's important when you start along this path is not to look at the 'perfect picture,' but to recognize that any incremental change you make along these lines will still bring your company tremendous benefit."[108] Process Optimization, Information Optimization, and Total Cost Optimization—Oracle has seen it all as a result of this monumental effort, and you can, too—one step at a time.

Beyond instance consolidation, it is time to take a fresh look at your technology infrastructure and critically review the rationale of your complete application footprint given the technological options available today. Of course any replacement decisions will be painful. There are always strong attachments to what's been constructed over time. Time, energy, dollars, and emotions have been invested in these systems and the integration that binds them all together. Unfortunately, none of that is relevant. What is relevant is whether or not you can optimize the environment by replacing and consolidating your systems across the enterprise. If nothing else, Sarbanes-Oxley requirements should make you review this architectural landscape, and force the question as to what will be the cost of achieving compliance with a systems architecture that is all over the map. Sarbanes-Oxley is a long-term reality, and it requires long-term rethinking of how we do business. A simple, consolidated IT infrastructure will certainly be an asset in meeting the compliance requirements of Sarbanes-Oxley, let alone the optimization targets which should really represent the long-term objectives of the company.

It should be recognized that for a lot of people and a lot of companies, a move toward system consolidation may be the very thing that makes them completely disposable. If an ERP supplier can provide adequate CRM capabilities to overcome the suboptimal components of an integrated environment, then who would ever invest in one of the CRM systems? There is an entire industry that will proclaim from the highest mountaintops the functional advantages created by this or that best of breed solution and how they far outweigh the offerings of the suite vendors. In some cases they may be right. In many cases, they're just blowing smoke to stay alive. Moreover, this dynamic affects individuals as well. Just as outsourcing may be the right move for a company, it also means that many individuals will lose their jobs. The same can be said of system consolidation. Fewer systems likely means fewer support personnel, or at least eliminating the support roles for the decommissioned systems. Remember the dramatic drop in IT personnel at Oracle during the instance consolidation project? This may be good for shareholders, but it's not so easy if your own job is on the line. Who will be motivated to make the "right decision" for the company if it means eliminating his or her own job or that of a close associate? Again, this brings us back to the role of the Process and Information Department. This group is empowered to look at the best interests of the company as a whole, and needs to be trained to maintain that view despite the impact it may have on individual colleagues. This dynamic cannot be underestimated as personal biases can certainly play a role in these decision-making processes if not proactively addressed by the PI Department.

There appears to be a fair amount of reluctance to this consolidation approach in the marketplace. Despite the obvious potential benefits, there is a sense that system consolidation will break more than it will resolve and the cost to replace will far outweigh the potential gains. Of course, these opinions are not relevant unless taken in the context of a framework with meaningful metrics to support the claims. Rarely is that level of analysis applied to these concerns. So let's take a look at a case where an integrated best of breed environment has been carefully and thoughtfully deployed, but where consolidation-based optimization opportunities are now in play.

Case Study: Best of Breed and Consolidation Opportunities at Stratex Networks[109]

Stratex Networks is a mid-sized high-tech company that, according to its Web site, designs, manufactures, and markets advanced wireless solutions for wireless broadband access, enabling the development of complex communications networks. Its solutions are used as complements and alternatives to fiber for last-mile access, wireless fiber transmission services, network backhaul, and interconnection in multiple communications applications worldwide. The company recorded annual revenue of $228 million in FY02 (down from $417 million in FY01). While based in the U.S., Stratex has more than 20 offices around the world and does the preponderance of its business outside of the North American market.[110]

Stratex provides a classic example of a best of breed environment, as seen in Figure IV-5:

Figure IV-5: Current Application Environment at Stratex Networks

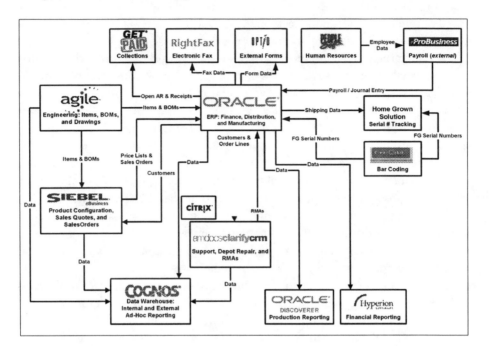

Diagram designed based on information provided by Stratex Networks, January 2003

Many of the decisions around the software selection and implementation of this best of breed environment occurred between the period of 1997 and 2002, and came under the direction of the CIO, B. Lee Jones. Jones was honored in 2002 by *CIO* magazine as one of the recipients of its *CIO 100 Awards*, where maximizing the value of an integrated environment was the main topic on which nominees were evaluated.[111] The Stratex environment grew over time in a period when the suite vendors were not able to supply complete end-to-end functionality. As Jones told me, "We didn't necessarily go with best of breed because we wanted to. We went there because the monolithic suite vendors couldn't support our needs. For certain key things, their solutions ranged anywhere from mediocre to dismal....Our projects are user-driven, focused on their requirements. If IT had forced decisions to use the suite approach back then, I would have ended up spending more in customizing the solution to meet their needs. That definitely was no way for us to go."[112] While the users drove the application requirements and system selections, Jones maintained ownership of the infrastructure, and here he made the conscious decision to standardize across the board. He selected Vitria as what he considered the best integration tool in the marketplace in 1999, and has leveraged that tool across each of his top-tier applications. All the core applications use Oracle for the database and Sun for hardware (Solaris for the operating system). Infrastructure standardization made the integration easier, and also enabled Jones to leverage specific support skills across multiple applications. This approach has made a big difference as headcount reduction in IT has become an economic reality at Stratex.

One of the strongest components of this best of breed architecture is that each of the major platforms exists in a single instance environment, supporting all users around the globe. So while there is integration between several of the applications, there is no need for any inter-platform integration. Jones is a strong proponent of the KISS approach to management and decision-making. "We debated the multi-instance approach, with different business owners having different opinions. But, once you go with multi-instance, you immediately get process differentiation, and once you start down that path, it's almost impossible to recover. Our choice was easy—the 'simple' choice of single instance architectures."

When I sat down with Jones, I asked him about his environment in terms of present capabilities and what options he might pursue in order to further optimize his environment. "The main thing I need to do is to upgrade our old version of Oracle (version 10.7, circa January 2000) to the Internet-based 11i,"[113] Jones told me. "That would open opportunities to optimize the entire environment and allow us to grow into some much needed capabilities." For example, PeopleSoft is currently in use as a stand-alone HR tool with a very limited number of users. When Stratex originally looked at Oracle for its HR solution in 2001, the company did not believe that the 10.7 version of Oracle HR could meet its needs. However, it also is not convinced that it is getting its money's worth out of the PeopleSoft solution, as the company is using only a small set of the available functionality. If Oracle was upgraded to version 11i, the Oracle HR solution would more than satisfy the company's functional needs and further optimize the overall environment.

- Opportunity One: Eliminate the cost of software maintenance and further support for the PeopleSoft platform, offset somewhat by the additional cost for Oracle HR. Net result would be positive based on:
    o Lower total cost,
    o Comparable process capabilities based on company requirements, and
    o Improved information as the employee master will now be fully integrated with the rest of the ERP platform with no additional integration for the company to build or maintain.

The second change would be to replace Clarify with Oracle Service. Clarify has been used at the company for nearly five years and was implemented prior to the Oracle solution, at a time when the company was using ManMan for its ERP infrastructure. Clarify is primarily used for service requests and depot repair functionality, as well as to initiate and track customer returns. While some of this functionality was rather immature in Oracle in version 10.7, it is much more robust in 11i and can certainly handle the specific needs of the Stratex Customer Service organization.

- Opportunity Two: Eliminate the cost of software maintenance and further support for the Clarify platform and the current two-way integration between Oracle and Clarify, offset somewhat by the additional cost for Oracle Service. Net result would again be positive based on:
  o Lower total cost,
  o Improved process capabilities with the fully-integrated, Web-based solution, and
  o Improved information, as now all service-related information will be fully integrated with the rest of the ERP platform with no additional integration for the company to build or maintain. This will consolidate an even higher percentage of customer-related information into a single system.

There are other long-term benefits of the Oracle upgrade to version 11i as well. The most compelling of these benefits revolves around out-of-the-box Oracle functionality that provides the foundation for automated communications with customers and partners, as well as self-service capabilities for employees, customers, and partners. Those capabilities are highly desired, but are not practical given the current release of software (version 10.7). In addition, implementing Oracle Service will also alleviate the need for the continued use of the Citrix solution, which is in place largely because of the network requirements for the Clarify application. That yields a third application that could be eliminated from the environment as a result of the Oracle upgrade and the corresponding consolidation of functionality within the Oracle Suite. These are all part of the plans for Jones and his team at Stratex.

With those changes, the environment would then look something like what is depicted in Figure IV-6:

Figure IV-6: Potential Consolidated Application Environment at Stratex Networks

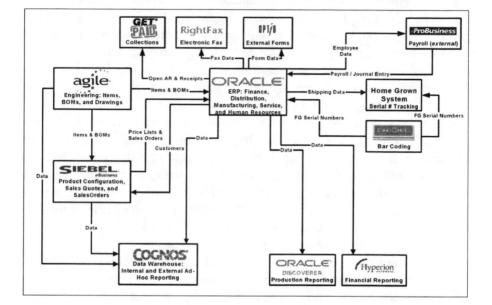

This would still be a best of breed environment, but based on a single-instance architecture, a common set of tools and hardware platform, and strong integration between just a handful of mission critical applications. That's pretty clean as far as best of breeds go. And the best of breed decisions here past muster within the context of the decision-making framework. Don't be misled by the number of "minor" applications resident in this integrated mix. Stratex has leveraged some of these minor add-ons to the Oracle environment (Optio, Right Fax, Get Paid, ClearOrbit, and Hyperion) for functionality that is simply not provided at a sufficient level by Oracle. If the Collections functionality in Oracle were able to match Get Paid, then Jones would consider replacing it. But it's still not there, even in 11i, so Get Paid will stay. The same could be said for Right Fax, Optio, and ClearOrbit. The point is not to eliminate *all* integrated applications—that may never be practical—but always to ask the question as to when it does make sense to consolidate, and to continuously evaluate those questions over time.

The same thought process can also be applied to the other major applications in the Stratex environment. Agile and Siebel continue to provide leading-edge functionality that is critical to the business processes at Stratex. Siebel is being used for a highly tailored product configurator solution that would be cost prohibitive to replace. This functionality could be redeployed using Oracle 11i, but it is a highly configured solution for which the replacement cost would be exceptionally high. The framework analysis agrees that it stays in Siebel, at least for the time being. Furthermore, while Oracle and several of the other leading ERP vendors are developing product lifecycle management (PLM) applications, none have reached the point of capability and maturity where a company like Stratex would be prepared to replace an installed package such as Agile at this time. Currently there is no compelling reason to make a change when viewed within the framework, and the decision to maintain these integrated solutions as part of an optimal architecture appears sound. That said, I asked Jones how he would implement the same footprint if he were starting today from scratch. His response: "It would probably be just Oracle 11i and Agile" for the application environment. In other words, even Siebel would be gone for the configurator and sales force automation if it weren't for how tightly that tool is already integrated into the environment. "The suites are just so much better today, so much more mature. I would still have our users deeply involved in the selection process—these are their systems, not mine—but I would expect much less need for the best of breed approach given the viability of the suites today."[114]

This is how to do best of breed really well: focus on top-tier applications, deploy them in single-instance architectures with a standard database platform, and provide the necessary integration with a single, powerful, and scaleable integration tool. Oh, and revisit the rationale for the environment mix on a regular basis to allow for further optimization by leveraging improved components of the architecture, such as with Stratex's plan for an upgrade to Oracle 11i and the corresponding decommissioning of PeopleSoft, Clarify, and Citrix. Other environments in larger companies may be more complex than the one presented here, but the concepts are the same. The professionals in the PI Department in all companies should look for enhanced capabilities by their core software suppliers that can provide opportunities to shut down additional platforms and the corresponding integration mess. When the time is right and the capabilities exist, these teams need to be ready to make the move and take advantage of the savings and operational improvements.

Finally, there is one additional component of the technology architecture at Stratex that merits attention; that is, the data warehouse. As Jones was going through his budgets with a fine tooth comb, it became clear to him that not having a robust data warehouse was costing him a lot of money. This was at a time when every dollar saved may equate to someone's job being saved, something that is very personal to Jones and drives him even harder to attempt to uncover every opportunity for savings. Prior to the widespread adoption of the Web-based version of the COGNOS data warehouse, Jones had to provide training for each of his core applications for many of his business users around the world, primarily just to satisfy their need for access to reports. Additionally, he had to support the license costs for all those users across each of these applications. By pushing the ad hoc reporting capability to the Web using COGNOS, Jones was able to significantly cut his training costs and his software license costs. COGNOS now has the largest user base of all the applications in the company, and at a dramatically reduced total cost compared to the prior situation. In addition, when Jones was recently faced with a sudden contractual requirement to extend information to specific external customers, he was able to leverage the COGNOS environment to provide a quick and simple solution. This also ensures that internal employees, sales reps, and these specific customers will all be referring to exactly the same data when discussing these accounts. That's a very nice step toward Information Optimization. Data warehouses, when done well, can be powerful allies on the path to Enterprise Optimization. In this case, the solution attacks all three components of the framework: dramatically lower total cost, improved processes for the user community in terms of getting access to data, and optimized information as the tool serves to consolidate all the data into a single, Web-based location.

Customization

Most of the discussion about suite vs. best of breed translates well to the debate over whether you're more likely to achieve optimal results when implementing "vanilla" software (i.e., based on the built-in capabilities provided by the vendor) or customized software. As seen in the best of breed approach, user communities that were not having their needs met by the suites pushed for point solutions that addressed their own immediate needs. In this context, these particular users may improve their short-term capabilities, but the costs will more than likely outweigh the benefits for the company as a whole, and may even yield long-term issues for the functional unit itself. Typically, you have the same constituents who pushed for a best of breed architecture also pushing for customized IT solutions. Business users often feel that they cannot work effectively within the confines of the package, and their simple workarounds are deemed unacceptable. In response, these users contact IT down the hallway to write some custom solution that appears to make their life easier, all in the name of Process Optimization. But at what cost? I wish I knew what the average *total* cost is for every $1,000 of software customization over the life of that solution. I contend that it's many times the base amount, in terms of headcount to support and maintain that customization, as well as all the elements it touches in terms of end-to-end processes and data integrity. The support costs alone go up dramatically (whether your support team is in-house or outsourced), plus these customizations often nullify your support agreements with the software vendors, largely putting you and your team on your own when problems arise.

What does it really mean when a user "can't live with" out-of-the-box functionality? Is the real statement "can't" or "won't" or simply "don't want to" live with the vanilla software? I'm the first one to admit that some of the modules in the major enterprise software applications are clumsy. But *unusable*? In most cases, that is definitely a stretch. Process Optimization is not just about getting every bell and whistle and form layout you've ever wanted. That would be nice, but decisions need to be made in terms of *all three* components of the framework, not just one. As was stated earlier, the "perfect process" in the eyes of a functional user may not represent an "optimal process" for the company as a whole. What does it mean for the company if Process Optimization increases by 10 percent as a result of some customization, but the impact on Total Cost and Information Optimization results in an overall hit to the company of 20 percent? Is that an optimal decision? Of course not. But in many companies today, that kind of approach would be approved because all anyone looks at might be the 10 percent process improvement being articulated by the functional team. This is how we end of with highly customized, best of breed (complex!) environments that become impossible to manage and fraught with issues.

With the sophistication of the enterprise systems today, coupled with the industry-specific versions and the industry-specific implementation knowledge of the system integrators, there is no reason companies that deploy Tier 1 systems cannot take the out-of-the-box approach and leave the implications of the custom work to someone else. In the past, one of the common reasons to customize these packages was that the system-mandated process flows were not flexible enough for the organization, or that the system didn't provide effective notifications related to these processes. In many cases these gripes were legitimate. However, advances in the technology in these two areas have been extensive with most of the top-tier platforms, now making it much easier to tailor the workflow of the processes *within* the confines of the package. This enables you to work with your functional colleagues, and/or your consulting partners, to optimize your business processes without tons of custom code. This flexibility may have been lacking in the past, but is definitely improving in recent incarnations of the enterprise software, now enabling adoption of embedded best practices, as well as making it easier to tailor these processes when necessary. Further, it is now fairly standard for these packages to support notifications (via e-mail, pagers, etc.) related to almost any stage in a process, often enabling managers to respond to those notifications without ever logging into the system itself. Coupled with the workflows, the system will place transactions on hold while notifying a manager for an approval, and then escalating that approval if the manager doesn't respond within a certain amount of time. All of this can be automated, including exception management, within the standard capabilities of these top-tier platforms. Does this still require some technical capabilities to pull it off? Usually, yes. But now it is within the standards and confines of the system itself, not an unsupported custom solution that creates havoc when you need to modify it (or fix it) down the road.

Here's my approach to requests for customizations. Rather than ask the user community open-ended questions such as, "What are your requirements?" or "What would you like the system to do?" I take the approach of, "Tell me why the out-of-the-box solution isn't acceptable?" or "What is it about the vanilla solution that won't work for you?" This puts the onus back on the requestor to make a compelling case, not the other way around. Someone needs to have an extremely strong argument to get me on his or her side to recommend a customization to the client. Remember, "complexity kills," and software customization is synonymous with environmental complexity. Of course there will be exceptions, and there are different kinds of customizations, some more effective than others, but the bar should remain high in all cases to present an argument not about what you want, but why the out-of-the-box solution simply won't work.

One of the typical reasons we face this issue in the system implementation business is that hands-on users simply want what they've always had in terms of functionality, process flows, and information reporting. How quickly these folks forget the pain it took to customize their legacy systems to get them what they have today, and most have no idea what the total cost of those custom solutions was. Why would you want to replicate that suboptimal environment in your brand new solution? Plus, perhaps the way you've managed to perform your processes in the past simply no longer makes sense, or may have never been optimal in the first place.

Decisions about customization must come back to the long-term impact on all three components of the Enterprise Optimization Framework. I'll take out-of-the-box software and flawless execution over a customization approach any day of the week, even if I have to make a few compromises in terms of process definitions to get there. Are there exceptions to this approach? Absolutely. The key is to treat customizations as exceptions and not allow them to become the norm. Make it difficult for people to justify the need to customize. Make them demonstrate the long-term advantage based on the framework. If they make the case, go ahead and have your outsource development team do its job. But set the bar high, and you will be served well in the end. And always be on the lookout for opportunities to decommission customizations in your complex environments when your vendor begins to provide similar capabilities in an upgraded, out-of-the-box solution.

The PI Department has a hand in guiding all of these decisions, all in the context of what is good for the company as a whole relative to the framework. The Process Department can't become biased for a customized process solution and lose objectivity when it comes to the overall cost of that solution. All members of the PI Department need to understand the implication of adding complexity to their environments and fight the urge to customize, knowing the long-term costs of that approach. It doesn't do the company any good to optimize a process if it has to suffer through off-setting (or worse) implications in terms of the other components of the framework. The PI Department needs to set these guidelines and then work with its colleagues to see the light in focusing on flawless execution of the solutions as originally intended, rather than constantly trying to alter the technology to do things in a manner they were not designed to work. *Keep it simple!* Leverage what others have done before you. Utilize "best practices" in the context of out-of-the-box solutions, and then focus on executing better than anyone else. These guidelines will help you optimize your organization far better than a never-ending battle of building and maintaining one complex custom solution after another.

Evaluating Suite vs. Best of Breed vs. Tools-Based Solutions

If you find yourself in the midst of an integration nightmare, rest assured that you're not alone. The question remains what to do about it. How can you optimize your environment in the context of the framework given your current level of complexity? I recommend the following decision-making hierarchy, which puts the maximum value on the options that are higher in the list. In other words, higher levels of Enterprise Optimization will be reached the more you can answer "yes" to the higher level questions for each opportunity being evaluated by your PI Department.

- Evaluate the degree to which your enterprise system supplier(s) can adequately support the required functionality.
    - o If no, then evaluate identified solution partners of your enterprise system supplier(s) to determine if any of them can adequately support the required functionality with prepackaged, integrated solutions.
        - ▪ If no, then evaluate other solution providers in the marketplace to determine if any of them can adequately support the required functionality with prepackaged, integrated solutions.

- If no, then evaluate independent tools vendors (ideally those that have partnerships with your core providers) to identify the best manner in which to build the solution on your own, or to customize an existing solution to meet the requirement.

The whole premise is reducing the complexity of these environments by offloading the integration components to someone who has already built, tested, and deployed them before. Complexity drives up costs, and drives out efficiency and effectiveness. It also severely restricts corporate agility and the ability to provide a single face to customers or partners. There will certainly be cases where you will not be able to answer "yes" to the top two or even three questions in the hierarchy above. All companies will need to face these challenges and deal with them in the context of the framework in trying to make an optimal decision given the available options at a particular point in time. But that doesn't mean we look to build custom solutions as our first option, at least not based on what's available in the marketplace today. Who knows, maybe in a couple of years I'll turn this decision-making hierarchy upside down and business process management and/or Web services-based tools (which will be discussed in detail later in this next section) will dominate this decision-making landscape. In fact, that would be ideal! But we need to be careful about jumping for solutions that are still in an early, emerging state. As has been stated several times, our decisions must reflect the capabilities at a particular point in time. At *this* point in time, custom tools-based solutions should be seen as the *last* alternative in the decision-making process.

Let's take a look at a couple of scenarios where an integrated solution does appear to make sense in the context of the framework. We already discussed a couple of examples in the case study around Stratex Networks. The core systems could not provide adequate support in the following areas:

- Bar coding
- Serial number tracking
- Collections
- Tax calculations
- Automated faxing
- External forms (invoices, sales order acknowledgements, packing slips, etc.)
- Payroll

A best of breed solution was needed to satisfy the business requirement, and integration was necessary to complete the solution. One of the advantages for Stratex, however, was that at least the integration leveraged a single tool, was built upon a common infrastructure (database and operating system) across all plat-forms, and each of the core solutions existed in a single-instance environment. In this case all four levels of the decision-making hierarchy listed above were needed (the serial number tracking system represented the homegrown, tools-based solu-tion). Just as Stratex is looking to replace significant portions of its best of breed environment today, it will continue to look for opportunities to replace more over time. Things change quickly in the technology world, presenting ongoing opportunities for optimization.

Looking at what some of the integrated tools and solutions have to offer, there are trends worth noting that make a tools selection more viable. Some things to look out for include:

- The rules governing specific processes are incredibly complex with a myr-iad of permutations.
- The rules can change at a moment's notice, and companies are required to be 100 percent up to date on these changes as soon as they are imposed.
- Audibility (information management) is essential when questioned by authorities.
- The penalty for non-compliance can be severe.

Think in terms of the areas such as payroll, benefits, taxation, and trade compli-ance. All of these processes require complex rules that can change at a moment's notice, and the last thing any company needs is a case of employee unrest due to system errors in their paychecks or their benefit statements, or problems with the government related to tax or customs. Further, it may make sense to identify a robust, external rules engine and process management tool for these processes in that *managing the content* becomes a critical component for success. In these cases, even if ERP suite vendors provide the rules engines for these processes, there is still that issue of content management (i.e., the regulations themselves). In the Enterprise Optimization Framework, it is very attractive to be able to outsource these entire areas where you can work closely with qualified partners to provide an overall solution. Complicated rules-driven processes, especially where the content management of the rules is a key component, may be one area where externalizing the rules management may prove to be the optimal solution, regardless of the functionality provided by your core systems. Content management is likely not to be a core competence of your organization, so why manage those tasks? Let the experts do it, and go for the integrated solution in a well-designed, straightforward manner. This makes perfect sense, and is why each and every opportunity needs to be objectively evaluated in terms of the overall impact on the three components of the framework. In order to truly make this straightforward, however, there is no question that the state of your technical infrastructure will have a role in this analysis. It will be far easier and less expensive to externalize and integrate any of these processes with a qualified partner if the required integration stems from a single source, rather than from multiple point-to-point solutions from around the globe.

The context of this discussion has primarily been about internal software utilization, as well as collaboration with various partners. So how does the application service provider (ASP) world fit into this mix in terms of integration? As stated in Section III, one of the major challenges in the early days of the ASP model was the lack of any integration capabilities beyond the specific solution hosted by the ASP. As we now start to see integration capabilities emerge for ASPs, how does that impact their viability as part of our application footprint? The answer lies in the basic analysis of the framework. If the ASP can provide an optimal solution, given all the factors regarding process, information, and total cost (including the ramifications in all three areas around integration), the ASP path may make perfect sense. The surviving ASPs have listened to the marketplace and are beginning to respond with integration capabilities that deserve to be evaluated. Plus, we're now seeing these growing service providers (such as NetSuite and salesforce.com) expanding the breadth of their offerings with enhanced end-to-end functionality. This move is positioning them to take on the enterprise suite vendors, and not just provide best of breed point solutions. This extended capability, if done right without loss of stability or over-complexity, may quickly further the maturation of this business model.

So now you're looking at broader, integrated ASP solutions, as well as the capability to extend that integration to other back office systems. This is a far cry from where we were just a couple of years ago, and at least merits the attention of the analysts in the PI Department. A problem may arise if you begin to partner with multiple ASPs or managed services providers. While the individual integration points may be viable, you should be cautious about extending this model too far, as this integration strategy may not scale very well across multiple platforms (at least not yet). In other words, be cautious about taking what are "simple" solutions on their own and creating an overly "complex" solution by tying too many of them together. But as these solutions continue to mature, both in functional depth and in ease of integration, they should at least be considered as alternatives in the overall context of the framework. Remember, the decision-making hierarchy listed above looks first to the capabilities of your enterprise system supplier(s). There's nothing that says your enterprise system supplier shouldn't be an ASP.

In the end, in all cases it's about providing robust technological services in a clean and simple environment. This requires constant analysis of the current environment and a willingness to put aside past decisions in favor of new options when they become available. It also means ensuring that the new options are truly viable, as risk and likelihood of success need to be integral components of the analysis of the PI Department. In other words, make sure the solutions you select are real and not just a bunch of hype.

The Future is Now...Or Is It?

This is not a book about technology. The focus has been around organization, decision-making, and strategies companies can adopt in order to achieve further levels of optimization throughout their enterprises. That being said, information technology absolutely plays a role in enabling many of the strategies that have been identified to move down this path of optimization. As such, the members of the PI Department need to have a keen awareness of what is available in the marketplace, and what may be on the horizon, as the basis for decision-making on the likely outcomes and benefits of specific opportunities. They don't need to be knee deep in the technology itself to be successful in this role. Rather, they need to understand the costs, benefits, and impacts of making information technology investments, and then to assign the appropriate resources (in-house or outsourced) to execute the delivery of those solutions. It's primarily the capabilities that need to be understood, but that's not quite all. As the technology marketplace evolves quickly from one innovation to the next, PI professionals need to be aware of the risks and rewards of being early adopters of new technologies vs. being laggards vs. being somewhere in between. I live in a consulting world ripe with early adopters, anxious to jump at a moment's notice on the hot new thing (whatever it is) in the firm belief that it's an opportunity to gain immediate competitive advantage. I've been through these exercises where they have worked like a charm, but I've also seen companies get badly burned by the latest innovation from a technology vendor. I try to be aware of the Gartner "hype cycles," and factor the maturity of a given solution into any objective calculations within the context of the framework. I don't need to be first or second with the "hot new" innovation, but I do aggressively look for early marketplace validation so that I can still be on the initial uptake of any technological wave. This gives me the opportunity to learn from the failures of others, but still be able to gain advantage over the competition. Typically, this is when the hype is wearing off and the real benefits begin to emerge. This is the case of an ongoing delicate balancing act where experience and industry insights prove invaluable for PI Departments and their companies.

We all want to achieve competitive advantage, and the latest and greatest movements in information technology often appear tempting as the "silver bullet" that is going to put us over the top. But there is danger in looking for that silver bullet (as discussed in Section II). First, it may not exist at all, or, more likely, someone says it exists but it really doesn't. We need to balance our trust in the statements of the leaders in the IT industry to make good on their marketing claims with the fact that many of us have been burned by taking on too much risk in these wonderful-sounding but immature offerings that ultimately do not live up to expectations (or not work at all).

No one can forecast whether or not you should be an early adopter—that is largely ingrained in you or your company's approach to the risk/reward continuum. But it is prudent when investigating new technologies to have a plan of action that includes the following steps:

- Understand the vision of the new piece of technology in the context of what it may be able to do to optimize your organization.
- Translate that vision to reality—what's real today, what will be real in the short term, and what will likely be real in the long term.
- Understand the track record of the solution provider in terms of being able to deliver on its vision.
- Understand what the path is around the vision with your customers, your partners, and within your industry.
- Understand what the analyst community is saying about the new technology (in the context of the track record of any particular analyst who is commenting on the topic).
- Investigate specific examples where another company (ideally one within your industry) has taken advantage of this new piece of technology, and understand any lessons learned from that company's efforts.
- Ultimately, have your PI Department prepare an analysis of expected outcomes (best case, worst case, likely outcome, and break-even scenario) within the context of the Enterprise Optimization Framework. Initiatives based on new technologies should have a higher bar for approval in that the likelihood of success is less well known than with more mature technologies.
- Finally, if you decide to pursue the initiative, be sure that you continue to track progress against your impacted metrics well after the delivery is complete to validate your assumptions and actual results.

The bar should be high when investing shareholder money. The "gut feel" approach to decision-making can no longer apply, particularly with respect to the latest technological innovations, which may sound like the perfect solution to the "gut" but may be more smoke and mirrors than anything else when you pull back the covers for detailed analysis. Early adopters may gain advantages, but they are also likely to suffer significant pain along the way, which may negate much of the actual value of those potential advantages. As always, have your Process and Information Department use the framework in a disciplined way, and let the metric-driven, analytical results guide your actions. Just as with any initiative, this is the surest way to making good decisions in your quest to achieve Enterprise Optimization.

At this point in time, there are a handful of exciting, innovative developments going on in the world of information technology. The remainder of this section serves to highlight three of these areas:

- On-demand services
- Web services
- Business process management

Each of these is in the early stages of development, and each has a hype cycle underway that cries out for caution. I will highlight the vision, as well as the reality for each of these solution areas. My advice: make yourself aware of each of these initiatives, but proceed with caution. Make sure you include risk analysis in the context of the framework and understand that there will be more failures than successes in the early goings. The job of the PI Department is to be aware of these (and other) initiatives, and be ready to jump if and when the solution area begins to gain traction and success in the marketplace.

On-Demand Services

Regardless of what the service is, ideally you would only use as much as you need, and you would only pay for as much as you use. This is the model for most of our commodity services, including electricity, gas, water, telecommunications, and others. In technology, the ASP model was designed in part so that you sign up for a certain number of users per month and that's all you pay for, and you could change that number on a monthly basis. In a world where accurately forecasting demand (for products or services) is extremely difficult, it is clearly advantageous to the consumer to only pay for those services that are actually consumed.

Addressing this challenge is largely the theory behind a new technology trend referred to as "on-demand services." IBM is arguably the leading advocate for this emerging solution, with HP and Sun Microsystems also investing heavily in this space, along with software powerhouses Oracle and Computer Associates, among others. IBM's on-demand offerings span multiple areas (see Figure IV-7), and now consume a large portion of the overall market strategy for Big Blue.

Figure IV-7: IBM's On-Demand Offerings

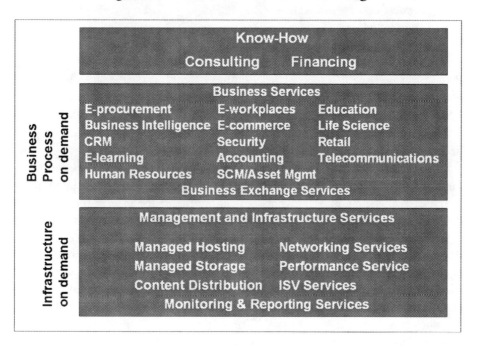

Source: IBM Website (ibm.com), December, 2002

According to the company, "The promise of on demand is that companies or institutions can respond dynamically to whatever business challenges arise. They can provide products and services 'on demand,' in real time. They can adapt their cost structures and business processes to reduce risk and drive business process improvement. They can optimize their IT infrastructures to cut costs and boost productivity. And they can be resilient—prepared for whatever challenges may arise."[115] Sounds right up the alley of the Enterprise Optimization Framework! This is a monstrous undertaking, requiring massive technological development and significant change management on the way to fulfilling the overall vision. Let's take a look at where we are today.

"In 2000, IBM created a series of internal divisions, now called Emerging Businesses Opportunities (EBOs), that focus, among other things, on developing new technologies for the different pieces of on-demand, including:

- Utility (essentially pay-by-the-drink IT)
- Autonomic (software that automatically diagnoses and fixes computer problems)
- Grid (pooling computers to form a single virtual entity)
- Business process integration
- Linux (IBM's answer to providing a single OS that can run on any type of computer, from a mainframe to a PC)

IBM says it will spend much of its $5 billion R&D budget on the EBO technologies in 2003."[116] This is a major investment around an entire strategy in IBM's quest to continue to dominate the global IT landscape.

There are certainly some notable achievements for IBM to date, including the success of WebSphere in the integration tools space and the continuing adoption of Linux throughout the industry. Neither of these has achieved true industry standards, but IBM's influence has certainly helped to foster growth and adoption in each of these areas. But what about those first three areas in the guts of the hardware and software solutions? IBM is already signing up companies in the "utility" framework for IT outsourcing. In December 2002, IBM agreed with J.P. Morgan Chase & Co. on a seven-year, $5-billion outsourcing arrangement based on the "pay as you go" model. Only about $1 billion of the deal is guaranteed based on fixed cost investments, with the rest being applied on a variable basis in relation to actual usage. The agreement covers data center operations, help desks, data networks and voice networks.[117] There's a lot to overcome here to get this to work, including issues around security, industry standardization, network infrastructure, software, etc., but if IBM can crack this nut then it will be well-positioned to take market share from its competitors. No longer would customers be locked into a flat rate that is probably tilted toward the provider so that it can adequately cover your anticipated needs (with a little headroom built in). Rather, you would pay for what you use, and nothing more. Not only can this approach to outsourcing benefit IBM as a first mover, but it can also differentiate itself in the marketplace as smaller competitors may not have the overall depth to be able to offer such a flexible service.

So once again we've got the vision, and with some of the large computer companies we've even got significant commitment and investment around the vision, but how close are we to real breakthroughs in this space? Skepticism abounds. We are still in the very early stage of development of on-demand and buyers need to be cautious about exactly what they're getting for their investment dollar. On-demand is about creating a whole new approach to the computing industry, so it's not just the technology that will be the stumbling block, but an entire mindset, as well. Even the pricing of the solution is turning out to be incredibly complex, since no one has been able to establish a universal metric for measuring the usage of computers. In telecommunications, we price by the minute. In electricity, we price by the kilowatt. These are pervasive standards. In utility computing, however, there is no standard, as this unit of measure has to account for data-storage capacity and processing power, and must be flexible enough to accommodate the shifting needs of customers. IBM has the "service unit," HP has the "computon," and Sun has the "Sun power unit," all of which are different and are further varied on a customer by customer basis.[118] The technology is challenging enough, but many additional aspects of this new solution will need to be resolved before the marketplace will be ready to jump on board.

Christopher Koch provided this perspective in a July 1, 2003, piece in *CIO* magazine:

> On-demand exists only in theory. And while CIOs during the years have managed plenty of difficult technology projects, implementing theories has never before been on their to-do lists.
>
> In this economy, CIOs who jump the gun on any of those technologies—or who let their CEOs and CFOs fire it for them—will pay dearly. The technologies for making what you have more efficient are untested, and most require consulting help. In today's economic environment, CIOs need to make sure that any experiments they undertake have clear business payback, and that's tough to do when the technologies are so immature. [Sounds like an analysis job for a PI Department and the Enterprise Optimization Framework!]
>
> What's clear is that right now e-business on-demand is not much more than a slogan. CIOs who think it's something more are looking through those magic business binoculars, darkly.[119]

On-demand solutions provide an attractive vision and are currently supported in the early development phases by the dominant player in the IT industry. Process, Information, and Total Cost Optimization are parts of the vision, but at what cost today, and at what risk level? We need to be cautious about the marketing and hype cycle associated with something as dramatic as on-demand. Yes, there are limited components that are viable today, but there remains a lot to overcome to bring the vision together (be it by IBM, HP, or any other solution provider willing to invest billions for a competitive edge in this space). This is again why we all need a PI Department that can uncover the reality and provide objective advice for business executives who may not understand the risks and ramifications of being an early adopter in this space.

Web Services

While I maintain that instance and systems consolidation is the optimal approach to technology infrastructure, there will continue to be organizations that reject this approach, or feel that they are unable to effectively unwind their complicated technology architectures. Many organizations remain committed to highly integrated best of breed approaches, so those environments need to be addressed as well in terms of the Enterprise Optimization Framework. One area generating a lot of excitement (hype?) with respect to enhancing integration capabilities is that of Web services, where the concept is that you can take advantage of new technologies that will enable you to utilize a common data element throughout your enterprise architecture, even if that data element is defined and stored in multiple applications. Here's one definition of Web services and how they work:

> Web services are software modules wrapped inside a specific set of Internet communications protocols and can be run over the Internet. In order for the Web service to be run, it needs to be described in detail so that other programs can understand what it is and know how to connect to it.…For a computer or program to use a Web service, it needs to be able to find this service description and then bind to it. To accomplish this, there are three key roles in the Web services architecture: Service Provider, Service Registry, and Service Requestor. Together, they perform three operations on a Web service:
>   1. **Publish**—The service provider hosting the Web service module creates an XML-based service description for the Web service. It uses the publish operation to make information about the service available so that it can be found and used.
>   2. **Find**—The service registry, using the UDDI protocol, makes service descriptions available so that Web services can be found and run. A computer or program can search for, and understand, what the Web service is, where it's located and how to link to it.
>   3. **Bind and run the service**—After the service requestor finds the Web service's description, it has the information it needs to run the Web service.[120]

That's the most straightforward definition I could find! Part of the problem has been all these acronyms. (See Figure IV-8 for some definitions of the key elements in the Web services vocabulary.) That being said, after sorting through the jargon, you can see some very positive opportunities in bringing Web services to life.

Figure IV-8: Most Common Web Services Standards

- XML (Extensible Markup Language)
  - o A markup language that structures information so that it can easily be extracted and used by other applications. It uses tags, as does HTML, but those tags are used to structure and define information rather than display it. Service descriptors that detail how Web services can be located and run are written in XML.

- SOAP (Simple Object Access Protocol)
  - o The protocol through which Web services communication takes place. It's used to exchange structured data between network applications. SOAP is used to publish service descriptions to a service registry. In fact, all interactions among service registry, service requestor and service providers are done via SOAP.

- WSDL (Web Services Description Language)
  - o The language used to create service descriptions of Web services. It can be used to describe the location of the service and how to run it, as well as what business is hosting the service, the kind of service it is, keywords associated with the service and similar information.

- UDDI (Universal Description, Discovery, and Integration)
  - o The directory technology used by service registries that allows the directory to be searched for a particular Web service. In essence, UDDI is a White Pages or Yellow Pages that can be used to locate Web services. There can be both private and public UDDI directories.

Source: *CIO* magazine, "The Promise of Web Services," April 15, 2002

As mentioned, one of our biggest headaches in the world of information systems is trying to connect those systems, moving data elements and transaction components from one system to the next. This traditionally has always been done in the context of hard-coded data mapping across often-disparate technology platforms. The promise of Web services is that we'll be able to define that element in the Web services environment as a common, single entity, and then share (and update) that entity in real-time across multiple applications. One early adopter success story of Web services can be seen at Dell, which used the .NET Web services technology from Microsoft to significantly enhance the customer experience and decrease the total cost of ownership in its popular web-based storefront. The original Web services that were developed included real-time tax calculation, shipping calculation, shopping comparisons, address verification, and order status. Now, these are services that are provided on many web sites, but the real-time integration has often been problematic when connecting with third-party vendors and solutions for the various elements of these services. The traditional approach has been point-to-point integration, often with hard-coded rules, which is time-consuming and costly to both develop and maintain, as well as very difficult to leverage from one integration solution to the next. The Web services approach at Dell enabled high reusability for each of these pieces, as well as dramatically lower total cost of ownership. Susan Sheskey, Dell's VP of Sales, Marketing, and Services IT, expressed some of the benefits of this approach. "By using Web services, we can develop programs in languages that are useful to a particular business need and share components across the enterprise." She added, "One of the advantages that we didn't anticipate early on with the adoption of Web services is the ability to build our way out of the legacy environment, one step at a time." Dell is now looking to continue the reuse of these services in extending these capabilities to its partners, suppliers, and customers. According to Sheskey, "The idea of build it once, update it quickly, and make it available for subscription for anyone to take advantage of whenever they need it is extraordinarily helpful."[121]

One of the compelling aspects of Microsoft's approach to Web services is that we will get a chance to have seamless integration between our business applications, our web applications, and our desktop applications, the latter of which are dominated by the Microsoft product line. We all love the ease of use and flexibility of products such as Microsoft Excel, but it's often a full development task to upload or download data from Excel into these other systems. How about running your planning organization on Excel, and then seamlessly integrating that data into your core information and web front-end systems? Most of us use PowerPoint, Word, Outlook, Internet Explorer, Visio, and Microsoft Project for much of our daily business activities, yet we have difficulty leveraging any of these assets outside of the Microsoft suite of products (at least without significant integration development). I would sure appreciate the opportunity to do my work in these familiar tools, and then use a Web services platform to propagate my data across various HR, budgeting, CRM, and billing systems. Maybe we could get rid of the term "working off-line" if these traditional "off-line" tools finally become seamlessly integrated with our core on-line systems.

All this being said, if the opportunities for Web services appear as rosy as just described, then why has adoption of Web services remained relatively light, with continued forecast from the analyst community indicating relatively slow adoption by mainstream businesses in the near future? There are, in fact, a number of inhibitors that must be understood before jumping onto the Web services bandwagon.

IBM's former boss, Lou Gerstner, provided this commentary when asked about integration and standards: "The process of integrating this technology and achieving the benefit is unbelievably painful for customers. The industry has been all about faster, faster, more function, more function. Most devastating from a customer point of view are the lack of standards and the lack of interchangeability. It is truly a mess. You wouldn't deliver steel to General Motors in a different form than every other steel company."[122] I wholeheartedly agree. The lack of standards has been a tremendous inhibitor to our collective ability to take advantage of the age of Internet computing, and Web services have yet to solve this problem. Giga Information Group put the challenge of bringing Web services to life in the following context:

> There is no common, agreed-upon definition of what a Web service is. Since there is no Web services "architect," there is no agreed upon definition of a Web services architecture. The Web services vision is being driven by multiple, sometimes conflicting, visions of what Web services are by vendors and users. This lack of a clear, common definition means that there are multiple logical Web services architectures being proposed by vendors and users. While there are still gaps where standards are needed, a more pressing problem is the increasing fragmentation and "niching" of Web services standards, tools, APIs and technology. We have multiple security standards being proposed, multiple business process management standards, even multiple standards for reliable messaging at the wire level. While it's certainly true that many vendors put out standards as proposals, in order to stake a position, and then work behind the scenes to get agreement, the problem is that user involvement typically comes very late in the process. The key Web services value proposition of interoperability is jeopardized.[123]

Part of the problem is that the leading software companies that are pushing for Web services standards can't agree on what those standards should be. Most troubling is that one of the key areas where disagreement persists relates to security. What could be a more devastating gap than security standards when it comes to Internet-based communication? It is true that we do have a few standards that are starting to gain traction, but only XML has made any material headway thus far.

Microsoft, IBM, Oracle, Sun, and others all have a stake in these definitions, but they also have competing interests, and these are typically not the sorts of organizations that have a great track record in coming together for the good of mankind. As such, we get .NET from Microsoft, which isn't quite the same as

WebSphere from IBM, which differs from the 9iAS solution from Oracle, etc. Then you've got application-oriented solutions such as NetWeaver from SAP and the process-focused Universal Application Network (UAN) from Siebel, all claiming to be based on Web services standards (whatever they may be). These are well-funded, ambitious offerings, and they may be able to provide some advantages within individual organizations or small networks of partners who all agree to the same platform. However, everything I see tells me that we're at least two or three years away from having true standards to help manage our broad integration challenges in an Internet-based environment.

I particularly enjoyed the way Steve Baloff, general partner at Advanced Technology Ventures in Palo Alto, California, portrayed Web services, and what we can expect in the near future.

> Web services is an amorphous blob of business apps, and different players define it differently. Ultimately it can be described as any application delivered over the Internet and accessed by almost any device, from PCs to mobile phones. What Web services can offer is a set of shared protocols and standards that permit systems to share data and services without requiring humans to broker the conversation. The result promises to be "on-the-fly" links between the online processes of different companies.

> The middleware vendors and system integrators have made fortunes, but for many businesses, the resulting mess of hard-coded, inflexible bindings between legacy and new enterprise software is certainly not the solution they dream about.

> The Web services dream, if fulfilled, could provide far more control for end users to assemble the needed building blocks that allow for tremendous flexibility and lower total cost of ownership. In today's world, the high-cost integration software and services that currently link enterprise applications are simply not sustainable. If it works, Web services will offer an escape hatch....[However,] while the promise of Web services is definitely attractive, the time frames and benefits have been overstated.[124]

In other words, beware the hype! Based on the evidence to date, we're a long way from reaching the goal in which Web services develop into a broad set of standards in which individuals can actually adopt and receive value. The concept alone is challenging enough, and industry in-fighting is making it that much more difficult.

As such, my skepticism abounds for the near-term prospects of Web services in the context of Enterprise Optimization. Experience has taught me to always be cautious about new technologies in the software industry. The concept of Web services has heightened my nervousness for three reasons in particular: (1) it requires cooperation between rivals in order to create true industry standards, (2) it touches on the most challenging component of the software landscape—integration between multiple systems, and (3) there has been very little progress in security standards, which continues to remain the biggest concern about doing business over the Internet. This combination is crying out for caution. The troubling aspect is that the vision of Web services is exactly what so many companies believe will be the answer to all their problems. That's what makes the hype so dangerous. Plenty of my technical colleagues for whom I have tremendous respect assure me that the concept of Web services is real, and that it will absolutely change the way we deploy technology. They may be right—eventually—but I remain skeptical and cautious about what to do *today*.

To this end, a review of technical architectures continues to be prudent in any best of breed shop. Analysis is called for, in the context of the Enterprise Optimization Framework, to determine the degree to which instances can be consolidated and systems retired to create the "cleanest" environments possible. This exercise will yield opportunities for optimizing the enterprise, both for internal operations and communications beyond the organization. In cases where multiple technologies are in play, standards should be adopted at least at the individual organization level. If your environment requires integration, you will serve yourself well if you standardize on a small set of integration tools and methodologies. Adopt what's common in your industry and what your primary partners are using. There may be elements of Web services solutions that have proved successful on a targeted scale in your industry that may be ready for adoption. Focus on those. Just as standardization of instances and systems can yield significant results, so can standardization of integration tools. Industry-wide standards for integration don't exist at this point, and we may be a long way from getting there. In the meantime, simplification and standardization of those environments that are within your control or sphere of influence are strongly recommended. This kind of approach will provide another key component in your ability to optimize your enterprise.

The issues associated with the lack of industry standards for Web services and overall integration technology do not stop at a company's firewall. The potentially larger benefits these standards will enable will be the eventual explosion of integration with external partners. Refer again to the "hype cycle" curve that was mentioned earlier. The Internet boom promised all kinds of breakthroughs in electronic collaboration, as customers, multi-tier suppliers, and various other partners would be connected in real time, providing extended visibilities throughout end-to-end process value chains. We started hearing about exchanges, e-hubs, and all sorts of other collaboration vehicles, all representing tremendous potential for companies and industries. Through effectiveness in our processes, data management, and technology architectures, we would have the opportunity at our fingertips to create value for our enterprises. We would be able to lower our costs. We would be able to dramatically improve our processes and the availability of critical information. We would be able to enable better decision-making. But, the fact is, we haven't achieved most of these results—a common theme to these recurring hype cycles. There are several reasons the promise of this phenomenon has yet to become a reality.

The first, as stated, is the lack of industry standards with respect to collaboration technology. The lack of standards is particularly troublesome as so many parties need to play together in order for this end-to-end collaboration to really work. If we want communities of partners sharing data to drive optimal decision-making, then all the links in the chain need to be connected. The lack of standards makes this extraordinarily complex and often cost prohibitive, as you end up with a myriad of point-to-point solutions based on the personal tastes of each of your external partners. At least within individual enterprises, or in small, tightly controlled networks, we have the ability to maintain control over the communication technologies, and can at least enforce our own standards. But when you start venturing into broader networks of communication, this becomes exponentially harder. This is one of the reasons why even the limited adoption of Web services today is predominantly limited to within individual organizations or in very small partner networks. (See Figure IV-9)

Figure IV-9: Integration Scenarios for Web Services Usage

Integration Scenarios	% Response
Integration or Development Within Your Enterprise	44%
Integration of Applications Between Fewer Than 10 Known Partners	22%
Integration of Applications Between More Than 10 Partners in Private	11%
Integration Within a Public Exchange	12%
Others/Don't Know	11%

Source: Gartner Group, "Systems Integrators and Users Advance Web Services Use in 2002," January 14, 2003.

Beyond the issue of technology and standards, there are other fundamental challenges in the marketplace inhibiting the pursuit of external collaboration. Many of these problems tie back to the ugly back-office environments of so many of our companies—in other words, totally independent of the technological challenges for enterprise-to-enterprise communication. Specifically, the back office components that are impeding progress in this area include:

- Lack of confidence in the quality of data
  - What's the point of providing insight into your information systems if the underlying data is untrustworthy in the first place? How many companies can honestly claim complete trust in their data? How about just marginal trust? How many companies are prepared to share data in which they lack confidence? Many of the companies that have invested in collaboration technology are unable to meet expectations in terms of benefits given the lack of quality of the underlying data. This is the critical responsibility of the PI Department in the area of Information Optimization. This means providing easy access to relevant data, as well as ensuring that the data is accurate and can be trusted. Far too many companies lack structure and discipline around the management of their systems, nullifying the opportunities for optimization. This diminished returns reality affects companies internally as well as externally, and remains a principal reason why we have not achieved the collective benefits around enterprise-to-enterprise collaboration.

- Multi-instance environments
  - The second phenomenon that has limited our ability to succeed in the external collaboration space is our back-office mess of multi-instance software platforms. Just as this inhibits our ability to achieve a comprehensive internal view of our global enterprises, it further impacts our ability to provide that view to our external partners. These partners want to do business with single entities, but multi-instance environments make this extraordinarily difficult and extremely costly. And in these difficult economic times, that means we're not likely to do it. Of course, the flipside provides the opportunistic view that yields advantages to single-instance environments that *are* capable of providing one face to the customer/partner and provide a platform in which external collaboration is significantly more viable.

- Complex internal integration
  - Along these same lines, we've got companies that support the highly integrated back-office mess, serving as another limiting factor in deploying external collaboration. As your data streams across multiple systems and goes through various translations, you limit your effectiveness in maintaining a clean and accurate data environment. This goes back to an earlier point where lack of data quality almost defeats the purpose of external collaboration. Data integrity is significantly more challenging (and costly) in highly integrated back-office environments, which serve as a contributor to data quality degradation. This kind of architecture presents technical challenges to the integration necessary for sophisticated, end-to-end data collaboration. More importantly, these architectures (especially in their extreme forms) often impact data integrity, which has an even deeper impact on the potential value generation which could be realized by way of external collaboration.

In collaboration environments today, typically you're faced with a collection of point-to-point solutions in which the individual connections are rarely leveraged for economies of scale. Rather, you're reinventing the wheel for each and every integration point with each and every partner. This approach is similar to our typical legacy mess for our internal architectures, with lots of confusing point-to-point integrations linking our systems together. This approach is neither optimal for our internal communications nor for our external collaboration.

We all need to clean up our back-office environments in terms of data quality and instance and system consolidation. Then we need to extend those same improvements to our collaboration environment. Industry standard technology would sure help bring this kind of structure to life, but in the meantime, partners need to work together (ideally at the industry level) in order to define at least a minimal level of standardization in order to get started building these communication networks. This is where corporate partners and industry groups are going to need to force the issue on Web services and other standards if these kinds of architectures are to become viable on a widespread basis. Without this pressure and cooperation, we'll never achieve the long-term vision of Web services, and our collective efforts toward optimization will be thwarted.

The fact is we haven't seen much progress in this area, which, frankly, is a crying shame. Partner collaboration (on the demand side as well as the supply side) presents one of the most powerful opportunities of the Internet age. This is where the Internet hype really has the opportunity to produce significant results. So much money is left on the table throughout these end-to-end demand and supply chains. Time is money, and the manual steps and human intervention required to move processes in and through various companies waste tons of time. We have the opportunity, with a commitment to discipline around processes and data, to drive cost out of our structures. Collectively we just aren't living up to the task, either inside or outside the firewall.

Those companies that are successful in this task have a clear shot at competitive advantage, at least in the foreseeable future. Marco Iansiti, a Harvard Business School professor, put it this way: "Business is becoming the art of managing assets that are largely outside your direct control—a broadening network of suppliers that provides you with what you need. So all you have left is the integration combination that makes the business run. If you don't integrate now, you're going to later, so you might as well think about it now."[125] But you can't just throw money at solutions like this. Without organizational discipline, specifically with respect to data and technical architectures, you have virtually no chance to succeed. External collaboration represents one of the true potential opportunities for the Internet age, and this is one area where excellence in integration is fundamental to success. There is no quick answer to the lack of industry standards. One would have to believe that market forces will provide a solution for us in the not too distant future. In the meantime, though, there's still so much we can do to gain value through partner integration based on the basic blocking and tackling that represents the roll-up-your-sleeves tasks of the PI Department. We need to do this as individual companies, and we need to do it as entire industries. This includes a company-wide commitment to data standards and quality, a company-wide commitment to efficient transactional processes, and a company-wide commitment to technical architectures that lend themselves to effective operation in these collaborative environments. Only then will we start to achieve the long-hyped benefits of external collaboration.

Business Process Management[126]

While Web services are designed to help standardize the means by which we integrate applications, business process management (BPM) tools take this game to a much higher level. The concept around BPM is that we will be able to provide business communities with a standard, easy-to-use set of tools whereby end-to-end processes can be modeled and maintained over time, and the tools will then propagate the changes for us throughout any number of systems that are used to execute the processes. Because BPM is based on standards, these end-to-end processes will not have to stop at the firewall, but rather will be capable of being modeled and executed with one or more business partners.

BPMI.org (the Business Process Management Initiative) is one of the entities aggressively pursuing the goals of BPM. It is a non-profit corporation whose mission is to "promote and develop the use of BPM through the establishment of standards for process design, deployment, execution, maintenance, and optimization....BPMI.org leverages those converging trends [in integration standards and protocols] by developing technologies that empower companies of all sizes, across all industries, to develop and operate business processes that span multiple applications and business partners, behind the firewall and over the Internet." The organization already has more than 80 members participating in this effort, including a who's who of technology companies that are leaders in the application, process, and integration space.[127]

Howard Smith and Peter Fingar are the authors of *Business Process Management—The Third Wave*, which explores many of the elements being pursued by BPMI.org. Smith and Fingar state:

> The third wave of BPM is not a fantasy, a false promise or hype. For BPM, like other true breakthroughs, is based on mathematics, specifically Process Calculi, the formal method of computation that underpins dynamic mobile processes, as opposed to static relational data....The radical breakthrough is that in the third wave, business processes are directly and immediately executable—no software development needed!
>
> BPM doesn't speed up applications development; it eliminates the need for it....The essence of the BPM innovation is that, based on mathematics, we now understand data, procedure, workflow, and distributed communication not as apples, oranges, and cherries, but as one new business "information type" (what technologists call an "abstract data type")—the business process. The recognition of this new fundamental building block is profound, for each element in a complete business process (the inputs, the outputs, the participants, the activities and the calculations) can now be expressed in a form where every facet and feature can be understood in the context of its use, its purpose and its role in decision making.[128]

They continue:

> In the era of the third wave, processes can be viewed by human users as information and by machines as executable code at the same time. An open standard is used for describing all processes. Process

design proceeds from both the top down—at the level of business strategy and business process design—and from the bottom up, at the level of leveraging existing IT systems.

In BPM, a rich process representation language can express any process and a dedicated execution environment can immediately put new processes to work. The third wave proves management is a straight through process—no translation into executable code is required.[129]

This is sure a heck of a lot more powerful than your standard workflow engines, which have already come a long way in making process flows more robust and flexible. If and when we reach the capabilities described above, we will have found the holy grail for business management and will truly empower business-focused PI Departments to dramatically expand process capabilities within (and between) their enterprises. This capability is a CPIO's dream—a set of tools that enables PI staffers to easily model and maintain complex processes that span multiple back-end systems with little or no assistance from technology-focused IT staffers. Process innovation will expand exponentially as the complexity and high cost associated with the necessary integration and customization typically associated with these advancements in today's world will become insignificant elements with respect to the requirements for deployment. These business systems will not only eliminate the latency associated with translating process definitions into deployed technical solutions, but will also eliminate the inherent limitations of the programming languages and application parameters that tend to be barriers to deploying processes as originally defined. Moreover, BPM will provide for the ability to execute simulations around new business processes so that we can model expected results based on user-defined parameters prior to actual deployment across the enterprise. With these simulations, as well as with analytical reviews of live processes, PI professionals will be able to analyze process efficiencies, identify bottlenecks, and make process alterations to address these constraints practically in real time. Agility, flexibility, reduced cost, reduced development times, optimization—BPM will lead to them all.

Smith and Fingar's book is an excellent vision for those of us who believe in the importance of processes and information in optimizing the environment for our organizations and industries. Just beware the hype! Smith and Fingar state that BPM is "the breakthrough that redefines competitive advantage for the next fifty years."[130] My question is: How many of those 50 years will we spend designing and building this solution as a practical set of tools before it is truly viable on a broad scale? There are targeted initiatives already underway with many companies that are piloting concepts related to BPM, but we are nowhere near the state of nirvana that is implied by Smith and Fingar in which all of our integration problems will become things of the past, and that modeling and implementing complex processes will be functions performed easily by business users virtually on the fly.

BPM is certainly not new. BPM tools have existed for years in a variety of forms, alongside custom business rules engines (BREs), which have been used to manage complex process flows and rules-based decision-making. Enterprise software vendors have enabled these kinds of tools within their packages for years as well, becoming more sophisticated all the time. For example, the management of purchasing processes and order management cycles, where transactions are automated to follow certain steps based on various conditions, has been common for years, and has become even more robust as workflow and alert management technologies have improved. The current iteration of the BPM movement is differentiated in that it advocates actually removing the process logic from the application layer and creating a new layer in the technology stack (data layer, application layer, *process layer*, and presentation layer). The intent is to define and maintain end-to-end processes in the process layer, which extends across all of the applications and data repositories needed for the execution of the processes. This is far beyond traditional enterprise application integration (EAI) or sophisticated application workflow. Finally, the BPM view extends beyond traditional EAI in that BPM encompasses end-to-end human-to-human interactions rather than system-to-system interactions. The tools being developed today explicitly include the human components of our processes, which are often the least efficient components of all. Just because we can optimize our system-to-system integration doesn't mean that we have truly optimized our end-to-end processes. That kind of optimization needs to include all the human interactions as well, and the BPM approach to modeling and execution is designed to do just that. Ultimately, BPM is an entirely new way of having our business (process) needs supported by our IT (technology) solutions.

While some advances have been made in this new and exciting area, we are still limited in our advancement and marketplace adoption. Many of the current efforts remain highly complex solutions that still require sophisticated technical skills for design, maintenance, and updates. They are currently far from the vision of BPM as being application-independent, user friendly, business process modeling and management tools that can be easily picked up by the business community. Moreover, the achievement of the end-state vision around BPM remains impeded by the overall lack of BPM standards. BPMI.org is just one of many organizations moving to create standards in the BPM space. While its list of members is broad-based and impressive, there remain a number of large and influential organizations that have not signed on to this particular initiative. This lack of agreement spans two areas: Web services (which represent a significant component of many BPM development efforts) and BPM technologies themselves. The lack of standards in the Web services category has already been discussed. With Web services specifically related to BPM, Gartner's "Hype Cycle for Web Services" places the timeframe for the "plateau of productivity" in the range of 5 to 10 years.[131]

Organizations like BPMI.org have helped progress the state of the art in BPM, and have mode some progress in the critical area of BPM standards, but we still have a long way to go. The furthest progress has probably been made in what is called BPMN (Business Process Modeling Notation), as the leading process modeling providers all appear to be moving toward universal adoption of this modeling standard. The benefit, of course, will be that users will be able to use their modeling tool of choice, and not worry about incompatibility when trying to leverage those models with their BPM execution engine of choice. The other area in which BPMI.org has advanced the state of the art is with its BPML (Business Process Modeling Language), which actually appears to be giving way to another standard (BPEL4WS), but was a major influence in getting the marketplace to adopt the pi-calculus view of BPM execution technologies. So while progress is being made, it's been slow and with considerable debate. And even with this progress, we're still a long way from the vision around holistic Business Process Management Systems (BPMS). BPMI.org itself recognizes the following areas as specific limitations that exist today:

- No standard way of sharing process diagrams
- No standard way of invoking business rules
- No standard way of managing workflow tasks
- No standard way of connecting to user interfaces
- No standard way of deploying processes
- No standard way of monitoring processes
- No standard way of analyzing processes[132]

There are more than one hundred vendors vying for market share in this space, ranging from small organizations with narrow targeted solutions to very large players seeking to develop full suites of BPM offerings. But having a universal, easy-to-use set of BPM tools will be contingent on the widespread adoption of standards, and likely a significant consolidation of these varied offerings. While we're slowly making progress, we're still a long way away from where we need to be. The Delphi Group put it this way: "Few areas of software will receive more attention in the coming months and years than BPM. Yet the greatest challenges in the BPM market are the very forces making it so attractive."[133] In other words, it won't be easy. So despite the fervent desire for such a solution, we'll need patience while we wait for a mature solution.

The vision of BPM is perfect in the context of the Enterprise Optimization Framework. The fact that we have some of the best and brightest in the world of information technology working on this set of initiatives is certainly encouraging. However, I must advise caution on expecting BPM to be a simple, widespread solution to your integration and process management nightmares. Some companies have found success in this area with limited, targeted uses. PI professionals must educate themselves on the claims in the marketplace, but also be prepared to ask hard questions about the viability of these claims. Find out about the success stories, and do so by delving into the details about what has been accomplished and how companies achieved their levels of success. *Skeptical optimism* is the way I describe this approach. And part of that approach is to always remember that what is not yet viable today may very well be viable in the near future. You can't take a static view of innovations such as BPM. Rather, they need to be re-evaluated over time as advances and breakthroughs are achieved in this complicated but potentially vastly beneficial set of offerings.

The real drawback to BPM is not that the technology isn't ready for prime time. That will come. It may be a year, it may be five years, it may be ten years, but there is enough vision, momentum, and desperate need in the marketplace that our chief technologists will figure out how to bring this vision into reality. The drawback to BPM brings us right back to where we started, back to specific actions we can all take right now to optimize our organizations. The focus on BPM represents a recognition of the fundamental importance of processes and information, as well as the pervasive challenges that exist across organizations in each of these areas today. The excitement is being generated based on the hope that technology will be able to solve many of these challenges for us. But nothing will ever be solved without a commitment to the basic fundamentals, which puts Process and Information Optimization at the top of the food chain in terms of the ability of an enterprise to thrive (or perish). The breakthroughs in enabling technologies, such as BPM, will never solve our problems on their own. Remember, systems and technology, in and of themselves, do not yield competitive advantage. They only serve as an enabler for competitive advantage, and must be coupled with optimization of processes, information, cost, and flawless execution. To have a shot at optimal results, our Technology solutions must be aligned with our organizational Strategy, Controls, People, and Processes. We need empowered CPIOs and PI Departments to lead our enterprise-wide efforts to optimize in the areas of processes and information. We need a commitment to a metric-driven decision-making framework within the context of generating bottom-line benefits for the organization as a whole. We need to implement these foundational changes now. We need to get moving on modeling our processes, identifying our weaknesses, and validating opportunities for immediate improvement. We need to analyze our processes and our corresponding system infrastructures and look for opportunities to generate enhanced efficiencies and effectiveness by way of standardization, consolidation, and overall simplification. The only thing holding us back is ourselves, and leadership can overcome that obstacle; in fact, it *must* overcome that obstacle if we're ever to optimize our environments. BPM will automate many of the solutions put in place by PI Departments in the future. BPM will make our lives easier and enhance our efficiency and effectiveness. BPM will enhance our ability to optimize. But BPM will be useless unless we also make the corresponding organizational and decision-making changes highlighted throughout this book. Those are the steps we can all take right now to optimize our capabilities in the marketplace. We must choose to pursue the path of Enterprise Optimization or Enterprise Extinction will surely be the result. The choice is yours: *Optimize Now—or else!*

Summary and Highlights

- In the context of the Enterprise Optimization Framework, organizations will find significant advantages in building their technical infrastructure, *to the greatest degree practical*, around software suites rather than best of breed solutions. Optimization can be further achieved with architectures constructed around single, global instances of this enterprise software.

- While some degree of technical integration is required in all of our companies, it also represents one of the greatest sources of suboptimal performance in the areas of process, information, and total cost across organizations today. In the area of application architecture, simplicity is our ally; complexity is our enemy.

- Companies that have invested in best of breed solutions, linked together via technical integration, need to periodically review the software landscape in the context of the framework, looking for ways to optimize via systems and instance consolidation. In the latter case, technological advances with software, hardware, and networking have made single global instances of enterprise solutions the preferred mode of deployment in terms of all three elements of the Enterprise Optimization Framework.

- Complex integration is the norm for technical infrastructures today. A number of movements have been initiated in the software industry and by specific vendors to make things easier and more effective for companies that employ this model. However, in many cases, the hype has been more prominent that widespread success.

  o In addition to internal integration, external collaboration has suffered due to the lack of standards in this space. But that is not the only thing that has limited expansion of external collaboration. Lack of confidence in the quality of data, multi-instance environments, and complex *internal* integration have all played a role in inhibiting companies from electronically collaborating with their business partners.

  o Companies should address integration solutions based on the following hierarchy:
    - Evaluate the degree to which your enterprise system supplier(s), which might be either internal or ASP-based solutions, can adequately support the required functionality.
      - If no, then evaluate identified solution partners of your enterprise system supplier(s) to determine if any of them can adequately support the required functionality with prepackaged, integrated solutions.
        o If no, then evaluate other solution providers in the marketplace to determine if any of them can adequately support the required functionality with prepackaged, integrated solutions.
          - If no, then evaluate independent tools vendors (ideally those that have partnerships with your core providers) to identify the best means in which to build the solution on your own, or to customize an existing solution to meet the requirement.

- On-demand services represent a technological advance in which companies will be able to treat information technology as a utility that can be turned on and off based purely on need, and will require payment only for what is consumed. Some of the dominant players in the IT community are leading development efforts in this space, but the solutions remain relatively immature in terms of widespread availability and practicality in the marketplace.

- Web services have been introduced as integration standards whereby companies will be able to leverage standard protocols to share data and process communication across multiple applications, regardless of the underlying platforms. The problem is that the definition of these standards has been slow to develop, with multiple competing standards resulting in the marketplace. Analyst predictions indicate a slow adoption rate for this potentially high-impact set of standards.

- Business process management (BPM) tools represent another area of technological innovation that sounds compelling but still resides in an immature state. BPM defines a set of standards whereby the business community will be able to define, maintain, and adapt end-to-end, cross-platform business processes without the need for radical IT transformation projects. There have been targeted successes in this area of technology, but we have yet to see the true vision of BPM come to life as a ubiquitous, comprehensive set of solutions.

- While we await technological advances in BPM, companies must start now on the principles related to Enterprise Optimization expressed throughout this book, which will be invaluable in their own right, as well as the necessary foundation for any BPM initiative.

- The Process and Information Department needs to be the focal point within companies to constantly stay up to date on what is real and what it just hype in the information technology landscape. There is a fine line between being an early adopter that gains competitive advantage vs. an early adopter that is crushed due to risking too much on an immature new solution. The answer lies in the Enterprise Optimization Framework, which provides a robust and disciplined approach to analyzing any initiative, regardless of maturity of the solution. It is this kind of concrete, objective analysis that will provide confidence in whatever decision is reached.

Final Thoughts: Ten Ways to Achieve Enterprise Optimization

1. Recognize that the position of Chief Information Officer is perceived and utilized in most companies as a tactical role focused primarily on technology and not on business. Companies should eliminate this role and replace it with a new, business-focused executive position that will be staffed by someone who can lead the company in its Enterprise Optimization initiatives. This person would be the Chief Process and Information Officer (CPIO).

2. Place the CPIO in charge of a new organizational entity that spans the functions and geographies of the organization. This Process and Information (PI) Department needs to be empowered by the company's senior executives to lead the organization in the following four areas:
   a. Process Optimization
   b. Information Optimization
   c. Information Technology
   d. Program/Project Management

3. Have the PI Department lead the effort to provide the definition and enterprise-wide adoption of meaningful corporate standards. Key areas in which to define standards include:
   a. End-to-end processes
   b. Data quality and responsibility
   c. Performance management metrics
   d. Project management governance

4. Recognize that investment decisions can no longer be made based on "gut feel." Project evaluation should be based on the Enterprise Optimization Framework, which states that initiatives should only be approved if the expected net result of the quantifiable impact on the company's processes, information, and total cost is positive.

5. Adopt a metric-driven approach to enterprise-wide management. Quantifiable metrics that are directly indicative of business value should be defined and then utilized to evaluate initiatives and personnel. This analysis will be most beneficial when it continues long after a project goes live, for it often takes months (or years) for the benefits of a project to actually kick in.

6. Recognize that the opportunities presented by offshore outsourcing have dramatically improved in just the last couple of years thanks to the widespread availability of high-speed bandwidth, as well as the abundance of high-quality, low-cost resources located across the globe. As such, PI Departments should immediately look for opportunities to outsource traditional information technology development, as well as transaction-oriented business processes that are not core to your company's business.

7. Further recognize that while there are tremendous opportunities available today in offshore outsourcing, those components evaluated for this solution must be considered in the context of *all three* components of the Enterprise Optimization Framework. In other words, it can't just be about cost. Skills such as business process expertise and program management have yet to reach the state of maturity with the offshore solutions and should be strongly considered for on-site retention.

8. Immediately engage a thorough review of your information technology architecture. Understand that optimization will likely be achieved in all three components of the framework by adopting and/or moving toward an environment that leverages single, global instances of a limited number of enterprise software platforms. A major component of this objective is to limit the requirements for integration between systems and complex, custom technical development.

9. Have the PI Department initiate an investigation into some of the newest innovations in information technology, including such areas as on-demand services, Web services, and business process management. Recognize that risk must be evaluated as part of the Enterprise Optimization Framework, and PI professionals should be cautious about spending shareholder funds on unproven technologies. PI Departments should constantly be evaluating new IT capabilities, but should look for validation in the marketplace of new solutions before jumping ahead with the so-called latest and greatest offering as soon as it becomes available. The PI Department must also

never forget that even though some of these technological innovations may be slow to develop, the foundational principles around Process and Information Optimization (independent of information technology) are available for immediate adoption and continue to lead organizations down the path of Enterprise Optimization while preparing for the technologies of the future.

10. Keep it simple!

Appendix A

Case Study: Integration vs. Integrated, That is the Service Question—Framework Analysis in Action[1]

Shortly after going live on its new ERP (Oracle) and CRM (Siebel) systems, a company in the high-tech industry found that there were clear deficiencies in the way its service orders were being processed, beginning in the ERP system and culminating in the CRM system. Linking service to the correct products in the order management system was clumsy and fraught with errors. Due to limitations in the system, custom-configured, non-validated fields were used to capture significant pieces of information. This led to a high volume of data inaccuracies, compounded by the fact that the data had to be "translated" in the integration between ERP and CRM. The Customer Service (CS) group was spending a disproportionate amount of its time correcting data errors in the CRM system. The CS team went to IT looking for a fix to improve this quickly deteriorating environment.

IT investigated the issues surrounding the complaints, and then called all the business owners together to discuss some alternatives. The prime suggestion was to implement additional functionality within the Oracle ERP system to provide more accurate data capture at the outset of the process. This company had not implemented the Oracle Service components of order management during its initial deployment, so was not able to take advantage of some of the additional functionality and validation available via this module. IT identified that by implementing Oracle Service, along with a modest amount of additional validation in the order management workflow process, a significant amount of the pain on the CS side would be diminished. At the end of this two-hour meeting, the IT lead asked for a show of hands whether or not the team would support this deployment in terms of a positive economic impact for the company. It was unanimous—everyone in the room raised a hand in support.

So, what were the results? We'll never know, because the project never got off the ground. This company required a business owner to prepare a business case justifying any IT project that would cost more than $100,000. This project was initially estimated at around $250,000, which included software costs and implementation consulting costs. While all parties in the initial meeting were aware of these costs and were in support of the project, IT was finding it hard to nail down an owner to work on the business case and to be the prime driver for the initiative. Customer Service felt that the Operations group (which included Order Management) should take the reins, as most of the enhancements would be implemented at the front end of the process. Operations had the opposite point of view, because most of the benefits would be felt by the CS organization. In fact, the workload in Order Management might actually *increase* due to the enhanced data capture requirements. A deadlock ensued in which neither side would opt to take ownership of the project (nor did either side want to allocate funds to pay for the project). It also didn't help that while a business case was required there was no standardized approach or template that had been created anywhere in the company for this purpose, and no one in this group was particularly motivated to chart this new path. The result: nothing got done and the project opportunity simply disappeared. Of course, the fundamental problem didn't go away, and the CS Department went on suffering with having to constantly correct mistake-laden data.

This example demonstrates a number of the common issues involved with getting a project off the ground. First, as with most organizations, this company was organized around functions and not processes. There was no CPIO or Process and Information Department to provide procedural oversight across the enterprise. As such there was no one to step up to ownership for the initiative. IT wasn't empowered in this role (nor was anyone else), so, lacking ownership, the opportunity simply went away. Moreover, there was no framework in place for this company to properly evaluate the initiative. Would this project have created value for the company? No one knows. No one truly investigated the matter as no guidelines were in place to facilitate analysis. As one IT lead in this company told me, "We could try to build the business case, but they don't really tell you much....Let's face it, IT projects are approved based on instinct. You either know it's the right thing to do, or not." Notwithstanding the widespread support of this sentiment at this company—and, one could argue, in the marketplace—I must wholeheartedly disagree. The problem is that companies typically aren't organized appropriately to make these decisions, and haven't implemented a framework in which to guide them through the decision-making process.

Let's assume the existence of a PI Department in this organization, which has enterprise-wide responsibility for project justification. And let's break down this opportunity in terms of the three-pronged framework to see what this company might have achieved if it had decided to move forward.

Total Cost Optimization

Let's begin with a detailed breakdown of the cost component of this opportunity, based on the framework provided in Section II.

Cost Component	Analysis	Net Impact
Software	Estimated cost for license and maintenance for adding the Oracle Service module to the rest of the company's current ERP software license.	$40,000
Hardware	No additional hardware required.	$0
Implementation Services (external)	Consulting fees were estimated for process design, system design, system configuration, three testing rounds, core team training, solution validation, and initial post-go-live support.	$215,000
Implementation Services (internal)	The consulting organization would provide approximately 80 percent of the implementation services, leaving 20 percent for company personnel. The cost for internal personnel for testing, validation, and training is included here. This is in the form of an opportunity cost.	$50,000
Integration Costs	Consulting fees were estimated for the enhancements required in the integration between Oracle and Siebel.	$30,000
Cost and Frequency of Future Upgrades	Negligible impact in light of the scope of this piece in terms of the overall Oracle suite of applications that has been deployed.	$0
Ongoing Support Costs	Negligible impact.	$0
Training	Estimated cost for employee supported end-user training.	$10,000
Decommissioned Systems	Small impact to decrease IT cost associated with troubleshooting errors in the interface between Oracle and Siebel.	($5,000)
TOTAL		$340,000

Based on this analysis, the net impact to the total cost of this solution is an increased cost of $340,000, most of which will be incurred during implementation. A portion of the software and consulting fees (including integration costs) will be capitalized as part of the deployment, so the first-year impact of this project will be approximately $185,000, with $165,000 depreciated over the following three years. Taking an aggressive view of return on investment, the company will raise the bar for project justification assuming the need to offset the entire $340,000 investment in the first year of service.

Process and Information Optimization

The primary sub-process affected in this case is part of the overall order-to-cash process, which includes the transfer of assets to the service install base, along with the information that entitles the customer to a certain level of technical support for a specific duration.

The primary process changes associated with this project will be in the data capture portion at the front-end of the process. With the deployment of the Oracle Service functionality within the order management module, the Order Administration team will now be required to add additional service contact data to the customer master prior to entering the order. This includes name, address, phone number, and e-mail address. This information will then be validated against the customer master as it is entered into the appropriate fields on each sales order. Furthermore, there may also be additional time spent up front verifying the serial number which connects a service contract to a particular product/customer combination. Order Admin was required to enter this contact and serial number information previously, but now will no longer have the freedom to enter the information into fields that are not validated. The errors that resulted from this "freedom" were what yielded many of the headaches at the back end of the process in Siebel and for Customer Service. In the new process, Order Admin will need to take the additional steps to ensure that it has the valid information or else the application will not accept the data as inputted.

The Customer Service team estimates that 60 percent of orders require some manual intervention to research and update before the service contract is valid in Siebel. The manual intervention takes an average of two hours, but typically spans three to four days on the calendar. This is where Information Optimization kicks in. It turns out that this calendar delay resulting from incomplete and invalid data streams represents a significant impact to the company in that customers are not eligible for service during this time period. (The technical assistance center, or TAC, was not authorized to provide service without a valid service contract in place within Siebel.) Customers who may require service in the initial set-up of their systems may be denied service because of the delay in getting the valid transaction processed in the system. The immediate result, especially for new customers, is anger and frustration. In addition, this process applies to service renewal orders as well. As a result, a customer who has properly renewed service within the correct timeframe may be denied service by the TAC simply because of the delay in the processing of the transaction. These delays and the confusion associated with them were creating such a customer satisfaction issue that the company began providing service to customers simply based on their word that they had bought or renewed a service contract. The result was complete lack of confidence in the data in the system and an abundance of free service being provided for fear of further deterioration of customer satisfaction.

Let's go back to the framework and the analysis for the justification of this project. From a pure process standpoint, there will be both increases and decreases in terms of the time associated with processing these transactions, depending on which functional organization is being reviewed. For example, the Order Management team will now take longer to enter sales orders because of the additional information captured and the additional validation that will take place for many of these data fields. Order Management will no longer be able to enter contact information via free-form text fields. Those service contacts will now need to be set up in the customer master and selected via a validated drop-down listing. Accuracy should increase considerably, but the data gathering and data entry time will increase as well. In addition, Order Management will be required to select the specific part numbers and their corresponding serial numbers for which the service is either being ordered or renewed. Once again, this information has been captured up until this point in text fields for which no validation was provided. A common source of the data inaccuracies is incorrect entry of part numbers and serial numbers.

Based on the process and data entry changes being prescribed, order management estimates a 15 percent *increase* in the time it takes to enter all of the information relative to a sales order. This is translates to a *decrease* in productivity by 15 percent for this capacity constrained group.

- Based on the number of order entry people and the cost of those resources, this implies a *decreased* annual benefit of $60,000.

On the flip side, you have the Customer Service organization, which believes this deployment will cut by two-thirds the number of orders that require manual intervention. So, while not eliminating the problem of invalid orders, it is estimated that the frequency will drop from 60 percent of transactions to 20 percent of transactions.

- Based on the number of Customer Service people focused on transaction processing and validation and the cost of these resources, this implies an *increased* annual benefit of $120,000.

Table A-1 displays the justification calculation based on the data gathered thus far in the analysis.

Table A-1

Total Cost Optimization		($340,000)
Process Optimization		
Order Management	($60,000)	
Customer Service	$120,000	
Net Impact		$60,000
Total Impact		($280,000)

The net result from the total cost and process-related impacts of this opportunity is therefore a *decreased* overall benefit of $280,000. Stopping here, the project would be rejected. But the PI Department wouldn't stop here in its analysis. The analysis would not be complete without factoring in Information Optimization and the positive impact it might provide.

Information Optimization provides a tangible benefit in two areas as a result of this project opportunity. First, the decrease in invalid transactions will increase the credibility of the data for both Customer Service and the TAC. Even though the company estimates that 20 percent of transactions will still require some level of manual intervention, the cycle time of that intervention will decrease, narrowing the window of opportunity for customers to actually call in for service during this timeframe. The immediate impact is that the TAC would revert to its original policy of not providing service without a valid contract in the system. Escalation managers would have the right to overrule that policy for the handful of cases that still fall within this window, so some degree of customer dissatisfaction may persist and need to be addressed, but the revenue leakage associated with unwarranted free service would be decreased significantly.

Quantifying this impact is not strictly science. Some assumptions need to be made in terms of increased service revenue and reduced service cost as a result of the Information Optimization associated with this opportunity, but that's what the PI Department is for. This group of professionals is tasked with this quantification exercise, which in this case is broken down as follows:

On the revenue side:
- Service revenue currently equals approximately $80 million annually for the company.
- Given that service is currently provided to anyone who claims to have a service contract, the CS organization estimates, based on research and experience over the last six months, that 10 to 15 percent of service callers lack a valid contract and are receiving free service. Taking the lower estimate and assuming that the TAC would be able to convert just

one-quarter of these people to sign up for a valid service contract, this would *increase* annual revenues by $2 million (representing a 2.5 percent increase on the whole). The team actually felt that the conversion rate would be much higher (possible twice as high), but this conservative estimate came with a higher degree of confidence.

On the cost side:
- Currently the TAC often finds itself providing service for customers who do not have a valid service contract.
- As the TAC is a capacity constrained organization, the time spent providing service on an unwarranted basis cuts into the time spent with customers who have valid support contracts.
- Based on the number of TAC personnel and the estimated time spent with customers who do not have valid service contracts, this implies an opportunity cost to the company of $100,000 for the worker time spent on these cases.

These benefits can be directly linked to the company's bottom line. The revenue opportunity is significant and ties directly into the top line of the P&L. The opportunity cost benefit is also not insignificant given the scope of the investment associated with this opportunity, and goes directly to the bottom line of the P&L, possibly in the elimination (or reassignment) of one full support position.

Table A-2 contains the summary of the analysis compiled thus far:

Table A-2

Total Cost Optimization		($340,000)
Process Optimization		
Order Management	($60,000)	
Customer Service	$120,000	
Net Impact		$60,000
Information Optimization		
Eliminate Free Service		
Increase Revenue	$2,000,000	
Opportunity Cost	$100,000	
Net Impact		$2,100,000
Total Impact		$1,820,000

Based on the figures compiled in Table A-2, the project should be approved.

However, before the analysis is finalized, one must recognize that the benefits of Information Optimization don't stop here. For at the root of this issue is the impact of customer *dis*satisfaction. What is the actual cost of denying service to a customer who has already purchased a valid service contract? How do you quantify that cost, and therefore quantify the benefit in alleviating that driver of dissatisfaction?

As with the previous case study, this is probably the hardest metric to obtain up front as part of the analysis, and will be the least scientific metric in the calculations. Nevertheless, it may also represent one of the most relevant portions of the analysis. What is the cost of a dissatisfied customer? How likely is it that continuation of these problems would send this company down the slow path toward enterprise extinction? In addition, are all customers equal in this equation, or do different customers require and receive different levels of service, regardless of the state of contract? It had already been determined that for "large" customers, service would be provided regardless of state of contract, although follow-up messages would be provided to the Sales organization to contact the customer about getting current on its support agreement. So the company had already made a strategic decision on how to handle this issue as it relates to customer satisfaction for its larger customers different from that of its small- to medium-sized customers. However, it was actually the smaller customers who were more likely to defect to the competition if they called in for service under a valid contract yet were denied it because of transaction delays in processing the data. These customers represented approximately 30 percent of overall sales, or $120 million in revenue. The CS organization estimated that based on complaints and some anecdotal evidence, that the company would actually lose business from 10 percent of the customers who were wrongly denied service, and that such an occurrence took place approximately 10 percent of the time. That yields a potential lost revenue stream of $1.2 million as a result of this process and information gap. Of course the long-term damage would be much greater than this, as the cost to replace these customers as ongoing revenue streams would also be significant.

As previously stated, this part of the analysis is the least scientific of the research to date, yet these conservative estimates are reasonable approximations of what the company expects to occur. The PI Department needs to apply its best judgment—often based on skepticism when precious shareholder funds are at risk. The conservative approach should guide the way based on the reasonable expectations for the group performing the analysis. Again, this is why multiple scenarios should be modeled before reaching any final conclusions or making any firm recommendations. In this case, these estimates may be the best the company can provide given the lack of measurable data to support the hypothesis. However, a company commitment to ongoing metric analysis provides the opportunity to validate many of these assumptions over time. It is certainly possible to identify a handful of key metrics that can be put into place to track the progress of this initiative, assuming that the project moves forward. Some metrics that can be tracked include:

- Number and percentage of transactions that need to be cleared out of the interface between Oracle and Siebel by the technical team for data errors related to this issue;
- Number and percentage of sales orders processed by order management that require manual intervention by Customer Service;
- Cycle time for when a contract passes from Oracle to Siebel (Operations to Customer Service) to its appearance as a valid contract for the TAC;
- Number and percentage of customers requesting service for whom the system indicates a valid contract does not exist, but it is identified that errors in transaction processing has actually just delayed the creation of the contract in the system; and
- Number and percentage of customers who are determined to have received free service because the TAC couldn't authoritatively determine if a support contract in fact existed.

With these metrics in mind, the PI Department can monitor systems for data, as well as assist the appropriate functional groups by providing tracking sheets to monitor those activities not specifically captured in the systems. Just recognizing the need to track the data will move things beyond the anecdotal foundation for the analysis and yield more reliable and tangible results. Yes, some extra research may be required to make these measurements accurate and meaningful, but that is a small price to pay considering the consequences at stake.

The final measurement to the scenario, as with many similar situations, is to measure customer satisfaction in surveys to the issue you're trying to address. Create questions for surveys that address particular issues such as this one, and track the results over time. Throughout the life cycle of surveys, it will be possible to correlate improvements in particular areas to overall customer satisfaction. Such surveys are strongly encouraged, along with tying survey questions to specific initiatives.

At this point, Table A-3 provides the following data points for the justification analysis:

Table A-3

Total Cost Optimization		($340,000)
Process Optimization		
Order Management	($60,000)	
Customer Service	$120,000	
Net Impact		$60,000
Information Optimization		
Eliminate Free Service		
Increase Revenue	$2,000,000	
Opportunity Cost	$100,000	
Customer Satisfaction	$1,200,000	
Net Impact		$3,300,000
Total Impact		$3,020,000

While it was the process component that initially drove the requirement, it was actually Information Optimization that would provide the real benefit of this investment. It's unfortunate that none of this was taken into consideration when the project was allowed to die because of lack of ownership. The business users were completely focused on the costs associated with the processing of the transactions. No one ever looked at the impact of the dirty data throughout the process, and therefore never thought to quantify the impact this solution could have had in eliminating some of the ongoing revenue leakage.

Once again, the point has been reached where the initiative should be approved based on the justification framework applied throughout this analysis. However, the PI Department analysis is *still* not complete. As part of the framework, the PI team always wants to take a step back and look at the longer-term opportunities created by any particular project. This is an organization that often works in the tactical world, but should always have its eyes on the overall strategic elements of any initiative. It is also tasked with looking from an end-to-end business perspective on project opportunities, and not limited to the context of functional silos. With this view, additional opportunities to have a positive impact on the bottom line were found to exist in this scenario.

It turns out that at the time of this analysis the company supported and maintained several hundred part numbers for service items. This impacted Document Control, which created the items and entered them into the company's information systems, as well as Marketing, which owned the price lists, which varied across geographies and customer categories. There was a tremendous overhead in creating and maintaining service items and price lists for one simple reason: service items were duration-based, with the duration of the service imbedded in the item description itself. In other words, the company had only about a dozen different service offerings in its entire portfolio. However, since for every unique duration for each of those dozen service offerings a new part number was required, Doc Control and Marketing found themselves managing several hundred unique service items instead of a dozen. This problem would have gone away as a result of the proposed project, since duration could now be captured on the sales order line in Oracle as a new, validated data entry field, and no longer have to be imbedded in the service part number. Doc Control and Marketing are also capacity constrained groups in this company, which has cut expenses (and personnel) to the bone. Freeing up time for these resources was critical in that they could be responsible for the delay of new products being introduced and available to the marketplace.

Furthermore, this analysis was extended to uncover a positive impact to the Finance organization, again with respect to this concept of duration. As each service part number contained the logic for the duration of the service, accounting rules needed to be created and attached to these items to reflect the appropriate revenue recognition rules. By taking advantage of this one additional Oracle field (service duration), the Finance organization could cease to support many of its system-based accounting rules, and instead rely on a *single* duration-driven accounting rule that would be applied to all service items. These elements of Process Optimization were never uncovered, because the Document Control, Marketing, and Finance organizations were not involved in the analysis. The existence of a PI Department would enhance the likelihood of filling this gap and ensuring a broad-based view of project opportunities.

Finally, there is one more long-term benefit that this solution could provide that would be uncovered only if the PI Department looked beyond the current scope of deployment and into future opportunities for Process Optimization. At the time of this analysis, this company had no capability to support on-line ordering for its customers. This was an important initiative for the company for the upcoming year, as a number of the company's largest customers had been demanding the ability to place orders on-line. While not going into the analysis associated with the justification for adding on-line ordering capabilities at this time (although it would make for interesting analysis within the framework!), it does beg the question of how the company would be able to accept on-line orders if some of the critical data elements were captured in custom data fields that allow for free-form text and, therefore, provide no degree of validation. If the Order Administration team couldn't get these orders right, how could customers be expected to do so when placing orders themselves? Even if the analysis above had indicated that the project was not currently warranted, it may still be required in the near future to support the deployment of on-line ordering. One must also consider the advantages created by the dramatic reduction in service part numbers for use in on-line transactions and how that would translate into a more pleasant customer experience. Customers could then select a level of service from only a handful of choices, rather than choose from a list of hundreds. This final area may not have had a direct bearing on the immediate question at hand, but if the above analysis were close, and on-line ordering was right around the corner, then this type of benefit may be sufficient to break the tie in terms of providing a thumbs up or thumbs down for the current opportunity.

Once again, before leaving this case study, it is necessary to explore the accuracy of the analysis above. As with any justification analysis, multiple scenarios need to be modeled in order to gain a true appreciation for the depth of possible outcomes. Further, the break-even analysis should be a required element of this discussion. In this case, taking an extremely conservative approach to the overall benefits, you could eliminate the opportunity cost of assisting non-paying service customers and eliminate the anticipated lost revenue stream of customers who might defect as a result of poor customer service. These factors are certainly relevant, but the accuracy of the calculations is somewhat questionable given the anecdotal nature of the base assumptions. Even if you assume that these components yield *no* value by way of this project, you would still need to convert just *0.3 percent* of customers who are currently receiving free service to paying for that service (that's *less than one-half of one percent*), and this project would be justified. Even under this extremely conservative analysis, the project should have been authorized. But since the analysis wasn't done, nothing happened, and the company's struggles simply continued.

Appendix B

Detailed Results of the Current State and Future Expected Benefits Analysis in the Case of Solving the Service Returns Calamity

The results of this analysis are summarized for each of the five functional units that will be impacted by this deployment. These functional units include:

- Customer service representatives (CSRs)
- Logistics
- Technical service representatives (TSRs)
- Shop floor
- Finance

Customer Service Representatives (CSRs)

Current	Expected Future Benefits
General Data Entry	**General Data Entry**
• RMA Entry, Material Movement, and Shop Floor Entry are entered into multiple databases (multiple Lotus Notes, Excel, Oracle) throughout the complete customer return process; 7 to 8 databases including Oracle in all.	• RMA Entry, Material Movement, and Shop Floor Entry are entered into **one** system (Oracle).
System of Record	**System of Record**
• Lotus Notes and Excel are not tied to the financial system of record (Oracle)— allowing financial exposure.	• Oracle is tied to the financial system of record (Oracle).

Current	Expected Future Benefits
360^0 View of Customer	**360^0 View of Customer**
• Manual.	• CSRs can have a full view of the customer **on one screen** having "Red, Green, Yellow" or value-based snapshot info on: 1. Repair Products 2. Expiring Contracts 3. Opportunity Size 4. Credit Hold 5. Account Status 6. Cancelled Orders 7. Shipped Orders 8. Late Orders 9. Back Orders 10. Booked Orders 11. Lapsed time since last interaction 12. Open Requests Having this "snapshot" allows the CSR to make decisions based on the status (i.e. notify customer that they are on credit hold, have expiring contracts, etc.).
• Single point of contact for the customer is difficult.	• Single point of contact in a call center type environment to answer most customer queries
Service Request Entry	**Service Request Entry**
• Not applicable. But this is currently a paper process for the CSRs. • There is no electronic method to capture every interaction with the customer	• Additional data entry is required of the CSRs to enter the Service Request. • Every interaction with the customer is captured and can be referenced by anyone having access to the application functionality.
RMA Entry	**RMA Entry**
• Information queries regarding RMA Planner or identifying what MBU an item belongs to was done through Lotus Notes / ERP—additional system maintenance. Note that this will no longer be the case since this information is available in Oracle. However, the same Lotus Notes / ERP is still used for other purposes. • RMA is entered using Oracle and interfaced to Lotus Notes based Tracking Database used for tracking the products. • Serial Number entry is done in a "Descriptive Flexfield" (DFF). • Other information used by Lotus Notes is entered in a DFF.	• Information queries regarding RMA Planner or identifying what MBU an item belongs to will be done through Oracle. • RMA is entered in Oracle, which is linked to the Service Request and tracked within Oracle Service. • Serial Number entry is done in a "Descriptive Flexfield" (DFF). • No extra information is entered.

Current	Expected Future Benefits
Work Order Creation	**Work Order Creation**
• Work Orders are required in order for the material to be moved from building "O" (Warehouse) to building "L" (MBU). This allows for a poor turn-around time. Average TAT 15+ days.	• Work Orders **do not** need to be created to move material. Material is moved immediately (within one day) into the MBU incoming RMA sub inventory.
• Manual creation of WIP Job.	• Auto creation of Repair and WIP Job.
• All repair details are captured in "Tracking" database.	• All repair details are captured on the repair that is linked to the RMA and service request.
Charge Capturing	**Charge Capturing**
• Repair costs are captured in either Lotus Notes or Excel in order for the CSRs to generate the charge to the customer.	• Repair costs are captured into Oracle in order for the CSRs to generate the charge to the customer.
Shipment Back to Customer	**Shipment Back to Customer**
• RMA Return order is created manually in advance and based on what needs to be done with the Customer request.	• RMA Return is created automatically from the charges entered into the "Repair," which ties back to the initial service request.
Install Base	**Install Base**
• It is auto populated but not used effectively.	• Track what items each customer has purchased for each of their sites. This historical information is valuable for up-selling and cross-selling (i.e. what units at what customer site are due for calibration?).
• Not applicable.	• When entering a Service Request, Oracle validates that the customer owns the product.
Interaction History	**Interaction History**
• Manual or hard copy tracked.	• Interactions with the customer are tracked electronically and are available to everyone in the organization provided with access.
Tracking by Serial Number	**Tracking by Serial Number**
• No functionality.	• Serial number is entered at the time of creation of service request and is tracked and maintained from the point the unit is received until the time it is shipped back to the customer.
• No functionality.	• One can easily track where the unit is at any given point in time
Performance Reporting	**Performance Reporting**
• Compiled manually from various systems	• Generated from system base on date / time stamp of all activities performed.

Logistics

Current	Expected Future Benefits
RMA Receipt into Building "O" • Material is first received into Lotus Notes database. Material is not received immediately into Oracle.	**RMA Receipt into Building "O"** • Material is received immediately into Oracle.
Material Movement from Building "O" to "L" • Material is not moved until a WIP Job is created. Material movement into building "L" can take up to two weeks.	**Material Movement from Building "O" to "L"** • Material moves within one day to building "L". The material handler does not need to wait for a WIP Job to be created.
Discrepancy Receipts • Managed using Lotus Notes database and e-mail. Material could be sitting on discrepancy shelf for a long time.	**Discrepancy Receipts** • Received into Oracle Discrepancy sub-inventory, this is visible to everyone in the organization and will be cleared within one week of receipt.
Shipments Back to Customer • After repair material is sent back to "O" (warehouse) and then it stays there until a pick slip is generated. Products can stay there for a long time.	**Shipments Back to Customer** • Only material that is ready to be shipped back to customer immediately is sent to "O" (warehouse).

Technical Service Representatives (TSRs)

Current	Expected Future Benefits
Service Request Entry	**Service Request Entry**
• Technical inquiries are captured in Lotus Notes.	• Technical inquiries will be captured into Oracle.
• Not applicable. The TSR will need to notify the CSR that an RMA is needed.	• Further, inquiries that result into an RMA will be tied to the original Service Request—allowing everyone in the organization access to what was said to and done for the customer.
360⁰ View of Customer	**360⁰ View of Customer**
• Manual.	• TSRs can have a full view of the customer **on one screen** having "Red, Green, Yellow" or value based snapshot info on: 1. Repair Products 2. Expiring Contracts 3. Opportunity Size 4. Credit Hold 5. Account Status 6. Cancelled Orders 7. Shipped Orders 8. Late Orders 9. Back Orders 10. Booked Orders 11. Lapsed time since last interaction 12. Open Requests Having this "snapshot" allows the TSR to make decisions based on the status (i.e. notify customer that they are on credit hold, have expiring contracts, etc.).
Historic Search on Common Problems and Solutions	**Historic Search on Common Problems and Solutions**
• Not applicable.	• Knowledge-based search capability.

Shop Floor

Current	Expected Future Benefits
Charges Entry • Charges are entered in Excel or Lotus Notes. • Lotus Notes and Excel are not tied to the financial system of record (Oracle)—allowing financial exposure to activities within WIP. • Manual approval process.	**Charges Entry** • Charges are entered into Oracle. • Oracle is tied to the financial system of record (Oracle). • System approval is required before charges can be billed to customer.
Track Product Location • Lotus Notes or Excel are used to track product location.	**Track Product Location** • Oracle is used to track product location.
WIP Job Creation • WIP Jobs are created for items that are not yet in-house to the MBU. The items are still in another building. Items can take up to two weeks to be moved from building "O" to building "L"—with the WIP Job being "idle" for that amount of time.	**WIP Job Creation** • WIP Jobs are created when the MBU physically has the item in-house and the WIP Job is created only for the product that needs to be repaired. There is no necessary delay from the time that the WIP Job is created to the time the product is worked on.
Quality Results • Entered as free text in Lotus Notes database or Word / Excel.	**Quality Results** • Entered for each unit / SN# in Oracle Service by selecting from a predefined list of values and can do analysis reporting out of that data.

Finance

Current	Expected Future Benefits
Data Entry • Financial reconciliation is made more difficult with the entry of information into multiple systems.	**Data Entry** • Since everything from creation of Service Request to RMA creation to RMA Receipt to creation of charges is entered into Oracle, financial exposure is limited.
System of Record • Lotus Notes and Excel are not tied to the financial system of record (Oracle)—allowing financial exposure.	**System of Record** • Oracle is tied to the financial system of record (Oracle).

Appendix C

The Capability Maturity Model for Software [2]

The following is a summary of the Capability Maturity Model for Software (SW-CMM), as provided by the Software Engineering Institute at Carnegie Mellon University (January 2003). The model describes the principles and practices underlying software process maturity and is intended to help software organizations improve the maturity of their software processes in terms of an evolutionary path from ad hoc, chaotic processes to mature, disciplined software processes. The SW-CMM is organized into five maturity levels:

1) **Initial.** The software process is characterized as ad hoc, and occasionally even chaotic. Few processes are defined, and success depends on individual effort and heroics.

2) **Repeatable.** Basic project management processes are established to track cost, schedule, and functionality. The necessary process discipline is in place to repeat earlier successes on projects with similar applications.

The key process areas at Level 2 focus on the software project's concerns related to establishing basic project management controls. They are:

- Requirements management
- Software project planning
- Software project tracking and oversight
- Software subcontract management
- Software quality assurance
- Software configuration management

3) **Defined.** The software process for both management and engineering activities is documented, standardized, and integrated into a standard software process for the organization. All projects use an approved, tailored version of the organization's standard software process for developing and maintaining software.

The key process areas at Level 3 address both project and organizational issues, as the organization establishes an infrastructure that institutionalizes effective software engineering and management processes across all projects. They are:

- Organization process focus
- Organization process definition
- Training program
- Integrated software management
- Software product engineering
- Intergroup coordination
- Peer reviews

4) Managed. Detailed measures of the software process and product quality are collected. Both the software process and products are quantitatively understood and controlled.

The key process areas at Level 4 focus on establishing a quantitative understanding of both the software process and the software work products being built. They are:

- Quantitative process management
- Software quality management

5) Optimizing. Continuous process improvement is enabled by quantitative feedback from the process and from piloting innovative ideas and technologies.

The key process areas at Level 5 cover the issues that both the organization and the projects must address to implement continual, measurable software process improvement. They are:

- Defect prevention
- Technology change management
- Process change management

Predictability, effectiveness, and control of an organization's software processes are believed to improve as the organization moves up these five levels. While not rigorous, the empirical evidence to date supports this belief.

Appendix D

Profiles of Contending Outsourcing Providers

There are a number of organizations attempting to become dominant players in the overall context of outsourcing services—far more than can be addressed in this book. In this appendix, I will feature a number of different kinds of organizations that are addressing the market in different but compelling ways. This includes two Western-based organizations and three India-based organizations. Some are dominant today, others are growing rapidly, and one is attempting to leverage its current assets and expand into certain components of the outsourcing arena. These organizations offer various components of the "stack" of offerings identified in Section III, with each looking to add depth at every opportunity.

These five organizations include:

- International Business Machines (IBM)
- Oracle Corporation
- Wipro Technologies
- Tata Consultancy Services
- Infosys Technologies, Ltd.

IBM (and SAP)

The first showcase is the broadest in this group in terms of the entire "stack" of outsource offerings, with an assist via a partnership with a dominant enterprise software vendor in rounding out the overall solution set. It includes two vendors built around an extremely tight partnership. These partners are IBM and SAP. IBM can offer *almost* the complete stack by itself. IBM dominates the worldwide IT outsourcing market with 22 percent market share in 2002, with $15.3 billion in revenue. Other than EDS (at $11.1 billion), no one is even close to Big Blue.[3] Outsourcing revenues accounted for roughly 40 percent of the overall services revenue produced by IBM in 2003.[4] IBM has long been a leader in data center management and hosting, and has been growing its application management offering in recent years. As far as the "stack" is concerned, you've got offerings across the board, strengthened further via acquisitions in recent years.

From a software perspective, IBM continues to own a significant share of the database market, supporting legacy mainframe systems on through the most modern environments with its DB2 and Informix brands. It has also strengthened itself in the tools business with the acquisition of Rational Software to go with its own branded tool kits. It continues to be a force in collaboration software with its Lotus brand. The only glaring omission in the IBM software equation, in fact, is a robust suite of business applications, which will be addressed in a moment in terms of the partnership with SAP. The rest of the software suite of offerings is robust and market-leading.

IBM Global Services is the largest services organization in the world. It became even stronger in 2002 with the completion of the $3.5 billion acquisition of PwC Consulting. This combination immediately strengthened the company's capabilities in systems integration work, as well as in business process outsourcing. PwC provides a growing presence in the BPO space, especially in the areas of finance and accounting, procurement, human resources, and real estate management. The combination also enhanced the company's overall capabilities in business process expertise and program management offerings. IBM is also moving aggressively to expand its offshore BPO capabilities, primarily through the $150 million acquisition of Daksh eServices, the third largest BPO provider in India. Upon the completion of this acquisition, IBM will have more than 15,000 people in India, with nearly half of them focused on BPO.[5] From a services perspective, IBM has the components of the "stack" solidly in place, with a market-leading position in many cases.

As mentioned, the one glaring omission in this portfolio is an offering for enterprise business software. IBM has primarily addressed this gap with an increasingly tight partnership with SAP, which remains the largest seller of business application software in the world. SAP is, at heart, a software company focused on business applications. Oracle has surpassed SAP as the second-largest software company in the world (SAP remains third—Microsoft is first), but SAP still maintains the top spot in terms of business application software. SAP recorded $2.6 billion in application license revenue in 2003 ($2.1 billion euros), compared to $1.6 billion in application license revenue for Oracle.[6] SAP has other offerings, including consulting services and training, but its prime solution in the marketplace is a robust, fully integrated suite of business applications.

SAP has many partners around the world for implementation and integration work, but its partnership with IBM appears particularly strong and compelling for the marketplace. IBM has built one of the largest SAP implementation practices in the world, with approximately 11,000 professionals spanning 160 countries in its global SAP organization. IBM not only has a strong implementation business around the SAP solution, but it also is a leader in joint development initiatives with this leading enterprise software vendor. Validating the strength of the relationship, IBM was named one of the inaugural recipients of the SAP Pinnacle Award for 2002, which is SAP's first Global Partner Award Program.[7] Given the depth and breadth of this partnership and the large installed base of customers, IBM has also put itself in a strong position to be the managed services provider of choice for customers who have adopted the SAP platform.

It should also be mentioned that IBM has strong partnerships with many of the other leading software companies beyond SAP, including Siebel (particularly with their new joint CRM OnDemand software as a service offering), PeopleSoft/JD Edwards, and other enterprise software vendors, including Oracle. IBM is also open to a mixed environment by supporting multiple applications for the same customer. Moreover, IBM is also by no means sitting on its merits as a leader in the industry. Part of its outsourcing strategy is its ability to lead and dominate in the area of "on-demand business." The details of this far-reaching initiative are spelled out in Section IV.

There is no question that IBM is well-positioned in this space, but its success in increasing market share is by no means a given. While IBM has been open to supporting its customers with best of breed environments, there is still a feeling in the marketplace that a choice to go with IBM as a single provider makes you subject to an aggressive push to adopt IBM products and services for all your solutions. This may be a good thing, or not so good, depending on the circumstance. Just be aware that the approach of "the IBM way is the only way" has been an issue in the past and that it may continue to be an issue in the future. In addition, IBM has the same challenge as other large companies that try to provide multiple solutions to a single customer. It needs to be able to break down its internal barriers and operate effectively as a single entity. For example, there was a lot of concern in the marketplace at the time of the PwC Consulting acquisition that it would be a tremendous cultural challenge to integrate the people and offerings of PwC Consulting with those of IBM Global Services. Without that seamless integration, there can be no leverage for customers. Early results appear to be that the acquisition has gone fairly well from an internal perspective, as IBM Global Services has even adopted some of the methodologies and go-to-market approaches of its newfound brethren. It's still too early, however, to tell if the integration of services will truly be seamless and provide both immediate and long-term advantages to customers, both in the case of the PwC Consulting and the Daksh eServices acquisitions. IBM is a very big company. That can be a good thing and can be a bad thing. It has the assets in place to dominate in the end-to-end managed services/outsourcing arena. But it must work effectively as a single enterprise in order to achieve the ultimate gains.

Finally, success will only come to those who earn it, and in this business you need to earn it every day of the year, in every facet of your end-to-end offering. IBM must also respect the price pressure coming from the aggressive service providers entering portions of this space from all corners of the world. To its advantage, IBM can leverage assets across its broad portfolio to gain market share in one area by bundling and discounting an entire package of solutions. This advantage may turn into an imperative based on the dramatic cost pressure in the marketplace today in order for the company to remain competitive against all challengers. IBM needs to be sure it can continue to expand its low-cost offshore technical capabilities as part of its offerings, and it must effectively integrate those service capabilities into its overall solution set. As mentioned, IBM is investing heavily in India, but it must demonstrate to the marketplace that it can achieve the same high-quality on-site/offshore success rate as that of the native Indian companies. As such, this expansion is an imperative that must be seamlessly integrated into its end-to-end offerings to be able to ward off the growing presence of the large-scale, India-based operations.

Oracle Corporation

The second intriguing supplier in the managed services space is Oracle Corporation. Oracle is not among the leaders today in providing outsourcing services. It is not a leader in IT outsourcing, applications management, hosting, or BPO. However, Oracle can be viewed as one of the few companies that has a chance to very quickly become a dominant player as an end-to-end provider in the managed services space given its current asset base and its apparent commitment to venture aggressively into this business. There is a lot of work to be done inside Oracle to be able to pull this off along the lines of becoming as much a service company as it is a software company, but the opportunity clearly exists for significant growth for Oracle if it institutionalizes a commitment to providing outsourcing services throughout its vast organization.

Oracle is the second-largest software company in the world, currently offering one of the most extensive suites of business applications, accompanied by its industry-leading database business. Oracle Consulting Services (OCS) has provided a strong presence in the system integration market for years, specifically in the area of consulting work that relates to Oracle's own software offerings. And while project management and business process expertise at OCS may not match the quality found in some of the other consulting firms, they still represent solid offerings within the overall stack of solutions from Oracle.

Let's start with the software component, which is clearly Oracle's leverage point in broadening beyond its base of offerings. It has the complete set of enterprise software solutions, including database, enterprise business applications, tools, and analytics. If, as it has proclaimed, Oracle wants to compete in the managed services space, it will need to do so by leveraging its existing installed base of customers, and provide a compelling argument along the lines of the Enterprise Optimization Framework. Oracle has already invested heavily in building critical mass of expertise in Bangalore and Hyderabad in South India, not only for software development, but also for application support. The company is hiring about 100 employees a month in India, looking to eventually double its Indian headcount from 3,200 to around 6,000.[8] This is helping make the total cost of the Oracle solution more attractive to customers. Moreover (and this is critical), Oracle is trying to change its method of writing, revising, and deploying software to make the entire process more seamless to the customer.[9] Today, the cost and energy to support Oracle applications can be overwhelming for individual companies. There is no way that Oracle will be able to make managed services a profitable offering without dramatic changes in the software itself. While the complexity of the software is such that it will never be self-sufficient, it needs to approach a level of stability and standardization at which the cost of support can be decreased dramatically. Part of this will come from low-cost support resources based offshore, but that alone won't be enough to sufficiently reduce the support costs. The software itself needs to become easier, less time-consuming, and less costly to support. If it doesn't, look out for the ASPs, which may not have the end-to-end depth of functionality of systems like Oracle and SAP, but appear to have resolved many of the issues that plague enterprise software vendors in terms of ease of maintenance and system stability. Frustrated customers have tolerated the maintenance issues with enterprise software because there haven't been viable alternatives that provide the depth and breadth of required functionality. As the ASPs try to take on companies like Oracle on the functionality side, the enterprise vendors will need to solve the maintenance challenges that permeate the marketplace today. And this just isn't from a customer point of view. If Oracle wants to provide the support for its customers, the support will have to be less costly, and that must come in part from increased quality of the product and a more simplified approach for maintenance and upgrades. Finally, Oracle also needs to find a way to provide this level of service not only for its small customers, but also for its large, most complex customers.

As mentioned earlier, Oracle has ventured into the operations/hosting arena on a couple of occasions in the last few years with various branded initiatives. These offerings have been mostly targeted at smaller companies that are looking for a pure out-of-the-box solution at a very low price point. The service level agreements are fairly basic, and neither extensive modifications to the systems nor external integration are allowed. While this kind of offering may be appropriate for relatively small companies, it may not be realistic for medium- to large-sized businesses. These companies require flexibility that simply isn't there. They require more complex support and assistance, along with more options on the software and integration side of the equation. Oracle recognizes this as a need and as an opportunity, and it has recently begun tailoring managed services offerings to its higher end customers. Oracle has invested heavily in a top-of-the-line data center. It has support resources (some onshore and some offshore) that can provide the appropriate level of support required by these more sophisticated companies. And Oracle has indicated that it will break down the walls across its organization on behalf of its customers. If the operations team needs assistance from the consulting services or software development teams, or vice versa, Oracle says it will get it. Traditionally, breaking down these barriers inside the large software companies has been a tremendous challenge, as internal performance metrics haven't motivated leaders to share resources across the company. Oracle has committed itself to this offering, and has indicated that it will drive that resource sharing from the top down if necessary, in terms of acting in the best interest of the customer. If it can't, it will fail.

The newest part of this equation at Oracle is clearly the operations component for medium- to large-sized companies. This will not be a slam dunk for Oracle. This is where the pure service component of the business kicks in, and Oracle will need to rally around that approach. Oracle will need to break down the internal barriers to leverage its resources across the company to make this work, because substandard performance by just one segment of the overall solution will bring this whole offering down like a house of cards. It will take a complete company commitment to the model and the vision. That being said, Oracle is one of the very few companies that can offer virtually this entire suite of solutions under its own brand. The only critical component for technology outsourcing that won't have an Oracle logo on it will be the hardware, for which Oracle has an excellent story to tell in terms of partnerships with Sun, Hewlett-Packard, etc. Other than that, you can get just about the whole boat from Oracle. One-stop shopping. One throat to choke.

There are a handful of potential inhibitors to Oracle's growth in this area. The first has just been highlighted in terms of complete company commitment around the total service-based offering. That vision will need to resonate throughout the Oracle culture in order to achieve success. As stated, this has been a frustration for Oracle customers in the past, long before the offerings in managed services operations. The disconnects between the sales, software development, consulting, technical support, and functional support organizations have sometimes been as wide as the Grand Canyon. Technical support may agree that you have a bug, but software development says you've got the functionality as it was designed. The sales organization may say something completely different in terms of its understanding on the exact same problem. And the consulting arm (or any other consulting partner engaged on the deployment) ends up stuck in the middle, along with the customer, just trying to get something to work. This kind of disconnect occurs all too often with Oracle and will absolutely kill the end-to-end managed services vision if companies entrust their entire infrastructure to this single company and receive this kind of service. If it can't operate as a single partner, then it provides no advantage over the combo approach of stitching together multiple agreements with multiple vendors. This gap may seem easy and obvious to overcome, but typical experience with software vendors, as well as many other suppliers that provide multiple solutions to the same customer, indicates that breaking down these barriers and legitimately becoming "one throat to choke" is a monumental task that requires the complete dedication of the entire company. It needs to start with the top-down strategic approach and work its way all through the metrics used to evaluate employees throughout the enterprise. There has been some positive movement for Oracle in this regard. Headlines such as the following, which appeared in *The Wall Street Journal*—"Oracle Puts Priority on Customer Service"—are noteworthy. As this article highlights, Oracle has revamped its sales and consulting organizations, and has brought in some new leadership to focus on this very issue.[10] But, again, the proof is in the pudding. Structural changes alone will not make the difference. The company needs not only to adopt this focus at the top, but then also to drive it effectively down through every facet of the organization.

Another area where Oracle must open up pertains to customers who have not bought into the complete Oracle software offering. Even those companies that are tried and true Oracle applications customers may still rely on at least some best of breed solutions that are integrated with the Oracle suite. In this case Oracle has two choices: (1) It can try to convince its customers that are looking for as much vendor consolidation as possible to swap out existing systems in favor of the Oracle products. Oracle will likely aggressively pursue this option and possibly at very attractive rates because this will allow it to kill two birds with one stone. It will significantly simplify the environment while picking up market share all at the same time. (Customers, of course, will have to analyze this kind of scenario in terms of lower Total Cost, further Process Optimization, and/or further Information Optimization, and make long-term strategic decisions as to whether or not this option makes overall sense.) Or, (2) Oracle will have to bite the bullet and agree to host and support other software companies' offerings and the potential integration engines that are required to link the entire solution together. At least during the period in which it is growing its managed services business, Oracle will need to strongly consider offering this flexibility for its customers in order to achieve dominance as a single solution provider. In addition, many of those customers who do buy into the Oracle approach will likely also opt to transfer systems over time onto the Oracle platform. They may not do that right away, but the case will become more compelling over time, especially if Oracle is able to achieve high levels of customer satisfaction across this suite of offerings, and if it can make the migration path low risk and cost effective.

Finally, while Oracle has some strength within Oracle Consulting in the areas of project management and business process expertise, it has little experience in the area of business process outsourcing (BPO). As highlighted previously, this has been a strength of many other service providers for years, and is often tied very closely to other outsourcing initiatives. Oracle can certainly attempt to dominate in its current stack of offerings without venturing into BPO, but it may be leaving some opportunities on the table. If the goal is a complete end-to-end outsourcing partnership, then Oracle may need to invest in extending its solution mix to include targeted components of BPO as well.

As mentioned, Oracle is not what you would consider to be a major player today in the managed services space. However, it does have many of the relevant assets in place, and an apparent commitment behind this initiative (along with more nearly $6 billion in the bank)[11] to seed the possibilities to grow rapidly in this area. It needs to make that commitment throughout its organization with cross-functional buy-in from sales, development, consulting, support, program management, etc. The internal metrics need to reflect this new approach to the marketplace, and all of the company's offerings need to align to this model. That means stable software with low support costs, yet still a high level of service. This will not be easy and may take some time, but the essentials are there for Oracle to make a run at the leaders in technology outsourcing and managed services.

Offshore Challengers

In Section III, I highlighted a number of the significant advances that the offshore service providers have been able to achieve in the last few years. I also highlighted some of their specific capabilities in terms of breadth and quality of various offerings. In this quickly evolving market, it is clear that the leading Indian companies do represent legitimate and immediate threats to some of the U.S.-based players that have traditionally been perceived as dominant in the outsourcing arena.

Specifically looking at the offshore outsourcing space, META Group identifies four organizations in the position of "leader" on a scale that covers *Presence* and *Performance* in the area of Offshore Application Outsourcing.[12] These four include:

- Wipro
- TCS (Tata Consultancy Services)
- Infosys
- IBM Global Services

Accenture falls just shy of the "leader" category, sitting instead near the top of the "challenger" rating. These organizations have all invested extensively over the last decade in building capabilities in this offshore model, and the native Indian firms have clearly entrenched themselves as legitimate competitors in specific solution areas to many of the other global consulting organizations, including those based in the U.S. It is interesting to observe these two worlds heading for a collision course in terms of breadth and depth of capabilities, as well as on the all-important criteria of price. The Indian organizations are trying to grow into the more sophisticated business-process and industry vertical areas of expertise and to build their global brands. These specific companies are beginning to become well known within the U.S. IT community, but they are still largely unfamiliar to other U.S. business executives. Meanwhile, the U.S. firms are trying to quickly develop their own offshore, low-cost, high-quality capabilities to pair with their traditional offerings. "Wipro…is charging upstream into consulting and other high-value services while its bigger American rivals are rushing downstream. Vivek Paul (Wipro's President) argues that *'both ends of the spectrum are racing for the same point. Neither strategy is easy. It's not easy to build a strong global-delivery model, and it's not easy to rent real estate in India and hire engineers. But, ultimately, the center point is where the big players will play* [emphasis added].'"[13] Some of the "big players" on the U.S. side have already been discussed. Now it's time to take a more detailed look at some of these offshore organizations, and examine some of their capabilities and opportunities in the marketplace, both for them and for their clients.

META Group provides ratings for many of the leading organizations in the offshore application outsourcing space. For an overview and comparison see Figures D-1 and D-2, which provide some high-level insights into five of the leading organizations in this space. All five are global players; three are based in India, and two are based in the U.S.

Figure D-1: Offshore Application Outsourcing *Presence* Evaluation for Leading Vendors

Company	Vision / Strategy	Channels / Partners	Awareness / Reputation	Geographic Coverage	Business Drivers	Industry Focus	Investments	Share	Services	Technology
Wipro	Good	Good	Good / Very Good	Good / Very Good	Good / Very Good	Good / Very Good	Good	Good / Very Good	Good / Very Good	Good
TCS	Good	Good	Very Good	Good	Good / Very Good	Good / Very Good	Good	Good / Very Good	Good / Very Good	Good
Infosys	Good / Very Good	Good	Good / Very Good	Good	Very Good / Excellent	Good / Very Good	Good	Good / Very Good	Good / Very Good	Fair / Good
IBM	Very Good	Very Good / Excellent	Good / Very Good	Very Good / Excellent	Good / Very Good	Very Good	Good	Fair	Very Good	Good
Accenture	Good / Very Good	Good / Very Good	Good / Very Good	Good / Very Good	Good	Good / Very Good	Good / Very Good	Fair	Good / Very Good	Very Good

Source: META Group, *Offshore Application Outsourcing*, February 10, 2003

Figure D-2: Offshore Application Outsourcing *Performance* Evaluation for Leading Vendors

Company	Pricing	Execution	Agility	Personnel	Financials
Wipro	Good / Very Good	Good / Very Good	Good / Very Good	Good	Very Good
TCS	Very Good	Good / Very Good	Good / Very Good	Good	Good
Infosys	Good	Very Good	Good / Very Good	Fair	Good
IBM	Fair	Good / Very Good	Fair / Good	Good / Very Good	Very Good / Excellent
Accenture	Fair	Fair / Good	Fair / Good	Very Good / Excellent	Good

Source: META Group, *Offshore Application Outsourcing*, February 10, 2003

Some general observations from these charts indicate that the U.S.-based firms appear to have slight advantages in the following areas over their Indian competitors:

- Vision/strength
- Channels/partners
- Geographic coverage
- Technology
- Personnel

The Indian organizations appear to have slight advantages over the U.S.-based companies in the following areas:

- Business drivers
- Share
- Pricing
- Agility

The other areas appear fairly balanced between the Indian and U.S. entities in terms of their offshore application outsourcing capabilities. The consistency of capabilities (strengths and weaknesses) for the U.S. leaders and the Indian leaders is noteworthy in terms of finding a one-stop shop for services. The conclusion, as highlighted in Section III, remains that a seamless U.S./Indian partnership that represents the "Best of Both Worlds" may be the optimal solution in the marketplace (at least right now in this rapidly maturing market space). PI Departments should keep this in mind when evaluating providers for end-to-end outsourcing offerings.

The following sections highlight the more detailed capabilities and characteristics of the three Indian-based companies just mentioned. Their success has been nothing short of phenomenal, as can be seen in their meteoric rise in revenue over the past five years (see Figure D-3). These companies (which are profiled in no particular order) have played a big part in changing the landscape for global service providers around the globe.

Figure D-3: Revenue Tracking for Infosys, Wipro, and TCS (1999-2004*)

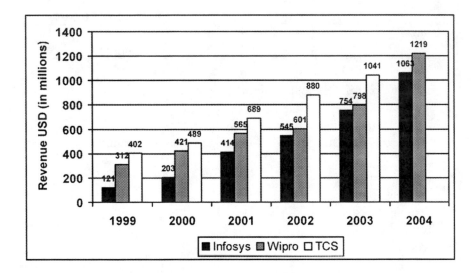

* Note: 2004 Revenue for TCS had not been announced at the time of publication

Data Sources: Information obtained from a combination of each company's web site and financial reports.

Wipro Technologies

"From the first day in dealing with Wipro, there's been nothing but quality, character, highest integrity, highest quality work. As a joint venture, you wouldn't find a better partner. As a supplier, you wouldn't find a higher quality partner."[14] That's the way former General Electric CEO Jack Welch described his relationship with Wipro—not a bad endorsement! Wipro has 30 offices worldwide,

17,000 IT practitioners and domain consultants, and more than 300 global customers. The company, which has been listed on the New York Stock Exchange since October 2000, has posted a cumulative annual growth rate (CAGR) of 45 percent over the last five years.[15] Again, not bad, for a company that was selling cooking oil and personal computers just about a decade ago.

From a services perspective, Wipro has three major offerings:

- IT consulting and services
- Product design services
- Business process outsourcing

These offerings are molded together into what Wipro calls the 2π Delivery Model, as shown in Figure D-4.

Figure D-4: Wipro's 2π Delivery Model

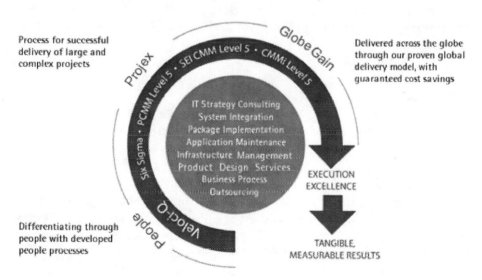

Process for successful delivery of large and complex projects

Delivered across the globe through our proven global delivery model, with guaranteed cost savings

Differentiating through people with developed people processes

EXECUTION EXCELLENCE

TANGIBLE, MEASURABLE RESULTS

Source: Wipro Technologies, October 2003

Referring to the "stack" of outsource offerings, it's just about all there, with the exception of enterprise business application software. Metrics from January 2004 indicate the following solution breakdown:[16]

- Custom Applications & Development=37%
- R&D Services=32%

- Package Implementations=11%
- IT Enabled Services (BPO and Call Center)=11%
- Additional Service Offerings=9%

Wipro appears well-diversified across many industry verticals, with no industry representing more than 17 percent of the business in the quarter ending December 2003. The top six industry verticals are as follows:[17]

- Telecom & Internet-working=17%
- Financial Services=17%
- Embedded Systems=15%
- Energy & Utilities=14%
- Manufacturing=14%
- Retail=12%

From a geographic standpoint, the work breakdown is as follows, with North America representing a strong majority of the business:[18]

- North America=64%
- Europe=30%
- Asia=6%

Specifically in the area of product development, Wipro has tailored its offerings by creating "development centers within its offices, each dedicated to a single important customer. The idea: to promote relationships that would create annuity revenue. Today in Electronic City, Wipro hosts development centers for Hewlett-Packard, General Motors, and dozens of other huge global companies."[19] Further, a commitment to quality is embedded into the culture at Wipro, as it is with most of its Indian rivals. The company has achieved Level 5 certification (the highest level) in the Capability Maturity Model (CMM) from the Software Engineering Institute at Carnegie-Mellon in *three* different categories—the first to accomplish this feat.[20]

A significant turning point for Wipro was when the company hired Indian-native Vivek Paul, now the company's president. Paul was a leading executive at GE Power Systems in the U.S. when he took over Wipro Technologies in 1999, which he decided to base in Santa Clara, CA, in the heart of Silicon Valley.[21] Paul, who was named one of the Best Managers of 2003 by *BusinessWeek*,[22] has been a key driver in expanding the global footprint for Wipro as it has continued to grow year after year.

The latest focus for Wipro has been in the area of business process outsourcing. The company acquired one of the leading BPO organizations in India, Spectramind, in July 2002. This 4,000-person organization has more than 100 clients worldwide, providing services in a wide variety of areas (see Figure D-5).[23]

Figure D-5: Wipro Spectramind BPO Set of Offerings

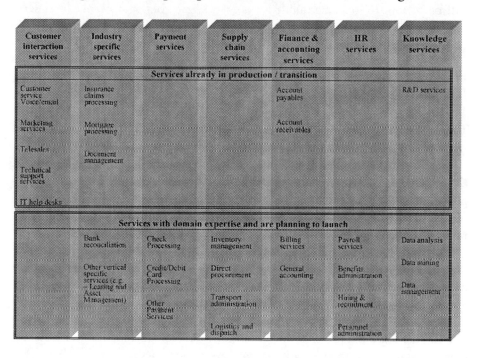

Customer interaction services	Industry specific services	Payment services	Supply chain services	Finance & accounting services	HR services	Knowledge services
Services already in production / transition						
Customer service Voice/email	Insurance claims processing			Account payables		R&D services
Marketing services	Mortgage processing			Account receivables		
Telesales	Document management					
Technical support services						
IT help desks						
Services with domain expertise and are planning to launch						
	Bank reconciliation	Check Processing	Inventory management	Billing services	Payroll services	Data analysis
	Other vertical specific services (e.g. – Leasing and Asset Management)	Credit/Debit Card Processing	Direct procurement	General accounting	Benefits administration	Data mining
		Other Payment Services	Transport administration		Hiring & recruitment	Data management
			Logistics and dispatch		Personnel administration	

Content Source: Wipro Technologies (wipro.com), December 2003

It is important to note that Wipro Spectamind's offerings are still evolving, as can be seen in Figure D-4 with the number of services identified as still *planning to launch*. Many of the BPO offerings from India are in this state; i.e., underway and available, but still immature, especially when compared to the maturity of the IT-related outsourcing capabilities. PI Departments need to be careful about many of these BPO offerings, especially as they extend beyond call center functionality. There is definitely more risk in these areas in the short term when compared to the services offered in the area of core technology support, although the ability for many of these organizations to come up to speed quickly in terms of repeatable, rules-based transaction processes is certainly impressive.

Wipro clearly has the complete set of outsource solution offerings. As with its Indian brethren, it will need to focus on building its brand and expanding the sophistication of its business-focused portfolio. This is what all the leading Indian organizations need to do now that they have established themselves as dominant in a vast set of commodity areas. There will still be growth opportunities in these commodity businesses, but the real challenge (and opportunity) will be to solidify that commodity base while growing into higher level services that can command larger margins and provide deeper penetration into customer accounts.

Tata Consultancy Services

Tata Consultancy Services (TCS), established in 1968, is a privately owned division of Tata Sons, Ltd., the main holding company of the $11.3-billion Tata Group. The "House of Tata" was founded by Sir Jamsetji Tata in the latter part of the nineteenth century. It started with textiles and went on to steel, electric power, automobiles, chemicals, and more. The group later diversified further, and it now has interests in financial services, hotels, telecommunications, and information technology. In all there are 80 companies in the Tata Group.[24]

For several years now TCS has been India's largest IT company, as well as Asia's largest independent software and services organization. The company services more than 1,000 clients in over 55 countries, with more than 20,000 employees around the world. The company has 15 centers in India alone that have been assessed at CMM Level 5, with more than 17,000 engineers operating in Level 5 centers, the highest number of any organization in the world. Growth has been a constant for TCS, with revenues doubling every two years for the past six years.[25] The company became India's first global billion-dollar software organization, hitting $1.04 billion in revenue in FY03.[26] The company's mission is: "To help customers achieve their business objectives, by providing innovative, best-in-class consulting, IT solutions and services. We shall make it a joy for all stakeholders to work with us." It was this second sentence that really caught my eye. There is clearly a strong cultural component to the success of firms such as TCS, including the overwhelmingly positive approach by its employees to the work they are performing. Often mission statements talk about enhancing relationships with their stakeholders, but I haven't seen many that take it one step further, to make it a "*joy* to work with us."

The company's model focuses on a variety of industry verticals, along with a number of service practices. This combination is portrayed in what it calls its "Web of Participation" (see Figure D-6).

Figure D-6: TCS' "Web of Participation"

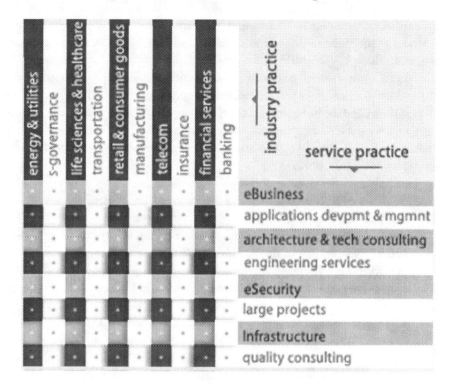

Source: Tata Consultancy Services (tcs.com), March 2003

TCS's venture into business process outsourcing comes in the form of a joint venture with Housing Development Finance Corporation (HDFC), India's premier mortgage finance company. The joint venture is called Intelenet. HDFC is a complete financial portal in itself with proven competencies in banking, insurance, mutual funds, asset management, and its core strengths: mortgage and properties. It brings to Intelenet its experience in customer management processes, back-office operations, and property management. The four main BPO solutions offered by Intelenet are:[27]

- Contact center management
- Back-office processing
- Accounting services
- Technical help desk

The theme of quality assurance carries through both TCS and this joint venture, Intelenet. In the case of the BPO joint venture, a 6 Sigma Framework is core to the culture of the organization, with rigid programs in place to monitor quality of service, and to provide the appropriate feedback and training to ensure a constant adherence to these high standards.[28]

The "stack" of outsourcing services is very much in place at TCS (again, with the exception of an offering for enterprise business application software). TCS is the largest of the Indian firms in this space, and continues to demonstrate impressive growth across its operations. So where does TCS go from here? Ajit V. Sawant, a TCS vice-president, published some comments to this effect in *The Economic Times* in July 2002.

> While the SEI CMM levels and Six Sigma have acknowledged India's ability to deliver quality, the challenge will be to move from the fundamental perspective of cost and create differentiators. Further, in the global IT market, the competition is still on cost—a replicable factor. In markets such as Singapore, companies from Philippines are apparently delivering the same as Indian companies but at half the cost.
>
> So what do we need to do? Focus on generating intellectual property, adopt vertical integration model coupled with domain knowledge, truly globalise operations, and make strategic acquisitions. The quality of business has to improve and substantial focus has to be on developing domain consulting.[29]

This is not a company, or an industry, that is going to sit idle and passively enjoy its recent success. It knows that commodity level businesses can rapidly gain market share, but their growth will only continue for so long as the barrier to entry by other companies (and other countries, in this case) is not high, and then margins can quickly erode. TCS and the leaders in the Indian offshore industry are aware of these facts, and are taking steps to find those hooks for differentiation and grow their capabilities to attack further business in other untapped areas. This approach will be needed for TCS to obtain its corporate vision: "To be Global Top 10 by 2010."[30]

Infosys Technologies, Ltd.

India-based Infosys Technologies was introduced back in Section III as one of suppliers of work for JDS Uniphase. The fact that Infosys has retained some of its combination of on-site, offshore presence at JDSU, despite the outsourcing of most of its IT services to Oracle, is indicative of the high-quality value-added services that the organization has consistently demonstrated throughout its tenure at JDSU. This company, which has been in existence for just two decades, and which was founded by seven "technocrats," has grown into an organization with more than 25,000 employees. Growth has been at 69 percent, on a compounded basis, over the last five years. The company has its corporate headquarters in Bangalore, with an additional 15 offices around the globe. Infosys was the first Indian public company to offer an employee stock option plan, and was the first Indian company to list on a U.S. stock exchange (INFY on NASDAQ). Most impressively, Infosys has been rated number one in the "Best Employers in India" survey conducted by Hewitt Associates two years in a row (2001 and 2002). As with its brethren, Infosys maintains a rigorous commitment to quality with an all-encompassing, metric-driven performance management program. The company has demonstrated this commitment on its way to receiving Level 5 certification in the CMM from the Software Engineering Institute.[31]

As with the other organizations, Infosys has a broad set of outsourcing solutions, leveraging its "Global Delivery Model," which balances a small set of on-site resources with the majority of its resources working in its offshore facilities. The core solution areas include:[32]

- Consulting and IT
- Product engineering
- Application product solutions (such as its enterprise banking solution)

As of March 2003, the portfolio breakdown is as follows:[33]

- Development=32%
- Maintenance=28%
- Package implementation=11%
- Reengineering=6%
- Consulting=4%
- Other products and services=19%

The largest of these industry verticals for Infosys is financial services, representing 37 percent of the business in FY03. Manufacturing (17 percent of revenue), telecom (15 percent), and retail (13 percent) are the next largest vertical segments.[34]

From a geographic perspective, North America dominates the landscape for Infosys, with the following global breakdown, also from FY03:[35]

- North America=73%
- Europe=18%
- India=2%
- Rest of the world=7%

An Infosys subsidiary, Progeon, represents the company's offering in the space of business process outsourcing.[36] The BPO solution set consists of the Industry Vertical Services shown in Figure D-7 and Cross Industry Services shown in Figure D-8.

Figure D-7: Progeon Industry Vertical Services

Banking	Credit / Debit card services Check processing Mortgage loan servicing Collections Customer account management Treasury operations management
Insurance and Health Care	Policy owner services Claims processing Transaction & re-insurance accounting Statutory reporting Annuities processing Benefit administration
Security	Client account management Corporate actions

Source: Progeon (progeon.com), March 2003

Figure D-8: Progeon Cross Industry Services

Customer Relationship Management	Customer support: Email • Customer service • Product support • Technical help desk Chat Monitoring
Finance and Accounting	Accounts receivables Accounts payable Tax processing
Administration	Benefits processing
Sales Order Processing	Quote through cash processes

Source: Progeon (progeon.com), March 2003

Once again, the consumer needs to be aware that these BPO offerings are brand new in the marketplace. Progeon was incorporated in April 2002 and is still ramping up the business with its first set of customers. However, the following statement from the customer sponsor of the very first client (a high-tech equipment manufacturer with operations in Australia, Holland, and the U.S.) certainly provides the sense that things are getting off to a good start:

> Thanks to both teams for one of the best implementations I've ever seen. Now to the next one. There is so much more coming, increasing challenges, but now more than ever I feel 100% confident we'll get there in a successful way. The proof is there, the role model is there, the team is there....It could not be better.[37]

Culture plays a big role in the success and growth at Infosys. A story from *Outlook India.com* put it this way:

> Enter Infosys City and the first thing that strikes you is the unconditional trust that every employee—from the receptionist to the management trainee to the mid-level manager—has in top management.

Everyone believes what the top management says. And everyone is suffused with a quiet pride in the organization and its achievements.

The official term for an Infosys employee is "Infoscion" and the word "scion," according to the Concise Oxford Dictionary, means a descendant, a younger member of (esp. a noble) family. Every time Infosys hires someone, it enters into an implicit social contract with that employee: give the company your best and the company will take care of you for all time to come. That's why India's best and brightest continue to work for Infosys (the attrition rate is a low 7.6 percent), although it's not the best paymaster within the industry and the share options are no longer as phenomenally lucrative as they were in, say, 1999.[38]

This is clearly more than an employee-employer relationship, and when the grab for the top talent is highly competitive, things like this make a big difference in being able to continue to expand and grow with high-performance service offerings. The importance of these personal relationships within the company extends to the service offerings and the company's relationships with its clients—a critical component in winning business (and repeat business) in this very competitive economic environment.

There you have it. Three fantastic success stories of organizations that started with very little, courted the best and the brightest, lived each day with a complete commitment to quality of service and a complete commitment to success (the success of its clients and the success of its people). These three companies are just some of the shining stars from India which have become competitors in the global landscape of outsource service providers. The question remains: Who will win in the end? On the one hand you have the American powerhouses (IBM and the former Big 5, along with some others, including software companies such as Oracle), which have well-established global brands and solid reputations in the marketplace for excellence across a number of solution areas. These organizations can offer business process expertise, along with vertical industry insight and the core guts of systems integration and core technical support (and enterprise software, in the case of Oracle). These companies are all at various stages of introducing extensive outsourcing capabilities, for systems and software related work, as well as BPO. Where these companies lag, and where they are struggling to remain competitive, is in the low-cost commodity components of their service portfolios. They're desperate to outflank the Indian firms and build the low-cost, high-quality offerings that are already mature with the Indian companies, and bundle those services with their higher end solutions. Over the last few years, the Indian firms have been winning the battle on the commodity side, and these victories have begun to take a hefty bite out of the traditional U.S. firms (as if the economic downturn wasn't enough for these organizations), but the U.S. firms are building (or buying) their own offshore capabilities at an extremely aggressive pace.

Then you've got the Indian firms, representing the one portion of the IT industry that continues to grow through the tough economic times. These organizations have established themselves no longer as "boutiques" around the globe. These are sophisticated businesses that have thrived based on wise investments, exceptional talent, and understanding what it takes to win work and then continue to win work once they are able to penetrate an account. It's come to the point where the U.S. firms are almost conceding that they can't win with their traditional on-site model when going head-to-head in the core technology space with these Indian organizations, so they are rapidly trying to develop competitive offshore offerings of their own. Similarly, the Indian firms, which remain immature in key areas of business process and end-to-end solution expertise, especially with respect to specialized knowledge in many industry verticals, are investing heavily on their own to build these skills and demonstrate to the marketplace that they can compete on all levels with their American competitors. After all, just as the Indian organizations have grabbed substantial market share in the commoditized technology space, there are plenty of additional companies in other countries (including China, Russia, Thailand, etc.) that are looking to outflank them on price in the technology commodity market. The Indian organizations must continue to expand their offerings or they will likely find themselves being squeezed from all sides. This is one of the reasons why the leading Indian firms have all launched BPO offerings in the last couple of years, trying to leverage their successes in core technology outsourcing into these process-oriented solutions, on the path toward complete end-to-end offerings.

It's the race to the center point, as Vivek Paul said. Will the U.S.-based global firms complete their set of offerings with the low-cost, high-quality commodity component before the Indian companies (as well as other firms around the world getting into this space) rise up and start taking share from their Western counterparts in process and industry focused offerings? Will we see partnership models and/or joint ventures capture this center point (as in the "Best of Both Worlds" case study in Section III), at least until the end-to-end solution offerings mature under the single brands? Who can get there the fastest while not sacrificing quality along the way? One can assume that it will be a highly competitive fight, and the jury is still out on who will be standing at the end. Those organizations that find themselves able to offer the "best of both worlds" at a competitive price will be well-positioned to win. Who that will be is still very much up in the air.

All of the organizations profiled in this section have a number of things in common:

- Breadth of offerings
- Global reach
- Commitment to quality
- Sound financial resources

Differentiation is established based on:

- Price
- Specific service offerings
- Brand recognition
- Reputation

All of these areas have been discussed. There is one area, however—maybe the most important of all when it comes to successfully providing services to clients on a long-term basis—that requires some additional attention. I'm talking about relationships. The key to success, ultimately, will be the ability of these organizations to truly adopt the service model and achieve a level of relationship with their customers that is rarely achieved in the business world; that is, becoming true business partners (as defined in Section III under the banner "The Essence of Partnership"). There are dozens of other organizations with intriguing opportunities to grow in the outsourcing arena. BearingPoint, Accenture, Hewlett-Packard, and HCL Technologies were highlighted in Section III, each of which has a compelling story to tell, along with some of the ASPs that persevere. Many others are in play as well. It's that race to the center for who can provide the complete depth of offerings (high-end to low), all at the highest quality and the lowest cost. And those that can provide these offerings in the true spirit of partnership will be the organizations with the greatest likelihood of winning.

Notes

Foreword

1   *Simplifying e-Fulfillment,* BPA Systems, September 2000.

Section I

1   Michael Hammer and James Champy, *Reengineering the Corporation—A Manifesto for Business Revolution,* HarperBusiness (A Division of HarperCollins Publishers), 1993, p. 27-28.

2   Ibid. p. 78.

3   Ibid. p. 28.

4   *Building the "Process Enterprise" at Canada Post,* Agenda: Business Process Management Conference 2003, Toronto, Ontario, Canada, July 2003.

5   Information related to Electrocomponents, plc was obtained primarily from the company's Web site (www.electrocomponents.com), including the company's 2003 Annual Report, which was listed on the site, September 2003. Background information was also obtained from Paul Harmon, *The Chief Process Officer, Business Process Trends,* September 16, 2003.

6   Lorraine Cosgrove Ware, "The State of the CIO 2003," *CIO* magazine, March 26, 2003. According to this survey, 47% of CIOs reported directly to the CEO.

7   Stephanie Overby, "The Incredible Shrinking CIO," *CIO* magazine, October 15, 2003. The article indicates that the percentage of CIOs reporting to the CFO jumped from 11% in 2002 to 22% in 2003.

8 Ibid.

9 Colin Powell with Joseph E. Persico, *My American Journey,* Ballantine Books, 1995, p. 255.

10 Eliyahu Goldratt and Jeff Cox, *The Goal,* Second Revised Edition, North River Press, 1992, p. 332.

11 This is a commercial standard developed by the non-governmental International Standards Organization (ISO) to address IT security and information integrity. It is based on the British Standard 7799, which was first developed in the early 1980s. IEC refers to the International Electrotechnical Commission, an additional international standards body.

12 Harold Kerzner, PhD., *Project Management, A Systems Approach to Planning, Scheduling, and Controlling, Seventh Edition,* John Wiley & Sons, Inc., 2001, p. 4.

13 Ibid. p. 325.

Section II

14 Christopher Koch, "It's Time to Take Control," *CIO* magazine, July 15, 2002.

15 Keith Regan, "Report: Half of Outsourced IT Projects Will Fail," *Ecommerce Times,* March 25, 2003.

16 Christopher Koch, "It's Time to Take Control," *CIO* magazine, July 15, 2002.

17 Ibid.

18 Forrester Research as depicted in *Business Process Management—The Third Wave,* Meghan-Kiffer Press, 2003, p. 161.

19 Dell Computer Corporation. 2003 Annual Report, April 2003, p. 3-4.

20 Andrew Park with Peter Burrows, "What You Don't Know About Dell," *BusinessWeek,* November 3, 2003.

21 Ibid.

22 Dell Computer Corporation 2003 Annual Report, April 2003, p. 6.

23 Ibid. p. 6.

24 Oracle Corporation Press Release, *Oracle Takes the Guesswork Out of Budgeting for Applications and Information Technology,* January 21, 2003.

25 Eliyahu Goldratt and Jeff Cox, *The Goal,* Second Revised Edition, North River Press, 1992, p. 301.

26 Ibid. p. 40-41.

27 Agilent Technologies, 10-Q filing with the Securities and Exchange Commission, July 31, 2002.

28 The California State University Press Release, "California State Univeristy Benefits from Audit of its Systemwide Technology Project," March 11, 2003.

29 Ibid.

30 Becky Bartindale, "Audit criticizes college spending on software—$662 million CSU deal questioned," *The San Jose Mercury News,* Page 1A (Main Section), March 12, 2003.

31 The California State University Press Release, "California State Univeristy Benefits from Audit of its Systemwide Technology Project," March 11, 2003.

32 Becky Bartindale, "Audit criticizes college spending on software—$662 million CSU deal questioned," *The San Jose Mercury News,* Page 1A (Main Section), March 2003.

33 All of the information in this case is adapted from another of the author's real-life client experiences. A few details have been altered to protect the confidentiality of the client, but the changes are only descriptive in nature and have no bearing on the merits of the case.

34 David Meister, *The Psychology of Waiting Lines.* Direct source: *Product Plus—How Product+Service=Competitive Advantage* by Christopher Whitlock, McGraw-Hill, Inc., 1994, p. 255. Original Source: *The Service Encounter* by Czepiel, J.A., Solomon, M.R., and Surprenant, C.F., Lexington Books/D.C. Heath. 1985, p. 113-123.

35 Dr. Harold Kerzner, *Project Management: A Systems Approach to Planning, Scheduling and Controlling, Seventh Edition*, John Wiley & Sons, 2001, p. 7.

36 Geoffrey Perret, *Eisenhower*, Adams Media Corporation, 1999, p. 435.

37 David McCullough, *Truman*, Simon & Schuster, 1992, p. 384.

Section III

38 Infosys Technologies, Ltd. Corporate Web site (Infosys.com), Frequently Asked Questions (FAQ) section, March 2003.

39 Jesse Drucker, "Global Talk Gets Cheaper: Outsourcing Abroad Becomes Even More Attractive as Cost Of Fiber-Optic Links Drops," *The Wall Street Journal*, March 11, 2004.

40 Jane Black with Manjeet Kripalani, "India: Hungry for Info Tech," *BusinessWeek Online*, March 4, 2003.

41 Pete Engardio, Aaron Bernstein, and Manjeet Kripalani; with Frederik Balfour, Brian Grow, and Jay Greene, "The New Global Job Shift," *BusinessWeek Online*, February 3, 2003.

42 Mark C. Paulk, Bill Curtis, Mary Beth Chrisses, and Charles V. Weber, *Capability Maturity Model for Software, Version 1.1*, Software Engineering Institute, Carnegie Mellon University, February 1993.

43 Compiled list of Organizations who have Publicly Announced their Maturity Levels after having an Appraisal Performed, Software Engineering Institute, Carnegie Mellon University, April 1, 2003.

44 Ibid.

45 Neeraj Saxena, "China a BPO Threat to India? Rubbish," *indiatimes Infotech*, August 19, 2003.

46 Mike Yamamoto, "Will India price itself out of offshore market," *CNET News.com*, March 29, 2004.

47 *MIS: Managing Information Strategies*, via BearingPoint Business Intelligence Group research.

48 Ibid.

49 Steve Hamm, "Can Salesforce.com Stamp Out Software," *BusinessWeek Online*, March 3, 2003.

50 "Benioff Backs A New Software Model," *eWeek*, March 1, 2002.

51 "Siebel Systems, Inc. to Acquire UpShot Corporation," Siebel Systems press release, October 15, 2003.

52 Erika Morphy, "NetLedger Rolls Out New CRM Features," *CRMDaily.com*, January 22, 2003.

53 Dennis Callaghan, "Salesforce.com Reaches Profitability," *eWeek*, March 3, 2003.

54 "PeopleSoft CEO knocks Web-based software," *The San Jose Mercury News*, December 9, 2002, p. 9E.

55 Erika Morphy, "Are ASP Users Marooned on an Island?" *CRMDaily.com*, January 29, 2003.

56 Ibid.

57 Salesforce.com's corporate Web site (salesforce.com), July 2003.

58 Upshot's corporate Web site (upshot.com), July 2003.

59 Erika Morphy, "Are ASP Users Marooned on an Island?" *CRMDaily.com*, January 29, 2003.

60 "PeopleSoft CEO knocks Web-based software," *The San Jose Mercury News*, December 9, 2002, p. 1E and 9E.

61 Andy Raskin, *Surviving in the Shadow of Siebel*, Business 2.0, June 2002.

62 Elliot Markowitz, "The World According to Tom," *CRM Magazine*, October 22, 2002.

63 David Bank and William Bulkeley, "In About-Face, Siebel to Deliver Software on Net," *The Wall Street Journal*, October 2, 2003, p. B1.

64 Carlye Adler, *The Fresh Prince of Software, Business 2.0*, March 2003.

65 Steve Hamm, "Can Salesforce.com Stamp Out Software," *BusinessWeek Online*, March 3, 2003.

66 All customer quotes in this section were obtained from the salesforce.com Web site (salesforce.com), July 2003.

67 Jim Steele, President of salesforce.com, interview with author, September 11, 2003.

68 Steve Hamm, "Can Salesforce.com Stamp Out Software," *BusinessWeek Online*, March 3, 2003.

69 "PeopleSoft CEO knocks Web-based software," *The San Jose Mercury News*, December 9, 2002, p. 9E.

70 Elise Ackerman, "Software rebel—Radical business model is winning sympathizers," *The San Jose Mercury News*, December 9, 2002, p. 8E.

71 Prepared by: RTI, Health, Social, and Economics Research (RTI Project Number 7007.011. Prepared for: Gregory Tassey, Ph.D., National Institute of Standards and Technology, Acquisition and Assistance Division, *The Economic Impacts of Inadequate Infrastructure for Software Testing*, May 2002.

72 Source: Accenture 2003 Annual Report.

73 Ibid.

74 *BearingPoint Opens India Global Development Center, Expanding AnyShore (SM) Outsourcing Solution*, Reuters, February 11, 2004.

75 Interview with L.S. Chen, Vice-President, BearingPoint Global Development Center (Shanghai), February 2004.

76 Ibid.

77 *BearingPoint Opens India Global Development Center, Expanding AnyShore (SM) Outsourcing Solution,* Reuters, February 11, 2004.

78 Pui-Wing Tam and William Bulkeley, "H-P Lands $3 Billion Contract to Manage P&G Tech Services," *Dow Jones Business News,* April 14, 2003.

79 Ibid.

80 Siobhan Kennedy, "HP Eyes IBM with Multibillion-Dollar Deals," Reuters, April 11, 2003.

81 Pui-Wing Tam and William Bulkeley, "H-P Lands $3 Billion Contract to Manage P&G Tech Services," *Dow Jones Business News,* April 14, 2003.

82 Robin Gareiss, "Analyzing the Outsourcers," *InformationWeek,* November 18, 2002.

83 "BPO Market to Reach $122B in 2003," earthweb.com, June 11, 2003.

84 Source: Lehman Brothers.

85 Source: India's National Association of Software and Service Companies.

86 "Outsourcing Worldwide Final Market Share," Gartner Group, August 2003.

87 Russ Banham, "Keys to Successful BPO Relationships," *CFO.com,* September 3, 2003.

88 IBM Consulting Services, *Best Practices of Leaders in Offshoring 2002 Survey* as found in *Offshore Resourcing: Once Adventurous, Now Essential for Financial Services Firms,* IBM Business Consulting Services (Shamus Rae, Lead Author), 2002.

89 Keith Ferrell, "Forrester: Business-Process Outsourcing is Overhyped" *TechWeb News,* September 2, 2003.

90 The information contained in this case is based on the personal experience of the author from April 2003 to July 2003.

91 HCL Technologies corporate Web site (hcltech.com), July 2003. The revenue figure includes results for HCL Technologies and HCL Infosystems.

92 HCL Technologies, July 2003.

93 Ibid.

94 Robin Gareiss, "Analyzing the Outsourcers," *Information Week,* November 18, 2002.

95 Most of the information contained in this case is based on the personal experience of the author from June 1999 to March 2003.

96 JDS Uniphase corporate Web site (jdsu.com), April 2003.

97 Oracle Corporation Press Release: "Oracle Helps JDS Uniphase Cut its Information Technology Budget by 60 Percent," February 18, 2003.

98 Paul Brinkley, Chief Information Officer, JDS Uniphase, interview with author, April 2003.

99 Ibid.

Section IV

100 Survey referenced in the following article by Jane Black and Olga Kharif: "The Battle to Streamline Business Software," *Business Week Online,* December 4, 2002.

101 "CIO Research Planning for the Economic Recovery," *CIO* Magazine, September 1, 2002.

102 Scott Berinato, "A Day in the Life of Celanese's Big ERP Rollup," *CIO* Magazine, January 15, 2003.

103 Bill Swanton and Wendy Davis, *Justifying ERP Instance Consolidation Requires a Strategic Business Goal,* AMR Research Report, 2003.

104 Metrics provided by JDS Uniphase. The 40% improvement in Customer Service efficiency is based on a flat level of total Customer Service transactions processed (within 1%) corresponding to a 40% decrease in Customer Service headcount over the same period of time. The 56% improvement in Accounts Receivable efficiency is based on a flat level of total Accounts Receivable transactions processed (within 2%) corresponding to a 56% decrease in Accounts Receivable headcount over the same period of time.

105 Paul Brinkley, Chief Information Officer, JDS Uniphase, interview with author, April 2003.

106 Ibid.

107 Oracle Corporation White Paper, *Keep It Simple: How Oracle Consolidated Its Global Infrastructure into a Centralized E-Business Architecture*, September 2000.

108 Ibid.

109 Information related to this case was obtained by way of interviews with the CIO of Stratex Networks, B. Lee Jones, during the period of January to March 2003.

110 Stratex Networks corporate Web site (stratexnet.com), February 2003.

111 Lafe Low, "15th Annual CIO-100 Awards—The Integration Imperative," *CIO* Magazine, August 15, 2002.

112 B. Lee Jones, Chief Information Officer, Stratex Networks, interview with author, March 2003.

113 Ibid.

114 Ibid.

115 "IBM Global Services helps customers uncover hidden value," IBM corporate Web site (ibm.com), July 2003.

116 Christopher Koch, "IBM's New Hook," *CIO* Magazine, July 1, 2003.

117 *The Wall Street Journal*, December, 31 2002.

118 Pui-Wing Tam, "Searching for the Kilowatt of Computing," *The Wall Street Journal*, July 17, 2003, p. B1-B2.

119 Christopher Koch, "IBM's New Hook," *CIO* Magazine, July 1, 2003.

120 "The Promise of Web Services," *CIO* magazine, White Paper Library, April 15, 2002.

121 "Dell Commits to a .NET-Connected Web Services Architecture," Microsoft Corporation, October, 2003.

122 Louis V. Gerstner, as told to *BusinessWeek* magazine in a Q&A with Associate Editor Ira Sager, "Lou Takes the Gloves Off," November 18, 2002.

123 Uttam Narsu, *The State of Web Services*, Giga Information Group, November 14, 2002.

124 Steve Baloff, "Investing in Web Services—Nobody goes there anymore; it's too crowded," *CIO* Magazine, September 15, 2002.

125 Lafe Low, "15th Annual CIO-100 Awards—The Integration Imperative," *CIO* Magazine, August 15, 2002.

126 The following sources were used in the preparation of this section: *BPM2003 Market Milestone Report*, A Delphi Group White Paper, 2003; Jim Sinur, *Business Process Management Goes Mainstream*, Gartner Symposium Itxpo, March 23, 2003; Michael Thompson, *Requirements for Effective BPM*, Butler Group, June 2003; and Howard Smith, Douglas Neal, Lynette Ferrara, and Francis Hayden, *The Emergence of Business Process Management*, Computer Sciences Corporation, January, 2002.

127 BPMI.org Web site, "Initiative," July 2003.

128 Howard Smith and Peter Fingar, *Business Process Management—The Third Wave*, Meghan-Kiffer Press, 2003, p. 20-21.

129 Ibid. p. 83-85.

130 Ibid. Cover.

131 "Hype Cycle for Web Services, 2003," Gartner Group, May 30, 2003.

132 Ismael Ghalimi, "Paving the Way for the BPM Revolution, Phase 2," BPMI.org, April 29, 2004.

133 Delphi Group quotation reprinted in *Business Process Management—The Third Wave*, Meghan-Kiffer Press, 2003.

Appendix A

1   All of the information in this case is adapted from another of the author's real life client experiences. A few details have been altered to protect the confidentiality of the client, but the changes are only descriptive in nature and have no bearing on the merits of the case.

Appendix C

2   Software Engineering Institute (SEI) at Carnegie Mellon University (sei.cmu.edu), January 2003.

Appendix D

3   Alorie Gilbert, "IBM cements outsourcing dominance," *CNET News.com*, October 2, 2003.

4   "IBM: A Detailed Look at Global Services—Meeting with Doug Elix," UBS Investment Research, December 9, 2003.

5   Satya Prakash Singh, "IBM acquires Daksh e-services", *The Times of India Online*, April 7, 2004.

6   "SAP Announces 2003 Fourth Quarter and Full Year Results," SAP AG, January 22, 2004, and "Oracle Corporation Q3 Fiscal 2004 Results," Oracle Corporation, March 11, 2004.

7   IBM Web site (ibm.com), December 2002.

8   Mike Tarsala, "Oracle to double work force in India," CBS.marketwatch.com, July 10, 2003.

9   Source: The Yankee Group, April 2002.

10   Mylene Mangalindan, "Oracle Puts Priority on Customer Service," *The Wall Street Journal,* January 21, 2003.

11 The estimate is based on the following information obtained from the Oracle Corporation 10-Q filed with the Securities and Exchange Commission on February 28, 2002: Cash and cash equivalents of $4,088M plus Short-term investments of $1,952M.

12 Dean Davison, *Offshore Application Outsourcing—METAspectrum Evaluation,* META Group, February 10, 2003.

13 Keith H. Hammonds, "The New Face of Global Competition," *Fast Company,* February 2003.

14 Wipro Technologies corporate Web site (wipro.com), March 2003.

15 Statistics all obtained from Wipro Technologies corporate Web site (wipro.com), December 2003.

16 "Towards Global Leadership," Wipro Technologies Corporate Presentation, obtained from Wipro Technologies corporate Web site (wipro.com), January 2004.

17 Ibid.

18 Ibid.

19 Keith H. Hammonds, "The New Face of Global Competition," *Fast Company,* February 2003.

20 Wipro Technologies corporate Web site (wipro.com), March 2003.

21 Keith H. Hammonds, "The New Face of Global Competition," *Fast Company,* February 2003.

22 "The Best & Worst Managers of 2003—The Best Managers," *BusinessWeek online,* January 12, 2003.

23 Wipro Technologies corporate Web Site (wipro.com), December 2003.

24 Tata Consultancy Services corporate Web site (tcs.com), March 2004.

25 Ibid.

26 TCS Press Release, "TCS India's first global billion-dollar software organization," June 20, 2003.

27 Intelenet corporate Web site (intelenetglobal.com), A TCS-HDFC Company, December 2003.

28 Ibid.

29 Ajit V. Sawant, Vice-President, TCS, "Exploding the myths of Indian IT," *The Economic Times,* July 18, 2002.

30 Tata Consultancy Services corporate Web site (tcs.com), March 2003.

31 Infosys Technologies Ltd. corporate Web site (infosys.com), December 2003.

32 Ibid.

33 Ibid.

34 Ibid.

35 Ibid.

36 Progeon corporate Web site (progeon.com), March 2003.

37 Rajiv Kuchhal, *Analyst Meet: Broadening the services footprint—Business Process Management,* Infosys Technologies Ltd., August 27, 2002.

38 Alam Srinivas, "A Debugged Operating System," *Outlook India.com,* January 27, 2003.

Index

0-595-66062-2

Printed in the United States
137156LV00001B/14/A